W9-DFE-992

Talk Never Dies

LAURENCE GOLDMAN

Talk Never Dies

THE LANGUAGE OF
HULI DISPUTES

TAVISTOCK PUBLICATIONS
LONDON AND NEW YORK

First published in 1983 by
Tavistock Publications
11 New Fetter Lane,
London EC4P 4EE

Published in the USA by
Tavistock Publications
in association with Methuen, Inc.
733 Third Avenue, New York,
NY 10017

© 1983 Laurence Goldman

Typeset by
Scarborough Typesetting Services
and printed in Great Britain at the
University Press, Cambridge

*British Library Cataloguing in
Publication Data*

Goldman, Laurence
Talk never dies: the language of Huli
disputes.

1. Ethnology—Papua New Guinea
2. Huli (Papuan People)   3. Land tenure
(Primative Law)—Papua New Guinea
4. Language and culture   I. Title
342.64′32′089912   GN671.N5

ISBN 0–422–78210–6

*Library of Congress Cataloging in
Publication Data*

Goldman, Laurence.
Talk never dies.

Includes bibliographical references and
indexes.
1. Anthropological linguistics—Papua
New Guinea   2. Huli (Papuan
people)—Language   I. Title
P35.5.P26G64   1983   401′.9
83–18294

Contents

Preface

This book is intended to provide a semantically and linguistically informed study of disputes among the Huli of Papua New Guinea. The theoretical perspective is tangential to those *idées reçues* embodied by the historically divergent traditions of dispute analysis in anthropology. In this regard, I have wholly embraced neither the approach of law-centred proponents – oriented towards circumscribing the legal as a 'generic field of study' (Roberts 1979 : 203) – nor the interests of process-focused research where 'rule-scepticism' (Gluckman 1973 : 614) is often evidenced by rejections of the need to elicit a *corpus juris*. Both substantive and processual paradigms converge when looking at language behaviour in the enactment and description of disputes.

The adoption of a sociolinguistic perspective complements the ethnographic data, which reveal that disputes and dispute-management procedures are defined and analysed through the activity of talk. Speech is both the resource and the topic by which disputants interpret and negotiate each other's actions. Furthermore, talk constitutes a powerful organizational model for inter-personal and inter-group relations that in other Highlands societies are articulated in terms of enemy/ally interactions. Disordered talk reflects disordered relationships in Huli. The interpretive frames used in this book were thus not conceived as methodological dogma, nor as a covert critique of alternative approaches to the analysis of disputes. The arguments put forward here stress the significant benefits to be gained from a *rapprochement* between discourse analysis and the study of disputes in culturally specific settings. Given the centrality of talk in the value system of the Huli, an analysis of disputing must in part be but an aspect of the study of conversation.

There are few precedents or guidelines specifically detailing how an understanding of disputes may be derived from, or demonstrated by, an investigation of the verbal interaction taking place within them. The *modus operandi* has been to elicit and describe the normative and lexical frameworks within which actors argue about claims. This has involved a consideration of the evaluative dimensions that are used to define the bounds of sense and nonsense in debate. The resources of the Huli language have been culled (but always presented in their performative contexts) to yield idiom, metaphor, and patterns of figurative or allusive speech. These have been analysed as an index of the stock of semantic discriminations concerning 'disputing'. I have located the focus on dispute texts within the wider system of speech forms and behaviour. In addition to my treatments of turn-taking, stereotypes, and the structure of mediation speeches, some consideration is given to the relation between form and content in Huli talk: that is, how speech is shaped by aesthetic norms as an appreciation of the extent to which ethno-poetics impinges upon our understanding of rhetoric.

The book is based on material collected between March 1977 and August 1978. I am indebted to the Anthropology Department of University College London, the Social Science Research Council, and the Central Research Fund for providing grants for the fieldwork.

I have benefited greatly from suggestions and criticisms made by many people. I am grateful to Professor John Middleton, Professor Mervyn Meggitt, Dr Philip Burnham, Professor Grant McCall, Professor Dell Hymes, Bambi Schieffelin, and Buck Schieffelin for their help, and a special debt of gratitude is due to Professor Andrew Strathern for encouragement, assistance, and incisive analysis of much of the material when it was first presented to him in a thesis format. I also thank Mike O'Hanlon for reading various chapter drafts and providing innumerable corrections and suggestions.

My understanding of Huli culture has been enhanced by the stimulating work of other researchers concerned with this particular culture, who have helped me before, during, and after my time in the field. My stay in Huli was facilitated by the generosity and friendship of Francis Leak, Father Malachi, Glenda Giles, Father Dominic and the Sisters of Koroba Catholic Mission, Ben Probert, and Murray Rule. Without their guidance and copies of language materials my task would have been a more arduous one.

Finally, I would like to record my appreciation of the help given to me by the people of Ialuba. In this respect special mention is due to Hunguru, Dalu, Degondo, Ago, and Mindi for their attempts to communicate Huli *mana* to me. I thank also Gulari Hidaiya who, in the capacity of friend and field assistant, made this book possible.

Abbreviations and notations

F = father
M = mother
S = son
D = daughter
B = brother
Z = sister
H = husband
W = wife
ch = children
/ in texts signifies the occurrence of pause in recitations
` A high-falling tone
– A level mid tone
´ A low-rising tone
→ An utterance to which the reader's attention is focused in respect of discussion about some particular aspect of discourse
[An occurrence of paired statements
ref. = refer
App. = appendix
D. = dispute number. D.2: 35 is to be read as dispute no. 2, line 35

. . . indicates omitted lines of discourse
  = indicates a lack of interval between the end of one person's
     utterance and the commencement of a second person's turn
  [straight brackets indicate the point at which overlap occurs
  :: stretching of the syllable prior to the colons

Acknowledgements

Parts of Chapter 5 were originally included in a paper entitled Speech
Categories and the Study of Disputes, *Oceania* (1980) Vol. L No. 3.

   I am grateful to the editor concerned for permission to include the
revised materials in this present book.

1

Introduction

'They are a most likeable people but are mecurial in temperament, very
emotional with a strong sense of personal dignity. I consider them quicker
to anger than the Kukukuku, but quick also to revert to calm. They love
gesture and oratory, yet become most uneasy at detailed questioning.'

(Sinclair 1955)

A theoretical perspective

A noticeable aspect of the anthropological literature dealing with
disputes is the reticence and failure of analysts to present 'case' data in
the form of discourse transcripts. Consideration of this singular
deficiency in an intellectual heritage spanning many decades, has
motivated many of the criticisms of traditional approaches and
analytical parameters central to the present study. For a sub-discipline
that is manifestly focused on the protracted verbal interchanges that
accompany situations of conflict, one must question the epistemic
status of dispute (or law) studies that ignore the dimensions of
language use and structure. The organizational and sequential
properties of talk about claims, rights, or obligations, are constitutive
phenomena meriting detailed consideration as contributions to an
understanding of how events and outcomes are determined by
speech. The preference for, and predominance of, condensed descriptive reports is attributable partly to the constraints of publication.
Nevertheless, the character of our case legacy also reflects a long-
established interest in the abstraction of norms and the interplay

between rules and praxis, rather than in the communicational framework that structures processes of rule negotiation and interpretation. Traditionally, the function of descriptive summaries has been to provide 'apt illustration'. This has ensured that, notwithstanding the advances made by the anthropology of disputes, the discipline cannot claim to be a 'working' one in terms of its case material. Its data base is not amenable to the processes of re-analysis and re-examination that might produce a counter-analysis: 'Transcripts, then, enable readers or hearers of an analysis to check out *both* the proposed reading *and* the proposed analytic apparatus with reference to precisely the same data as those in which they were based' (Atkinson and Drew 1979 : 27). The lack of provision for, or indulgence in, retrospective evaluation represents a serious indictment of current procedures of anthropological case presentation.

Disregarding the possibilities offered by providing even *one* complete dispute transcript, researchers have created a veritable cemetery of skeletal cases. These are rarely exhumed for the purposes of pathological examination, precisely because their corporeal form cannot serve to answer the questions engendered by detailed post-mortem inquiries. Such descriptive reports are specifically designed in accordance with the prior interests of the ethnographer, and his or her evaluations of what is important about any stream of events. Whilst cross-disciplinary interests are frequently thwarted by the format of data presentation, each new study generates further dead matter. Dispute cases cannot be subjected to further examination by readers without recourse to the analyst's private field notes. It can certainly be argued that our understanding of dispute processes has been impoverished by a doctrinal adherence to précis. Access to empirical material is curtailed to the detriment of an appreciation of how language influences actions and results in respect of (a) the formal, structural, and sequential properties of settlement-directed talking; and (b) the organizational features of any litigant's claim presentation. Explanatory models may be judged to have relevance or applicability in other cultural contexts, but the problems of demonstrating that 'fit' are replicated where case data are given as short descriptions. Our reliance on the ethnographer's descriptive and analytical competence remains constant as an acceptance of decontextualized assessments. With specific regard to the corpus of dispute accounts, anthropology has yet to furnish a fruitful data base that may benefit from multi-disciplinary dialogue. The high degree of resource deprivation increases readers' distance from the situated actions of any dispute. For researchers, successive descriptive and editorial decisions introduce a level of distortion in addition to the perennial problems of translation. Significantly, it is almost inevitable that an analysis will fail to explore the sense in which disputes – as episodes of speech exchange – are minimally constituted of sequentially arranged turns at talking. In this book I will argue that we are only likely to comprehend the logic of dispute in any culture if our approach is consonant with the place and value of talk in that system.[1]

The plea for transcript collection and presentation is not simply an academic exercise in circumscribing the analyst's privileged access to information. In accepting this methodological precept one embraces a radically revised set of research topics and foci, centrally related to the verbal apparatus used to communicate, and negotiate, conflict. We are constrained to locate mediation processes, and the sense in which the role of 'mediator' can be defined as a set of linguistic options, within an encompassing system of speech norms. What engages our attention is the manner in which the structure of dispute talk is responsive to indigenously perceived problems and tasks associated with debate, as well as debate about claims, in multi-party settings. Given that a dispute may constitute one type of 'talk situation', consideration is due to the models of ordered debate oriented to by participants, and to how the semantic and lexical frameworks are utilized to evaluate argument for the apportionment of credit or discredit. A systematic approach to the distinctive and structural features of verbal interaction in forensic contexts is thus a natural departure point for a discipline concerned, to a large extent, with extended verbal interchanges. To endorse such research interests is to argue the significant gains to be had from a *rapprochement* between the ethnography of speech and the ethnography of disputes.

The impetus for changes in our approach to disputes derives both from externally articulated reflections and recommendations, and from internally voiced dissatisfactions, and I would like to consider these two aspects in the present discussion.

(1) That dispute analysts have been unable to tell us very much about how language makes a difference in who gets what is perhaps hardly surprising. Indeed, it reflects the low academic prestige and analytical priority accorded to studies of conversation until the last decade. It is only recently that the investigation of discourse and supra-sentential structures has extricated itself from the orthodox linguistic concerns of

grammar and syntax within the boundaries of a sentence. The convergence of disciplinary interests on the phenomenon of language use in culturally specific settings thus challenges anthropologists to make verbal practices in disputes a topic for reflection, research, and report. The neglect shown to the centrality of talk in interaction is also attributable, as Harris (1981) and Atkinson and Drew (1979) have argued, to the ethnographer's tendency to examine that which is noticeable, exotic, or oddly apparent about any social setting. The fact that participants engage in talk to resolve their differences has remained a 'taken for granted' aspect, treated as a residual explanatory problem. Thus case summaries report that 'big-men of the group attempt mediation', or 'when the parties had reached agreement then . . .'. The contributory significance of that 'discussion' is sacrificed for an interest in outcomes rather than modes of production. The manifest role of talk as 'constitutive of social order' (Atkinson and Drew 1979 : 235), resulting from (or embedded in) disputes, has thus been largely neglected. This is despite the fact that many cultures conceptualize a dispute as a taxonomically discrete speech situation.

One response to the need to look more closely at these 'taken for granted' features has been the work of conversational analysts. From their detailed investigation of the nature of turn-taking and speaker transition (see Sacks, Schegloff, and Jefferson 1974) has come the suggestion that speech exchange systems might be cross-culturally compared in respect of various turn-allocation parameters. In the context of such preoccupations with how talk is managed, and indeed with whether discourse in some settings displays a distinctive syntax, we can reformulate certain of the traditionally conceived questions that have been the kernel of our sub-discipline. The problem of whether Western jurisprudential concepts are applicable in other cultures is thus secondary to an explication of those disjunctions and continuities that may subsist between 'legal talk' (or dispute talk) and 'ordinary dialogue' in any ethnographic context. That is, we need to know how such a distinction is formulated and utilized as a dispute management technique which assesses contributions and claims as appropriate / inappropriate in specific circumstances. To what extent does such a contrast, if drawn, relate to a pre-specification of turn-order and turn-type? In these respects, a sociolinguistic analysis of disputes reflects an involvement with the dimensions of comparison between institutionalized processes of conflict resolution that is free from the definitional quandaries concerning the nature of law or legal arrangements (see Goldman 1980).

By explicitly focusing attention on talk, and 'what people expect of talk' (Harris 1981 : 1455), we begin to appreciate the complex factors that impinge upon the structure of claim presentations in any dispute. First, we have to ask whether the evaluated differences between claims reflect cultural ideas about verbal and non-verbal acts. Second, by attending to detailed verbal interchanges we can explore the types of predominant claim patterns as reflecting structured choices from culturally defined (and personally perceived) options. Moreover, we seem better prepared to assess how participants react to a familiar *case profile* (a sequenced ordering of claims), as well as how emergent resolutions relate to specific *claim types*, their *probable frequency of occurrence*, and their *positional incidence* in any dispute. These concepts are explained in more detail below. The contention that there should be more sociolinguistically and semantically informed analyses of disputes does not reflect a submission to fashion – the view that 'conversation seems likely to be the vogue research topic of the 1980s' (Harris 1981 : 1455). Rather, it is founded on the belief that our understanding of disputes and their settlement is enhanced (in ways detailed throughout this book) by a focused examination of the dominant communicational medium used to declare normative breaches.

(2) The argument, then, that the anthropology of disputes should pursue directions, and embrace analytic frames, engendered by specialisms concerned with language and meaning in sociocultural contexts (such as ethnosemantics, conversational/discourse analysis, ethnography of speech) would appear to be timely. The disquiet expressed by many researchers that this domain of enquiry is in need of remedial attention is reflected in the comment of Roberts that 'established techniques are repeated and consolidated' (1981 : 490) but not progressively developed in new directions. In this regard, the case for 'speech' oriented investigations is strengthened by the fact that they inevitably confront questions outside the two paradigms that have constituted our intellectual bequest from Malinowski and Radcliffe-Brown, through Gluckman, Bohannan, Nader, Fallers, Moore, Hamnett, and others. I refer here to the contrasting theoretical concerns of 'substantive' and 'procedural' models (see Goldman 1980 : 209). In the former instance, conversationally constituted analyses are concerned to ensure that rule elicitation proceeds by

detailing the speech context in which norms are announced. Furthermore, there is a specific interest in the routine nature of the speech environment in which norms are utilized, and an appreciation of the relation between their form and content. In the latter case, the researcher attends to the structure of talking to demonstrate how participants orient to perceived and expected strategies relating to blame attribution and deflection, claim presentation and resolution, and ideas about ordered and disordered debate in regard to the organizational tasks associated with dispute settings.

While a sociolinguistic perspective requires an account of rhetoric – of the Aristotelian divisions of the 'political' (the do and do not), 'epideictic' (censure and praise), and 'forensic' (attack and defence) – it also clearly reaches beyond the scope of studies of political oratory. A wider range of discourse phenomena other than purely persuasive modes of talking are subjected to scrutiny. The possibility is entertained that the whole of a dispute talk might realize a determinate structure, or, more probably, that there are 'recurrent routines, sections and sets of sections that have an implicit syntax' (Hymes, personal communication). This re-conceptualization of themes and problems in the anthropological study of disputes has historical roots in the seminal works of Albert (1972) and Frake (1969). Their respective interests in the cultural patterning of talk, and the semantic features that underlie labelling activity and lexical domains, represent fruitful lines of enquiry that have paradoxically remained neglected within our sub-domain. It is thus only recently that dispute analysts have again suggested that their specific interests in decision-making processes should be located within a description of the total speech framework (Roberts 1979 : 44), and that 'there is a strong argument for looking much more closely than has generally been the case at what people say and how they say it in the conduct of disputes' (Roberts 1979 : 205). This nexus of 'speech'-related foci structures the approach to Huli disputes adopted in this book.

A critical assessment of prevailing conventions in case presentation must of course be balanced by an acknowledgement of the irreducible (and perhaps ultimately indescribable) complexity of any stretch of dispute talk. This complexity has to be confronted, albeit in a piecemeal fashion. Accepting that our province of study is founded on the analysis of conflict cases, an insistence on transcript-based treatises defines a standard of acceptability and admissibility of the kinds of 'reports' that we can justifiably call 'cases'. While recognizing that any description of a dispute is in different degrees incomplete, paying attention to what is actually said permits an appreciation of the multi-dimensional character of the data base. In this regard, it might prove more advantageous to have a few complete (however one defines this notion) cases, rather than the multitude of summaries typical of most dispute/law-centred studies. There are two specific areas where the implications of this methodological shift are likely to be felt. First, if one accepts that adjudicators' or mediators' contributions are 'invariably a most difficult part of understanding the disputing process' (Gulliver 1982 : 566), then this is frequently because the verbal contexts of assertion and commitment are rarely subjected to detailed investigation. Clearly, it is important to determine the possible designs a speech can take in respect to types of participant status, and the extent to which this data reflects, linguistically, predominant structural choices in any interaction. Moreover, we need to expose the interactional sensitivities of actors to disagreement, censure/praise (of others or self), and other forms of deference behaviour. Specifically, attention must be paid to levels and modalities of commitment to blame imputation, as well as the linguistic format and force of suggested resolutions. In response to these problems, Chapter 2 attempts to provide an outline of the salient properties of Huli language in relation to speech behaviour and the communication of meaning. I consider the dominant interactional categories and routines that are functionally appropriate to settlement-directed talking. That is, the extent to which stereotype expressions ('gambits') reflect a framework of expectations about the orderly debate of rights, norms, and claims, and how they semantically frame information in accordance with a cultural determination of what is important.

A second implication of the polemical stance against case summaries (in the particular respect of the talking that may accompany conflict) concerns the principles on which critical reviews are often conducted. The staid replication of presentational formats reflects, to some extent, the dependency of our discipline and its reference frames on the evaluative judgements made by researchers. One might question here, on two counts, the sense in which such positive assessments as 'rich case materials' (Gulliver 1982 : 566) adequately convey the hiatus between descriptive reports and transcript-based texts. On the one hand, no case is intrinsically richer than another, while on the other hand it seems preferable to reserve such eulogies for data that more faithfully reproduce the experiential complexity.

Ease of comprehension and expression should not take precedence over the immeasurable gains in understanding to be had from detailing the performative character of disputants' arguments. This is a methodological corollary of the point that incriminatory and defensive postures frequently reflect litigants' appreciation of the importance of form to content, and, importantly, the strategic value of specific locales in a stream of talk. A demonstration of the sequential structuring or patterning of moves and counter-moves by participants requires presentation of dialogue. These dimensions offer a fruitful basis for cross-cultural comparison between conflict management processes in Western courts – how verbal interaction is organized in judicial settings (see Atkinson and Drew 1979) – and native contexts such as the Huli.

The application of sociolinguistic precepts to the field of disputes can also yield insights into the meaning of social interaction in other contexts. As it is always necessary for anthropological analyses of conflict to sketch the broader sociocultural factors that affect the structure of argument – for example, the stereotypes used in the attribution of praise or censure, and the degree to which speech is instrumental in marking status contrasts (see Chapter 5) – various sub-themes can emerge that are relevant to the overall place, role, and value of talk in that community. In this regard, my analyses of 'talk about talk' and various linguistic repertoires associated with Huli modes of criticism reveal levels of consistency and congruency in the semantic dimensions they embody; moreover, these axes underlie the indigenously perceived (and verbally declared) structural homologies between the behavioural domains predicated on pigs, paint, and parlance. These three 'substances' are utilized in systems of exchange so that they form a unitary social source for metaphorical abstraction and symbolic statement. They are interchangeable modes of self-presentation. Manipulation of pigs or paint (a metonym for 'decoration') is construed as a form of surrogate speech.

Interactions with pigs, paint, and speech seem to be ordered by the same framework of motives, conventions, and values that index a shared reticulum of meanings. Of particular importance here is the way in which the discrete environmental categories of *anda* ('home/private') and *hama* ('public') organize processes of production and display such that male reputations register increments of prestige or praise. The subsistent parallels with ethno-ethological models of bird of paradise behaviour constitute the symbolic motif of *man* : *bird* that permeates much of the metaphorical language of disputes. These themes are central to an understanding of the cultural patterning of speech in Huli, and these 'zones' define degrees of appropriate and acceptable behaviour by specifying rules for the apportionment of credit or discredit. At the level of talk about claims, I have attempted to categorize the grounds of evaluation, for *anda* or *hama* contexts, in accordance with the 'sufficiency' of any contribution. I suggest that the actions of crediting appeal to truth-sufficient, type-sufficient, and role-sufficient norms. These interpretive procedures are, as I explain in subsequent chapters, dependent on context and dispute-type. Data presented in Chapter 5 support the contention that, consequent upon a degree of formal scheduling, these sufficiency dimensions are most likely to be defined and announced at the outset of any dispute: they are used to orient participants to a set of debate terms. It is precisely in the phases of debate concerned with assessment that we can understand how the speech genre taxonomy is used as a grid for defining speech aberrations and infelicities in case presentation.

The present study is thus concerned with the concept of normative breach on two distinct, but related, levels: behavioural delicts that lead to situations of settlement-directed exchange, and those normative violations associated with processes of claim presentation. This interrelationship between how something is said and what is said, between form and content, is a particularly important focus for any analysis of Huli culture. The reason for this is simply that norms in all fields of social action, and indeed even the diacritical features by which Huli assert their cultural identity, are expressed in formulaic terms which Huli call *pureremo*. The semantics of such kin categories as cross-cousin (*hanini*) or non-agnatic cognate (*aba*) can be discovered and articulated only in regard to their respective *pureremo*. It is an intrinsic part of the meaning of such relationships that members may engage in pre-patterned communicative routines according to the circumstances described in Chapter 3. This phenomenon constrains us to consider the following problems. First, what stylistic aspects (particularly the segmental and non-segmental phonological correlates) of this linguistic variety are important to the maintenance, expression, and strategic value of such norms: what mnemonic functions can we attribute to particular aesthetic patterns? Second, is there a level of differentiation between ideal statements and formal performances concerned with censure, reprimands, or reminders to others of their obligations? In each chapter emphasis is placed on the degree to which speech evidences a structuring by aesthetic principles. This is in accordance with the following prominent features:

(1) An unexpected degree of frequency of certain artifices of sound which elevate the sound-meaning relationship above the level of arbitrary connection. Specifically, the lexicalization of antonyms and synonyms, minimally-distinct pairings and prosodic phenomena (such as tone contrasts) appear iconically to indicate a high level of correspondence between semantic, syntactic, and phonological structures.

(2) Empirical data show that types of aesthetic patterning and sound-symbolism tend to cluster around articulated contrasts that have a determinative influence on the structure of dispute speeches. They represent a strategic nucleus of rhetorical devices that reflect back on the cultural importance attached to particular oppositions. Most noticeable, in this context, is the distinct phonological patterning of contrasts that relate to the male-female distinction as manifested, for example, in kinship terminology (see Chapter 3).

(3) There is a sense in which all explanatory and ratiocinative models embody a cultural aesthetic manifested in the distinctive linguistic garb of the component cognitive contrasts and axes. This may well reflect their functional adaptation to rhetorical motives and situations. In Chapter 5 I concern myself with certain occasions when vocabulary switching is either mandatory or preferred. It is thus a further ingredient of the critical reaction to the mainstream of dispute analysis that these parameters are too often not considered.

Examination of various lexical systems has revealed a consistent set of ideas about how the Huli comprehend the relationship between disputes, settlement processes, and outcomes. A fundamental aspect of this conceptual system is the centrality – as an absolute presupposition – of the sexual disjunction and its attendant scheme of values. This cultural motif is identifiable both as a constituent feature of the data and a discursive instrument. Importantly, it is associated with an uncompromising ideology of pollution that pervades all contexts of Huli behaviour, and articulates the social implications of female sexuality. In connection with the function of language as a medium of discrimination, and the ubiquity of a stigma philosophy, attention is given to correlating role differentation along sexual lines with patterns of speech use. In the context of disputes, it is clear that males have a powerful lexicon for expressing the negative dimensions to events, people, or verbal acts that cause disorder. The male-female distinction is also a constituent semantic feature of *anda* and *hama* as spatial and conceptual poles. To the extent that the Huli are concerned in most activities with the maintenance of boundaries, situations of breach, defilement, or disorder are verbalized in the lexis of pollution. This is one further basis for the imputed homology between the three semiotic sub-systems of pigs, paint, and speech. Exchange behaviour in epideictic contexts (*hama*) must conform to norms governing 'dirt' (Douglas 1966). The display rationale is a conscious ordering of actions to achieve and demonstrate states purified of aberrancy. This necessitates utilizing one's best pigs, feathers, or words. The idioms of deviance are patently couched in terms of contamination and illness. Data pertaining to 'talk about talk', anger, shame, insult, and lies testify to the very real equivalences between the pathology and treatment of sickness and speech.

Settlement-directed talking is thus oriented to the eradication of anomaly – situations where transactions breach defined boundaries. Deviance is controlled through specific rituals of separation and sanitization. This cultural identity between dispute management and 'dirt elimination' is intertwined with the frequently declared notion that such processes should constitute acts of exchange. Attributions of censure and praise are based on an implicit division between actions that reflect the axiomatic norm of 'reciprocity' (Goldman 1980), and those based on an egocentred appropriation of decision making. This is semantically embedded in the terminologically distinguished conditions of any talk about claims; the central opposition is between *bi* (orderly talk or debate) and *lai* (argument), where *lai* is a contracted form of *lai ha* – 'to finish saying'. Argument begins when people perceive that speech reciprocity no longer obtains. Dispute settlement in Huli is thus concerned with control of impurity. It proceeds through application of situational definitions and norms governing appropriate and acceptable issues or behaviour on *anda/hama*. Vocabulary changes are one means of identifying 'sanitization' mechanisms; processes of aesthetic engineering are indexed by the prevalence of euphemism and employment of valued lexis. As a corollary of the premium placed on 'high' speech forms (detailed in Chapter 5) during claim presentation and debate, there is an emphasis on switching to these 'linguistic equivalents of disinfectant' (Leech 1974 : 53). The field of action and meaning concerned with the relation between *injury* : *healing* provides the Huli with a code for conceptualizing the relation between *disputes* : *dispute settlement*. Compensation – embracing notions of restoration, rehabilitation, and reparation – represents a healing mode, an application of 'medicine' symbolized by pig-transfers. The context-specific lexis of indemnity is full of terms derived from the field of talk about sickness and health. Whilst these themes reflect an ethnosemantically in-formed approach to disputes, there remains to be considered the dominant theoretical frame adopted here and the associated problem of substantive units.

The sequential properties of claim profiles

While few anthropologists have made verbal practices in disputes a topic for sustained empirical research, there does exist a corpus of sociolinguistic literature specifically concerned with the systematic description of conversational order in naturally bounded settings. A comprehensive review of ideas common to discourse analysis or the ethnography of speech is beyond the scope of this introduction, but certain methodological premises that have influenced the interpret-ative frames I adopt do deserve comment. The analyses mentioned above assume that talk may, in any given context, manifest a discern-ible and describable order; patterning is anticipated, not an *a priori* presupposition. Moreover, it is frequently argued that abstracted structural principles are an implicit feature of indigenous concepts of orderly debate. For the most part, models of spoken discourse have been developed in contexts that have conventionally defined bound-aries: opening and closing routines, participant statuses and limi-tations, and constraints regarding topic introduction and development tend to be easily identified precisely because they reflect a degree of institutionalization. The 'chalk and talk' setting of the classroom has thus been central to the development of models associated with the Birmingham analytical tradition (see Coulthard, Montgomery, and Brazil 1981). Attempts to generalize from specific cases to a broader theory of discourse structure typically confront two problems. First, that any model of regularized interaction reflects a set of stylistic options that are rarely relevant to casual conversation. Second, not-withstanding current lack of agreement on the substantive units of importance, definitional categories of one language can be notoriously difficult to identify (in terms of given diacritical features) in data gleaned from another culture.

From the notion that certain utterances reveal an *adjacency pair* format – for example that questions are regularly followed by answers, or invitations by an acceptance/rejection (see Atkinson and Drew 1979) – researchers have put forward models of increasing complexity that disclose the elemental nature of verbal interchanges. Clearly, while much of the talk in Western courts tends to be organized in terms of question-answer dialogic units, and participants may attend to this format as a constraint on speech, informal conversation does not consistently conform to such patterning. Furthermore, in Huli disputes there is no devolution of responsibility for any choreographic direction of floor-taking. Not only is rule elicitation problematic in such contexts, it is also unlikely that any text can be shown to be determinatively organized to the same degree as the didactic dialogues between teacher-pupil, or the inquisitorial interactions between examiner-witness. Nevertheless, the overall perspective of discourse as 'speech exchange' is one that is particularly useful for a study of Huli disputes which are defined as contexts for the 'sharing of talk'. In addition, the primary focus on sequential structures – how and in what sense one unit follows on from another – that characterizes most conversational analyses, opens up some exciting possibilities for an understanding of multiple-claim disputes beyond the extended-case parameters of participant relationships, manipulation of response options, or chronologically interlinked cases.

If it is the case that 'sequence' is a critical and strategic property of participants' models of talking, and one that is pertinent to the presentation of claims and defences in Huli disputes, then it is important to delineate the sequence-relevant levels. Sequential structures can thus be elicited in regard to the following.

(1) The order of those constituent units that compose a *turn* (an unbroken stretch of talk) which we might describe as types of move or speech act. The 'folk' repertoire of interactional categories consists, in Huli, of substantive discriminations and evaluations of 'talk' (*bi*) described in Chapter 5. Analytically, the notion of a claim can be conceived as one type of move similar to accusations and blame rebuttals. Importantly, then, the confrontational framework of defence, admission, charge, and complaint is not lexically indexed in Huli.

(2) We can attend to the synchronization of turns at speaking and

rules governing the transition from one turn to another. Furthermore, in respect of the transactional categories mentioned above, there is a possibility that certain moves are ordered relative to moves in a previous turn. That is, participants design their turns according to their placement in a sequence of turns and to their expectations about the projected turns of others. What is said in any turn reveals an appreciation of the overall purposes of that talk and the speaker's sensitivities to the avoidance or furtherance of various moves (see Pomerantz 1978a, 1978b). For example, the avoidance of self-praise in speech and decoration can be specified in respect to the sequential ordering of verbal and non-verbal turns (see Chapter 5), as can the general preference for blame deflection in disputes.

(3) At the supra-turn level certain macro-structural patterns may possibly be abstracted from any transcript as an analytical finding. Equally, such a model may be indigenously acknowledged to serve as an orientation for the direction of members' contributions. I have shown elsewhere (Goldman 1980) that Huli explicitly state that settlement processes should conform to the progression: '*tene tai bira / tene goda handama* ('to search for the source / to dig up the sources') → *bi tale bule / yabu lole* ('to share the talk') → *manani daba bule* ('to choose according to customary norms')'. The sequential properties that subsist in these units and levels shape the production of meaning and speech, speech about certain topics, and the presentation of self with speech. I cannot conceive of any alternative or acceptable 'case method' other than one firmly rooted to transcript data, which can adequately demonstrate, or test in a way capable of assessment by readers, the explanatory value of sequential patterning or the strategic value of particular locales in any stream of talk.

The most important facet of disputes in New Guinea is that they are typically multiple-claim affairs. Past grievances are invariably resuscitated, so that the overall structure is a complex web of claims and counter-claims, and the overt issues expressed may have little bearing on the underlying bases of tension. My argument is that these facets have been treated as reflecting a cultural mode of repartee. It has not been recognized that the sequential structure of claims in any litigant's posture constitutes an important phenomenon that deserves examination in its own right. Neither have descriptive accounts addressed the question of how outcomes specifically relate to this matrix of claims, while correlational parameters have completely ignored the incidence of a claim in a sequence of like units, or as part of a system of optional claims. In accordance with the need to develop a more powerful apparatus for dealing with these features, I have used the following rank scale whereby each unit relates to a subordinate one in terms of a 'consists of' relationship: *dispute*, *profile*, *claim*. These descriptive categories may be defined as follows.

Dispute

One type of 'speech situation' (Hymes 1972 : 56) concerning disagreement or conflict between two or more parties regarding an alleged infringement or denial of rights. In a general sense, the term refers to a stream of verbal and non-verbal events that the Huli acknowledge manifest an aetiological connection. The unity of any manifold is expressed by such phrases as 'this trouble belongs (*naga*) to X', where X may be a person or important issue. A dispute, then, is a construction from known entities, a unit abstracted from the flow of interaction between specified people. In this book, 'dispute' also denotes the speech events at which people discuss their claims, and which are regulated by conventions of appropriate speaking. This is consonant with the Huli classification of such encounters as discrete 'talk' (*bi*) situations. The criteria that distinguish a dispute from other occasions of verbal interchange are (1) topic focus; (2) participant categorizations: for Huli there are always two 'talk sources' (*bi tene*), while mediation proceeds by membershiping oneself as a 'middle-man' (*agali dombeni*); and (3) a shared attendance to a single sequence of turns at talk as the accredited outcome-oriented conversation. Concurrent dialogue is often present but it is muted, and does not affect the audibility and clarity of the main stream of speech. These features are the recognition cues by which members segment their speech environment into discrete units associated with different normative frameworks.

In the ethnographic context of Huli, a dispute is largely an open state of talk with few restrictions on accretion or depletion of participants. Where a dispute follows on immediately from some other talk situation there does arise the problem of boundary demarcation. There is a marked absence of opening or closing rituals in Huli disputes which can index transitions in the way that 'Be upstanding in court' (see Atkinson and Drew 1979) appears to do in English courtrooms. The task of precisely determining when a dispute has begun is made all the more difficult by limitations imposed by fieldwork circumstances. It is often the case that a researcher arrives on the scene once a dispute has already got under way. However imperceptible the drift from, say, casual chat to a dispute may be, it is the tacit agreement to sustain that single sequence of exchanges that separates the two situations.

Profile

Any dispute consists of at least one, and frequently two, litigant profiles. That is, a syntagm made up of claims that represent structured choices from the paradigmatic options open to any disputant. The profile is partly dependent, then, on historical circumstances.[2] The sequential and strategic aspects of claimants' profiles are indigenously understood and expressed through a locative terminology (see Chapter 5) in which the constituent units are weighted in terms of their relative values as *tene* ('cause / reason / origin').

Claim

This is the minimal unit concerned with the demand for acknowledgement of, or recompense for, breaches of rights or obligations. A claim is defined by virtue of its potentiality for occurrence in a profile. The notion that claims are interchangeable in any multiple-claim presentation is belied by the fact that certain claims recurrently appear in particular positions in dispute profiles. Like linguistic units, the claim is amenable to analysis along syntagmatic and paradigmatic axes (the chain and choice dimensions).[3]

The crux of the analysis undertaken in this book concerns the relationship between the semantic morphology of claim types, and the sequential properties of claim profiles. I shall try to show the importance of the locale of an item in a sequence of similarly constituted units. Furthermore, I argue that the *positional incidence* of a claim in a profile affects the outcome of that claim and the dispute of which it is a part. It is important to repeat that notions such as positional incidence – which parallels the locational frequency of occurrence with which a given letter appears in a word – are part of members' ratiocinative resources for handling a proliferation of claims advanced by any litigant. In so far as sequencing is an intrinsic aspect of the empirical data, I have presented the statistical features of claim incidences (see Appendix 5) in a way that most faithfully reproduces that order.

The fact that certain claims routinely appear in particular 'priority' positions in any profile reflects an appreciation of their differential semantic weighting in regard to impression management techniques. Not all claim types have equal efficacy, import, or valency within any given culture. Their non-equivalent status is thus likely to vary according to (a) the relationships a claim contracts with other like units in any syntagm; (b) conventional values attached to that claim type outside the actualized profile; and (c) the degree to which the structure of any profile is responsive to the profile of an antagonist in any dispute.[4] These factors define the sense in which certain claims are *preferred* for use in particular strategies. Preferred orders of claim presentation are thus also evident from the design features of any profile in which they occur. It should be clearly understood that the term 'preference' refers to a structurally ingrained property of profiles, not a 'speaker's psychological disposition' (Atkinson and Drew 1979 : 59). Furthermore, on account of this fixed preference structure speakers anticipate that litigants will manipulate the sequence of declared claims.

I suggest that the approach outlined above advances the uncritical application of such traditionally conceived parameters as relationship between disputants, grievance type, dispute process, and sanction (see Starr 1978 : 111, or Young 1971 : 116). It seems to me an oversimplification and distortion of the empirical data to allow a dispute to be descriptively categorized, and statistically computed, as a unit of a certain type, where a multiplicity of claims are 'rooted in the same set of grievances', and thence to subsume this matrix under a single rubric determined by the nature of the 'precipitating offence' (Young 1971 : 117). We cannot profess to have explained, in any degree, a situation of multiple claims by concentrating on only one part of the sequence, or indeed by reducing this matrix to a single descriptive category. Moreover, a dispute may commence with a claim that becomes progressively subsumed within other claims, and both the outcome and settlement process may not at all reflect the nature of the precipitating offence. The only proper unit of accountability is the claim. By retaining the rank-level discriminations between dispute-profile-claim one can more rigorously correlate the relations between claim type, positional incidence, and resolution form independent of any notion of 'precipitating' breach. This avoids the perils of reductionism whereby a multiplicity is treated as a logical whole. The analysis offered here is unlikely to represent the whole answer, but it seems to me to suggest one way in which we can begin to confront the complexity of our raw data. It attends to the central problem of how the structural properties of disputes affect the peculiarities of outcome forms in different, culture-specific situations.

Without pre-empting later discussion, a brief outline of one claim type may serve to strengthen the arguments I have presented. In Huli, insult claims constitute the third most frequent category of indemnity issue. Sixty-seven per cent of all such claims I recorded occurred in the initial position of any profile; 83 per cent of all insult claims were renounced by litigants. In accounting for this systematic feature of profile shapes – which seems to reflect a preference for initiating a dispute with an insult claim – recourse can be had to the semantic salience of such verbal acts in the culture. The power of words is thus attested to in the metaphorical language about talk 'hitting', 'killing', or causing 'sickness' (detailed in Chapter 5). Despite such efficacious idioms, the injury done by insult (judged from the high rate of renouncement) seems somewhat transitory in terms of a compulsion to compensate or pursue damages. Reference to its position in claim sequences suggests that insult is here peculiarly responsive to strategies in which more 'important' issues (in the sense of their political or economic ramifications) can be sequentially deferred until later in the debate. Importantly, and in contrast with the constraints imposed by the question-answer format of Western court-talk, disputants know that the opportunity to air other claims will always arise. On account of a power to evoke immediate reactions of disapproval, and a relatively uncomplicated causal aetiology, insult claims occupy priority locales in any profile. Once debate with opponents is under way, other issues emerge and the insult claim becomes dissipated in the matrix. Data regarding other claim types also reveal significant relationships between sequential properties and resolution forms.[5]

All of this serves to indicate the importance of an attendance to the relative semantic evaluations of verbal and non-verbal actions in any culture. It also reminds us that the structural features of disputes have to be elicited with a view to the general organizational patterns of talk in such settings. The constraints of Western courts operate to restrict the range of issues that can be talked about, when people may take a turn, and what kind of turn their utterances must constitute. The setting-specific tasks of debate concern the elicitation of detailed information about events and people, the rejection of unacceptable evidential statements, a constant recapitulation of the finer details of any set of actions. While the question-answer format seems functionally adapted to the achievement of such ends, its close ordering properties force defendants to manage information in the form of replies. Because the defendant has also to direct himself to an examiner's specific request for certain details or a yes/no response, he is restricted in talking about matters of his own choice.

For an understanding of the verbal interaction of Huli disputes, this adjacency pair format is largely redundant. Very often it is the total matrix of contention issues between parties that is considered relevant. There is an expectation that by allowing disputants progressively to reveal claims through reciprocal dialogue, the *tene* ('source/origin/base/cause/real') of the dispute will eventually emerge. This expectation is particularly clear from a reading of D.2 (p. 158). In accordance with the purposes and tasks of such speech events, the structure of talking is quite different from that which obtains in 'court' type institutions. The turn-taking system is based on the principle of self-selection rather than pre-allocation; there is a concomitant absence of lexicalized labels for confrontation routines, or the interactional moves associated with adversarial systems. One corollary of this lack of explicit direction concerns a sensitivity to blame attribution and to overt disagreement with others. Participants rarely make reference to a previous speaker's contribution, and the markers of dissent have the property of referential indeterminancy (see Chapter 2). The overall character of a dispute talk conforms to a series of contributions where people often simply talk for the sake of talking. It is a forum for self-presentation and the attainment of prestige through the display of 'good speaking'. The determination of liability for compensation is thus an outcome that emerges from suggestions which are posed, presented, and offered for consideration. It is the sense of an event rather than its detail which is critical. In line with these facets talk is delivered *at* an audience rather than always directed *to* specific individuals. These observations appear to explain Sinclair's comment regarding the reactions of Huli to detailed questioning. Their uneasiness reflects the low incidence of such interrogative techniques. The Huli system affords participants a greater strategic potential and opportunity for counter-claim manipulation. Equally, it allows interactants to utilize a range of defence moves in different sequential locales.

My intention here has been to define areas of importance, suggest terms of description, and locate a pool of hitherto neglected foci that are the concern of this present investigation. The study of disputes should be, in part, but an aspect of the study of conversation. This ethnography is developed in line with the inclusive concepts and categories relating to the field of talk. The socio-legal research currently being conducted into the distinctive nature of talk in

Western courts provides one source for fruitful comparative work. This argues for a revision of those traditional problems relating to the applicability of Western jurisprudential concepts to native systems. The basis of comparison is transformed to how and why talk in different problem-solving contexts is structured in varying ways.

The ethnographic setting

The Huli are one of the largest cultural groups in the Southern Highlands Province of Papua New Guinea, and now number over 80,000. They inhabit an area of approximatively 2,000 square miles. In the north there is an uninterrupted flow of population between Huli and Duna country. Most inhabitants of Tanggi (see *Map 1*) are thus bilingual. The territory is divided administratively between the Koroba sub-district and the Tari sub-district. The first outsiders to contact the Huli were Hides (1936) and O'Malley in the early 1930s. Subsequently patrols by Sinclair (1955, 1957, 1966, 1973) and others resulted in the establishment of Government stations at Tari (in 1951) and Koroba (1955). The majority of my fieldwork time was spent in Ialuba valley (*Maps 1* and *2*) which represents the last Huli community west of Koroba.

Though the period of contact has been relatively short, changes to the social and economic fabric of the society appear to have occurred rapidly. A widespread network of roads has considerably increased mobility and it is not uncommon to find Huli in the capital Port Moresby, or Hagen. Most areas are serviced by aid-posts, local schools, and mission stations. Despite the virtual cessation of warfare, economic development has been slow in comparison with other Highland groups but includes cattle farming, cash-cropping, coffee plantations, and silk-worm projects. Traditional trade routes varied according to location. In the Koroba district black-palm bows and bird of paradise feathers came largely from the Duna, salt from Enga, and Tigasso tree-oil from various groups west of Levani referred to as Dugube. Nowadays it is common for Kaluli from the South to trade bows, string-bags, oil, and hornbill beaks with Huli as far north as Tanggi.

The majority of Huli are now nominal converts to various denominations (e.g. Catholic, Wesleyan, and Seventh-Day Adventist) and few people perform the traditional rites and spells that formerly accompanied both secular and religious activities. The large-scale fertility cycles of Tege (Glasse 1968) or Dindi Pongo (Goldman 1979)

Map 1 The Huli of the Koroba area

have not been practised for at least a decade. Nevertheless, the belief system remains intact and exerts a powerful determinative force on everyday behaviour. Moreover, where imported materials and methods prove unsuccessful, resort is made to the older, indigenous conventions. In the field of sickness and healing most areas can boast a few ritual practitioners versed in the re-ordering of one's relationship to *dama* (ancestral spirits and other supernatural beings). This breakdown in the framework of discipline is more noticeable in respect to male than to female adolescents. In pre-contact times young boys would undergo initiation into the Haroli cult which was concerned with the promotion of individual beauty and bodily health. In the various purification rituals that attended membership to this order the hair on one's head was a prime focus for attention. The sociocultural meanings surrounding this cult have persisted and Huli men take a great pride in their appearance. Wigs are worn as part of everyday dress and are frequently decorated with various ferns and feathers. The complex symbolism surrounding self-decoration in Huli is briefly touched upon in Chapter 5.

The Huli are subsistence farmers utilizing a bush-fallow technique devoted to sweet-potato cultivation. This is supplemented by taro, sugar-cane, pandanus, and various leaf vegetables. The system of horticulture includes ring-barking and burning (*e hiraya*), composting (*o dabia*), fallowing, mounding (*mondo*), and drainage. A differentiation is made between three types of garden: those made in the swamp (*lara*), those that lie immediately outside of a house (*gama*), and the larger mound tracts (*mabu*) which may be scattered in several places. Spades and steel axes have replaced the wooden digging-stick and stone axe. With a lack of distinguishable seasons there is little variation in the economic activities of Huli and there is certainly no annual horticultural cycle. In most communities small 'markets' operate once a week, and are occasions on which people meet to sell produce, exchange news, and pursue claims and grievances. Hunting for marsupials, snakes, cassowaries, and bird of paradise is more common in border areas like Ialuba, but is not of great dietary significance. Development has not been uniform over the whole area and change is most evident the closer one is to a government or health centre. Money (Kina) is now generally accepted as a substitute for the exchange mediums of pigs and cowrie-shells.

The origins of the Huli are obscure, though culturally and linguistically they are closest to the Duna and Ipili Paiela (Enga). Indeed, their myths stipulate common origins for these three cultural groupings. The area lies at an altitude of between 1,500 and 2,100 metres above sea-level. Rainfall averages 2,500 millimetres annually, while temperatures vary between 7°C minimum and 27°C maximum. The topography ranges from flat grasslands to hilly and precipitous terrain. One finds sinkholes, escarpments, volcanic ranges, and limestone outcrops;

the dense rain forests that often form a boundary between communities give way to small valleys. A rapid growth in population over the last twenty years, coupled with an appreciation of the new economic potential of land, has increased the pressure on resources in certain areas. While these factors will have affected the relative frequency of certain claim types, generalization for the whole area is difficult. In small communities such as Ialuba land disputes were still uncommon.

The structural organization of the Huli conforms to the patrilineal-patrivirilocal patterns typical of such Highlands tribes as the Enga, Melpa, and Daribi. Land is divided amongst discrete clan units. In three important respects the Huli deviate from regional patterns. First, they lack exchange cycles such as *te* (Enga) or *moka* (Melpa). Second, most males have a good knowledge of genealogical history, the generational depth of which is quite atypical for the region. Third, there is an explicit ideology of ascribed leadership which is focused on an individual referred to as a 'headman' (*agali* (man) *haguene* (head)). There are other men of importance in any community but it is the presence of this office of leadership which distinguishes the Huli political system from those constituted around the 'big-man' syndrome. With the exception of warfare, the operational spheres and functions of any incumbent remain the same and are described fully in later chapters. Onto this traditional system has been superimposed a multi-layered structure of legal institutions. These range from the appointment of land mediators and the provision for locally elected councillors, to land courts, local and district courts, and village courts. By means of this complex referral network a dispute may be subjected to a number of different settlement agencies and processes. The predominant feature of Huli social structure is the manner in which it articulates the male-female disjunction. In most of their daily activities the sexes are rigidly separated on account of an uncompromising philosophy of female pollution. Men and women maintain separate houses, and cook and consume food in the privacy of their own environments. An analysis of the structural importance of these principles is presented in Chapter 3.

The Huli are well-known in the anthropological literature of New Guinea through the publications of Glasse (1959a, 1959b, 1965, 1968). I have forsaken a lengthy introduction to Huli culture here since this would replicate the fine accounts of Glasse. In addition, the minutiae of daily life will emerge from a reading of data presented in the following chapters. The first systematic work on the language was carried out by Rule in 1954 with further research by Cheetham (1977a, 1977b) adding considerably to our understanding of this system. Huli is a Non-Austronesian verb final language which has been classified as a member of the Enga-Huli-Pole-Wiru family (Wurm 1961). It is typified by extensive vowel harmony rules, a high level of phonotactic restriction, and the presence of contrastive tone. This latter aspect is discussed in some detail in Chapter 2 since it forms part of the aesthetic model governing the relationships between meaning and form. Most Huli are monolingual but are acquainted (in differing degrees) with neo-melanesian pidgin. Talking is an extremely important activity in this culture. Words are conceptualized as mediating elements between an actor and a desired state of affairs. The proclivity for indulgence in assessments of verbal products reflects the salience of reflexivity (talk about talk) in the language. It is the elaboration of vocabulary sets and levels, the metalanguage used to convey the presence of aesthetic properties, and the separation of 'saying' from the 'said' that indexes the attention of Huli on the substantive nature of verbal interaction.

Notes

1 The position adopted here is consonant with ethnomethodological critiques of 'documentary' sociology. Whilst the argument is not a new one, the dearth of transcript cases in the dispute literature renders this re-statement timely. It seems clear that in order for our discipline to engage in fruitful dialogue on a corpus of detailed cases, there is a need to create the research 'mentality' that accepts the limitations of descriptive summaries relative to the reproduction of actual talk. This applies to both case collection and presentation. Furthermore, even where the focus of interest lies in the types of cultural distortion evidenced by memory cases, it may be significant to examine the stylistic choices adopted in the recounting of events as against those utilized in reports that occur in disputes.
2 The notion of *profile* refers specifically to the verbally actualized sequence of claims presented in any dispute. There may well be a case for suggesting that litigants also have non-activated profiles constructed from their option sets but not utilized. In so far as such psychological phenomena present the researcher with problems of independent verification and recording, I have not given any consideration to this possibility in this book.
3 The definition of this unit here does not exhaust the problematic nature of separating a claim from a 'passing reference' to a still smouldering grievance. Since members are also faced with the same identification problems the most reliable discrimination procedure is to assess how forcefully the issue is pursued and what reactions it engenders among the participants. It should be understood that the structural frame outlined here was

not conceived as an attempt to import linguistic models to the study of disputes. The analogies are an outcome of the properties of the empirical data which, as I have reiterated throughout the introduction, are well understood by Huli disputants.

4   This latter dimension is one that I was, sadly, unable to critically evaluate in this study. Quite simply, reliable statistical results depend on the avail- ability of a good data core. It would have required a longer fieldwork period to conduct such an analysis but clearly the interrelationships between profiles in any dispute is a question deserving of attention, and one hitherto unformulated.

5   Within the confines of this study it was not possible for me to give a full treatment of all the results derrived from the methodology adopted. In this regard, a detailed consideration is given to insult claims in Chapter 4. From an examination of *Table A1*, however, it can be seen that damage by pigs represents the most frequent category of claim (17 per cent) during my fieldwork time. Like insult, there is an immediacy about this type of issue in the sense that it is invariably presented in the initial locale (94 per cent) of any profile. It is rarely utilized as a form of counter-claim or resuscitated matter in disputes between the same parties. In the main such indemnity demands are privately sued (71 per cent) with a high overall outcome of renouncement (54 per cent). On account of the frequency of such incidents, people are generally reluctant to press claims for compensation from first-time offenders, knowing the likelihood of finding themselves in the same position at some future time. 50 per cent (see *Tables A2, A4, A6*) of renounced claims concern first offenders. Significantly, 14 per cent of all such claims were brought by women, the highest number of female com- plaints I recorded. This tends to emphasize the importance of their role in pig-husbandry. Clearly, one can appreciate here the relationships between positional incidence of a claim in a profile, semantic weighting, and out- come type.

2
A framework for talking

'At the very least, we hope to have shown that a rigorous
understanding of the methodic bases of action and order in courts
is unlikely to be arrived at independently or in advance of an
adequate understanding of the organisation of verbal interaction.'
                                        (Atkinson and Drew 1979 : 216)

A Huli dispute is conceived and constituted as a distinct type of 'talk
situation', the outcomes of which are defined as products of distributional and exchange patterns of speech. It thus seems appropriate
here to allow an analysis of disputes to include a consideration of discourse structures. Conversationalists habitually organize their speech
in terms of language-specific options that realize culturally salient
precepts. These cognitive principles are typically embodied in certain
pre-patterned expressions that function as types of openings, closings,
and parenthetic modulations. Such stereotypes represent an accumu-
lated corpus of strategies derived from recurrent contexts of talk. They
have proved, historically, to be 'functionally appropriate' (Coulmas
1981 : 2) for argumentation. The production of understanding and
meaning in verbal interaction concerns the display of competence –
presenting information in accordance with expectations of patterning
and what is important in talk. As both a resource and topic, participants use talk to accomplish order. They 'display to each other their
analysis, appreciation and use of that orderliness' (Schegloff and
Sacks 1973 : 290).
    The coherence of any stretch of discourse is thus partly sustained by

routinized speech forms which facilitate the flow of talk and turn-taking. They further provide a comprehension frame, or map, for semantically structuring what is said. An analysis of disputes must consider how the language of conduct, as well as the conduct of language, is culturally patterned by evaluated differences between distinct forms of 'doings', and some attention is due specifically to the way in which stereotypes, which mark boundaries between topics and between topic and speaker, articulate assessments of behaviour. Through this type of study we can perhaps glimpse the interplay between cultural patterns of speech and the underlying system of values or *Weltanschauung*. Beyond a consideration of how the various phrasing units encode notions about conduct lie two other issues. First, whether certain linguistic options can be identified as predominant in specific talk contexts; and second, whether these options express 'ritual constraints' (Goffman 1981 : 19) on interpersonal communication in disputes. That is, how far are the patterns of talk delineated below an index of people's sensitivities to directness, deference, or politeness in verbal interaction?

The problems defined above seem particularly critical for an understanding of Huli disputes where talk evidences a high degree of structuring with prepatterned expressions. For the most part (though not exclusively) these phrases function to reformulate and restate prior statements in terms of the primary categories of thinking (*mánda*), saying (*lá*), and doing (*bia*). The act of 'saying' is verbally represented in Huli as an explicit performative that is ubiquitous in most stretches of talk. These three modes of *doing*, as manifested in semi-fixed expressions, function as categories of comment. Information is packaged by anaphoric forms that constitute a type of 'subsidiary' discourse (Coulthard, Montgomery, and Brazil 1981 : 36) to the mainstream of topic development. They serve to talk about talk. In retrospective fashion, many of these formulae say again what has been said in accordance with a value system that evaluates different kinds of action. The expressions or 'gambits'[1] considered in this chapter thus 'gloss' propositions by indicating how that information is to be received, that is, whether the statement forwarded is an opinion, guess, belief, or assertion, and whether it is verbal, object, person, or action-oriented. It seems prudent to initiate a discussion of these processes by fixing upon some of the key distinctions relating to talk.

Figure 1 Doing and saying

A   *Bi*
System   'word', 'language', 'topic', 'talk'
                                            |
Process   *Lā*
                            'speak', 'say', 'verbally make'
                                            |
                                  Bi ogo dagua lā
                                  'talk this   like say'

B   *Lā*   :   *Bia*
          'do verbally'   'do non-verbally'

C²   *Lā*   :   *Lá*
          'say/speak'   'to cause to', 'to bring into effect'

Bi and Lā

The notions of *bi* and *lā* express a separation between language-system and language-behaviour. In Huli, the taxonomic systems for speech evaluation, analysis, and description are predicated on the substantive domain of *bi*. In language used to talk about talk, attitudinal import or comment is articulated by means of adjectival qualifications of *bi* (i.e. *bi* + modifier). The process of speech production, as marked by the verb *lā*, is not an action capable of the same degree or kind of assessment. What is said, and the fact that it is 'said', are what constitute potential topics for debate, rather than the manner in which things are said. There are not different ways of saying in Huli, only the saying of different 'words' (*bi*). The distinction between *bi* and *lā* is pervasive and irreducible in the language system. References to speech or soundmaking always keep distinct product from process: *Bi tê lāro* ('I am saying a folk-legend'); *Bi yobage lāro* ('I am saying a veiled talk'); *Bi illili lāro* ('I am saying taboo words').

The langue/parole dichotomy, and how it is defined and realized in any system, is clearly an important dimension of comparison between languages. For example, in Kaluli (another Southern Highlands society: see Feld and Schieffelin n.d.) the corresponding constructions for *Bi ndi lāga* ('One says a secret talk') and *Bi ko lāga* ('One says a mispronunciation') are contrastingly compounded with *sama* ('say') as descriptions of how speaking is performed. A similar order of divergence is indexed by the way the two cultures formulate modalities of soundmaking. The Kaluli differentiate modes of utterance as adverbial distinctions of the manner of speaking; the Huli formulate comparable differences as aspects of the substance 'talk' (*bi*):

Bi hagare lāra	'He is saying a whisper-talk.'
Iba gana lāra	'He is singing' ('causing' (*lāra*) + 'water' (*iba*) + 'in the drains' (*gana*): figurative).
Bi ga lāra *ó lāra* *ù lāra*	'He is saying a shout-talk' (the substantive terms are onomatopoeic).
gau lāra	'It is saying "*gau*"' (describes the time as early morning. '*Gau*' is the talk of the Alua (honeyeater) heard at this time of day).

These interlinguistic differences seem related to systematic contrasts in speech poetics and style between the two cultures. The Huli indigenously define their stylistic system as firmly located at the rank level of words (*bi*) (see Chapter 5). This is partly evidenced by the proliferation of functionally differentiated eulogistic lexicons. For Kaluli, expressive forms appear anchored to modes of soundmaking. It may be that these differences in metalinguistic outlook further correlate with differences in speech behaviour in disputes.

Consistent with this lack of emphasis on speech processes, Huli has few explicit expositives relating to the actions of 'commenting', 'evaluating', 'interpreting', 'mentioning', 'confirming', or other illocutionary forms common to the conduct of debate in Western courts. Only the act of 'saying' is lexically realized. Importantly, this economy of speech-act descriptors appears functionally related to cultural preferences for preserving a degree of neutrality and detachment in accounts of behaviour. Reported speech is always cited directly in the object position, followed by the appropriate form of the verb 'say' (*lā*); this unit is then semantically framed by further occurrences of *lā* as an explicit performative/description for the action of speech just performed:

Bi   ogoni dagua nalabe   laya   larogoni
'talk this   like   don't say', he said, I am saying.

The focus of attention in any report of speech is on what is 'said', and quotations are always 'direct'. The separation of content from performance is paralleled by a reporter's disaffiliation from that which he is reporting. Comment, opinion, evaluation, or other expressions of attitude are not lexically articulated in the process of reporting.[3] As a corollary of this there is little disagreement or debate in disputes about what precisely was said or the manner in which it was said. Inferences about speakers' intentions are made directly from the reported utterances. The glossing stereotypes that are most prevalent in the environment of reports restate that a stretch of talk was actually 'said': *ani lene* ('thus it was said'); *au layago* ('this is what was said'); *ogo dagua lalu* ('it was said like this').

A dispute, as one exemplification of *bi*, is not terminologically structured or divided into episodic phases. There is no schema that classifies talk in the confrontative and processual terms common in the language of our own court systems. Contributions are thus not located within an interactive framework of 'justification', 'defence', 'examination', or 'accusation'. The substantive bias of the system reveals itself through assessments of topic definition and presentation, and aspects of the relation between speaker and speech.

In respect of a speaker's act of assertion, communicated by the performative 'say' (*lā*), there are in Huli (additional to verb-final suffixes of tense, mood, person, number, and voice) a number of important final suffixes expressing emphatic and evidential aspects:

no suffix: evidence on previous knowledge ('I know that . . .')
-go/goni: emphatic (for action or state)
-rua (present third-person)/*-yua* (past third-person): first position suffixes added to the verb stem which indicate evidence based on perception other than sight.
The following suffixes may be appended to either verb or non-verb statements:
-da: evidence of an occurrence is based on visible results
-ya: statement based on previous evidence no longer visible
-bada: suffix of possibility.

From these linguistic markers of epistemic modality (the knowing and believing aspects of assertion) we may say that the Huli system of *lā* is one of objective modalization (see Lyons 1977 : 799). The categorical I-say-so component is an inalienable aspect of uses of the verb 'say' in Huli. It shows a commitment by the speaker to the factual nature of the proposition; Huli speakers do not lexically express reservation about information given. Importantly then, assertion is always an unqualified act in Huli speech. There are statements of qualified factuality but not qualified assertion. The I-say-so (neustic) component in acts of *lā* are always categorical, while the it-is-so (tropic) can be qualified in respect of the evidential aspects described above. This structuring of where assertion and doubt are located in utterances relates fundamentally to recurrent uses of *lāro* ('I am saying') as an explicit performative in talk. The value and importance of assertion (as opposed to statements of opinion, hearsay, or tentative inference) in Huli is thus indexed by the use of the stereotype 'I am saying' as opening, closing, and parenthetic expressions. Presentation and assertion of self demands that the speaker make explicit what is being done in any utterance – i.e. 'saying' – and who is performing that act. As will be evident from the textual data given throughout this book (e.g. Appendix 4), the importance of 'I am saying' (*lāro*) as an act of self-declaration seems confirmed by its relative frequency of occurrence.

The prevalence of surface forms of *lā*, as making explicit *what* one is doing in any utterance, and the fact that it cannot be qualified, highlights the relation between language structure and language use. Verbal action is of paramount importance in the value system of this culture as a vehicle for control and assertion. *Lāro* ('I am speaking') appears to mark the interdependence between these values and patterns of speech behaviour. The systematic delimitation of modality in respect of neustic/tropic clarifies for an audience what pertains to the speaker (commitment), and what relates to content. Assessments of each are done on the basis of different criteria. This linguistic feature is clearly a crucial aspect of the presentation of accounts and reports in disputes.

Huli has no comparable subjective modalizations (or words describing attitudes) of 'wonder', 'doubt', 'imagine', 'presume', 'suppose', or 'believe' that intimate diminished assurance or tentativeness. There are no contra-factive forms such as 'I wish . . .'. From an examination of the list of stereotype expressions (see *Table 1*, p. 46) we may note the marked absence of the opinion frames that typify comparable lists of English formulae (Keller 1981 : 98: 'I have reason to believe . . .' or 'I am pretty sure . . .'). The Huli system appears then to be designed to elicit fact and incident (and more especially, what has been said), rather than attitude, opinion, or doubt.

These observations bear directly upon the evaluation of this system with regard to forms of politeness. From an emic standpoint, talk demands some management of the potential strains between acting in a direct, assertive manner for self-advancement, and a need to avoid giving offence by the adoption of a blunt posture. This is not an *a priori* presupposition about behaviour in Huli, but is explicitly acknowledged and verbalized by actors with reference both to talk and to non-verbal interaction such as decoration (see Chapter 5). A balance is achieved between these constraints by forms of mitigation or downgrading that have to be defined in any specific cultural context. In talk, the directness of the unqualified status of I-say-so is offset by the qualified manner of the it-is-so component in any utterance. There are many parallels in other aspects of talk. For example, from the set of linguistic options for claiming a turn at talk, the majority of devices used in disputes (see *Table 1*) appear to embody the value and necessity of competitive assertion. Once a turn is commenced however, the content is organized in terms of impersonal norm formulae and recurrent use of disjunctive formats that present possibilities and choices to participants. The directness of language used to obtain turn incumbency is balanced by modes of indirectness once 'space' is secured. The speaker, moreover, establishes a distance from, and diminished responsibility for, content in reports of speech. The theme of assertion is indeed common to many of the New Guinea Highlands cultural systems: 'Independence and assertion in speech and action are functionally valued in this egalitarian society' (Feld and Schieffelin n.d.).

Lā and Bia

These two terms mark the distinction between 'saying' (*lā*) and 'doing/making' (*bia*) in respect of verbal and non-verbal acts. Unlike usages of *do/make* in English, *bia* has a more restricted collocational scope in that it cannot occur in constructions concerning the production of vocal sounds. The sentence (see *Figure 1*)

> bi   ogo *dagua bia*
> talk this like   make
> ('make a talk like this')

is inappropriate and deviant in Huli. Additionally, *bia* cannot be substituted for states such as anger (*keba*), refusal (*manga*), or pain (*tandaga*) which compound with the verb stem *ha* ('stand/be'). *Bia* occurs then as a component of verb forms signifying the 'doing' of something. It can function as a stand-in for any episodic verb including acts, happenings, actions, attempts, omissions, achievements, and accomplishments. As with the verb for 'saying' (*lā*), utterances based on *bia* are prevalent in subsidiary discourse (talk about talk) and most usually have an easily identifiable syntactic independence. Many of the routinized expressions cited in *Table 1* act as glossing or focusing devices that repeat/rephrase a preceding statement to reiterate that something was 'done' or 'said'. The initial discourse statements become an object for further reflective talk or comment as articulated primarily through *lā* and *bia*. This is done, as we have seen, in accordance with the general orientation of the system for eliciting fact rather than opinion, attitude, or comment. Two short examples can (as a preliminary to later discussion) serve to illustrate these points:

TEXT 1 : D.3 : 36–47
1 *Abago ina lelo hondo ha*
   Aba, to let me speak you wait
   tene Ibai āba ibugua layagoni . . .
   the source Ibai's father has said . . .
5 *tene ina howa larigola oba haya*
   the source was from what you said, and they laughed
   ibu ere mbira hayago ibu oba hoya hayada
   the ones that were behind him they laughed (as we can see: *da*)
→ *au biyadagoni*
10   that is how it was done
   agali biago ibu
   that man
   oba howa hayago
   when they had laughed
15 → *agi larube toba howa haria nawi nu tombe lāru lāruago*
   'What did I say; not knowing I went where there was no track', he is
   saying (we can hear : *rua*)
→ *ogo dagua layago*
   like that he said
20 *bi mbira ibugua udu iba pirayagola pene biarubi lene biaru*
   one talk down there was about the flood, those were said
→ *mbira lene biago layagola*
   one thing was said, and then when that was said
   i nde tabirene lalu
25   then there was a joke said
   ina mbalini piyagola howa . . . (pause)
   when the sister had gone . . .
→ *au lole naga larimagoni*
   for to say like this we are talking

TEXT 2
1 *nogo wariabu mende ogonibi minigo iginigo Homai yalu pene*
   the second Wariabu pig was given and carried by the boy Homai

nogo wariabu tebone ogonibi minigo Taro ibu yalu pene
the third Wariabu pig was given and carried by Taro
5   *nogo wariabu mane Garua hame tini*
the fourth Wariabu went to Garua's father
→ *ani bigi bini laro*
thus it was continually done I am saying
→ *au bialu*
10   therefore it was done like that

(Field data)

Part of the organizational work in dispute speeches consists of focusing participants' attention on things 'said' and 'done' through routine expressions that log, reflectively, the progression of reported events. In the above texts we can observe how such 'ritualised gambits' (Lyons 1977 : 53) (Text 1 : 10; 19, Text 2 : 8; 10) constitute a subsidiary discourse to the main flow of propositional information. They tend to be located at the boundaries between topics:

TEXT 1
8   the ones that were behind him they laughed (as we see: *da*)
10 →   that is how it was done
15   'What did I say; not knowing I went where there was no track',

and function to review the main discourse by 'expanding it, modifying it and evaluating it' (Coulthard, Montgomery, and Brazil 1981 : 37). What is noticeable, in the context of Huli speech, is that the items that 'gloss' what has been said to have been said or done, are predominantly structured around the categories of *lā* and *bia* (see *Table 1*). In this regard, subsidiary discourse not only re-evaluates the development of a speech, but clearly abstracts categories of action that are culturally salient. Such gambits are interactively designed to provide a measure of cohesion to speech in regard to expectations about order.

It seems important to recognize both that the items of subsidiary discourse function to review, rephrase, and summarize talk, and that they perform these tasks in language-specific categories. With reference to the opening paragraphs of this chapter, *lā* and *bia* provide a semantic frame for communicating propositional information. Hearers are given a map for plotting the 'said' and 'done'. This appears to constitute one dimension for understanding the interplay between cultural patterns of speech and value concepts. For Huli, types of action (and their evaluated differences) are more significant than objects, people, attitudes, and manner. The topic of gambits and their functions provides an interface between discourse analysis and the study of disputes. It forces us to consider cultural assessments of different modes of 'doings'.

Other units based on *lā* and *bia* function as linking clauses between topics under discussion and the development of new points. Linking clauses most typically include, in a different morphological form, the key categories of *lā* and *bia* found in glossing units (which repeat, rephrase, and comment on the 'said' and 'done') that may precede them. Moreover, the above texts reveal a concern with what will be 'said' (Text 1 : 28) as a prospective structuring of future talk. We may note the use of evidence suffixes attendant on reports of direct speech (Text 1 : 15) or events (Text 1 : 6).

'Saying' and 'doing' constitute the rudimentary behavioural concepts that underpin the habitual structuring of speech in Huli. Their purpose is to order talk so as to reflect expectations about the presentation of content. The focus of utterances is thus on what happened, what was said to have happened, and what was said. This is consistent with the 'event-dominated' character of non-Austronesian languages such as Huli. In the context of the present analysis we may further add a pronounced indulgence in verbal retrospection. The style of forensic rhetoric in Huli is rooted in the categories of *bia* and *lā*; they constitute a 'semantic frame map' (Keller 1981 : 97) that communicates what is being said about some information. *Doing* and *saying* are modes of producing material effect on the world and relationships. As such, they represent salient acts for re-emphasis and evaluation. An outcome to any dispute is dependent on the prospective structuring of talk. This is conveyed by those stereotype conclusions (see *Table 1* : 3(c)) which offer a 'plan':

o *binidagoni*   *lamiya larimibe laro*
Oh done (we have seen: *da*) let's say, did we say, I am saying
('I am saying, did we say "Let us say it was done (on the visible evidence)?"').

It would be wrong to infer from the 'routine' nature of such gambits a semantic redundancy, a total loss of literal meaning. Such devices are indeed polyfunctional and capable of carrying many different kinds of meaning.

While on one level we can thus equate *lā* and *bia* in respect of certain discourse functions, it is the evaluated contrast between speech and action that is philosophically fundamental to assessments of behaviour and events. How their relationship is defined is a critical parameter for studies of disputes. One central hypothesis demonstrated in this book is that the saliency of 'talk' in Huli is indexed by the frequency of insult claims. Moreover, on account of the existential status of verbal action, this type of claim has a positional frequency of occurrence such that it is habitually utilized as an opening type of claim in any given profile of multiple claims. That is, claims about 'what was said' have a positional priority in disputants' strategies relating to multiple-claim presentation. It is at this level, then, that a knowledge of language structure and behaviour – and specifically the distinctions of 'talk' (*bi*) and 'saying' (*lā*)/ 'saying' (*lā*) and 'doing' (*bia*) – are essential to the interpretation and analysis of dispute processes.

The particular nature and quantity of claims in any dispute reflects aspects of interaction, past and present, between the parties. The sequential structure of those claims expresses the cultural system of evaluations concerning 'doings'. The positional incidence of insults (their place at the head of any list of claims being pursued by any disputant) also reflects their relatively uncomplicated causal aetiology – their 'factuality' in respect of something that was 'said' alienated from complications of attitude or intention. Claims of insult have an ability to evoke immediate reactions of disgust and disapprobation. In so far as words (*bi*) alone have material reality and effect for someone, other considerations of manner, opinion, or attitude are irrelevant. This partly accounts for the substantive bias inherent in language structure and behaviour relating to *bi* ('words/talk'). While from an etic standpoint we may assert that saying is absolutely always 'doing', we need in any setting to define what that 'doing' consists of, and what implications arise.

Importantly, as I have argued elsewhere (Goldman 1980; and see also Strathern 1981 : 10), the Huli do not contrast men of actions (*bia*) with men of words (*bi*). In this culture, actions do not speak louder than words, and words are not said to be 'translated' into actions. For Huli, saying and thinking (*mañda bia*: literally 'doing knowledge') are not quiescent states but modes of 'doing'; speech is not 'insubstantial' in comparison with actions. Contrasts of control, effectiveness, and substantiality are made within each mode of 'doing' rather than between them. Speech is evaluated against other speech, or thought against other thoughts. Saying words is a production of material effects. The full implications of this system of assessment are detailed in Chapter 5, but in the following text we have some idea of how the effective/ineffective dimension is used to attribute the quality of 'manhood':

TEXT 3
1   *Ai i ore agali ndo*
   You are not a man
   ti agali ndo
   they are not men
5 → *au larimago*
   we are saying like that
   Mana li ngagome
   with the *mana* (custom) that is there
   ina bai holebira
10   you will throw it down
  → *au lalu bai harimago*
   when that has been said and we have thrown it down
   i agalida lelo
   then we will let you say 'I am a man'
15 → *biaga biago*
   that is what we used to do
   i agalida lelo biago
   to let you say I am a man
   ina duria maria mule pu
20   you go and give five or four (pigs)
  → *au layago*
   it has been said like that
   bi dindi naga ogoria howa
   for the talk on the land
25   *daraboli naga howa*
   for the trouble
   o haguene biago howa bi ogo hangu bule pudaba
   from the headman there is only this talk, 'Go and do it'
  → *au layago*
30   it has been said like that
   mo wa harigo?
   you threw it away? (rhetorical question)
   ndo
   no
35   *ina mbira mule pu*
   you go and give one (pig)
   ibugua kira mule pu
   he will go and give two (pigs)
  → *au layago.*
40   it has been said like that.

(Field data)

The speaker contrasts the effectiveness of giving pigs (an indication of 'manhood' (*agali*)) with the ineffective action of 'throwing away'.

One course of action is assessed against another. We may note the recurrent use of gambits centred on 'saying' and 'doing' that function as boundary markers between topic statements. Topic structure is something that I will discuss more fully later. At this juncture it is relevant for my analysis of *lā* and *bia* to consider how these semi-fixed expressions frame statements that are presented in a paired format. The implicit syntax of the speech reveals linked formulations, a repetition of binary units for each new topic statement. There is a progression:

(1)	*the present state of matters*	*Gambits*
	'You are not man' ⎱	
	'they are not men' ⎰	'we are saying like that'
(2)	*conditions for attributing*	
	manhood	
	'mana . . . thrown down' ⎱	
	'let you say I am a man' ⎰	'that is what we used to do'
	'let you say I am a man' ⎱	
	'give five or four pigs' ⎰	'it has been said like that'
(3)	*types of claim for which talk*	
	has been said	
	'for talk on the land' ⎱	
	'for the trouble'	
	'from the headman'	'it has been said like that'
	'go and do it' ⎰	
(4)	*something that shouldn't be*	
	done	
	'you threw it away' ⎱	
	'no' ⎰	
(5)	*two conclusions*	
	'you go and give one' ⎱	
	'he will go and give two' ⎰	'it has been said like that'

Each topic may be stated in retrospective or prospective terms, but they seem invariably to retain a bipartite format.

We can perhaps relate this structure to the nature of Huli dispute management processes, which are oriented to achieving agreement by consensus rather than by obedience to imposed judgements. The coda of most speeches that define outcomes (see Chapter 5) articulates a set of alternatives by employing the disjunctive 'either . . . or . . .' form. Despite the grammatical guise of the two conclusions in Text 3 (35–8) as compound commands, they are 'suggestions' rather than enforceable directives. The uncertainty about how they will be received by disputants is balanced by the security that derives from (a) references to norms of *mana* (7), and (b) the structuring of talk in terms of *lā* and *bia*.

This discussion has abstracted some of the ways in which Huli conceptualize 'saying' as a kind of 'doing'. Talking is a social action, and the dispute is one 'talk situation' for self-presentation. 'I am saying' (*lāro*) functions here as an assertive speech act, an explicit performative marker that is also descriptive of a 'naturally consequent performance' (Austin 1962: 65). Saying gives words material reality as things that can be evaluated as registrable on personal reputations. A man is measured by the measure of his words (*bi*). On account of the systematic distinction between the I-say-so (*lāro*) and the what-I-say (*bi*) components in any utterance, the act of assertion in Huli is not qualified for manner or attitude (i.e. reservation, opinion, doubt, or tentativeness). What is assessed are kinds of words (*bi*). The effectiveness of verbal 'doings' is partly demonstrated in the cultural patterning of, and responses to, insult. In this regard, the metaphorical language of pain and sickness provides an expressive medium for Huli talk about talk. Speech and pain are conceptually equated as affecting people in precisely the same ways. Saying gives existential status to words and its causative force is nowhere better articulated than in Huli concepts about *gamu* ('spells') discussed below.

Lā and Lá

In addition to the senses in which *saying is doing*, we may further distinguish contexts in which there is a saying *of* doing (statements made in non-verbal behaviour such as self-decoration), and a saying *while* doing (Paine 1981 : 19). The interplay of speech and action is particularly evident in Huli spells (*gamu*), which are a prerequisite for success in most fields of endeavour. It is not unusual for a Huli man to 'hold' (*yi*) some twenty or more spells, verbal formulae that mediate between an actor's aims or purposes and their attainment. For the most part, Huli spells conform to object- or person-addressed commands. The hoped for action or result is defined as an activity or a state of affairs that the speaker wants the target to achieve, or refrain from. The speaker's epistemic warrant for making the spell derives from its manifestation of *mana* ('custom, lore'). In terms of content we can differentiate between statements that define specific actions: *action-oriented commands* ('go like the cassowary/go like the wild dogs . . .'); and *state-realization commands* ('be like . . .') which order or invoke a particular state of affairs. These are ideal types and there are many spell statements that fall in the middle of the continuum as both explicitly doing an action and stating a result. The preconditions that obtain for the success of a spell relate to proper performance. The efficacious power of a rite reflects then the interdependence between *bi* ('words') and *lā* ('saying').

This interdependence between content and performance is paralleled by that of verbal and non-verbal components of any magical routine, both of which are denoted by the term *gamu*. Saying and doing are fused in a way that emphasizes their complementarity. Speech is an integral part of actions directed to bringing about something. Saying invests the analogic and metaphoric processes of spell language with causative power that seeks to control people, events, and objects. *Gamu* realize an attempt to recreate and reorder a natural or present state of relationships.

In these linguistic routines and other discourse, the phrase 'I am saying' (*lāro*) is understood to cover two quite separate, but related, functions: (i) the utterance of sounds and an expositive act of assertion; and (ii), as a verbal clause of existential-causality, the production of material reality. These two meanings, and the systematic nature of their association, are given separate lexical status in the language as tonally contrasted word-forms (see *Figure 2*).

Figure 2   Tone units

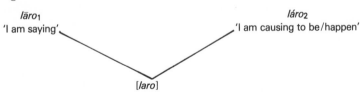

$lāro_1$
'I am saying'

$láro_2$
'I am causing to be/happen'

[*laro*]

The way in which phonemic tone in Huli systematically differentiates between related meanings of what we might otherwise consider as a single polysemous lexeme, is central to an understanding of speech and meaning in this culture. Many of the interpretive hypotheses adduced in this book are based on the significant senses in which this prosodic system interweaves similarities of form and meaning. By way

of introduction to the discussion of tone we may briefly consider the
following spell.

TEXT

Māli Dagia Gamu (Dance (*māli* + platform (*dagia*) + spell (*gamu*): the
spell as a preparatory basis for public performance)

Auwa pugu   *lāro*
Auwa waterfall (like) I am causing to be
Yambala pugu   *lāro*
Yambala waterfall (like) I am causing to be
Biri pugu   *lāro*
Biri waterfall (like) I am causing to be
Bagoma pugu   *lāro*
Bagoma waterfall (like) I am causing to be

Informant: Anya Imane (Tobani clan)

The spell is stylistically typical of its genre, showing marked lexical
and phonological patterning. A single idea is formulated and then
reiterated through parallel repetition – repeated syntax with oneword substitutions which are, in this case, fictitious waterfalls. The
names fall into rhyming pairs based on assonance (*Auwa/Yambala*)
and alliteration (*Biri/Bagoma*). We can again observe a tendency for
statements to be paired as binary forms even though the topic is not
here structured in dualistic terms. The spell is used to imbue the
performance of a dance with the valued properties of waterfalls. The
alignment of the two domains by analogic processes is mediated by
the semantic features of movement (cascading) and fluency. These
properties were identified to me in the speaker's exegesis.

State-realization is explicitly accomplished here through *lāro* ('I am
causing'). In these contexts it embodies the implicit causative power
of *lāro* ('I am saying'). That is, the unstated first-person performative
I-say-so is embedded both in the talk-situation of spells, and in the
naturally consequent act of utterance. Saying gives material reality to
the metaphoric process. In much the same way, 'I am causing' is a
semantic component inherent in 'I am saying'. While each has a
degree of realization in the other, they are tonally differentiated
(perhaps as surface forms of *laro* (*Figure 2*)) because the separate
components do not always coalesce. Thus the verb stem *lá* ('cause')
compounds with the stative stem of other verbs to give the meaning of
'to cause to . . ./to leave . . .' that does not reflect a verbal act. To
assert that there is a semantic relatedness between the tonally distinguished terms is not etic construction. However, we need to

examine in some detail how far this relationship between meaning and form is a systematic aspect of the language, and what criteria justify relatedness of meaning.

The presence of lexically significant contrastive pitch is widespread among the non-Austronesian languages of New Guinea. Huli is a region of known occurrence. Tone languages differ in the degree to which pitch is important semantically, and there is some basis for regarding tone as a secondary feature of the Huli language. Three contrastive pitch levels were identified – high, mid, and low – utilizing substitution-frames and toneme identification procedures outlined by Pike (1948). The results and conclusions reached, in respect of toneme attribution, accord with those initially formulated by Rule (1954). In over 95 per cent of the sample collected (with an approximate upper limit of perhaps some fifty words) semantic relatedness could be posited between word-forms whose meanings were distinguished by tone.

Within the context of knowledge about Huli culture it was immediately evident that such contrasted lexemes were, in the main, of fundamental significance to indigenous discourse about kinship relations, decoration, and social interaction. The morphological reflection of semantic relatedness made it reasonable to postulate that this prosodic system correlated with the cognitive status and cultural salience of the lexical distinctions it made. The following compilation serves then as a résumé of the tonally marked contrasts that underlie some of the interpretive statements made in this book. The brief formulations appended to each set, explaining the area of semantic coalescence, should be understood in the context of the fuller ethnographic expositions given elsewhere in this book.

Yári$_1$ (cassowary) : (decoration) *Yàri*$_2$
[The sense in which 'I am decorating' means 'I am becoming a cassowary']
Mañda$_1$ (hair/wig) : (knowledge) *Mañda*$_2$
[The sense in which one's hair/wig displays a state of knowledge and maturity]
Heǵe$_1$ (swear words) : (tongue) *Heǧe*$_2$
[The sense in which swear words are located in, and derive from, the tongue]
Hambu$_1$ (sorcery) : (lips) *Hambu*$_2$
[The sense in which this genre of sorcery has a power that is performatively, as well as mythically, related to 'lips']
Hame$_1$ (father) : (desire) *Hame*$_2$
[The sense in which an agnatic ideology normatively defines relational and residence preferences]

$M\grave{a}li_1$ (celebratory dance) : (death platform) $M\grave{a}li_2$
[The sense in which $M\grave{a}li$ traditionally followed the death of an enemy, and in which the decorated death platform is, metaphorically, a celebratory act for the dead]

$Wa\tilde{n}dia_1$ (woman's house) : (to avoid/go around) $Wa\tilde{n}dia_2$
[The sense in which the inter-sex ideology defines female associated objects as items for strict avoidance]

$`A\hat{b}a_1$ (father) : (mother's brother) $A\bar{b}a_2$
[The sense in which a person has "two fathers" (Wagner 1967 : 77; 124) as defined by cultural notions of substance and consanguinity]

$\hat{U}_1$ (shout/yodel) : (song) $\bar{U}_2$
[The sense in which, as speech modes, they fall into the format of call-response moves with pronounced use of falsetto (Pugh-Kitigan 1975 : 80)]

$L\bar{a}_1$ (say) : (cause to) $L\hat{a}_2$
[The sense in which 'saying' is an existential-causative]

It is clear from the data that we are not dealing with homonyms, nor, in a strict sense, with a single polysemous lexeme. Tonal contrasts mark the senses in which the meanings of derivationally related terms are similar and yet different. Furthermore, this is systematic in the language. Relatedness of meaning is not here posited as a pre-theoretical, *a priori* assumption. The criteria for attribution must be clarified. Two specific problems, detailed by Lyons (1977 : 552), are involved. First, semantic relatedness or metaphorical connection are not quantifiable concepts, but matters of degree. Second, native speakers' intuitions or responses to questions invariably resulted in indeterminate and confusing results. While acknowledging that 'semantic relatedness' is a problematic concept for anthropology, the inferences I have drawn concerning the operation of tone in Huli depend on three criteria, which provide varying degrees of corroboration:

(1) That in the context of what is known about the interlinguistic aspects of tone (see Pike 1948), the Huli system is not unique. Importantly, similarities of form or sound permit guarded inferences concerning relations of sense. Placed within the framework of other data relating to poetics (see Chapter 5), one can demonstrate that the relation between form and meaning is not completely arbitrary in Huli. The tone system functions alongside such devices as minimally-distinct pairings in the lexicalization of synonyms/antonyms, and the binary facets of eulogistic vocabularies. They seem all to express the high degree of correspondence between semantic, syntactic, and phonological structures. It appears reasonable to view tone differentiations as another facet of sound-symbolism in the Huli language.

(2) The attributions of semantic relatedness reflect interpretations about Huli data. Further to my discussion of *láro* ('I am saying') and *láro* ('I am causing'), we may briefly examine the example of *hége* ('swear words') and *hège* ('tongue'). *Hége* is used for lexically specific profanities and expletives; it always describes a verbal act. *Hège* can be used metonymically for most articulatory organs and idiomatically for 'talk'. Invariably, it has derogatory import most graphically expressed in the phrase 'poison tongue' (*hège tomia*: tongue-poking). The semantic connotations of each term are embedded in its corresponding, but tonally contrasted, analogue. Each has representation in the other, but the shades of difference are marked by prosodic contrasts.

(3) The semantic equivalences embody themes and motifs that, to judge from relevant literature, are clearly of regional significance. For example, the association between 'cassowary' (*yári*) and 'self-decoration' (*yàri*) (see Chapter 5) is made by most cultures of the New Guinea Highlands (see Gell 1975). The sense in which mother's brother (*aba*) is a kind of 'father' (*aba*) appears central to Daribi kinship (Wagner 1967). The meanings conveyed by the tonal pairs accord with regional-wide cultural statements; the manner in which they are linguistically represented is perhaps a mode of expression peculiar to the Huli.

The above discussions provide a firm basis for understanding the logic of talk in disputes. The fundamental relationships between *words/saying*, *saying/doing/*, and *saying/causing* underlie the very nature of how speech is designed in regard to dispute resolution. The equivalency of thinking (*mánda*), doing (*bia*), and saying (*lá*) is contextually modified by the pre-eminence of talking for handling claims. In summary, we may briefly compare the culturally standardized expression of *mana* (custom, cultural ways: the amorphous repertoire of conventional norms) with a segment of text from a dispute:

Bime   *mana*   *lole*
with the talk the *mana* will be said
halime   *hole*
with the ears it will be heard
deme   *de hondole*
with the eyes it will be seen
minime   *mitangi bule*
with the mind it will be reflected upon

Culture (*mana*) is actualized through talking and the perceptive faculties. The repetition of syntactic form,and alliteration between agentive and verb, highlights the associative link between cognition and *mana*. For debate, however, thoughts must be coupled with words:

> *Ai agali kemago au biaga ka*
> ai men who are here this is what we used to do
> *agali mbira bi nalaga*
> there will be one man who never used to talk
> *mini biaga*
> he used to do with the mind
> *bi mini la harume biaga birima ka*
> we are doing what we used to do with the talk and mind together.

Gambits

The term 'gambit' (see Keller 1981) refers here to certain phrasal constructions which, as we have already observed, play an important role in structuring talk in disputes. They represent implicit agreements about how information is to be packaged for communication. In so far as they reflect a 'conception of a social system' (Coulmas 1981 : 2), they do so in Huli by embodying evaluative judgements about words and action. A striking feature of the gambits listed in *Table 1* is the repetition and fixity of lexical phrases based on the verbs *la* (say) and *bia* (do). It needs to be emphasized that the capacity of such gambits to indicate how statements are to be understood is determined as much by the lexical item used as by context. To the extent that the English gambits 'I presume', 'I believe', 'I imagine', or 'I wonder' can be said to express an element of doubt, reservation, or tentativeness, they do so partly through contrast with substitutable terms like 'assert' or 'convince'. The corollary of this perhaps obvious point is that the gambits considered here fall into a different category of stereotype phrases from those socially obligatory formulas related to greetings, farewells, apologies, or expressions of gratitude: gambits do not suffer the same degree of loss of 'literal' meaning, nor does their absence result in social censure. It is because recurrent expressions can be placed along a continuum in regard to their 'formulaic' character, that we can discuss the semantic aspects of gambits – in

Table 1   *Gambits*

---

1 Topic evaluation

(a) Disagreement (turn-beginning devices only)

(*bi*) *agueni ndo* / *ogoni ndo* / *au bule ndo* / *ndo laro* /	'not like that / I am saying that is not the talk'
nakarulape	'that is not enough'
hariga tara	'that is on a different track'
bamo / *yamo* (*wa habe*)	'that is nothing, throw it away'

(b) Agreement (turn beginning devices only)

karulape laro	'that is enough (good) I am saying'
nde / *e au laruguni*	'yes, I have said like that'
ogoni dege	'just that / that's right'
bayele / *henene*	'good / that's the truth'

(c) Restatement / summation / emphasized aspect / repeats

ani au agua ogoni } *lalu lene laya* } *laro*	'it was said like that I am saying'
au lari hendene	'it has been seen that you said like that'
au laramagoni	'we are saying like that'
ani au ogoni dagua } *bini biya bigi bini*	'thus it was done'

(d) Personal evaluation

bi ayu larogoni	'The talk I am saying now'
ogoni naga laro	'I am saying for that subject'

(e) Origin / causes / reasons

tene ogoreni howa	'The source is from there'
bi tene mbira laro	'I am saying one of the sources'
kuniore yido	'I am holding one bone (important thing)'

(f) Speaker: Information monitoring / knowledge

o larogo hale keni	'can you hear what I am saying?'
manda bidebe?	'can you follow / understand me?'
toba harama	'we are in a state of ignorance about that'
manda bedo	'I know'
hendeni	'it has been seen'

---

2 Topic development

(a) Establishing connection to previous topic

bi mbira ore piaruagoni pu gimbu bilo	'My talk will meet one talk that has gone there'
inaga bi helowa tago bilo laro	'My talk will mix in there I am saying'

Table 1—*continued*

2 *Topic development*

agali ibugua udu layago	'I am coming on the tail of what that man
mbira ina ere haro	has said down there'
(b) Listing	
mbira . . . mende	'one/first . . . second'
dugu mbira . . . dugu mende	'one path . . . second path'
haria mbira . . . haria mende	'one track/way . . . second track'
(c) Linking clauses	
au biyagola howa	'and since it was done like that'
au laragola howa	'and since they are saying like that'
ani bialu	'having done like that'
bi ogo dagua lalu	'having said a talk like that'
(d) Reference to norms	
mana li ngagome	'the *mana* is there'
mana ayu wirimagoni	'the *mana* we have put there'
mana bai hole	'the *mana* will be thrown down'
bamba mana ogoni dagua	'the *mana* from before is that'
bi ani laramali	'we used to [customary mood] say a talk like that'
ogo dagua biaga	'we used to do like that'

3 *Prospective strategies of action*

(a) Proposals for claim renouncement	
wa hamabe au lowa larama	'we are saying did we say "throw it away"'
wa ha loleberebe?	'will you say "throw it away"'
(b) Reciprocity	
au bulebira manali tigua	'this is the way it will be done, the *mana*
yabu lole/tale bule larogoni	men will share the talk, I am saying'
bi mo tale buleberema	'we will take and share the talk'
ogoni dagua tale bule	'You will share it like that'
(c) A plan	
ayu au/ani/agua/ogo dagua buleberema	
'Now like this/this	is what we'll do'
agua larimagoni au lowa lamiya	'since we have said like that let's talk'
agua loleberema	'this is what we'll say'
ogo dagua biama/lama	'do/say like this'
ogoni dagua lama lo larama	'we are saying to say "say like this"'
bi hale ho bule	'we'll hear the talk'

Table 1—*continued*

---

3 Prospective strategies of action

(d) Choice
ogoni dabole ladaba laro	'I am saying speak to choose'
bi ogoni daba	'choose on that talk'

---

4 Turn-taking stereotypes

(a) [I want/am taking this turn: first starter]
ina mbira laro	'I am saying something'
bi mbira laro hondo ha	'I am saying one talk, wait'
emene mbira laro	'I am saying a little something'

    [I want/am taking this turn: second starter]
ayu ina galone mbira laro	'now I am saying something important'
agali bi tene lo wiaro	'I'm placing my speech to say the source'

(b) [I want/am keeping my turn]
ina lelo hondo ha (be)	'To let me speak, wait'
ina larogo laga laga ndo	'I am speaking, don't all keep talking'

(c) [Let him/her have the turn/finish a turn]
ibugua lela	'let him/her speak'
bi ina unu larigo lai ha	'finish the talk you have said'
bi laradege lole lelo dai	'To let her say the talk she/he is just
nabi hondo ha	saying, don't reply back, wait'

(d) [Don't interrupt my turn]
bi la pugua nabi	'don't cut (interrupt) my talk'
i ala marobi hole	'I will first finish off'
bi wa (habe)	'throw away your talk'
iname labe lo hondo ha	'we'll say speak so wait'

(e) [I want to/am completing my turn]
ogoni hangu/bi ogoni hangu laro	'that's all/that's all the talk I am saying'
bi ogoni dege laro	'there is just that talk, I am saying'
bi au laruguni/ laramagoni	'a talk like this I have said/we are saying'

---

turn-taking, topic presentation, and evaluation – and make inferences about their levels of directness or deference.

Table 1 represents a preliminary inventory of gambits gleaned from a corpus of dispute transcripts. For the most part they relate to opening, closing, and parenthetic functions. Many of the gambits can be used to signal a variety of intentions so that their categorization under a particular discourse strategy does not preclude a capacity to signal some other action. For example: 'I am coming on the tail of what that man has said down there' (2 (a)) can, as an turn-entry utterance, also communicate a claim to take the floor (i.e. 4 (a)). For a study of verbal interaction in disputes, a model of such regular expressions identifies some of the key transactional tasks performed in reaching outcomes. Their frequency reflects the recurrent nature of situations of talk where reference to norms (2 (d)) or origins (1 (e)) is organizationally adapted to dispute settlement. In a system of debate where *who* speaks, and *when*, has been pre-determined, or where there is some explicit choreographic direction of turn-taking, one would expect a comparative list of gambits to include forms such as 'Would John now speak . . .' or 'The next speaker is . . .'. What is evident from *Table 1* is that the taking of a turn at talk proceeds through self-selection principles. Clearly then, an inventory of gambits can tell us much about how discourse is organized and how a proposition is 'framed' in respect of topic-related factors, or a speaker's attitudinal stance.

	TEXT 4	*Gambits*
1	*I HALE KEMIBE?*	1 (f)
	are you listening?	
	AI AGUA LAMA	1 (c)
	this is what we are saying	
5	*BI LARIMAGOLA LALU*	2 (c)
	since what we have said is said	
	numba committeeru agali kanegeru wali dabu biagaru	
	the committee elders and men who used to marry others are here	
	inaga bi wa	
10	throw your talk away	
	bi wa howa bi ayu	
	when you have thrown the talk away this is the talk now	
	Mindi ibugua howa bi laro au laruago	
	Mindi has said 'I am talking', it is said	
15	*INA BI OGO DAGUA LARO*	1 (c)
	this is the talk I am saying	
	AU LALU ibugua bi damenego ogoria ibu ngelai ha	2 (c)
	when he has said, all his talk leave here	
	ogoria ngelai haragola howa	
20	and when they have been left here	
	O AYU INAME MO TALE BEREMAGOLA HOWA	2 (d)
	and then now we are sharing the talk	
	ibu bi habale larua hayago lalu haruagoni	
	the talk that he said before	
25	*ibugua ibu honowinigo hari hiduali hondoledago napole*	
	his daughter is hidden in the clouds, 'she won't go away'	

AU LAYAGOLA HOWA	1 (c)
thus he said like that	
O AU LALU HAYAGONI	2 (c)

30   and when that had been said
i mama ndo
'You are not my father' (she said)
i mame
'You are my penis' [see Chapter 5]
35   *au layago Atabi ibugua*
that is what Atabi said
ibu ainya abála naga gubalini unugua mbira padago
there is something inside her mother's and father's heart
ina dodole pu layago
40   'Go and break it', she said
ai nogo i handabelo liguria haru ibu pu pole poro layagoni
'You will see the pigs (marriage), I'm going to get them'
o biagoni haru ibu wiya
for those pigs she has brought them here
45   *ai i wane napole layeria*
while she was saying 'My daughter won't go'
ayu o lalu kagoni
we are now here

O LARUGONI	1 (c)/(d)

50   that's what I have said
pole layagome wini laruabe?
she has said 'I am going' – will that prevail?
napole layagome wini laruabe?
the mother has said 'You won't go' – will that prevail?

55 *handa miya*	3 (c)
let us see	
INA BI LAROGO OGO DAGUA LARO AU LALU	1 (c)/(d)
The talk I am saying is like this I am saying	
iname bi hangai nahama	

60   we are not blocking the talk

OGO DAGUA BIAMA LARO	3 (c)
Let's do like this I am saying	
OGONI HANGU	4 (e)
that's all	

Text 4 represents a fairly typical speech that is not overtly patterned by rhetorical devices such as parallel repetition or use of 'high' vocabulary. By plotting the occurrence of gambits against the text we can elicit some of the structural modes pertaining to speech in disputes. All the mediation speeches considered in this book exhibit, to a greater or lesser extent, a meta-schema of moves that corresponds to the following format:

(1) statements about the present state of affairs (Text 3 : 1–4; Text 4 : 24–7)

(2) statements about what should not be said/done (Text 3 : 31–4; Text 4 : 60)

(3) statements about what should be said/done (Text 3 : 7–20; Text 4 : 10–22)

(4) statements about prospective conclusions (Text 3 : 35–8; Text 4 : 51–6).

The relation between 'how things are' (1) and 'how things will/might be' (4), balances the relation between 'what should not be said/done' (2) and 'what should be said/done' (3). Most typically, moves in the categories of (2) and (3) may make reference to injunctions about speech or action that are stressed by the use of gambits related to norm invocation (e.g. Text 3 : 7; 15; 27). The binary aspects of this framework of moves are replicated at the infra-structural level. That is, each move is composed of statements that are themselves presented in a binary format as example/counter-example, assertion/denial, or other forms of positive/negative exposition. These contrastive propositions are 'framed' by gambits that indicate an evaluation of things 'said' and 'done', or comment on the statements in ways defined in *Table 1*. Gambits, as constituents of 'subsidiary' discourse, appear to mark boundaries between topics (the subjects of paired statements) and the overall structure of moves which the speaker performs. The patterns elicited above are particularly clear in Text 3 (Texts A–E, Chapter 5), and Text 4:

32	'You are not my father' ⎫	
34	'You are my penis' ⎭	'that is what was said'
52	'"I am going" – will that prevail?' ⎫	
54	'"You won't go" – will that prevail?' ⎭	'let us see'

Given the highly unpredictable nature of speech, the extent to which randomly considered texts do appear to reveal the above organizational features represents a finding of some significance. We begin to appreciate just how far conversation in Huli disputes is a structured activity. The interplay between the constituent structure of mediation moves, and the contrastive binary statements which compose those moves, is marked and facilitated by the organizational functions of gambits.

Part of the explanation for this system resides at the level of language structure and rhetorical patterns for communicating information.

I discuss in some detail later how certain semantic dimensions used in speech evaluation are defined in contrastive terms. Notwithstanding these parameters for interpretation, the prevalence of conditional and disjunctive propositions in moves that present 'conclusions' (4) seems to define the role of mediator (*dombeni*) as a set of linguistic options. Importantly then, acts of assertion in claiming turns and recurrent uses of the categorical 'I am saying' (*lāro*), are attenuated by what happens in the progression of talk during that turn. Because mediators are not judges, outcome options are posed, presented, and suggested, but not directed as enforceable 'law'. To reiterate a previous conclusion, the coda of all mediation speeches express outcome possibilities in a pair format:

TEXT 3

36   'You go and give one pig'   } 'it has been said like that'
38   'he will go and give two pigs' }

TEXT 4

52   'She has said "I am going" – will that prevail?'   } 'let us see'
54   'The mother has said "She won't go" – will that prevail?' }

As the dispute system is indigenously conceptualized as a forum for speech exchange, the language options that prevail will reflect orientations towards achieving agreement and consensus. By examining the verbal detail of speeches in the above manner we can show, in a substantial way, how outcomes materialize through language use.

From the gambits given in *Table 1* we further note the absence of modalities of 'opinion' or 'doubt'. In the speaker's commitment to what he says there is a separation of the categorical I-say-so (neustic), from the qualified it-is-so (tropic) and what-is-so (phrastic). Therefore, one of the means by which the speaker attenuates his mode of assertion is by maintaining a degree of detachment from the 'said' of his speech. This is achieved through frequent invocations of impersonal norm formulae or gambits during the course (i.e. in moves 2 and 3) of his talk. A measure of detachment is consequential on direct quotation (Text 4 : 14; 31–2; 42) where the actual words are given out for others to draw inferences. Again, these linguistic devices appear to mediate the conflict between the need to be direct and forthright in interaction and the need to avoid being considered offensive. The devices used to manage these constraints, both in speech and non-verbal behaviour, implicitly delimit levels and locations of commitment. The speaker gives an unqualified commitment to the act of assertion, but an assertion of qualified factuality to the statements he makes. The endorsement of alternative actions/proposals is categorical but the mooted possibilities are given the force of suggestion rather than commands.

Some gambits, such as linking clauses in Text 4 (5; 17; 30), also function to provide the speaker with a measure of time to think about what to say next. Other gambits constitute important sequential devices which signal the boundary of, or end to, an utterance or turn at talk. The parenthetic use of *láro* ('I am saying') in Text 4 (15; 49; 57; 61) marks completion of both the sequence of mediation moves and the turn. The ubiquity of *láro* as a token-reflexive performative measures the degree to which speakers constantly reaffirm their participant status. 'I am saying' expresses the individual's involvement in the stream of communication. Its recurrent use as a statement-final verb (and thus as an optional turn-exit device) bounds the verbal performance of the speaker at that particular point in the debate. The final act of a speech in Huli is thus an act of assertion which makes explicit the fact that someone is 'saying words'.

In so far as talk in disputes reveals itself to have a high degree of structuring that is (from preliminary investigation) similar to talk in other situations, the often-drawn distinction between 'formal' and 'everyday' speech becomes somewhat blurred. It seems preferable to attend to the manner in which the elicited structures differ in various contexts or between the differentiated genres. In this respect it is instructive to contrast the roles played by forms of *lá* ('saying'), as a termination device, in talk situations apart from disputes. I shall briefly consider the organizational frames of folk-stories (*bi té*) and wailing (*O*).

Bi té

Bi té are legends, myths, and stories told at night by men or women to children or adolescents. In their most stylistically appreciated form these narratives are delivered in a melodic recitation style. Narrative conventions are restricted to choice of pitch levels and use of a topic 'frame' that is constantly repeated throughout the performance. Statements then are bounded in a cellular structure that allows variation only in the particular morphological form of *lá* ('saying') chosen:

$$
\text{Nde nigureni...} \atop \left. \text{'And then down} \atop \text{there'} \right\{ \begin{array}{l} \textit{laya lama agini} \\ \text{'we are saying it was said like that'} \\ \textit{lea laya} \\ \text{'it was said it was said'} \\ \textit{larugo abiyeni} \\ \text{'I said it was like that'} \\ \textit{haya laya} \\ \text{'it was said it was there'} \\ \textit{lene laya} \\ \text{'it was said it was said'} \end{array} \right\} \begin{array}{l} \text{...e} \\ \text{(refrain)} \end{array}
$$

These frames serve to segment the development of themes into manageable units which are thereby given emphasis. They clearly parallel some of the organizational functions discussed for gambits. Indeed, in one sense frames are like some pause phenomena, dividing talk in a 'piece by piece' fashion which allows speakers time to plan further talk. This is particularly important for *bi të* which can last for a few minutes or several hours.

The terminating phrasal component (based on 'said') has sequential implications. A situation of story-telling is conceptualized in exchange terms. Listeners are enjoined at the start of a narration (under sanction that the narrator's parents might die) verbally to acknowledge their monitoring of the talk by timely interjection of the monosyllabic assent lexeme *e* ('yes'). This is uttered after such phrases as *lene laya* (see above) and functions to finalize metre. Phrases compounded with the verb 'said' thus mark boundaries in the exchange activity between speakers. They operate in precisely the same way as *läro* ('I am saying') in naturally occurring conversation. The discontinuity in meaning between occurrences of forms of *lä* ('say') in different talk situations relates to the relative fixity of the frames in which they are member elements. In *bi të* and *wali-o*, meaning is perhaps primarily contextual rather than literal.

Wali-o

Mourning laments are sung only by women. They may precede death, occur immediately afterwards, or be sung sporadically for many years in accordance with feelings of grief. Death-wailing may be performed by a single mourner (Appendix 4, Text C) or a group of women (Appendix 4, Texts A–B). There are two distinct forms: (1) sung lines which are terminated by a group refrain consisting of the vowel /ɔː/; or (2) a sustained holding of /ɔː/ on a single pitch punctuated by short pauses.

Thematically, laments range from expressions of personal sorrow to covert accusations of those held responsible for someone's death (Pugh-Kitigan 1975 : 55):

> *Gunini Urulu ngi -o*
> Give us Gunini and Urulu (names of enemy warriors) . . .
> *Gulu Wambia bialu ibini ngi-o*
> Give us the men dressed in lesser bird of paradise plumes.

The dead are extolled by recounting their sojourns in places that are associated with 'fertile' objects: 'fruit' (Appendix 4 Text A : 18–20), 'water source' (Text A : 21–3), 'mushrooms' (Text A : 24–26; Text C : 23–25), and 'figs' (Text C : 30–3). Certain cultural themes are implicitly alluded to in the texts cited in Appendix 4. First, there is the general equivalence between hair and strength which explains the idiom of 'cut hair' (Text B : 8–11) in reference to death. The departed are implored not 'to let the side of your "hair" go bad in the foreign land' (Text A : 1–2; Text B : 3–4). The Samson motif is embedded within a more profound semantic association between *mañda* ('hair') and *mañda* ('knowledge'). A second theme is the metaphorical links between humans and birds. The mother's imprint on her environment is likened to birds' 'footprints' (Text C : 56–65), a term which is figuratively used for 'evidence'. The grief felt by the mourner is expressed as the 'bitter taste of Taro'. A third motif concerns the importance of talk. The performer in Text C conducts a conversation with the dying mother in which reference is made to previous entreaties that the woman should 'make a talk'. Through talk, an individual exercises the capacity to effect people and things. An individual's talk represents personal *mana* in which resides a spiritual residue for others to reflect on. The essence of lines 79–94 (Text C) is embodied by the title of this book – 'talk never dies'.

With respect to the stylistic structure of *wali-o* we confront again the prevalence of 'I am saying' (*lāro*) as a termination marker of statements, verses, and genre performance. Here, as in *bi tê*, *lāro* is a fixed performance convention which jointly actualizes acts of assertion and communion. Following the verbalization of *lāro*, co-wailers participate by sustaining the pitch of the final phoneme /ɔː/ of /lʌrɔː/. In such contexts the phonological properties of *lāro* are suited to the overall nature of the speech event in which it is sited. An examination of the three lament transcripts given in Appendix 4 reveals that this is a systematic feature of this genre. For example (Text A : 28):

> *Dibawi nano ombe wane*   *lāro*   – *o*
> 'Dibawi mushrooms daughter (of) I am saying' – *o* (group refrain).

In so far as *o* is an acknowledgement of grief, as well as understanding, it parallels the assent lexeme *e* in *bi té*. There is then a degree of structural correspondence between the two genres. Similarly, the speaker recognizes the need of listeners to know when a sentence, verse or performance is completed by marking termination with *lāro*. This device is 'recipiently designed' (Atkinson and Drew 1979 : 202).

Turn-taking gambits

Turn completion devices are but one aspect of the turn-taking system which governs the distribution of speaking rights. That is, how talks are co-ordinated so that there is an orderly transition from one speaker to the next with a minimum of overlap or prolonged periods of silence. The call for anthropological analyses of disputes to confront turn-taking by examining how the 'techniques for claiming turns are differentially employed' (O'Barr 1976 : 417) has met with little systematic response. Nevertheless, a study of these organizational mechanisms is fundamental to an understanding of information management and control. Furthermore, turn-taking represents an important comparative parameter for cross-cultural analysis of dispute systems.

In this latter respect, the seminal work of Sacks, Schegloff, and Jefferson (1974) indicated that speech exchange systems appear to range along a continuum defined by certain speaker selection techniques. They distinguished between systems based on complete pre-specification or pre-allocation of turns according to some distributional rule, and those systems in which allocation is locally managed on a turn-by-turn basis. That is, the present speaker may select the next speaker or, failing that, speakers are free to self-select at a suitable 'transition' place in the stream of talk. Conversations are organized then on the basis of single-speaker turns and an orientation to the maxim that 'only one speaker speaks at a time'. Evidence that this norm constitutes an important dimension of patterning in multi-party discourse can be gleaned from situations of 'breakdown'.

In Huli, certain gambits (*Table 1* 4(b), (d)) are routinely employed to correct interruptions or stop simultaneous talk. Indeed, persistent periods of violation (as in heated insults) are described as *lai* ('finishing talking': see Chapter 5) – 'disordered speech'. Moreover, repair mechanisms operate in situations of overlap such that one speaker generally ceases talking or is urged to 'wait his turn'. Overlap is more prevalent in systems where turns are distributed on a turn-by-turn basis. They most typically occur at those transitional locations where speakers compete for the 'floor'. Thus, either (1) speakers incorrectly project the completion of a turn which results in premature interruption; or (2) several speakers simultaneously self-select whereupon other devices are called into play so that only one claimant emerges from a short period of multiple overlapping. Interruptions are frequently censured with such retorts as *agali ibunaga bi nalabe larogo mo ko holebira* (the talk belongs to that man, don't talk or you will make it bad). To 'cut' (*pugua*) someone's talk is to interrupt the expression of personality. It is also to breach the fundamental norm of a Huli dispute that talk should be 'shared'.

An analysis of turn-taking encompasses a consideration of the interplay between synchronization (timing and sequencing of turns) and principles of structuration (the design components of turns and their interactional functions). It is because a study of verbal interaction in any setting must detail the meshing of these two levels that wholesale comparisons between the discourse of Western courts and, for example, New Guinea Highlands 'moots' is unlikely to prove fruitful. The organization of talk in judicial settings is, as Atkinson and Drew (1979) have shown, structured by pre-allocation of *turn order* (between examiners and witnesses) and pre-specification of *turn type*. Talking predominantly consists of sequenced utterances that are minimally recognized as 'questions' and 'answers'. Useful as the adjacency-pair format (i.e. question-answers/invitation-acceptance or rejection/accusation-denial or admittance) is for the analysis of talk in courts, a Huli dispute cannot be accounted for in terms of such neat dialogic interchanges. Talk in disputes seems closer to a conversational model where people acknowledge a 'state of talk', and often simply talk for the sake of talking without responding to identifiable first-pair parts such as questions. The overall pattern has less 'ping-pong' (Goffman 1981 : 35) than talk in courts. Furthermore, as will become evident, a dispute in Huli is far removed from those classroom situations that have served discourse analysts so well. Given the very real problems attendant on explaining the whole of a text in terms of a single exchange model, it seems preferable to concentrate attention on sections and sets of sections in any dispute and to relate these to participant role definitions and organizational tasks.

A focus on turn-taking gambits evidences an appreciation of their communicative and strategic functions. They constitute evolved linguistic responses to recurrent organizational problems associated with talking in multi-party settings. Without some acknowledged (albeit implicit) system for signalling intentions about talk, an unfettered process of self-selection would result in chaos. Gambits serve to dissect a state of talk into ordered and disordered conditions. From an analytical standpoint, they can also shed important light on 'politeness' phenomena.

The Huli refer to the locational aspects of a turn by means of the words *are* ('hole') or *henge* ('space'). The contribution that is made in any turn may be described as *dagia* '(platform'/'floor'). From its traditional contexts of occurrence, *dagia* can be seen to have the same figurative meanings attached to 'platform' in Western political discourse. In such descriptive phrases as *agali dagia* ('men's platform': sexual intercourse rites), *wali dagia* ('woman's platform': bridal decoration rites), or Máli *dagia* ('the platform for Mali dancing'), *dagia* connotes a series of rites and spells that are a preparatory basis for presentation and display. It is a statement of policy about how things should be. In the context of disputes, *dagia* is conceived of as a rostrum for personal assertion and preparation for repartee.

Given the cultural importance of taking the 'floor', it is noticeable that in the turn-taking gambits cited in *Table 1* there is a marked absence of verbal deference forms. The first person present active *bi mbira lāro* ('I am saying something') is declarative of an action and intention to claim the turn. It is frequently followed by the imperative *hondo ha* ('you wait'). While syntactic form is not a reliable guide to speech act status, this gambit was not (in any of my data) uttered with the normal question intonation. In a dispute one does not request speaking rights, one usurps space, since everyone is entitled to a say. Turn-taking is a context where assertion is at a premium. There is then a lack of distributional direction by any single person, and those formulaic expressions allocating speaking rights (*Table 1* : 4(c)) are not responses to person-specific requests for turns. Because turn incumbency is a right, the inventory of turn-taking gambits is not structured in regard to degrees of politeness (e.g. 'excuse me but . . .'; 'may I just . . .' or 'could I interrupt . . .'). In line with this observation I would further argue that choice of a particular surface form of gambit is determined by synchronization factors (e.g. another speaker starts to talk) rather than attendance to rules of conversational etiquette.

One important caveat to the above is that our interpretations of what is said encompass an understanding of what can be said. The turn-taking gambits represent types of predominant stylistic choices from a reservoir of underlying linguistic options available for the same tasks. For this reason a repertoire of different forms might be expected to prevail in other talk situations. Against the background of assertiveness in disputes, one can place, for example, the explicit request for speaking permission, frequent in informal conversation:

bi mbira loabe?
talk something will I say?
(future tense, first person question requesting immediate response)

One preliminary conclusion that emerges from the data thus far examined concerns the contrast between levels of directness in obtaining a turn, and what one does with the turn. In the face of competition for talking-space Huli adopt an assertive stance; once that space has been secured what is said is couched in attenuated terms. This model parallels decoration behaviour (see Chapter 5) such that once the opportunity for display has been achieved men modify the icons of self-assertion. The cultural weighting of directness is circumscribed by notions of appropriate context.

The attenuation of directness once talk has commenced is consistent with many of the structural patterns elicited earlier. Following on from the above conclusion we do not find in Huli speeches any perfunctory routines of apology for speaking. Contributions are not characterized by a prefacing period of excuses (as among the Merina (Bloch 1975 : 7)). The expectancy framework regarding deference behaviour is quite differently defined and located. To infer from this absence of permissive and request modes (in turn-taking) a degree of 'impoliteness' would be to ignore the ethno-semantic dimensions underlying assessments of these types of action. Claiming a turn is an act displaying *hongo* – commitment, strength, and 'push'. The presentation of content requires a modicum of sensitivity to the constraints on excessive assertion. I attend to some of the cultural implications of commitment in the next section.

In the context of the above observations, second starter techniques (*Table 1* : 4(a)) attest to the importance of self-assertion for achieving turn incumbency. Speakers may override a first starter who has self-selected by raising their voice and/or using such commands as 'You wait' (*hondo ha*). These devices may occur together with an explicit self-crediting phrase. By indicating that a talk is 'important' (*galone*), or may identify the 'sources' (*tene*), the speaker offers the prospect of implications for the allocation of responsibility. This introduces an element of uncertainty and expectation which can often prove effective in wresting a turn from a previous starter. The first speaker thus gives way in the face of a higher level of commitment to blame allocation from another speaker. To supersede a first speaker demands 'push' in the sense of showing one's talk to be important through acts of self-praise.

One area where this directness is modified is in the opening gambits which intimate agreement or disagreement (*Table 1* : 1(a)–(b)). These contrast with more explicit positive and negative evaluation terms (see Chapter 5) in respect of (i) their sequential position as turn openers; (2) a tendency to consist of only one or two words; and (3) having the property of referential indeterminacy. They function as general terms of assent or dissent which do not dissect a previous turn in respect of the detailed propositions that are evaluated. Along with such appositionals and turn beginning devices as 'o' or 'ai' that occur in most speeches, their impairment by overlap does not affect the development of the sentences that follow (Sacks, Schegloff, and Jefferson 1974). These markers of assessment are thus functionally adapted to the task of turn-taking. They provide time for conversational planning. In their negative guises, their indeterminacy does not evoke immediate reactions that might culminate in overlapping talk.

Finally, we may note the absence of apologetic or gratitude gambits (*Table 1* : 4(e)) when signalling verbal closure. The most frequently used expression for marking completion of speech is (in full or contracted form):

bi   ogoni hangu lāro
talk this   only   I am saying
(that's all of these words I am saying)

It is clear from the occurrence of the substantive *bi* that what is finished are words/talk, not the activity of production. From the data available (see Feld and Schieffelin n.d.) it would appear that similar termination devices occur throughout the region (e.g. the Wahgi *embe ere nint* – 'that's all' (M. O'Hanlon: personal communication)). In the context of Huli disputes, this gambit represents a linguistic option that contrasts with common conversational forms where the activity of talk is concluded: *lai haro/lairi haro/la maro bero* ('I am finishing/concluding saying'). Choice of gambit in disputes is thus partly determined by contextually defined notions of appropriateness; a specific talk is finished but the option remains open for further 'saying'.

Speech genres

The preceding discussion of gambits has highlighted the extent to which disputes are a type of verbal playground for the acting out of ritually relevant expressions. They are also contexts in which specific modes of speech can be said to be appropriate or inappropriate. The Huli taxonomic system of genres is presented in *Table 2*. As lexical items used in the description of performances they embody conventional knowledge about the interdependence of form, content, and situation. The taxonomy is used as a grid to analyse, evaluate, and segment verbal interactions for the purposes of praise or censure. It is this aspect of the genre system that I shall focus on here, leaving more detailed analysis of style and content for separate discussion.

In many cultures there operates a *type-sufficiency* norm whereby speech format is assessed as conforming to, or deviating from, situationally appropriate invocations of genre. For example, the terms 'prayer', 'lecture', 'sermon', 'performance', or 'cross-examination' can be used as rhetorical labels for 'extreme' talk. There is something overdone or infelicitous about their use in certain circumstances. Censure in this environment carries the import of such colloquialisms as 'this is neither the time nor place' – where 'time' refers to a sense of occasion. Censure is, then, one of the cultural implications of inappropriate genre usage: discourse can be negatively described through innuendo and sarcasm:

MALIYAGO: For planting coffee there is a place
For planting casuarina there is a place
For planting pandanus there is a place
HELAGO: Are you making *mana* to me?

(D.2 : 28–30)

Table 2   *Huli speech genres*

Damba bi (close down (*damba*) + talk (*bi*))
Performed on occasions of war or compensation; delivered by headmen only; uttered in a fast, loud, rhythmical fashion; each phrase is marked by a half-turn of the head; high degree of lexical and syntactic patterning with pronounced use of the eulogistic lexicons of *kai* and *bi mone*; symbolic and analogical facets of topic are said to reflect *yobage* ('veiled talk').

Malu (ancestor / before (*ma*) + long (*lu*))
Recitation of clan genealogy that occurs as a separate part of accounts concerning land and ancestors; performed in public only on occasions of land dispute between sub-clans or clans; delivered by headmen who have an acknowledged right to use this genre; generation enumeration is slow and deliberate with a rising intonational contour over first-parts, followed by a voiced pause and then falling intonation over ancestral names (see Chapter 4).

Bi tê (talk (*bi*) + story (*tê*))
Folk stories told by either sex to young people at night; often sung in a melodic recitation style; statements are framed by narrative conventions which provide participants with sequential cues to acknowledge comprehension through the timely monosyllabic interjection of *e* ('yes'); can be of varying length and often include conventional character descriptions (*pureremo*) of *Iba Tiri* and *Baya Horo*.

Bi tene / tene tê (talk (*bi / tê*) + origin / source (*tene*))
Oral history and myth; frequently conceived of as the property of particular clans; can be sung; imparted to others usually during educational sessions at night; may utilize words from any of the 'high' vocabulary levels.

Wali O (women's (*wali*) + lament / wail (*O*))
Performed both before and after death of a relative; can be a communal chant incorporating individually recited lines, or a monologue (*dugu*); verse structures are built on parallel repetition with substitutions of similar sounding synonyms which are members of the paradigmatic sets of *kai* words; can be used as a vehicle for expressing accusations against some group held responsible for a death and thus may include *yobage*.

Pureremo
Conventional formulations of norms or cultural truths; used during the transmission of information in any context where such stereotype expressions exist for the topic under discussion; predictable word order and content; syntactic structure variable and resembles *gamu*; characterized by predominance of alternative vocabulary items.

Gamu
Spells that are a ubiquitous component of actions, in any domain, which seek success; utilizes the 'high' vocabulary forms; repeated syntax linked to distinct metres; objects of purchase or inheritance.

Table 2—*continued*

Dawe

Generic term referring to individually named sub-species of chanting as well as the speech event itself: a) *dawe* – courting songs; verse structure usually six or seven lines only and dictated by *kai* paradigms; predictability of syntax and content allows co-participants to enter a verse in unison with the lead singer after the first line. Two forms are commonly recognized: (i) *ū wai* – 'song (*ū*) + fighting (*wai*)': opposing groups attempt to compete for females through song which often progresses into licensed verbal abuse (ii) *wali ibilo* – 'women (*wali*) + to come (*ibilo*)': songs which attempt to allure women quickly. Traditionally, only married men were allowed into the song-house (*dawe anda*), and performances were always at night. b) *gereye* – form associated with Dugube and performed as part of the *dindi pongo* rites; often referred to as *hewabi bi* – 'foreign (*hewa*) + talk (*bi*)' c) *bilagu* – part of the sequence of rites to ward off ancestral spirits; consists of a lengthy recitation of land names; performed for several hours by one or two men.

Maliyago's speech is like the kind of homily a father would give to a son. Helago's (his brother) sarcastic response questions his right to make such a speech, suggesting that Maliyago is using a language style inappropriate to his 'station'. In the same dispute, a further speech by Maliyago outlining land rights prompts the response: *I Malu larebe?* ('Are you making Malu?') (D.2 : 415).

Malu is a speech form restricted to headmen in situations of inter-clan land disputes. Again, Maliyago is 'out of order' in respect of a status warrant to perform Malu. Talk that demonstrates excess may often be labelled *Dawe* (*Table 2*), the semantics of which parallel the implications of the Western idiom 'to make a song and dance' about some matter.

The relation between genre and occasion can best be detailed by examining data on *Damba bi* (*Table 2*). Traditionally, *Damba bi* occurred in situations of war or compensation to exhort men to fight or collect pigs. *Damba* means to 'close down / close over' thus marking the sense in which such speeches foreclosed any further talk about an issue. In disputes it is common to find this label applied in a literal or figurative way for talk that 'covers up' some matter, or 'shouts down' another contribution.

In the performance of *Damba bi* the speed of articulation is rapid, volume is loud, and each phrase is accompanied by a turn of the head to the right. In disputes, such interpretive processes can have an effect on the outcomes of claims.

Damba bi are now rarely made in Huli, and the two texts cited in

Appendix 2 are atypical in respect of traditional context (Text 1) and naturally occurring performance (Text 2). Nevertheless, they do convey the stylistic essence of this important verbal art form.

(1) *Text 2*. Despite its artificial construction, other men from the same clan as Gurubugu identified parts of the speech as having been delivered following the famous incident detailed by Sinclair (1966). The speech has two basic themes. First, the speaker asserts himself as a man of knowledge by referring to ritual customs associated with land fertility rites (lines 1–5). This theme is continued towards the end where cultural differences between the Huli and Duna are explicated in terms of 'decoration' (lines 33–41). Each sentence consists of 'stock phrases' employing a specialized eulogistic vocabulary. This establishes control of conventional modes of presenting the topic of decoration. The assertive tone of the speech is evident in the self-praising utterances (lines 42–3): 'My mind is straight/I used to plant the Habono tree' (specific ritual sequence of Tege). This assertiveness is also marked by the imperative mood (lines 30–32) and is implicit in the very act of *Damba bi*. In this regard, *lāro* ('I am saying') would be redundant. The second theme concerns the necessity for compensation. The metaphorical language equates thus: men (*agali*) = marsupial (lines 6–9; 27–9); bamboo containers (*be*) = pigs (lines 15–18), such that the action of collecting bamboo vessels and making a 'lid' figuratively expresses the need to gather pigs and 'close' (*damba*) the issue. Importantly, this type of compensation is denoted by the label *damba abi*. The semantic notion of 'closure' common to the action of indemnity, the objects utilized (*nogo damba*), and the speech form that verbally urges their actualization, is expressed through the repeated use of the same term *damba* ('to close').

(2) *Text 1*. The significant feature of this speech, despite the unorthodox context, is the marked syntactic continuity with the type of mediation speeches thus far examined. Topic structure revolves around the contrast of motherhood versus fatherhood. This theme is developed in terms of pronounced binary statements:

1	His mother and father . . .
2	That woman's mother and father . . .
3	When one says mother
4–7	Children will be born . . .
8–11	Anger and displeasure . . .
12	They should sit down
13	They will stay
14	When one says father

The cultural value of 'mother' is defined in terms of procreative functions and discipline. The 'father' is linked to ritual objects used in child-rearing rites (*Ma Hiriya*: lines 15–16) and items of adornment (lines 17–18). The coda evokes natural images of abundance to reassure the woman that she will bear many children. Each half of a binary pair may itself be expressed in dual or quadripartite format based on parallel repetition – repeated syntax with one- or two-word substitutions. The syntactic pattern is determined by the structure of the poetic vocabulary sets used (see Chapter 5). Similar-sounding synonyms are members of a paradigmatic word set and function as substitute lexemes in parallel statements. The words constitute rhyming pairs. Binary forms occur then at both the rank level of statements and words:

'Children'
4 ⎡ *Gili*
5 ⎣ *Gawali*   (alliterative)
6 ⎡ *Barina*
7 ⎣ *Bangale*   (alliterative)
'Anger and displeasure'
8 ⎡ *amba tambo*   (reduplicative)
9 ⎣ *hembo lembo*   (reduplicative)

Precisely the same stylistic features are evident in Text 2 where one can note the pronounced use of repeated syntax ordered by a eulogistic lexicon. For example, *Godane–Galuni* (alliterative), *Tirane–Hengedane* (assonant: lines 15–18).

Because a genre is defined on a number of levels, a speech need only simulate a few of these defining criteria to be subject to the censorial labelling process. In Huli disputes, the incongruity caused by deliberate facsimile may also result in humour:

This is an extract from a dispute concerning a marauding pig which belonged to Hedange and was said to have eaten some chickens in another person's garden.
PAYAWI: When a certain man from this valley comes then let's settle this when a woman is there
when a man is there
when a middle-man (mediator) is there from
Koma
Ibu
Mata   (sub-clan names of Koma clan: *Diagram 2*)
Aguene
then there will be a talk here
so who is going to be there then?'

HEDANGE: For man's compensation
let us see the nut trees
let us see the man's body
let us see the talk, we have said
so we are seeing the talk now
the men are there
let's go
AGO: (general laughter from participants) *Damba bi larego?*
('Are you saying a *Damba bi*?')   (Field data)

The abberrant nature of Hedange's speech is due partly to the irrele-
vance of its content to the issues at stake. The statements were delivered
with staccato phrasing, typical of *Damba bi*, and in a loud assertive
manner calculated to produce humour. The rhetorical exhortation
'let's go' does not relate to any plan of action, and references to
compensation are there to add authenticity. The speech is thus both
type-insufficient – as an inappropriate invocation of genre – and
role-insufficient – as a talk unlikely to help realize an outcome to the
dispute. What is interesting about the first speech is that it too is
characterized by repeated syntax where statements stand in a balanced
and structured relationship to each other. These bipartite patterns are
constant in Huli talk (of all forms) and thus cannot serve as a criterion of
differentiation between 'formal' and 'everyday' speech. What seems
important to our descriptions is the relative fixity of structural devices,
the overlay of intonational and kinesic phenomena, and indigenous
evaluations of appropriateness in performance.

I have been concerned in this chapter to consider some of the key
concepts, terms, and distinctions relevant to an understanding of dispute talk. Talk, as we have seen, is one medium for the expression of
culture (*mana*) – *bime mana lole* ('with the talk the *mana* will be
said'). The notion of *mana* informs all aspects of social behaviour.
The Huli conceive it both to order – as a normative repertoire – and
to explain – the raison d'être for routine actions – their lives. It is
reasonable to postulate that *mana* is morphemically constituted of *ma*
('before') +*ne* (noun specifier). The semantic concept of 'looking
back' – historical retrospection – is evidenced in related terms such
as *malu* (*Table 2*: speech form listing ancestral clan predecessors),
mama/mamali (ancestors), or *mame* (father). *Mana*, in the sense of
norm and custom, derives its epistemic validity and status from
association with ancestors. In its verbal expression it attests to the Huli
phrase *bi na homaga* – 'talk never dies'. As 'tradition', *mana*
is internally differentiated through specifications of relevant

domain: *dama mana* – beliefs and rites concerning the supernatural; Haroli *mana* – practices relating to the bachelor cult; *ndi tingi mana* – rites of marital intercourse. That is, in any sphere of interaction *mana* stands for the set of behavioural prescriptions and verbal practices that embody statements about cultural uniformity and continuity.

Mana functions as a symbol of identity and integrity at successive levels from the individual to the tribe. It affords the Huli the criteria for self-definition: *ina mama mamali naga mana ogome mo mbiyaore kemagoni* ('the *mana* of our ancestors makes us one'). Differences of knowledge and behaviour are rationalized as differences of *mana*; this systematic ambiguity allows both for statements of cultural homogeneity and explanations of idiosyncratic forms. In speech contexts *mana* encapsulates a socio-historical accounting of knowledge. The cultural salience of this concept is to some extent indexed by the habits and processes of verbalization. The expression of *mana* in all forms involves (as is evident throughout this book) linguistic routine. Norms, and especially those invoked in disputes, exist as formulaic and pre-patterned speech where rhetorical efficacy is matched by an aesthetic appreciation of linguistic form.

The Huli conceive themselves to be different from the Duna, Dugube, and Obena by virtue of their *mana* as expressed through material culture and decoration. These symbols of cultural identity are to the fore in the following conventional formulations (i.e. *pureremo*: *Table 2*):

TEXT 5
Hulu Gomaiya o manda dania / aulai / Hewari babu / time ende gili / gulupobe / hiliyula / gauwa / nogo ere mame / hirulaya
The Huli with hair bound with rope / decorated with yellow everlasting flowers (*helichrysum bracteatum*) / with purple everlasting flowers / arrows with decorated shafts / pan-pipes / double-stringed musical bow / jew's harp / with aprons of pigs'-tails / with drum.
TEXT 6
Mirila o ayu warabia / dambele atoba pindi baro / ega malungu / tumbudi tangi
The Duna with their form of axe / with their aprons made of this species of string / feather worn in the hair / string-cap.
TEXT 7
Obena o poromali / herele ibi / dombo puli / ngegoye yandere
The Enga with this dance style / salt / small cowrie shells / spear made from a Lai tree.

TEXT 8
Dugu Yawini o aminemo / ayu aimena / langa bima / digi dobo / biango
neria / wabe dalumu nguira / migilini / mandambu / mbulu uru abiyene
The Dugube with their tree oil / axe / bow / species of cane / dogs'-teeth neck-
lace / bamboo through their nose / hair style / shouting style / killing stick.
TEXT 9

Dugu Yawini	*labanda*
The Dugube (build houses) in trees with sago fronds	
Duna	*tawa anda*
The Duna (build houses) with roofs of pandanus leaf	
Obena	*gambe anda*
The Enga (build houses) with roofs of pitpit	
Huli	*dange anda*
The Huli (build houses) with roofs of kunai	
Honebi	*gaba anda*
The administration (build houses) with tin roofs.	

These fixed verbal forms focus on aspects of culture that are amenable to observation. The phrases in Texts 5–8 are typified by eulogistic synonyms. Text 9 is particularly remarkable for the way Huli have adapted a distinguishing feature of administrative culture into a traditional poetic form. Presenting oneself is a matter of identity negotiation and talk seems clearly to represent an important means to this end. However, the above texts (also Appendix 2 Text 1 : 17–18; Text 2 : 33–42) also reveal the value of decoration as a marker of identity. This parallel between talk and decoration, and more especially the semantic dimensions that underlie behaviour with these two substances, constitute one of the sub-themes of this book.

Notes

1 The treatment of gambits in this chapter is an attempt to indicate the importance of a study of semantic frames for dispute analysis. Presentation of data follows the format used by Keller (1981). I conducted little systematic work on informal conversation but my initial impression is that there is little discontinuity in speech patterns between naturally occurring talk and debate in disputes.
2 I have consistently marked tone only in this chapter. Elsewhere in the book occurrences of *la* will, unless otherwise stated, always refer to the verb 'say'.
3 I did not conduct research into paralinguistic and intonational features. Therefore, much of the argument concerning attitudinal import may well have to be modified in the light of future research into these parameters of meaning.
4 The tonal distinction between *aba* (F) and *aba* (MB) is consistently made by Rule (1954 : 29; 32; 34).

3
Talking about relationships

Igiri yagua danda danda
In the case of a boy then bows bows
Wandari yagua damba damba
In the case of a girl then bride-price bride-price

Much of the talk in disputes is concerned with the assessment of outcomes and actions. These discursive processes are founded on a cultural system of deontic norms that ascribe behavioural patterns to specific social categories. Whether it be a self-declaration of status – 'We *middle men* who are here . . .' – or a definition of litigants' relationship, identifying and allocating category membership is part of the interactive work of dispute management. In this regard, kinship and descent constitute lexical resources for status and role delineation. We may isolate two aspects of this category collection in Huli. First, the underlying principle of consanguinity is structured by notions of transmitted substances. Second, the normative injunctions relating to category-bound activities, whereby exchange behaviour can subsequently be rationalized through the kinship idiom, are encoded in verbal forms. The perspective I adopt here is therefore concerned to detail the stylized discourse routines that Huli use to communicate the category-bound nature of social obligation.

The importance attached to particular strands of kinship is indexed in this culture by the existence of standardized speech formulae (*pureremo*).[1] These, as will become evident, articulate (often metaphorically) the affective and normative dimensions of a particular relationship. As rhetorical strategies, verbal routines are used to enforce conformity by publicly re-presenting an acknowledged order to dispute participants. This interdependence between processes of category definition and pre-patterned speech is illustrated in the following extract relating to the kin category *aba* (non-agnatic cognates):

TEXT 1
My *aba* will cook (the compensation pigs)
⌈ Dali Tiabuli and
⌊ Dali Libi and Lobe both are following (me)
⌈ Hoga Handalu and
⌊ Dali Hui
→ ⌈ Like the feathers of the baby cassowary they have come into my bag [i.e. I
   ⌊ have taken responsibility for them]
→ ⌈ Like the feathers of the baby cassowary they have been planted on my wig
   ⌊ [i.e. I have placed them in a central and important location]
→ ⌈ When we had arrived you came and stayed like a little root that had gone
   ⌊ inside me
→ ⌈ *Aba*, you are staying on top of me, I am saying [i.e. we are staying together
   ⌊ here]
   Aba, we'll fetch and drink water from Yalibi river [i.e. when you kill pig]
   Your forehead has become dark [i.e. you are with shame]
⌈ Kill one pig now
│ In the case that you don't kill pig tonight then tomorrow you will kill and
⌊ give pig
   That's all.

The first part of the speech is a creative adaptation of a standard interactive routine typical in disputes between *aba*. It is not simply that attendant obligations are reiterated through formulaic speech. More importantly, these speech acts are an intrinsic constituent of the meaning of Huli kin terms such as *aba*. To talk about kinship in Huli is to engage in an activity which makes explicit the sense in which structured verbal interaction is a model for ordered relationships.

Despite the voluminous literature on New Guinea Highlands descent systems, and the wide appreciation of the link between rhetoric and kinship, attention to conversational routines has (judging from the paucity of texts) remained of secondary importance. With the notable exception of kin terminologies, explications of the cultural logic of kinship have tended to by-pass speech behaviour as a critical expositional parameter. For the Huli data, we cannot easily divorce (for example) an imputation of siblingship between cross-cousins from the performative contexts in which such equivalences are announced or encapsulated. The indigenous models of structure emerge then as constructions from discourse so that we are constrained to describe related speech patterns and to account for the interplay between form and content. There are two further respects in which the data indicate how kinship is a mode of organizing, and talking about, talk.

(1) Central to the field of kinship is a distinction between relationships that are 'tied/bound' (*bai leda*) and those that are not. This idiom, which marks off consanguineal from affinal relations, is applicable at different levels of the topic hierarchy. This corresponds with a subdivision of the kin lexicon according to whether reference is made to (a) *unit structuration* – category and group terms that are indissolubly fused to land and residence ideologies; or (b) an *ego-focused matrix* of relationships. Each of these levels is structured by sets of contrary propositions that explain the 'negotiable' face of social structure. The significance of exploring the commutable nature of consanguineal and affinal principles derives from the inferential framework attached to these respective axioms. At the level of unit structuration, patrilines that are immutably linked as 'consanguineals' acknowledge patterns of speech deference, and performance rights to specific verbal genres, in disputes. Category specifications in respect of paired ('tied') units relate directly then to the organization of turn-taking as well as to the design and content of what is said in turns. Perhaps somewhat uniquely in terms of Highlands ethnography, collecting speech-focused data reveals more than the centrality of the verbal medium for communicating kin norms. Kinship is also a mode of structuring talk. This perspective clearly has repercussions for comparative analyses concerned with the interrelationships between dispute management processes and descent structures.

(2) The kinship ideology of the Huli is constituted as a set of inferences from certain presuppositions that are not subject to debate or questioning. These function to synthesize, stabilize, and systematize reality. One such absolute presupposition is the distinction between male and female. This dichotomy, and its related scheme of values, is fundamental to most Melanesian cultures. I shall be concerned to expound the senses in which the oppositions of *anda* (private/home space)/*hama* (public/display ground), *homa* (death)/*habe* (life), *darama* (blood)/*kuni* (bone), *yamuwini* (non-agnatic cognates

related through a female agnate)/*tene* (agnates), and *damba* (bride-price)/*danda* (bows) manifest the multidimensionality of the female–male distinction. The sexual dichotomy is both a constituent feature of the above pairs and an identifiable discursive instrument in Huli culture. The unity of the set of distinctions is a characteristic possessed by virtue of having been reproduced in accordance with this rule of synthesis. The social distinctions, inequities, and imbalances associated with sexual discrimination reveal a coherent set of beliefs about the nature and implications of female sexuality. Language use and structure is one medium for the inculcation of stigma philosophies. The structure of kin category labels, language about women as well as language used by women, and contexts where choice of lexeme is restricted, all embody the interplay between a dominant ideology of pollution and rhetorical modes of expression.

Genealogical terms and ideas of procreation provide a convenient point from which to discuss Huli conceptions of 'kinship'. The most salient descriptive terms are as follows:

Bai leda refers to consanguineal relations. *Bai* means to be 'tied' as in *ho bai* ('to tie the struts of a house').

Daba signifies 'generations' and invariably compounds with numerical adjectives in genealogical reckoning (ref.D.1). *Daba* denotes both a species of vine and, as in the verb *daba ha*, to a state of being 'tied with cane'.

Damene expresses cognatic kinship. Its inclusive range derives from the word stem *dama* meaning 'big/everything'. Further specification of bilateral kin is achieved by qualifying *damene* with the words *ainya* (mother)[2] or *aba* (father) to refer to maternal or paternal kin respectively.

Tagini refers to close cognatic kin. It is morphemically compounded of *taga* ('shame') + *ni/ne* (noun specifier) which intimates a range of prohibited sexual relations. Incest is referred to by the phrase *wali tagini* ('woman shame').

Aria is co-extensive with *damene* as a general term for consanguineals. The word is most likely a contraction of *haria/hariga* ('tracks'), a common idiom for kinship in Highlands societies such as the Kuma (Reay 1959 : 65).

The central notion of 'tying' expresses Huli ideas of connection. Relationships of kinship, as well as talk (see Appendix 4 : C : 79–94 where the alternative terms for talk are names of vines from which rope is made) are conceived as 'ropes' that bind two entities. Two further idioms recur in disputes to express relationships. The first is *anda* ('house/inside') which signifies membership and incorporation as in *andahane* (house (*anda*) + inside (*ha*): 'neighbour'), *anda hene ha* ('he stays inside' i.e. within the localized descent unit), *anda ibu* ('come inside': into a conversation) and *anda tambira* ('inside (*anda*) + cold (*tambe*)': a phrase used as a substitute for the name of any dead cognate, which is avoided for fear of spirit invocation). A second common idiom is that of 'bridge' (*togo*) used for both cognatic and affinal ties. Like 'tracks' (*aria*), there is a figurative allusion to the sense in which people and goods mediate between connected points.

Paralleling the Melpa term *mei* (A. Strathern 1972 : 8), the Huli word *hana* ('carried') can be used in a variety of contexts to express (a) childbirth (*honowini*: carried (*hono*) + placed (*wini*)); (b) transportation of live animals in a string bag (*taba hana*); (c) payment of death compensation (*agali hana*: man (*agali*) + carried (*hana*)); and (d) performance of bridal rites for another (*nu hana*: string bag (*nu*) + carried (*hana*) – a reference to the black string bag given to the bride to cover her breasts until after the birth of her first child). The notion of 'carrying' shows the connection between a physical act and (as in the $\overline{aba}$ text cited above) responsibility/liability for the results or objects of such acts. A child is believed to be formed by the coalescence of maternal and paternal substances. A man's semen travels down from the head in sexual intercourse to form the bones; a mother's blood contributes the fat and flesh. The conceptual equation of maleness and bone explains references to agnatic descent categories as 'one-bone people'. The procreative contribution of men has a permanence that contrasts with the dissipation of blood and flesh both before and after death. The logic of kin relationships compounds this fact by circumscribing genealogical limits to ties based on 'blood'. The different implications of substance transmission provide a basis for the calculation of certain compensation payments given when either bones are broken or blood is spilled. As part of the web of linguistic and semantic discriminations surrounding the male–female opposition we may note the sense of 'importance' and 'strength' associated with phrasal lexemes based on 'bone':

agali kuni ('strong/important : *danda kuni* ('strong/well made
  man')   bow')
dindi kuni ('ancestral land') : *bi kuni* ('important/main talk').

In this context we might also contrast patrilateral: matrilateral ties in terms of the (morphemically conveyed) affective notions of 'desire' (*hàme*: see also Chapter 2):

hàme ('father') – *hàmene* ('brother') – *hàmeigini* ('father–son: Clan')

and 'sympathy' (*dara*):

darama ('blood') – *daramabi* ('red')

Much of Huli talk about relationships and category-bound activities can be accounted for in terms of this schema of attitudes.

From the many rites that follow childbirth we may briefly consider two that relate directly to our understanding of Huli kinship and the social ideology predicated on the male/female distinction. On the morning of the fourth (for a girl) or eighth (for a boy) day after birth both parents traverse *kebe haria* (tracks along which the Huli progenitor Kebali first travelled) strewing leaves from a Balimu tree and reciting the spell given below. The rite represents an invocation of fertility, the suffusion of human actions by models of mythical reproduction. I collected many sample texts in the Koroba area which showed little variation in either theme, structure, or, importantly, coda:

TEXT *Balimu Pudaga* or *Habua Pu Gamu*
Bebali Puni Bebe Yame poro/Habolima poro/biango hiwi poro/Wabia gabua poro/dudu andu poro/nogo taro poro/dali pari poro/wai puya poro/igiri yagua danda danda/wandari yagua damba damba.
Like the cassowary in Bebali Puni (Dugube), go/like the dwarf cassowary, go/like the wild dog, go/like the wild pig from Wabia, go/like the wild dog, go/like the wild pig, go/like the snake, go/like the snake, go/in the case of a boy then bows bows/in the case of a girl then bride-price bride-price.

While the literal meaning of *poro* is 'I am going' the lines are uttered with the force of a command. An opposition of wild versus domestic underlies the references to animals that symbolize strength, freedom, and aggression. These attributes are associated with the ancestral period known as *ma naga*, 'the taro time'. The binary aspects of theme and syntax parallel structures present in speech in disputes. The quadripartite constituents cassowary, cassowary/dog : pig – dog : pig/snake, snake are balanced in the final phrases by an equipollent contrast of male : female. Boys represent 'bows', a symbol of help in disputes and thus ultimately 'talk' (see Appendix 3 : 2 where bow is used figuratively for 'song'). Male adolescents are referred to as *danda homa* ('one bow') and marriage is signified by the phrase *danda pole* ('going to the bow': Appendix 4A : 14). Girls, in contrast, represent incoming bride-price. These truths are structured in much the same way as outcome options are presented in disputes. They are alternative-indicating with a high degree of syntactic and phonological (the assonance of *damba* : *danda*) symmetry. These devices constitute both a cultural mnemonic and a means of message intensification. It is not uncommon for Huli spells to end with a traditional saying providing an insight into cultural values unattainable through question–answer formats. We might reformulate this aphorism in terms suggested by Milner (1971 : 256):

Igiri yagua	*danda danda*	+	'In the case of a boy then bows bows'
+	+		
Wandari yagua	*damba damba*	+	'In the case of a girl then bride-price bride-price'
+	+		

(Both sons and daughters have their complementary values as children)

The structure of the opening *aba* text reveals a similar ordering of bipartite statements of theme culminating in a disjunctive conclusion

'In the case that you don't kill pig tonight   (–)
then tomorrow you will kill and give pig'   (+)

These verbal patterns are pervasive in Huli speech irrespective of context or genre.

On the same day as the above rite, *Ma hiriya* ('burning of the taro') was performed as an invocation of ancestral 'strength'. Burnt taro was lightly scraped onto an infant, to the accompaniment of the following spell:

TEXT *Ma hiriya gamu*
Urubu gele bi mero / Urubu hegele bi mero / Bai mope bi mero / Bai hinini bi mero / Kilape gege bi mero / Kilape hongode gege bi mero.
(Informant: Hunguru-Koma clan)

The initial terms of each phrase represent 'praise' (*kai*: see Chapter 5) lexemes for birds of the Lorikeet family. The format shows 'praise-name pairing' that parallels ancestral name pairing in the *aba* text cited above. Beyond this, however, we can note the manner in which the man–bird motif articulates the cultural significance of sound production, of 'talk' (*bi*). The clause *bi mero* means both 'I am *getting* the talk' and 'I am *giving* the talk of these birds to the child'. Maturation is thus firmly linked to speech development in a way consistent with the importance of talk as a mode of adult self-presentation.

Through *gamu*, talk is used to reproduce itself. From the above data we can see that rites constitute an expressive medium for evaluations of gender as well as statements about valued attributes.

Unit structuration

The Huli are divided into named patrilineal clans that are associated with territories referred to here as 'parishes'. The segmentary structure of the clan provides an organizational model for the sectional divisions of a parish. Huli use the term *hameigini* ('father (*hame*) + son (*igini*)') to denote both the agnatic descent category and the local settlement with which it is linked. The androcentric bias embedded in, and displayed by, unit category labels is consistent with the cultural values given to the procreative functions of males. In this regard, 'bone' and 'father' symbolize a strategic nucleus of related idioms pertaining to notions of descent unity:

Hameigini mbiyaore harali ogoni kuni mbiyaore ni howa igini damene honowinidago kuni mbiyaore gai bini. Hameigini hame mbiyaore laga.
The *hameigini* (clan) that is there is one; from the one bone all the sons are born, they are broken off from the one bone. The clan is 'one father' it is said.

(Field data)

Identification with an agnatic category, as defined by a principle of descent, is expressed through the medium of ancestral patronymic prefixes. These are retained and inherited without regard to the residential or economic association maintained with the 'source land' (*dindi tene*: locus of a clan's property and ritual interests). In valley communities such as Ialuba, the clan-segments and clan-parishes may be referred to by a 'neighbourhood' term compounded of a place name and the suffix *li* ('people of').

Interrelationships between clans occupying contiguous territories are often (though not invariably) ordered in accordance with a binary schema whereby one clan is *tene* ('source/origin/base') and the other *yamuwini* ('nothing/woman (*yamu*) + placed (*wini*)'). This structural alliance – such as obtains between Hiwa : Koma and Dugube : Tobani in Ialuba – represents a fusion of genealogical and sociological components. Clan-pairing derives from an historically defined creative affinal link between an incoming ancestral deity (*dama*) and a sister of a resident deity. The progeny of such mythical unions, often incestuous (*tagini*), mark the division between *dama* and 'man'. Agnatic descent remains the principle of differentiation as the two units confront each other as distinct patrilines. The alliance is defined in terms of kinship; the clans are linked as immutable '*consanguineals*' rather than perpetual affines or parts of a cognatic descent category. The aetiological accounts of ancestral unions (see D.1 p.128) compound these facts with distributional patterns of land, ritual, and talk. In this regard, the precedence of *tene* is not that of a wife-giver but of a land-giver, and the binary schema provides a rationale for subsequent settlement and territorial rights. This relational model applies only in the context of land disputes. The immutability of this alliance is not reproduced at the level of individual marriages, where ties of consanguinity created in the next generation link a network of people but not their respective clan units.

The terminological duality of *tene/yamuwini* embodies a similar order of systematic ambiguity as *hameigini*. The opposition is predicated on the conflation of male/female and cross-sex sibling-ship. The resultant social classifications reflect progenitorial myths in the differentiation of 'base/source people' (*tene*) and those 'placed by women' (*yamuwini*). This semantic component of 'placement' underlies evaluations of precedence that are a corollary of historical patterns of land transference. Moreover, the relative weighting of *tene/yamuwini* – separating 'primary' from 'secondary' land owners – is reflected in the pejorative connotations of the morpheme *yamu* ('nothing/worthless': see *Table 3*, p. 95). The fusion of gender and locality biases is thus terminologically institutionalized. Notwith-standing these observations, the fixity of clan-pairing is an inferential model constructed and expressed through a specific discourse mode known as *malu*. Where accounts of land inheritance become a topic of dispute (as in D.1) there is a challenge to the specific applicability of the *tene/yamuwini* schema. This reinforces the important point that this dualistic model is tenable only in the context of historically defined patterns of land allocation. A second source of threat stems from internally expressed contentions that (for example) Hiwa *tene* and Koma *tene*, as distinct patrilines, are not immutably linked as 'consanguineals'. The logic of such statements is founded on oscillations in the way social identities are defined as *tene*. The term is used to denote both a mother's brother's patriline (in the case of clan-pairing) and one's own agnatic descent category. Emphasizing unit differentiation entails categorizing members of, say, Hiwa as

Figure 3   Unit structuration

KOMA   HIWA
TOBANI   DUGUBE

◄—— Land-takers   ◄—— Land-givers

Yamuwini   Tene
Female   Male
Sister   Brother

The nexus of *aba* kinship

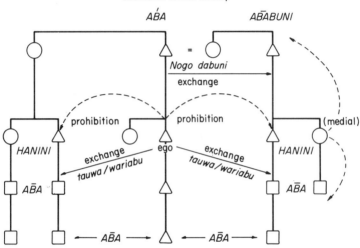

classificatory 'wife's-brothers' (*balibuni*), thus isolating the incidence of ancestral affinity. The implications of stressing unit independence are to deprive Hiwa of rights to speech precedence and public recitations of *malu* in inter-clan land disputes. Clearly, configurations based on the categories of unit structuration cannot be divorced from contexts of discourse about them.

The 'negotiable' face of such structural models seems, as previously contended, to derive from the convertible and contrary nature of those propositions from which they are inferred. The Huli notion of *tene* – alongside the parallel idioms of Melpa *pukl* (A. Strathern 1972), Duna *tse* (Modjeska 1977), and Daribi *page* (Wagner 1967) – encapsulates a doctrine of causality which distinguishes between 'origins' and 'sequence'. In respect of discourse about the relationships of people, events, or people to events, *tene* is used to attribute causation, ownership, and responsibility. As shown below, the dual applications of a number of related terms expresses the sense in which the primordiality of 'females' is sometimes declared and deferred to, and sometimes masked. Often these competing perspectives are expressed through symbolic inversion as in the behavioural fields of decoration – the ritual meanings surrounding Huli wigs – talk – the content of certain proverbs – and myth – themes of fertility and death. There is a structuring of those occasions when the values attendant on the sexual disjunction are attested to and validated. These perspectives appear to isolate structurally the creative (and historical) tie of affinity from the sequence of agnatic descent.

male	*female*
Tene	*Tene*
father's clan	mother's brother's clan
land-giver: sequence	land-giver: origins
Aba	*Aba (buni)*
father	mother's brother
land-owner (*dindi aba*)	land-owner (*dindi anduane*: land (*dindi*) + breast (*andu*) + inside (*hane*))

The equation of MB and F as respective male representatives of two *tene* lines seems to constitute the semantic relatedness between the two tonally contrasted '*aba*' lexemes. Ego has two 'fathers' and two '*tene*'. In a further sense, and paralleling Daribi notions (Wagner 1967), they are consanguineal parents of ego who uniquely fuses bone and blood substances as devolved from mother and father. Moreover, the same lines reflect 'responsibilities' of matrilateral and patrilateral kin which are embedded in the two complementary terms for 'ownership' (i.e. 'father' and 'breast'). Indeed, members of Koma may metaphorically refer to their relationship to Hiwa by such statements as 'I have taken the breast from him' (Goldman 1981a : 403), which conversely expresses Melpa formulations (said by an MB about an ZS): 'These children are fed by my breast' (A. Strathern 1972 : 20). The conclusion that emerges from data thus far presented is that the Huli system demonstrates structural principles common to many Highlands societies.

The *tene/yamuwini* polarity is also used to relate classes of parish member. The terms refer respectively to an aggregate of domiciled or affiliated people sharing patrilineal descent from a founding ancestor, and a class of non-agnatic cognates related to these latter individuals through a female agnate. Importantly, at this level the classes do not oppose each other as distinct patrilines, nor are the membership rights of *yamuwini* defined or phrased as founded on cognatic descent from apical ancestors. Descent confers entitlement to parish membership only for agnates. Cognates may affiliate, initially, through ties to a specific ego that directly reflect the attendant obli-gations of cognatic kinship and its cultural implications. This reticulum of interpersonal 'ropes' (consanguinity), in regard to land grants and usufruct, is encapsulated by the designation *aba* and communicated through the associated *pureremo* analysed below. *Yamuwini* is thus a categorical construction derived from the behavioural meanings attached to *aba* kinship. The terminological separation of *tene*/*yamuwini*, as a unit structuration schema, from the creative and constituent ties of *aba* consanguinity, is analytically critical. *Yamuwini* is not a category label that can be employed *prospectively* to claim rights to land usage. The oppositional frame is a *retrospective* gloss of the manner in which the classes residentially compose the parish. It is an ideological schema pertinent to discourse about land, war, compensation, and ritual where emphasis is placed on unit denomination and complementarity. Therefore, far from constituting a relevant recruitment idiom, *yamuwini* represents the culminative implications of *aba* kinship underscored by the cross-sex principle. Non-resident or non-affiliated cognates are not included in this class. Linguistic and behavioural data pertaining to *aba* removes the last vestiges of morphological correspondence between the Huli and the descent systems of the Kwaio and Choiseul (see De Leper-vanche 1968 : 186; A. Strathern 1972 : 186) where cognatic descen-dants 'are not to be refused' (Scheffler 1965 : 48). These observations explain such common statements as: *Yamuwini ti aba tara, ti hameigini tara, ti wi tarame honowini yamuwini* ('Their father is different, their clan is different, they are born from a different penis'). Non-agnatic cognates are not 'one father' with *tene*, but a composite class of the *hameigini* as a parish settlement. The idioms of unity are here territorial rather than genealogical.

The fusion of locality and descent notions is graphically depicted in that classical Melanesian metaphor of the 'tree':

'The clan (*hameigini timbuni*) stays like the base (*tene*) of a tree, we are staying together like the trunk. The sub-clans (*hameigini emene*) are there like the branches (*ginigene*); those who are born later continue to stay like branches. They may get lost or they may stay; the main base will not get lost. The first tree that is there will continue to bear fruit. The base (*tene*) stays like that, as the first man on the land. We are staying on the ancestral land (*dindi tene*).'

(Field data)

The terms 'big' (*timbuni*) and 'small' (*emene*) discriminate higher from lower segmentary units. Agnates (*tene*) stay on the land as 'base' (*tene*). Genealogical charters (*malu*: ref. D.1) are structured in accordance with the lines of patrilineal descent. Ideally, only the headman (*agali haguene*: 'man (*agali*) head (*haguene*)') of each clan-parish – a position based on descent and primogeniture – has the authority to use this knowledge in disputes. There are men of prominence in every parish but the office of headman is hereditary and not subject to competition. The incumbent symbolizes clan *mana* as the repository of myth and genealogical information relating to the socio-historical origins of people and land. In this respect, and indeed the remarkable depth of genealogies (see D.1), the Huli do not conform to the 'big-man' systems described for other Highlands cultures.

The clan retains ultimate title and dispository rights over land but allocation of land-use rights is the prerogative of individuals. Both men and women may grant usufruct or bequeath gardens to kin and non-kin without the need for formal decision processes. Many Huli maintain gardens in a number of parishes and there is a high toleration of multiple-parish affiliation. In Ialuba, some 10 per cent of adult Koma males had gardens in other parishes but the range of choice rarely exceeds three. The flexibility in residence choices partly reflects norms entailed by affinal, cognatic, and friendship ties. Practical demonstrations of 'allegiance' are, however, demanded in certain situations of conflict. In extreme instances, support of an opposing unit can result in temporary expulsions of parish members. The overall position of non-agnatic cognates is frequently phrased as follows:

TEXT 2
⎡ don't do wrong things
⎣ don't say (wrong things)
→ *ibu hanuni haga mandagi kebagoni*
  he [i.e. cognate] used to stay in the middle, we are together
⎡ when he is doing bad things there
⎣ when he is stealing women

⌈ when he is stealing and eating pigs
⌊ when he persists in this
'Go to your father's land', we used to say.

Yamuwini have secondary status in the parish, reflecting the manner in which women are said to be 'under the legs' (*ge pouni ha* (D.3 : 461)) of men. In the context of discourse about land, people may refer to themselves or another by such phrases as '*i/ibu ainya*': I/he is mother'. This is a contraction of an optional and expanded statement '*i ainya dindi ko*': 'I am on my mother's land' where mother is a female agnate of the clan parish. In the case of more distant female links the appropriate generation term can be substituted for 'mother' in the above formulations. These descriptive expressions do not have the status of category labels nor do they imply any ranking of *yamuwini*. Similarly, the Huli do not categorically differentiate modes of residence that are associated with some attenuation of rights. Such phrasal lexemes as *tagira hene* ('he stayed outside'), *bamba hene* ('he stayed a long time') and *ibu pu bu dai bu* ('he comes and goes': i.e. between parishes) – referred to by Glasse (1968 : 24–5) – are not used to discriminate specific classes of residential 'affiliant'. Notwithstanding the flexibility in residential patterns and choices there is an ideologically articulated stress on patri-virilocal settlement:

TEXT 3
⌈ Don't stay for a long time (on the mother's land)
⌊ after you have stayed for some time then continue to return here
⌈ when you have gone to your mother's land
⌊ then stay for ever on your father's land
⌈ go to your mother's land
⌊ stay on your father's land.

Unlike the majority of texts presented in this book, Texts 2 and 3 above were collected in informal interviews. When set out with a lineation appropriate to Huli speaking, it is remarkable that again they display an implicit syntax characterized by binarism. One of the dominant explanatory hypotheses forwarded in this book is that in 'consensus'-oriented dispute systems, the presence of disjunctive conclusions is functionally related to the necessity for option-presenting outcomes. A disputant is given either/or choices. The lack of judicial authority seems correlated with an absence of outcome formulations couched in the imperative mood. The binary nature of theme and topic appears structurally related to the articulation of choices. I argue in Chapter 5 that in the universe of speech evaluation the organizational patterns reveal a high degree of correspondence between semantic, syntactic, and phonological structures. In the context of talk about kinship and residence, the mental and verbal furniture seem determined, in no small degree, by aesthetic considerations. The ethnomodels – in common perhaps with all explanatory frameworks – express a cultural aesthetic that invests interrelated sets of contrasts with distinct linguistic characteristics. In this area of discourse about relationships we can perceive a reduction of arbitrariness between form and meaning. It is not simply that binary patterns are 'good to think', for they can also be 'good to say'. It is this inter-dependence between the two, as realized in the textual data cited in this chapter, that is crucially important for understanding the rhetorical efficacy and dynamics of models.

Two further category labels deserve brief comment. The first, *tene hamene* ('source brother'), denotes certain long-established *yamuwini* who, through successive generations, have stayed on the land like *tene*. The criteria of continued residence and association defines the sense in which they are 'just like *tene*' (*tene ale dege*): '*Tene hamene* have forgotten their fathers' land, they stay like the base'. They are quasi-*tene* only in respect of *tene* as a class of parish member, not a descent category (see Keesing 1971 : 131). The second class, *wali haga* ('women (*wali*) continue to stay (*haga*)': i.e. a source of marriageable females), is composed of affinally related residents and non-kin. This category term is also used synonymously for any *hameigini*.

By comparison with the substance repercussions of 'bone', the ramifications of 'blood' in Huli are somewhat complex. Not only are sub-clans metaphorically conceptualized as 'branches', but there is also acknowledgement that female agnates' blood creates separate patrilines. This is symmetrically reflected (FZ = MZ = MB) in the kin term *magane* ('mother's brother') – a generic word for 'tree branch'. Paralleling the Melpa construct *mema tenda* (A. Strathern 1972 : 15), Huli idioms of 'one blood' signify an agnatic descent category, its inclusive interpersonal relationships, and a range of cognatic kin. Despite these similarities, in Huli cross-cousins' children are said to be of 'different blood' (*darama tara*). To comprehend the rationale behind the genealogical limits of this idiom it is necessary to inter-relate certain aspects of marriage norms, kin terminology, and bride-wealth practices.

The Huli marriage rules prohibit unions between agnates,

consanguineals related as second cousins or closer, and (ideally) people who fall into the categories of *tene* or *yamuwini*. In this latter case the limits are imprecise so that with increased genealogical distance there is a mitigation of disapprobation. There is a tripartite classification of pigs given in bride-price transactions:

Collective terms[3]

Nogo Wariabu₁ ('pig (*nogo*) woman (*wari*: form of *wali*) + compensation (*abu*: a form of *abi*)')[4]

or *Nogo Dabuni* ('pig (*nogo*) marriage (*dabu*)')

or *Nogo Hende* ('pig (*nogo*) pig rope/tied up (*hende*)')

or *Nogo Damba* ('pig (*nogo*) closed down (*damba*)')

Sections

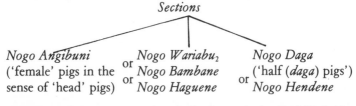

Nogo Aṅgɪbuni		Nogo Wariabu₂		Nogo Daga
('female' pigs in the	or	Nogo Bambane	or	('half (*daga*) pigs')
sense of 'head' pigs)		Nogo Haguene		Nogo Hendene

The sectional divisions are made principally on the basis of diminishing size. Norms relating to the distribution and consumption of bride-price concern only *nogo wariabu₂* thus reinforcing the extent to which this section represents the essence of marriage transactions. The relevant rules may be stated as follows:

(a) all agnatic kin and immediate cross-cousins (*hanini*: see Figure 3) are prohibited from receiving or eating *wariabu₂* under the dual sanctions of shame (*taga*) and deafness (*hale pai*)

(b) *wariabu₂* pigs should be distributed to the *aba* class of kin

(c) these pigs should be both killed and consumed by *aba*.

The injunction that agnates and cross-cousins cannot receive *wariabu₂* clearly discriminates those 'who may eat' from those 'who may not eat'. The division occurs precisely at the limits where 'one-blood' ties are commonly acknowledged to finish. The further prescription that this section of bride-price must be both killed and eaten is a means of enforcing the conceptual break between cross-cousins and cross-cousins' children who are not 'one-blood' with ego. Were agnates or cross-cousins to collect *wariabu₂* it would intimate an incestuous act tantamount to 'eating the bride's vulva' (Glasse 1968 : 57). In this context, the bride is considered as a 'sister' by both ego and ego's cross-cousins (i.e. Z = MBD = FZD). For these kin classes *wariabu₂* are conceptualized as *anguatole* ('jumped over/crossed over by women'). The pigs are 'contaminated meat' through association with a female sibling, and 'trouble' (*anguatole*) in the sense that any retention would deprive the *aba* of their rightful pigs.

Importantly, precisely the same rules apply to compensation pigs given when illicit sexual relations have occurred. This payment is called *nogo tauwa* ('pig (*nogo*) testicle/male (*tau*) + placed (*wa*)'). The pigs must again be killed and consumed by *aba* whose rights are said to have been infringed by the delict. The accordance of bride-price norms and compensation injunctions emphasizes the degree to which the former is itself a category of 'indemnity' transfer, a facet morphologically displayed in the term *wariabu*.

The extension of these prohibitions to cross-cousins is explained by their 'sibling-like' status. Indeed, sibling terms may be used in this relationship, thus indicating an Hawaiian element in what is essentially an Iroquois-type kinship terminology. The behavioural analogues of this equivalence are crystallized in conventional formulations (*pureremo*) that may be rhetorically fashioned to strategies that define obligations between people. These pre-patterned speech acts are category-bound, as the following *pureremo* indicates:

Hanini ogoni o i gubalini ore
this cross-cousin is my very heart
Humbirini hariani iya haru
we'll be together on the road to Humbirini (place where souls migrate)
iya mandagi gai buledago lowa
we'll meet up together it is said
hamalu howa ibu ala piyayagua
if he should die first
o i mani ibule
then I will come later
ibugua ira deladagoria pole hariani ibu holebira
while I am on the road he will be making fire there
ina howa homeneyagua howa
if I should die first
o hariani i koria ibu ibiragola
then while I am there he will be coming
iya mandagi bayele howa
we will stay well together.

The mutual obligations between *hanini* are symbolized by 'fire-making'. The very existence of a verbal ritual for this kin category measures the degree of importance they hold in the web of consanguinity. This same complex of affective and attitudinal dispositions in regard to cross-cousins were traditionally dramatized in the degradation rites of Tege where attempts were made to 'shame' initiates. Male transvestites – called, significantly, *wali hanini* ('female cross-cousins') – would enter an initiation house (*guru anda*) to shame young boys by simulating sexual intercourse with them. The meanings of this ritualized humiliation derive from the incestuous associations attached to female *Hanini* as cross-sex 'siblings'.[5] Furthermore, this Tege sequence was referred to as *wariabu₂ hoge* ('the bride-price trick'), an explicit acknowledgement of those prohibitions which obtain between *hanini* in respect of *wariabu₂* pigs. This kin category represents a functionally significant class for shaming rites intended to inculcate secular morals.

In the same way as cross-cousins are associated with siblingship and prohibition, as communicated through verbal and non-verbal rituals, so the centrality of *aba* ('cross-cousins' children') in exchange behaviour is articulated through the cultural medium of *pureremo*:

Aba hanuni
aba middle
(these relatives are centrally related and placed with respect to me)
E tabaya   hanuni
fertile gardens middle
(they stay on the fertile gardens in the middle of my land – a reference to one's obligations to provide *aba* with land if they request it)
Homa embo hanuni
forehead   middle
(they are in the middle like one's forehead – the forehead is considered the locus of truth and is here invoked to symbolize the cultural veracity of one's obligations to *aba*)
Wandari wariabu₂   hanuni
girl   bride-price pigs middle
(the *aba* are in the middle with the bride-price – the meaning of this phrase incorporates the polysemy of *wariabu* as the 'middle' section of bride-price pigs)
Galu Wabia   hanuni li   hengedagoni
Lesser bird of paradise middle on top has been planted
(they have been planted on my land in an analogous manner to the planting of Lesser paradise feathers in the middle of my wig)
Homa haguene   hanuni
skulls of the dead middle
(they will be in the middle with the dead skulls – a reference to the mutual obligations between *aba* to decorate the skulls of respective relatives in a Tege rite known as Homa haguene Tege)

Like many of the institutionalized norm formulae considered in this book, the striking economy of style belies the complexity of meaning. The repeated notion of 'middle' – which occurs also in Text 2 – expresses geographical contiguity, a physiological location where truth is visible (i.e. between the eyes), and the concepts of unbiased, sharing behaviour. The fundamental truths of this kin relationship, the ensemble of category-bound obligations, are metaphorically summarized in an idiom that conveys Huli doctrines of veracity (see Chapter 5). The text represents an ideal formulation of the *aba puremo* which can be balanced against the extract cited at the beginning of this chapter. The latter is fashioned in accordance with specific confrontation exigencies. The constancy of analogy in the two texts is illuminating. A metaphoric identity is conjured between the placement of *aba* in the 'middle' of one's land, and the actions of 'planting' feathers in the middle of one's wig. The fulfilment of kin obligations presents the self for assessment in a fashion analogous to modes of self-decoration. The communicative rituals of *puremo* do not simply index the ethos of *aba* and *hanini* relationships. They constitute definitional criteria: to be consanguineally related is to have the potential for engaging in routinized speech, just as to be affinally related prohibits joking and naming with opposite sex affines.

The above linguistic formulae clarify the degree to which the claims of non-agnatic kin regarding residence and refuge are normative entailments of a reciprocal and bilateral system of cognatic kinship (*not* cognatic descent). Viewed from the perspective of a parish's system schemata, matrilateral and patrilateral *aba* are categorically differentiated should they affiliate to ego's settlement. In the former case, they are classed as *wali haga* ('marriageable'), and in the latter instance as *yamuwini*. This triadic classification of parish members isolates the sequential implications of 'bone' (through patriliny) by counterpoising it against complementary categories. This conceptual and terminological format – *female : male : female* – is organizationally fundamental at the levels of (1) unit structuration, (2) bilateral consanguinity, and (3) affinity:

(1)   *Yamuwini*   .   *Tene*   .   *Wali haga*
        ('woman placed')   : ('male/agnate') : ('woman continually
                                                           stay')

(2)   *Aba*   *ego*   *Aba*
        (any alter who, in an   (any matrilateral
            ascending   alter consanguineally
        genealogical chain,   related to ego:
           relates to ego   :   'male'   : M = MB = MZ for
        through a real or   kin two or more
           putative female   generations
              agnate)   removed)
(3)   *ego*   *Imane*
                              'male'   : ('women (*ima*) + of
                                              (*ne*)' = affines.
                                            Ima cognate with
                                            Duna (Modjeska
                                            1977 : 100) and Mae
                                            (Meggitt
                                            1964b : 194))

The sexual dichotomy is semantically replicated at each discourse level and thus appears axiomatic. The *pureremo* texts, as types of native exegesis, further delineate the connection between marriage practices and the nexus of *aba* kinship. In this regard, Glasse confused the analytically and operationally distinct systems of *aba*/*wariabu*$_2$ and *tene*/*yamuwini* when he stated that transfers of bride-price stress the complementarity of the unit categories 'in the parish' (Glasse 1968 : 57). The exchange relationships of *aba* empirically cut across territorial boundaries, since not all of one's cognatic kin will live in the same parish. In addition to the fact that *yamuwini* and *aba* are not coterminous (since matrilaterally related *aba* and non-domiciled patrilateral *aba* are not *yamuwini*), the *tene*/*yamuwini* schema is not a relevant frame used by Huli to conceptualize or talk about bride-price.

What further terminological evidence can be adduced in support of the postulation that the sexual division is both an absolute pre-supposition and a classificatory axiom? This Iroquois-type system con-forms to the principle 'once cross always cross' (Scheffler 1971 : 248) but the mode of extending the 'cross' versus 'parallel' distinction beyond the level of first cousins is (by comparison with other High-lands Iroquois systems) quite idiosyncratic. *Aba* can be used to denote cousins of either parent and (where real or putative consanguinity is acknowledged) any terminal alter descended from a FZ, Z, MZ, or MB.

The scope of this sexually undifferentiated (but sexually defined) category isolates ego's agnatic kin from cognates related through a 'female' consanguineal. This accords perfectly with the *exchanges* of *wariabu*$_2$ between *aba* which constitute acts of unit definition. They ritually separate 'bone' people from 'blood' people. The distinctiveness of ego's agnatic line is maintained against the patrilines of his *aba* by enforcing consumption of 'polluted' meat. *Aba* are not party to the prohibitions of siblingship so that the killing of *wariabu*$_2$ symbolically breaks the ties of siblingship that subsisted in the previous generation between *hanini* ('cross-cousins'). With reference to *Figure 3*, the nexus of *aba* relationships and behaviour appears as a dialectical interplay between affinity and consanguinity. The sibling tie that is breached at the parental level is re-established in the next generation through cross-cousinship, and then severed again by transfer of 'tainted' meat. The oscillation of exchange-prohibition-exchange – which directly parallels Wagner's (1967) structural analysis of Daribi kinship – is terminologically realized by the equation of MB (*aba* (*buni*)) and MBSch/MBDch (*aba*) in contradistinction to X-cousins (*hanini*). Moreover, the medial position of *hanini* between two *aba* – on both the matrilateral and patrilateral sides – may be reflected semantically in the closeness of the terms *hanini* ('cross-cousin') and *hanuni* ('middle'). Given the prevalence of this concept of 'middle' in Huli talk about non-agnatic kin (e.g. see *puremo* texts above), and the quite regular vowel substitutions of /I/ and /ʊ/ in aesthetic speech forms (see Chapter 5), my speculation has firm foundations. These interpretive insights expose the structural principles determining the ascription of certain behaviour to specific kin categories.

Importantly then, at the level of the first descending generation *aba* is used to denote cross-cousins' children, FBDch, Zch, and MZDch/MZSch.[6] That is, children of matrilateral parallel cousins are classed as 'cross-sex' kin. Without invoking the notion of 'primary' kin-term meanings, the MB-ZS relationship is a nodal point in the reticulum of *aba* relationships. The differential affective weighting is here terminologically marked by the presence of the intensification morpheme -*buni* ('on one's heart': see Appendix 1: note 1).[7] Obligations between MB-ZS are correspondingly stronger with respect to land-use and gardens. Statistical data (Goldman 1981a) indicate that this tie is more frequently used than others as a basis for residence changes. Indeed, 53 per cent of *yamuwini* from two Ialuba parishes were living on M/MB land. This internal division of the '*aba*' class accords with conventionally defined behavioural discriminations between MB and other *aba* who have reciprocal obligations concerning bride-price and ritual decoration of skulls.

Notwithstanding the lack of a one-to-one correlation between kin category and social role, the *pureremo* texts suggest the notion of 'exchange' as an underlying motif of *aba* relationships. *Aba* receive *wariabu₂* on the basis of past transactions which may have involved various types of compensation or funeral payments. The referential indeterminancy of this kin term allows for a considerable latitude of choice as to which *aba* will actually be recipients. The culturally defined norms are given specificity through individual interpretations. A transfer of *wariabu₂* may thus reflect previous exchange activity between the participants or indeed their ancestors, or it may form part of a new initiative. In either case, genealogical proximity does not confer precedence over other *aba*. Significantly, however tenuous the consanguineal relation is, the fact of exchange determines the use of *aba* as a retrospective gloss. The term becomes a basis for knowledge about activities between people. This indeterminancy is further manifested in other lexemes sharing the same word stem, for example, *abago*, which is used like the English 'thingummybob' or 'what's-his-name'. To differentiate between cross-cousins' children and other *aba* – or to separate genealogical from classificatory uses of other terms – the qualifiers *ibini* ('real/itself'), *tene* ('source/base'), *dege* ('just/exactly') or *ore* ('very') can be appended.

On account of the identity discriminations within *aba* it is imperative to avoid reductionist arguments whereby all *aba* are assimilated to some 'primary' category such as MB/F/ZS or cross-cousin. Continuities and discontinuities of meaning need to be carefully plotted against terminological variations as was done for the suffixed morpheme *-buni*. Within this framework, *aba* (F)/*aba* (MB) contrast in respect of tone and reciprocal status. A degree of semantic relatedness, such that F and MB share a common role identity for any ego, is a deduction that proceeds from an understanding of the semantics and aesthetics of tone in Huli. That is, the inference forms part of a system for predicting meaning and form. To augment such arguments, there is the further point that ego uniquely fuses bone and blood lines. The corollary of this cross-substance tie is that a person is said to have two 'fathers' (or conversely two 'mother's brothers'), two 'owners', and two *'tene'*. In these respects the Huli show a high degree of morphological correspondence with the Daribi

(Wagner 1967 : 77, 124); importantly, these meanings are linguistically manifested. Because MB gives 'breast' to a ZS, he has two 'sons' (*igini*). The absence of a communicative routine between these kin (such as the *pureremo* for *hanini* and *aba*) seems correlated with conceptions about the impact of MB-ZS on the production of conflict. Disputes with other *aba* are more frequent, are more likely to culminate in unit opposition (since *aba* may belong to other parishes), and directly impinge upon wealth through norms pertaining to bride-price. Nevertheless, strategies of dispute mediation may still verbalize equivalences between kin categories and their affective / behavioural milieu.

The principles that order Huli relationships share the presupposition of the sexual dichotomy and its culturally defined system of values. One distinctive feature of the definitional axes under discussion is an elaborate ideology of pollution. The stigma philosophy that surrounds 'female sexuality' is, as I have shown, terminologically institutionalized in the labels of unit structuration. The associated concepts of inequality and imbalance have the 'dignity of a spiritual principle not to be challenged by women or compromised by men' (Buchbinder and Rappaport 1976 : 31–2). The maintenance of 'boundaries', whether located in the dispute or kinship systems, is a means of coping with contagion. In this respect, 'agnation' is sanitized and separated from that which is female through the medium of 'meat' and the actions of 'consumption'. The kin terminology would appear to uphold the discrete nature of these zones by differentiating agnates from other consanguineals (*aba*) and affines (*imane*). The cross-sex principle is again dominant in the terminological sphere. It is noticeable (see Appendix 1) that a spouse's sibling (*mbalibuni*) and a cross-sex sibling (*mbalini*) share the same kin morph; indeed, all affines are 'of women' (*imane*).

While it is the case that the various sets of contrastive terms have a mutually reinforcing function in the inculcation of a stigma ideology, different contexts stress different aspects. For example, in the *Ega Dole* rite – traditionally part of a Tege sequence concerned with the promotion of well-being among parish section members – *tene* representatives would hold the shoulder part of a pig and shout 'father father' while *yamuwini* held the lower legs uttering 'mother mother'. This symbolic statement of the interdependence of maternal / paternal ties emphasizes the positional primacy of 'male'. The marriage system, however, appears to be founded on the principle of sibling exogamy. Many of the Huli origin myths detail an incestuous union between cross-cousins (e.g. Gangamina and Garimone (see D.1.)) as an historical determinant of marriage norms. Indeed, I have suggested that *wariabu*$_2$ exchanges are best understood as a sequence of breach – re-establishment – breach of siblingship. Cross-cousins' children mark the cessation of sibling ties created by marriage; they represent a point at which agnation becomes isolated from the web of consanguinity. Obligations between *aba* are a 'residuum of the claims existing between their parents' (Wagner 1967 : 127). The 'polluted' nature of bride-price pigs derives specifically from the shame attached to sibling incest – consuming these pigs is a symbolic act of intercourse. Inasmuch as Duna practices parallel those of the Huli, the 'explanatory blockage' (Modjeska 1977 : 208) of why Duna men say they are eating the bride's vagina is clearly resolved by the analysis I have offered above. Different contexts present alternative representations of the sexual dichotomy. The Huli data forces us to recognize that the meaning of kin terms and relationships is often indigenously defined in terms of structured speech that declares truths about obligations. It should also be emphasized that language use and structure provide diagnostic evidence for prevalent ideologies of inequity.

Linguistic discrimination and inter-sex relations

The Huli have a dominant ideology of pollution – a set of ideas articulating a conception of social order within which 'female'-associated actions and objects have pejorative connotations. Because ideologies are linked to the interests and policies of social groups, and inculcated through educational institutions, language is an important medium for discrimination. Linguistic disparities will reflect social distinctions, inequities, and imbalances. In this regard the rhetoric of male–female interaction reveals a coherent set of beliefs about the nature and implications of female sexuality. This level of semantic consistency is exhibited in idiomatic and terminological phenomena associated with anger, sickness, and trouble, oral history, and contexts where people deal with each other's sexuality. There is a marked sexual segregation in everyday behaviour and Huli women occupy a marginal politico-jural status. In the context of New Guinea Highlands literature (see Brown and Buchbinder 1976) it is common for the male/female distinction to be associated with the oppositions of *strength-decay*, *dominance-subjugation*, *purity-pollution*, and *fertility-death*. It is less common, however, for the semantic, symbolic, and metaphoric aspects of these dimensions to be described from a sociolinguistic perspective.

Aetiological narratives (*tene te*) relating to cultural statements of gender clearly demonstrate an institutionalized level of vocabulary switching – from 'neutral' to 'pejorative' terms (see *Table 3*). The dogmas of pollution and contagion are given continuity through oral instruction. Among Highlanders, causal explanations for a supposed historical transition from a time of immortality to mortality frequently involve ideas about snakes and 'renewed skin' (see Wagner 1967 : 40 and Modjeska 1977 : 30). Furthermore, females cause death through inappropriate 'verbal' responses. The resultant syndrome establishes a connection between females, feminine speech, and normative breach that underlies systems of censure and praise in disputes. Huli myths represent a predilection for explanation in terms of 'first causes'; they manifest the workings of the cultural doctrine of *tene* ('base, origin, source'). But myths also function to maintain the integrity of beliefs as a rationale of social behaviour. The following 'base story', which accounts for the occurrence of death, is widely known:

The first woman gave birth to the first child. While she was with the baby a man came and addressed her as 'Mother of Life!' (*Habe Ainya*: stay (*habe*) mother (*ainya*)). He called out once, twice and kept calling this name. She did not move and she did not say anything. This is the way the first man came and called her. He uttered this name so that the child would have it, but she just stayed silent. He turned the name around

→ (*beregeda*) and addressed her as 'Mother of Death!' (*Homabe Ainya*: death (*homa*) mother (*ainya*)), to which she responded 'Yes'. He had carried some clear water (*iba*) to give the child but because the woman had answered to the name 'Mother of Death' he threw the water away. The snake drank the water and so he does not die but simply casts off his old skin. Huli die because the woman answered to the name Mother of Death and the baby was given breast-milk (*pipini*) instead of the water the man had carried.

(Informant: Kabo–Pina Clan)

This central Huli myth incorporates the framework of ideas that structures social organization in this culture. If I am concerned in my analysis with oppositions it is because the Huli too express the relationship between life and death as one that is 'turned around' (*beregeda*). It is further important to know that fertility/death are twin aspects of women, each being emphasized in different contexts.

In the above myth, the theme of mortality appears to be ordered by the following equations:

Condition	Agent	Causal substance	Consequence
Death (*homa*) :	Woman (*wali*) :	Breast-milk (*pipini*)	: Mortality (Huli)
Life (*habe*)	: Man (*agali*)	: Water (*iba*)	: Immortality (snake)

Death is an outcome of the properties of women, and is contrasted with the life-giving agency of water, seen as external to man. The contaminating and debilitating aspects of 'breast-milk' are conveyed by the predetermined choice of the lexeme *pipini* – which refers both to milk and to fluid secretion at death (see *Table 3*) – in contrast to the neutral phrase *andu ibane*. The ideology of female pollution is couched in a pejorative code that is routinized in myth as an educational medium. The fecund associations of water (*iba*) are semantically realized in the terms for semen (*wi ibane*: 'penis water') and, in its 'fertile' guise, breast-milk (*andu ibane*: 'breast water'). The same ambivalence characterizes ideas about female blood. Strength may be alluded to by the phrase *darama bere* ('blood is sitting'), but female blood may also be used for poisoning and sorcery. These meanings are separately conveyed by the loaded terms *hugu*, *liano*, etc. (*Table 3*).

Significantly, the association of snake and water in the above myth is a recurrent motif of purification rites that are metaphorically conceived as a 'peeling of dead skin'. In the event of illicit sex, *tini gamu* ('intestines (*tini*) spell') may be resorted to. The intestines are associated with decaying substances; only women may receive and eat the intestines of pigs. Water over which a spell has been cast is given to the afflicted male to drink:

TEXT *Tini Gamu*
*Buni o poro / bune o poro / wani o poro / wa karayeke o poro / dalege o
poro / dali pari o poro / anga ungu pini ndibu / anga ungulu pini ndibu / gege
wagia pini ndibu / baya waya pini ndibu / . . .*
I'm peeling away the liver / I'm peeling away the liver / I'm peeling away the skin of the sun / I'm peeling away the skin of the flying beetle / I'm peeling away the skin of the snake / I'm peeling away the skin of the snake / I'm closing and making firm the roots of this pandanus / I'm closing and making firm the roots of this pandanus / I'm closing and making firm the roots of this pandanus / I'm closing and making firm the roots of this pandanus.
Informant: Puguraba (Koroba)

Table 3 *The lexis of female sexuality*

Neutral/primary terms →	Alternative idioms →	Associated meanings
Wali ('woman')	[*Angibuni* *Gende Yamo* *Bai Yamo*	(a) female gender (b) anger (c) pus/toxic (d) sow (pig) *yamo* ('nothing'): a *tayenda* (forest language) term *yamo* ('nothing'): a *kai* ('praise') term
Darama/Yada ('blood')	[*Hugu* [*Tomia/Liano/Pogaga*	(a) menstrual blood (b) secretion from sexual organs (c) anger poisons
Wali Tabira ('menstruating woman': *ta* (emit) + *bira* (doing))	[*Wali Guya* *Pugua Bira* *Pobo Ha*	*wali* ('woman') + *guya* ('cooking/heating') (a) strike out (b) erase (a) heat (b) anger
Andu Ibane ('breast milk')	[*Pipini*	(a) white substance secreted at death
Igini Beda ('pregnant': *igini* (child) + *beda* (seated))	[*Yamo ko*	*yamo* ('nothing') + *ko* ('bad')
Wali Mo Wini ('non-agnatic cognates': *wali* (woman) + *mo* (made) + *wini* (placed))	[*Yamouwini/Yamuwini*	*yamo/yamu* ('nothing') + *wini* ('placed')
Wali Pindu ('vagina': *wali* (woman) + *pindu* (possessions/things))	[*Hamba* *Ponde* *Koyale*	possibly related to *bambu* ('lips')/*bambu* ('sorcery') *po* ('lid') + *nde* ('twisted') *ko* ('bad') + *ya* ('held') + *le* ('thing'); as in *koya* ('to deceive')

Renewal of life is here achieved in a way analogous to the 'shedding of skins' by snakes. The polluting effects of intercourse are countered by making firm one's metaphorical 'roots'. We may again note the marked 'pairing' of terms – *buni / bune* : *dalege / dali pari* : *anga ungu / anga ungulu* – which is an invariable feature of Huli spells.

The imbalance of male / female is reflected in the different verbs used to describe people's whereabouts. For males, statements utilize the particle *ka* ('stand'), while for females the appropriate verb is *beda* ('sitting'). Men are *haguene* ('head') and women *erene* ('tail'); the former walk at the front (*bamba*), the latter behind (*ma*). Dreams in which a tooth is lost from the upper jaw are held to signify the impending death of a paternal relative; a tooth lost from a lower jaw means the death of a material relative. Further contexts of institutionalized inequality can be seen from *Table 3*, in which we can again note the disjunction between the neutral *wali mo wini* ('women placed') and the category label *yamuwini* ('nothing / women placed') for affiliated cognates related to a female agnate. These data establish a consistent set of ideas about female sexuality, concepts that have engendered a quite separate vocabulary, which trades on the negative import of its terms.

While this ideology is uniform, it is not ubiquitous, for there is an explicit notion of the ritual / mythical primordiality of females. All the symbols of fecundity have their own 'origin myths' which are widely known. In this respect the Huli nevertheless have a concept of factual purity and accuracy. The 'best' accounts are owned by the clans historically associated with specific sites (for example Karua clan of Levani where mineral oil is obtained) or ancestors. This compartmentalization of knowledge (see Goldman 1979) indicates the degree to which talk is a model of unit interrelationships in Huli. The series of etiological narratives I collected concerning Haroli (Appendix 6 B: bachelor cult concerned with the promotion of growth and beauty), *Anga* (pandanus), *Mbagua* (tree / mineral oil used for body decoration), and *Hiwa* (sago) – recorded in Goldman (1981a) – displayed a number of common motifs. In every case the items had their genesis in female 'blood' and were sub-divided into male : female species.

item	*female*	*male*
sago	*komaiya*	*yai*
pandanus	*mundia*	*lo*
oil	*ligabi*	*yola*
Haroli	*igiri more*	*hare*

Importantly, the interaction of males with the above items is hedged with ritual and prohibitions on swearing (*hege*), speech that is inappropriate in the company of 'women'. There is a separation along sexual lines between the production processes and the subsequent use and display of these materials that we might characterize as the control (through ritual) and exploitation of female power by men.

The construction of sexually constituted zones informs all areas of Huli behaviour, so that the kinship system described here appears as yet another expression of the need to isolate androcentric concerns from female pollution. The corpus of myths relating to fertility symbols all elaborate a cultural presupposition concerning the relationship of women to social disorder. Deviance is defined in a lexicon that articulates the stigma attached to women. The control that males exercise over females, in myth or social actions, is over women as 'norm breakers' (Keenan 1974 : 137). The use of violence in the Haroli text cited in Appendix 6(B) is a response to an act of 'pollution'. The rituals that attend male use of female-associated objects are thus procedures for decontamination. One corollary is that 'dispute management' describes actions for eliminating 'dirt'; public space should be sanitized from the pollution of uncontrolled speech or behaviour. The lexicon of female sexuality is utilized to define what is unacceptable and inappropriate: censure is most typically expressed by the attribution of 'female' characteristics.

Talking about sexual intercourse, in the context of a public dispute, demands a 'sanitization' of vocabulary used in 'private' situations. The high incidence of euphemism and metaphor thus correlate with a topic that represents an area of discomfort, strain, and anxiety. The conventions of debate constrain participants to avoid the low-valued terms of *hège* ('swearing': see Chapter 5) for forms that are the 'linguistic equivalents of disinfectant' (Leech 1974 : 53):

Ina howa eberere gambe te Tele Tele habale wiaru handa walia
I used to see and find the Tele Tele bird putting eggs in the pitpit.
I anga hangama/I kopi hangama
You were planting nut trees/you were planting coffee; or

The Kope Alua bird (honeyeater) is the one who sleeps in pandanus trees.

Language change is both an index of the Huli sensitivity to 'contaminating and disordered' substances in public exchanges, and a means for controlling potentially polluting actions. Indeed, the following spell text clarifies the sense in which sexual intercourse is one theatre in which males negotiate the female threat to a physically and socially defined order:

TEXT *Ndi Tingi Gamu* ('secret (*ndi*) body (*tingi*) spell')
The spell was traditionally intoned by men before intercourse. Mud and leaves were frequently rubbed over the penis. The rite formed part of *Agali Dagia* ('men's platform'), given to males approximately one year after marriage. The potential fertility of a union had first to be proved by tending special gardens and pigs before consummation of the marriage.

The spirit Ni and his wife Hana/you two have said poke/ you have said poke like a murmur/you have poked and shaken/on the trunk of the Tale tree/on the trunk of the Tale tree/Ni and Hana both/you have played on the sand/you have played on the compost/you have played on the gravel/you have played on the mud/with the charcoal of the Tege Walu tree/with the charcoal of the Tege Mugudila tree/with the charcoal of the Tege Lai tree/it is shining bright and you came carrying it/it is dazzling and you came carrying it/it is burning bright and you came carrying it/with the sap of the Wabulu cane/with the sap of the Galoma cane/with the sap of the Gibi cane/I am breaking and extinguishing it/I am breaking and extinguishing it/I am breaking and extinguishing it/the crackle and the hiss I am extinguishing [*ti tau*, *tigi tugu*, *ti te* are reduplicative aesthetic forms for 'crackle'])/I am extinguishing it and making it cold.
(Informant: Hiwa Tege (Pina Clan))

Ni and Hana are a pair of ancestral progenitors who are acknowledged to have given this 'talk' to man. The fertility of their union is invoked in the first part of the spell where the verbs 'poke, shaken, and played' are euphemisms for sexual intercourse. 'Clean' language preserves the sanctity of this verbal medium as an item of public currency. Allusions to mud, gravel, sand, and compost are references to the fecundity of the sexual act. Charcoal symbolizes the penis, which is strong and hard like the various trees mentioned. Phrases signifying the properties of brightness and burning relate directly to 'heat' produced by female sexual organs. The extinguishing of this 'fire' by semen (i.e. sap) is a metaphor for the male's control of female potency.

Not only is this symbolism indigenously undestood, it is also re-affirmed in the menstrual rites of women.These were performed to prevent men from being burnt (*do*) or scorched (*dalu*). Ideally, the male was supposed not to sleep for four days, during which time he would recite spells to cleanse his eyes (*De domalu gamu*) and 'open' his nose (*Ngui dugua gamu*) to counteract the 'taint' emitted by his wife. Having 'open' eyes and nose was vital for men: 'we do it so we can smell pig and see cowrie shells'. The idioms of contamination are most clearly articulated in post-intercourse spells, where pollution is said to 'stick/adhere' (*para*), precisely the same term used to describe an imputation of 'blame'. A woman's taint is figuratively expressed as dirt (*dodo*), sourness (*kau*), and mess (*kilandu*), which have to be scraped (*kedo*), cleared (*ndoa*), and cut away (*gundu*). As will become evident, evaluations of talk and action in disputes are couched in the codes of pollution and sickness. The mechanisms of compensation and resolution are conceptualized as 'healing rites' because illness is the dominant metaphor for disordered relationships.

The configuration of meanings surrounding the physiological functions of females is underpinned by a generalized notion that they display a lack of 'control'. Males insist, as they do in Duna (Modjeska 1977 : 164), that women have no *mana* ('knowledge/custom/talk') and so they are precluded from participation in decision-making relating to war, disputes, or compensation payments. These convictions have lexical representation and institutionalization in the language of anger, sickness, and trouble. In disputes, males are provided with a powerful rhetorical weapon for acts of censure that attribute cross-sex characteristics. Deviance or uncontrolled speech are glossed with polysemous terms (see *Table 3*) that (a) are female associated, and (b) carry a semantically debased value given to neutral terms only through paralinguistic means. The routinization of inequality is the basis of a semantic relatedness between the tonally contrasted pairs (see also Chapter 2).

wañdia ('woman's house'): wañdia hia ('to avoid/go around')
(The sense in which female associated objects are to be avoided.)
kebā ('anger'): keba ('woman's digging-stick')
(The sense in which this tool is often used in anger, as well as associated with frustrating work.)

The terms for anger in *Table 3* – *hugu*, *angibu*, *pobo* – signify 'heat' produced by menstruation. Huli poisons are based on the toxicity of female blood – emphasizing the association of death and inherent substances. Men and pigs are believed to be frequently attacked by malevolent spirits variously named Wali Nguni ('Woman (*wali*) taint (*ngu*)'), Wali Boleme ('Woman will hit (*bole*)') Wali Kaiya, and Duna Wali ('Duna Woman'). Only females are subject to this type of possession.

Behavioural prohibitions reflect the high degree of sexual segregation maintained in this culture. Women should not cross a bridge while men are underneath; they should not pass by seated men; they must refrain from stepping over food, weapons, or men's bags, and not give food to children from under their sleeping platforms. These injunctions prevent contamination that results from exposure to female genitalia – a 'passing through the thighs of women'. Significantly, this metaphorical notion is a facet of the term *anguatole* ('crossed over/jumped over') used in disputes to signify both a state of prohibition and a breach of norms. *Wariabu*₂ pigs are *anguatole* for agnates and cross-cousins. As polluted meat they are referred to as 'smelly' (*ngubi*). Clearly, disordered states are glossed with 'female' terms: *ngu* ('female taint'): *ngui* ('nose'): *ngubi* ('smelly'). This compartmentalization of gender prohibitions is further indexed by descriptors – such as *galo bira* – which are used specifically in talk about the delicts of women. What needs to be emphasized is the degree to which the conceptual separation of sexually associated norms is verbally marked. The range of prohibitions relating to joking, sitting, and naming in the context of affinal relationships (see Glasse 1968 : 60) is best viewed as an outcome of the inter-sex ideology I have been examining. These norms operate with regard only to opposite-sex affines. The rules of uxorilocal residence whereby a man should refrain, under sanction of *burayu* (illnesses of the chest), from eating *hai tigu* (species of red banana), *tia horia* (marsupial), *tiabu banguma* (species of papuan asparagus), and *nogo buni* (pig's liver) reflect beliefs about the danger of women *per se* rather than any notion of 'marrying one's enemies'. The qualities respectively of redness, small size, softness, and location of spirit attack all signify aspects of the female gender.

A code of social control

The behavioural phenomena I have been examining express the concern of Huli with 'boundary maintenance'; situations of breach, defilement, and disorder are expressed in the lexis of feminine pollution. This is the metalanguage of social control which attempts to define and deal with asocial actions by invoking the syndrome of female heat in relation to concepts of anger, dispute, sickness, or other manifestations of deviance. Dispute management is but one expression of the ritualized treatment of 'space' which involves the apportionment of credit/discredit, or praise/censure according to constraints defining what is appropriate and acceptable in discrete categories of environment. The semantic dimensions that underlie processes of evaluation – such as those of control, futility, and covertness (see Chapter 5) – articulate culturally-specific polarities, which I argue have a determinative influence on the prevalence of binary structures in dispute speeches. Importantly, these contrast sets can be shown to embody the scheme of values attached to the male-female opposition. The talk of Huli disputes thus appears as a creative dialogue with spatially defined impurities which, while not necessarily conceived as female engendered, are nevertheless expressed in the language of contamination.

The considerable attention given to gender-based distinctions by anthropologists who have worked in the New Guinea Highlands testifies to the axiomatic status of male/female in the production of meaning. To show that a stigma ideology is linguistically manifested (not, from a sociolinguistic viewpoint, a novel argument) focuses our attention on the dynamic properties of the sexual dichotomy as a discursive and pragmatic instrument. Language use and morphology work against the treatment of women as persons able to participate in politically constituted decision-making. The tenet that women have no *'mana'* reinforces male dominance in disputes so that the participant status of any female is limited to her direct involvement as a claimant or defendant (i.e. as one of two *tene* 'sources of a dispute'), or as a witness when specifically called to make some contribution. Talk, as a powerful medium for discrimination, is thus utilized to separate men from women and, more significantly, women-like men (i.e. those who display verbal or non-verbal deviance) from real men. The very notion of a dispute is, as I later demonstrate, metaphorically couched in terms of pollution and heat. Settlement-directed talking is here oriented to the eradication of anomaly that results when transactions breach defined boundaries. Consistent with the Huli ideology of pollution, disputes represent 'matter out of place' (Douglas 1966 : 35) so that dispute-management describes procedures for 'dirt-elimination'. An examination of the disputes presented in this book reveals the sense in which resolution processes are composed of rituals of separation and sanitization of speech or behaviour. The systematic ordering and classification of phenomena accords with the spatially and conceptually defined spheres of *anda* ('house, inside, private'): *hama* ('cleared ground, public'). This environmental categorization is central to the organization and production of most activities in Huli and Duna (see Modjeska 1977). *Hama* refers both to a geographically located ceremonial ground associated with sub-clans, and the 'public' aspect of any transaction which need not necessarily be conducted on an actual clearing.

Anda and *hama* are, as previously indicated, inextricably bound to the sexual distinction. *Anda* signifies the private world of domestic activities and arrangements, the unseen, unrecorded, and 'covert'. Any pollution that may derive from interaction between the sexes is a matter for personal action. *Hama* represents the epideictic arena, a forum for presentation of self and display. The conduct of bride-price transfers, important rituals, and disputes on *hama* invests these activities with the characteristic of having been 'publicly' recorded. There is public accountability of one's product, an unwritten affidavit of display that adds to personal reputation and renown. Increments of prestige attach to males, and *hama* is almost totally appropriated by males. Actions are here not only subject to the constraints of excess, but should conform to an axiom of reciprocity. That is, *hama* circumscribes fields of exchange. The ethos of *hama* – expressing the quintessential importance of exchange in Huli – decrees that actions subject to public scrutiny and evaluation should be conducted with materials that are the best one can command. In this respect, one can appreciate the imputed homology between the semiotic systems of pigs, paint, and parlance. The Huli conceive an identity between display modes of decoration, exchange of pigs, and oratory, all of which demand the use of 'high-valued' items. These three spheres provide a unitary source of metaphor and figurative allusion in which one's talk is equated with one's decoration, or pigs are symbolically identified with wigs: 'You (Gangaro) have said the pigs there have been put on like the decoration on a Haroli wig and you are waiting' (field data). Pigs, paint, and parlance are all substances used when 'coming outside' to present oneself through display. In every case, what is brought to *hama* must be decontaminated of any impurities that linger through association with *anda*, and thus women. There is a conscious ordering of behaviour to achieve and demonstrate a state of being 'sanitized' of pollution. The prevalent motif of man-bird in Huli culture is directly linked to these discrete environmental zones. The parallel of male bird of paradise displaying to females on separate display grounds – frequently cleared/cleaned of rubbish first – reinforces the symbolic processes detailed in Chapter 5. It is precisely because these meanings colour the entire spectrum of behaviour in Huli, and *hama* displays have an aesthetic rationale that an analysis of speech must here account for the importance of form in relation to ecological models.

Dispute settlement techniques are thus oriented towards maintaining boundaries by apt use of assessment strategies. Domain transitions in decoration are marked by changes from *tene* to *hare* wigs, pan-pipes to bows, and silence to speech, and to traverse the zones of *anda*/*hama* in respect of a dispute is also a rule-governed activity. A transition should be marked by a change in vocabulary from the talk of 'small children . . . women and daughters' to the talk of 'men'; from the use of *hege* ('swearing') to the high-valued lexicons of *kai*, *mini mende* and *bi mone*. Correspondingly, *anda* is associated with the futile, covert, and uncontrollable while *hama* invites a display mode of rhetoric and oratory. The dispute process is thus largely devoted to the separation and sifting of issues to appropriate zones in an attempt to sanitize *hama* of the contamination produced by domestic quarrels. Vocabulary changes are thus one form of disinfectant. This identity between dispute settlement and rituals of sanitization provides a new dimension in this cultural context to the often quoted formulation of Llewellyn and Hoebel (1941) that law functions to 'clean up social messes'.

Disputes thus represent the anomaly of 'matter out of place'. Disapprobation is qualified so that admonitions take the form of 'argue at home' rather than 'don't argue'. A dispute has both ordered and disordered conditions, a distinction conveyed by the terms *bi* – an exchange of talk – and *lai* – 'when the saying stops': argument begins when ordered reciprocity ceases. The control of impurity proceeds by defining the norms governing acceptable and appropriate behaviour on *hama*:

> There is a *mana* for man and wife that shouldn't be said on the public place.
>
> (Field data)

> This is going bad. You brought the talk from home (*anda*) out onto the cleared place (*hamani*).
>
> (D.2 : 155–57)

The *actes juridiques* of the Huli forensic system involve the application of such grids as *anda*/*hama* to define verbal and non-verbal infelicities.

In so far as these social spheres describe fields of dominance it is important that we understand the sense in which the 'origins of

production are obscured' (Modjeska 1977 : 271) by male appropriation of exchange and prestation. The products of female labour are
exploited by males for political purposes. The values that accrue from
these actions attach only to males; the possibility of female participation is not existentially defined. Open inquests into men's status,
renown, and network ties are legitimized by ideological tenets concerning *mana*. We may surmise that the monopolization of exchange
on *hama* – whether in the context of pigs, paint, or parlance – is
perhaps a mode of assertion and achievement of power in the face of a
culturally stated female primacy. The control of, as well as through,
language gives rise to stereotype female accusations of male bias and
obfuscation. Incriminatory and defensive speech patterns reveal the
motif of 'concealment'. *Figure 4* depicts the significant dimensions of
meaning that inform 'evaluation' processes. *Anda* signifies the zone
of private actions. Negotiators involved in determining the number of
bride-price pigs to be transferred are 'secret men' (*ndi ali*), just as the
performance of personal intercourse rites keep integral a 'secret body'
(*ndi tingi*). The application of decoration is similarly restricted to
'private' places so that, in both cases, commuting from *anda* to *hama*
is a conversion of negotiation/application/non-display to dis-
play/presentation and transaction. The zones are tightly defined and
any breach of the ground rules of transition may engender abuse and
shame. To engage in debate the covert must be made 'open'. The
patterned expectations of duplicity show that all *anda* behaviour cannot be publicly witnessed.

Figure 4   Environmental categories relevant to pigs, paint, and parlance

The semantic dimensions that structure procedures of sanitization
are discussed separately in Chapter 5. These define what is to be put
in quarantine and what may be permitted to 'come outside'. While I
am primarily concerned with the verbal interaction of disputes,

reference can also be made to my analysis of Haroli decoration for a further context application of the above model. The polarities discussed here show how deviance and conformity in disparate modes of action are assessed in accordance with a unitary set of behavioural parameters and evaluative axes. The linguistic conventions and routines of dispute management reflect the need to safeguard against category confusion. Importantly then, notions of validity and rationality that operate in the different zones can be shown to exhibit 'field dependence'. Verbal strategies of accreditation are managed in accordance with a corpus of norms that is fixed in the transcendent structure of debate. Given that the actions of crediting / discrediting or censure / praise are central to the conduct of argument, we can categorize the grounds of evaluation according to the *sufficiency* (degree of acceptability) of a stretch of discourse. Attribution of credit may thus appeal to:

(a) *truth-sufficient norms*, whereby statements are assessed against context-dependent concepts of evidence regulating what is admissible as truth;

(b) *type-sufficient norms*, whereby the speech format is adjudged to conform, or deviate from, situationally appropriate invocations of genre or topic; or

(c) *role-sufficient norms*, against which dialogue is measured as realizing or promoting the organizational purposes and tasks of that setting.

This schema seems cross-culturally applicable.[8] The conventions may be differently defined according to the vagaries of occasion and claim topic. The Huli data indicate that these norms are most likely to be formally announced at the outset of any dispute. As the result of a degree of scheduling and formality, orators (with reference to all three sufficiency dimensions) set the terms of debate to which speakers should direct their contributions. Beginnings tell an audience what to expect as well as what is required.

The sufficiency framework is thus articulated in accordance with the *anda* / *hama* polarity. The schema provides a dimension for comparison between evaluative processes in Huli moots and those that obtain in Western courts. We can briefly examine a few parallels.

Truth-sufficiency

Atkinson and Drew (1979) have convincingly demonstrated the 'exclusionary' character of evidential forms in courts. These seek to prohibit what are, in everyday conversation, considered adequate grounds for blame allocation or deciding matters of fact. The conventions of veracity here preclude hearsay, opinion, gossip, etc. Control of information offends against the 'proprieties associated with normal interaction' (Atkinson and Drew 1979 : 34) by restricting the freedom of participants to give accounts in their own words. The disjunction between the canons of objectivity pertaining to *hama/anda* in cases of sexual delict is the difference between being 'caught with the hand' and simply 'being seen together'.

Type-sufficiency

During the phase of court examination, turns should be minimally designed as either questions or answers. This format is attended to as a constraint so that any deviation from 'type' may engender complaint and censure. An examiner can refuse to accept a reply as constituting an 'answer' (see Atkinson and Drew 1979), or move to have additional information struck from the record of proceedings. Similarly, a witness may interpret certain questions as tantamount to a blame allocation and organize his reply accordingly. Clearly, participants orient to the type-sufficient norms appropriate in a specific setting. While the organizational structure of verbal interaction in most Huli disputes does not exhibit the A-B-A-B patterning of Western courts, attempts to use or imitate a speech form that is inappropriate or inexpedient in a particular context may be subject to discredit. The rhetorical strategies associated with infelicitous speech are examined more fully in Chapter 5.

Role-sufficiency

The evidence of witnesses in court should ideally present facts without explicitly fostering an interpretation of blame or liability. Judges may admonish witnesses, directly or in their summing-up, by stressing that a witness assumed the role of an advocate. The judge thereby conveys attention to certain organizational tasks associated with specific participant roles. In the New Guinea Highlands, reference is most typically made to role-sufficiency through enunciation of ideal rules about talk being 'open'. Emphasis is given to the counternormative aspects of concealment as inimical to resolution processes. The discontinuities between the two systems should not, of course, be minimized; nevertheless, the schema allows us to plot these in a manner that focuses attention on subsistent levels of similarity.

In this latter regard, a degree of similarity obtains between the opposition of *anda/hama* and the frequently drawn socio-legal contrast of mundane/legal. Both distinctions are part of the cognitive equipment of participants, in that behaviour in 'public' forums is constituted as a response to the insufficiencies of domestic/mundane language. The talk of courts – and perhaps even the question-answer format – has evolved as a continuing response to the inadequacies, flaws, and '"troublesome" properties of ordinary talk' (Atkinson and Drew 1979 : 8). The sanitization processes are intended to create objectivity, the separation of opinion from fact, the eradication of doubt, and the provision of impartiality. These ends are partly dependent on the capacity of the law to delimit areas of ambiguity in mundane talk. The structural edifice of objectives and values pertinent to Huli *hama* are, I would contend, defined quite differently, and are interwoven with an ideology concerning male and female. Vocabulary changes that are a prerequisite for creditable performance cannot here be accounted for in terms of the 'open-textured' character of ordinary language. Behavioural conventions and constraints have a rationale that is articulated in accordance with ethno-ethological models relating to display and aesthetic actions. Furthermore, because mediators wish to avoid direct imputations of blame, there is a diminished degree of specificity in respect of factual information about some event and gauging consistency in any account. This correlates with a reduced prevalence of question-answer frames as *the* organizational device for structuring talk.

As we have seen, an uncompromising dogma of pollution underpins a language code that supports the exercise of political power by men. The situational ethics of *hama* stipulate that blame deflection is a preferred response to any accusation. Individuals should attempt to remove public registration of a private state of impurity. Blame sticks (*para*) to one as a taint (*ngu*), an index of contamination. In the sequential environment of blamings, actions that disavow a fault imputation have positional priority over actions that acknowledge fault. This predisposition towards blame deflection is evident from the case material presented in this book. It can also be inferred from the properties of turns in which acknowledgement of fault is declared; that is, self-blame has a 'dispreferred' status. There are no terms expressing the concepts of admission, confession, or apology. Acknowledgements of blame are accordingly declared in turns that are privately (*anda*) constituted acts of pig exchange. Expectations of mendacity and deceit are a cultural manifestation of the survival value of falsehood in Huli disputes. This compartmentalization of appropriate behaviour on *anda/hama* extends to the type of claims that may be aired in public. Domestic quarrels are frequently classified as *anda* – dirty linen should not (in Huli) be washed in public.

The insufficiencies of *anda* further reflect the cultural motif of exchange; speech reciprocity is a fundamental axiom of the resolution system. The public debate of claims provides for institutionalized mediation through the auspices of the participant status *dombeni* ('the middle men'). Where speakers self-select to pass comment or suggest a plan they do so by giving themselves membership as *dombeni*. The failings of a two-party system of settlement are that it leads more frequently to intractable positions and non-verbal conflict:

TEXT 4
1   You know which pig is eating the chickens
    your pig ate them
    your pig ate them
    when you say like that then you two are going to fight
5   from there you two will cover the truth and lie
    it wasn't my pig
    it wasn't my pig
    let us leave those talks we are saying.

(Field data: Dalu)

Hama is an epideictic domain, a context of assertion that is constrained by conventions relating to exchange and excess. The acts of assertion are deliminated to the 'I-say-so' component of statements and do not realize themselves as binding decisions or authoritative promulgations. The paradox of talk on *hama* is located in levels of attenuated commitment such that there is avoidance of disagreement, direct attributions of blame, naming names, and evaluations of truth/falsehood. Speakers display an acute sensitivity, when assuming the role of mediator, to the ascription of liability. How speech in disputes reflects these sensitivities forms the subject of many of the chapters in this book. Most typically, speakers will simply present the alternatives, reiterate maxims, and indicate topics for discussion. That which is said is asserted; the content reveals an attenuated level of directness:

TEXT 5
Puma is not here, only Tandale is here
the *mana* is that we should share the talk

we should share the talk
that we are not going to say [i.e. because Puma is absent]
5   Puma has been looking after these two people
→ they are saying the truth?
→ they are saying lies?
→ Puma he will say [i.e. when he gets here]
when that has been said
10   then we are going to share the talk
Puma will say it is a bad thing you have been doing
you have pushed this man out like a pig that bites another
my brother has been doing a good work, he will say
no
15   you have been doing a bad work, he will say
when that has been said
then the ones who used to share the talk will share the talk.

(Field data: Dalu)

The topics I have been considering provide a general background to themes that emerge elsewhere in this book. Of crucial importance is the determinate linguistic expression of the male-female distinction. The semantic structures I have isolated correlate with specific phonological and prosodic devices. We might further list other pairings (see Appendix 1) related to the sexual disjunction:

Aba (F)	*Aba* (*buni*) (MB)
Ababuni (MB)	*Arabuni* (FZ)
Mama (male cognate of	*Baba* (female cognate of
+1/+2 gen.)	+1/+2 gen.)
Aba (F)	*Ama* (M)
Hambiya (B)[9]	*Hagiya* (Z)

Theories concerning the psycho-linguistic origins of this format are frequently defined in terms of patterns of child speech, an hypothesis that may also account for the prevalence of reduplication (see *Table 5*). Whatever the merit of such explanations, they must be separated from the fact that Huli acknowledge, in their metalinguistic terminology, such phenomena to display aesthetic form. Data presented elsewhere in this book demonstrate the 'systematic' nature of minimally-distinct pairings within a framework of language and meaning. These devices are used to convey semantic relatedness. The prevalence of these patterns across the kin terminology reflects the strength of the axiomatic contrast of male-female in opposition to other classificatory criteria. The cognitive unity of the contrasting terms is conveyed by a sharing of sound sequences; the differentiation of meaning is marked by a minimal deviance in the phonological shape. The affective weighting of patrilateral-matrilateral ties seems similarly indexed by structural parallels between phonology, syntax, and semantic import. The essential opposition of attitudinal stances can be profitably stated again:

'desire/liking' (*hame*)
hame ('father') – *hamene* ('brother') – *hameigini* ('father-son/clan')
and 'sympathy/sorrow' (*dara*)
darama ('blood') – *daramabi* ('red')

These observations tend to support the contention that semantic fields and explanatory models are often ordered in accordance with aesthetic principles. The degree of credibility that can be attached to the inferences of semantic relatedness reflect, in no small part, the prevalent and systematic nature of these patterns in the production of meaning within Huli culture.

Notes

1 It will be readily apparent to students of New Guinea Highlands social structures that data presented in this chapter and elsewhere portray a radically different system from that described by Glasse (1959a, 1959b, 1965, 1968). The disagreements extend beyond a refutation that the Huli have cognatic descent to matters of empirical fact (e.g. Goldman 1980 : 217) and theoretical interpretation. I do not consider these discontinuities to in any way reflect the temporal or geographical circumstances of our respective studies but locate them at the levels of ideology, language structure and use. For analytical and expository purposes, to retain a unity of focus, I have refrained from continually indicating specific points of conflict unless by so doing it clarified a particular argument.

2 This is one example of the kind of misunderstandings of language use referred to in Note 1; *Ainya damene* ('maternal kin') cannot denote, as Glasse (1968 : 26) contends, sister's sons. In accordance with this observation there is no ranking structure of non-agnatic cognates.

3 Much confusion can arise when discussing Huli bride-wealth where the extensions of *wariabu* are not consistently separated. The reader is advised to pay careful attention to occurrences of *wariabu*$_1$ and *wariabu*$_2$.

4 Changes from /I/ to /ʊ/ occur quite regularly when compounding takes place, or simply as an aesthetic rendering. For example, Huli to Hulu as in Hulu *wane* ('Huli daughter'). The statement that Huli conceive brideprice to be a form of compensation payment is thus consistent with the nature and meaning of all *abi* payments.

5 The social function of this ritual transvestism was noted by an early patrol officer to Huli: 'Men who are skilfully dressed to have the appearance of

women enter the *Guru anda* . . . the effect on the young initiates appears to be a practical moral story to the effect: don't have anything to do with women or else' (Hoad 1957 : 8). To this perceptive interpretation I have added the importance of the fact that they appear as 'cross-cousins' in a rite associated with the meanings of *wariabu₂*.

6 The use of *aḇa* for MZDch/MZSch is quite consistent with their cross-sex genealogical derivation. Nevertheless, the terms for son and daughter (which apply to FBSch) constitute an optional usage according to the frequency and quality of contact with the above.

7 The kin terminology surrounding the plexus of *aba* relationships bears a striking morphological correspondence to that of the Mae (Meggitt 1964). The Mae suffix-*ngge* operates as an 'intensifier' (Meggitt: private communication) for MB/FZ in precisely the same fashion as the kin morph *-buni* in Huli (see Appendix 1, Note 1).

8 The logical properties of the schema express the invariant bases of all crediting procedures. Consider the statement 'a lighted cigar was dropped' as an account of why there is a hole in a carpet. Along the axis of *truth-sufficiency* one might place utterances relating to evidence – visible or otherwise – that a cigar was indeed dropped. A *type-sufficient* argument would attend to the practical requirements of the public to whom an explanation is given. Namely, that the format 'a cigar was dropped' is required/acceptable rather than 'there is a hole in the carpet because its fibres were converted into carbon and gas through a specific chemical reaction'. A *role-sufficient* statement would be sensitive to demands that an explanation should explain. In this context one might adduce a general law of the form 'whenever a lighted object is dropped on a floor a hole will appear'.

9 The alternative kin-terms given here and in Appendix 1 can be distinguished further in respect of contextual usage and degree of affect. For example, *hagiya/hambiya* are specific terms of endearment for siblings. As such, they are often used in disputes to convey sarcasm. *Aḇa/hame/taribuni* (F) respectively express increments of austerity and respect. *Taribuni* is mostly used to refer to a dead father in eulogies. This whole subject is complex and deserving of separate treatment. It should thus be understood that the presentational format of kin-terms in Appendix 1 does not imply an equivalence of affective import.

4
Talking about land

Bi   nahomaga
Talk never dies
Ibu wiago haga
It stays always
(It will always stay)
Igini hondo mulebira
Son to   it will be given
(It will be given to the son)
Ibu aba   ibu bamba honowirago
His father he first   born
(His father that was born first)
hondo honowialu   bi ibu honowirago   miaga
to   the one born talk he the one born gives
(gives his talk to the one he has given birth to)
Bi   nahomaga
Talk never dies
Wiabo haga   nga
Stay   continue that is placed
(What is placed there will continue to stay)

Sacred geography

The notion of *mana* symbolizes the cultural integrity of Huli, as well
as encapsulating a socio-historical explanation of knowledge. The
epistemic status of *mana*, as verbally realized, derives from concepts
of perpetuity attached to the 'talk' of ancestors. It is the distribution
of types of talk that provides a model for social order and the interrelationships of people, clans, and tribes. The Huli universe is
bounded by the Duna to the north, Enga in the north-east, and a

number of separate peoples (Bosavi, Kuali, Kora, Tinali, Agala) to
the west and south referred to collectively as Dugube. These denominations depend on geographical position. Tari Huli refer to Huli of
the Koroba sub-district as Duna, despite their acknowledged common linguistic and cultural identities, while Koroba Huli use the
same term for people who inhabit the region north of Tanggi (see
Map 1). Central to Huli cosmology is the belief that these four tribes
have common origins, linguistically marked by the appellations *Hela
Huli*, *Hela Obena* (Enga), *Hela Duna*, and *Hela Dugube*. In some
etiological narratives Hela is an original Huli progenitor, though
other informants understood the prefix simply to encode common
descent.

The stratum of belief and myths pertaining to Huli origins is
known as *dindi pongo* ('the knot of the land' (Goldman 1979)). The
spatial and chronological dimensions of this universe of discourse
articulate the times, events, and places that structure Huli ritual.
Dindi pongo incorporates a sacred geography (see Gossen 1974 : 9) in
which dispersed landmarks and sites have assumed ritual importance
through their association with the actions and abodes of ancestors.
These sites tend to be distinguished as major or minor shrines, according to their significance in the cosmological scheme. Furthermore, the
principal sacred places are believed to be linked by a subterranean
network of 'roots' (*pini*), and an encircling and intertwined 'snake
and cane' (*puya gewa la*) (see Goldman 1981a : 77). Periodically,
following some natural catastrophe or depletion of pigs or people
through sickness, a major earth ritual was performed that involved, in
strict order, a multitude of clans from the whole of Huli territory and
indeed Duna.[1] The complexity and sheer scope of the myths relating
to *dindi pongo* requires a treatise that is beyond my present concerns. In the following exposition I attend only to the broad
principles as they specifically relate to (a) the inter-clan land dispute
given in D.1; and (b) the importance of form for cultural retention
of knowledge.

In the indigenous sociology of knowledge Huli clans are informally
ranked according to which parts of this origin myth they 'hold' (*yi*),
and their traditional roles in the cycle of fertility rites. Clan headmen
are repositories of both their clan histories and *dindi pongo* myths.
While these two dovetail into each other, the latter was never utilized
for public debate about land rights. One corollary of this extraordinary
system of *bi* ('talk') is that certain Huli headmen have a region-wide

status associated specifically with their understanding of *tene te* ('origin stories') and their possession of rites and spells (*gamu*) central to the production of health and fertility. Although these ritual practices have ceased, the system of knowledge is being perpetuated and used to support political aspirations and land claims. An awareness of the economic development and potential of the Star Mountains has engendered a new movement among Huli for an autonomous 'Hela' province within the established Southern Highlands Province. The headmen who hold the *dindi pongo* are thus gaining a new reputation, divorced from the traditional context of ritual. Their exclusive control of these etiological myths, and indeed the exclusive rights to performance, have renewed the political currency of *dindi pongo*. This mythical tradition reflects in part the Huli predilection for explanations in terms of 'first causes' (*tene*) that appears also to correlate with the importance (and indeed length) of genealogical knowledge.

While the specific details and 'correct accounts' of *dindi pongo* are thus privileged information, the nature of the system is public knowledge, encapsulated in *pureremo* (see *Table 2*). Most Huli men can recite the formulaic presentation of clan names considered central to *dindi pongo*. In the following text the clan name is signified by the construct 'x's son (*igini*)', where x is a well known predecessor or pair of ancestors. For identification purposes the clan names have been inserted in brackets.

Alu Daiya *igini* (Dagabua)/Goya Piliya *igini* (Kobiya)/Wara Lambiligo *igini* (Ware)/Hiliwa Mugu Himugu *igini* (Dugube-Bebe: D.1 : 493)/Nogo Yabe *igini* (Bai)/Gai Magare *igini* (Yangali)/Yalidima Aluya *igini* (Kokoma)/Gambe Amaiya *igini* (Pela)/Uruba Tele *igini* (Huri)/Mali Mandala *igini* (Bari)/Abo Auwira *igini* (Wenani)/Gubara Goli *igini* (Toleni)/Bai Daro *igini* (Luguni).

The marked assonance and alliteration that occurs among the paired ancestral names – for example, Mugu Himugu/Mali Mandala/Gubara Goli – indicates a level of aesthetic determination in genealogical charters. Reference to D.1 : 483–97 shows a degree of replication in speech forms associated with ancestral reckoning. The prevalence of name-pairing based on rhyme appears to relate to the mnemonic value of such devices for retaining a vast corpus of oral traditions and spells.

The original progenitors of the Huli are collectively referred to as *dama*. These have male (*hangu nana*) and female (*hana wali*) counterparts which are believed to co-exist with same sex spirits (*dinini*). They act in concert to cause sickness and misfortune to humans. Minor *dama* include Edepole ('broken back': it has a fossilized manifestation), Dindi Ainya ('earth mother'), Wanelabo ('two daughters'), and Heyolabe. Certain *dama* had material representation in stones collectively termed Lidukui ('the bones (*kui*) of Lidu') – for example, Ni Tangi ('the sun's hat': mortars) and Ni Habane ('the sun's egg') – that were owned by clan sections and kept in sacred sites called Lidu Anda. At the apex of the pantheon of deities are Iba Tiri, Ni, and Kebali. The primal myth recounting the incestuous relation of Ni and his sister Hana has been recorded by Glasse (1965 : 34) and referred to already in Chapter 3. Accounts of the progeny from this union commonly include the following initial names and divisions:

Figure 5   Section of a Dama genealogy

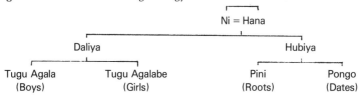

The schema clearly shows that aesthetic engineering is an important determinant of the construction of Huli reality. Again, these devices of rhyme[2] are significantly located around male-female oppositions. For clans that trace descent from Ni, the genealogy provides an explanation of the use, by agnates only, of the prefixing denominations Hubi (e.g. Hubi Koma or Hubi Tobani: clans of Ialuba) and Dali (as in Dali Gopia, Dali Lai, Dali Mandi, or Dali Piliba: clans of the Tari sub-district). In so far as the *mana* regulating relationships and interaction are thought to have been given to man by these ancestors – as for example the sexual intercourse rites detailed in Chapter 3 – they have also determined man's metaphorical 'roots' and the 'dates' pertinent to life-stage rituals.

The myth of Ni and Hana represents only a small part of *dindi pongo* and is counterbalanced by beliefs concerning the *dama* Kebali. There is general consensus in the Koroba area that this deity originated in the west, and that its mythological origins are known only by 'Hiliwa Mugu Himugu *igini*' (Irugua of Ialuba: ref. D.1). *Dindi pongo* is thus a mosaic of mythical themes assimilated from a number of neighbouring cultures. These themes have been interwoven and fused by the Huli predisposition for the delineation of ultimate 'sources' (*tene*). Different themes and emphases emerge according to the locations of informant and anthropologist. To the north of Koroba station the dominant myth of *dindi pongo* recounts the journey of a Duna pig (Nogo Para Tambugua) and lady (Memeleme) which bore the Huli clans Korawi, Koraiya, and Muguaiya. These themes recur in minor rituals of fertility and child-growth that attempt to re-create the state of primal fecundity. Other Huli clans are commonly acknowledged to be associated with the myth of Baya Baya (Glasse 1965 : 46), a small boy who was inadvertently murdered. While there was some variance in names and events in the cross-referenced myths I collected, invariably the narrator would employ certain routine formulations as evidence of both his control of *mana* and his credibility. The myth of Baya Baya is normally prefaced, or has a coda, which states the 'sons' (*igini*) responsible for murdering the boy: Abua Auwira *igini*/Koroba Koli *igini*/Bai Daro *igini*/Bai Hangali *igini*. The mother of this child is said to have caused the extinction of Hugu Humburu clan through the following curse:

Home pobe / *ba pobe* / *hengi   pobe* / *garengi pobe* / *yageyage*
Die   go   / kill go   / indecision go   / hunger go   / mate
biabe / *naga naga biabe*.
do   / consume   do.

When I presented informants with alternative accounts of myths they had given me, they rationalized the variations by stating simply 'that is his *mana*'. Provided a narrative contained certain of these core *pureremo* people were reluctant to explain apparent contradictions in terms of possible falsehood. The resolution of differences is achieved by reference to the infinite variability of personal *mana*. Truth is relative, provided that its verbal expression conforms to a recognizable pattern for communication.

There is a timeless aspect to the period when earth was inhabited by *dama*. Genealogical charters always make a sharp break between deities and man. The formal counting of generations concerns only the latter. The following short extract is part of Irugua's *dindi pongo* myth which directly relates to D.1. Considerable editing is involved in the division of a myth for 'public' and 'private' consumption. Significantly, the following is considered 'sacred' knowledge and omitted from Irugua's speech in D.1:

1   The first person on the land was a woman called Mbidumbi
    The land was wet and muddy so she collected it all in her string-bag and
    hung it up to dry.
    She made drains in the land, and she made mountains.
5   She bore *dama* Kebali and Hiẁa. For Kebali and his wife we say Ome and
    Kome.
    Kebali bore all the animals and he bore the snake (*puya*) and the cane
    (*gewa*) that run below the ground. Kebali followed on top down to Tari.
    Kebali's daughter was Dangeme who went and married a man in Pureni.

An elucidation of the main points of this tract are necessary for an adequate understanding of the topic format of inter-clan land disputes.

Line 1: The name Mbidumbi is closely associated with Mt Mbiduba (see *Map 1*) and represents, in Huli cosmology, a terminal pole to Mt Ambua in Tari. They respectively indicate the places where the sun sets and rises and are thus ritually linked to the *dama* Kebali and Ni (*ambua* is also the term for 'yellow', the colour of the sun (*ni*)). The opposition between these two deities serves as a metaphor for the conflict between descended clans in D.1.

Line 2: states the theme of primal chaos out of which order was manufactured.

Line 4: announces the association between *dama* and drains. Identifying these historical links is a critical part of case presentations relating to land claims.

Lines 5–6: reveal the sacred 'second names' (*mini mende*) for Kebali. In Huli, synonym systems are generally indicative of the contextual importance of 'concealment'. A distinction is made then between deistic names that can be used in ordinary conversation, and a sacred vocabulary invoked for selected ritual purposes.

Lines 7–8: formulate the central belief of a snake, entwined by cane, that links the sacred sites of Huli. Traditional prophecies of impending doom, a latent aspect of *dindi pongo* philosophy, stipulate that when the two ends of the circumferential snake and cane break apart, the death of mankind is imminent. The sense in which these two components 'bind' the world together is perhaps reflected in personal decoration. Cane belts encircle the waists of

Huli males while snake-skins are utilized to keep wigs on the head. Both items thus bind the body in an analogous fashion to the cosmological principle outlined above.

Lines 8–9: make reference to the journeys of Kebali. These 'tracks' are regarded as sacred places at which certain child-birth rituals are performed (e.g. *Habua pu:* see Chapter 3), and along which the Dugube and Duna used to travel for Dindi *gamu* ('earth spells'). The names of these paths are encoded in the following *pureremo* that displays a quite typical collocation of rhyming lexemes:

> *Puya Gewa la* ('snake and cane')/*Bai goba Balimu la* ('rotten wood of the *Bai (Castanopsis acuminatissima fam. Fagaceae)* tree and the *Balimu* plant')/*Biango Borere la* ('dog and marsupial-cat (*Dasyurus albopunctatus*)')/*Auwa Gauwa la* (tracks in Ialuba: see Map 2)/*Hagalabo Tegelabo la* (tracks in Wabia)/*Agapia Kirabo la* (tracks at Lake Kopiago, Duna).

On one level these appellations are regarded as variant names for Kebali, while on another level they manifest an imposition of cosmological unity.

Line 9: indicates that the continuation of the Kebali myth is held by people from Pureni (see *Map 1*). The sense in which *dindi pongo* presents itself as a homogeneous, yet fragmented, corpus of myths is thus partly realised in the inconclusiveness of any segment. Each myth is conceived to be sequentially related to others, which is precisely the pattern of topic presentation found in D.1.

Pureni is the site of perhaps the most remarkable of all shrines – Kelote, an historical vatican of the Huli. The site is owned by Dagabua clan whose elevated status derives from their previous role in ritual re-creations of the genesis myths. The accounts I recorded (see Goldman 1979) begin with the daughter of Kebali – Dangeme or Dangi Tene – relating how she ate only the wild species of food: *tumbu* (taro), *pili* (sugar-cane), *garua* (banana), and *hima* (sweet-potato). This period is known as *Ma Naga* ('taro time') or *Ira Goba Naga* ('the time of rotten wood') and is acknowledged to predate the introduction of sweet-potato proper. As will become evident, claims to historical precedence on land are based on defining who introduced the first sweet-potato vines to whom. The chronological division of 'wild' versus 'domestic' subsistence is symbolically restated in fertility rituals as well as organizing genealogical reckoning in disputes.

The centripetal tendency of the cosmos underlies beliefs surrounding Kelote. This focal site is frequently referred to as *dindi hanuni* ('the middle land'), *dindi pini* ('the root of the land'), *waya humbi* ('the shield') or *ira kelo* ('tree support': a support of the universe). Kelote is thought of as a metaphorical tree – medial between earth and sky – from which four roots radiate out to Duna, Dugube, Huli, and Enga. The major rivers of these four cultures – Tagari (Huli), Baro Wainya (Enga), Iba Ainya (Dugube), and Honowaga (Duna) – have their confluence in a tree known as Ira Hale. These waters are cleaned by the *dama* Iba Tiri and bound with cane. They are believed to rise up to a mythical place in the sky called Daluyeli from where the waters fall as rain: Daluyeli *pu tara* – 'the people in Daluyeli are urinating'. Most displays of oratory make some explicit or oblique reference to Kelote to demonstrate an understanding of *dindi pongo* philosophy (for example Appendix 2; 2 : 1).

The mythical system of *dindi pongo* imposes a geographical and conceptual unity on the Huli universe. Relationships between people and units are integrated within a framework ordered by the distribution of 'talk'. This system of ideas is perpetuated through the educational medium of *pureremo*, a conventional encoding of knowledge. The occurrence of this genre in any domain of talk indicates that which is for public assimilation and communication. Information is both created and determined in accordance with specific aesthetic norms. The following *dindi pongo pureremo* reveal then the interplay between the dictates of stylistic construction, and thematic perspectives relating to an encompassing sacred geography.

TEXT A

Mogorowada	*puni*	*mogo biamiya*
In Mogora (Fugua) swamp		let us meet
Daliwane	*puni*	*dai lamiya*
In Daliwane (Koroba) swamp		let us run
Iba Haiya	*puni*	*haiya lamiya*
In Haiya (Tari) swamp		let us scatter
Halunamu lani		*namu lamiya*
In Halunamu		let us sink it into the ground
Abe Bebetene		*bebe biamiya*
In Bebenete (Tari)		let us 'straighten' the land.

The format of the text is based on a cluster of sequenced phonological similarities between toponyms (the initial phrases) and the adjunct clauses which all refer to particular ritual actions associated with the cycle of earth rites. The formation of actions and ideas seems regulated here, as in many other Huli contexts, by aesthetic considerations. There is a similar pattern of phonic relationships in the next widely known extract which outlines how simultaneous fires were lit at the poles of the world for *dindi gamu*. The smoke from these fires is said to appear at various central sites thus realising the essential unity of the cosmos. Again one may note the property of rhyme between toponym and the species of tree that was burnt in that place.

TEXT B
Mbidubani   Gabi tugu de lolebira   o Bebali Puni
At Mt. Mbiduba the Gabi plant will be burnt o Bebali Puni (Dugube)
tagira pole
it will come out
Bebali Puni   Balimu de lolebira   o Kelote tagira pole
At Bebali Puni the Balimu plant will be burnt o Kelote it will come out
Kelote   Ira Kelo   de lolebira   o Bebenete   tagira pole
At Kelote the Kelo tree will be burnt o Bebenete (Tari) it will come out
Bebenete   Bai   de lolebira   o Mbidubani
At Bebenete the Bai (fam. *Fagaceae*) tree will be burnt o Mbidubani
tagira pole
it will come out.

The political importance of *dindi pongo*, and the status accorded to certain clans as a result of this system of 'shared' power, can be appreciated from a reading of D.1. What seems important is that we grasp the sense in which the roles of headmen are firmly linked to the inheritance of 'talk'. They function both as a repository of clan knowledge, and as a representative in fertility rituals associated with making the 'land' right (*gini*), straight (*bebe*), or clear (*hagama/haiya*). This is explained by the fact that clan *mana* inevitably form part of the supra-structural level of knowledge outlined above. The significance of this interplay, and the exclusive performative rights held by headmen in respect of their clan histories, can be gauged from D.1.

Ialuba

Ialuba valley (see *Map 1*) is situated in the Koroba sub-district of the Southern Highlands Province, twenty-five miles by road from either Koroba or Tari government stations. The valley floor measures approximately fourteen square kilometres and is divided by the river

Kemo (see *Map 2*). About 760 Huli inhabit Ialuba, which is territorially divided into six named clan units – Hiwa, Koma, Tobani, Dugube, Wida, and Pina. Mission influence in the valley dates from 1963 with Wesleyan and Catholic churches (*haus lotu* (pidgin)) having been established on the east and west sides of the Kemo respectively. Ialuba represents a border community, both geographically – lying on the western edge of Huli – and socio-economically, having no aid-post, school, or sustained commercial development. Four of the above-mentioned clans relate to each other as *tene* and *yamuwini*, both Koma and Tobani tracing descent to a female agnate of Hiwa and Dugube respectively. These genealogical ties are reflected in clan names; Koma is often referred to as Hiwa-Koma, and individual members as Hubi-x (agnates only) thus signifying patrilineal descent from Ni (see *Figure 5* and *Diagram 2*). The names of Hiwa or Koma ancestors are prefixed by the appellation Tugu – as in Tugu Yogoye or Tugu Doge (see *Diagram 2*) – which again emphasizes the relationship between these clans. The segmentary structure of these descent units is depicted in *Diagrams 1, 2,* and *3*, for which the following points should be noted. First, kinship ties between *dama* are putative; the same informants are rarely consistent in their accounts at this level. Degrees of accuracy and consistency are socially required only where reckoning begins in dispute contexts. Second, recitations of genealogical ancestry always preserve the division between *dama* and men, the conceptual imposition of ordered relations is relevant only to the latter. Third, the noticeable occurrence of the same progenitors in the Dugube and Hiwa schemes – for example, Tugume, Yogoye, Mone, Tirane and Dongoma Puali (*Diagrams 1* and *2*) – indicates the extent to which such charters are subject, over time, to alteration in accordance with political ends. This explanation is indigenously stated in D.1 which represents a conflict for ownership of 'names' as much as for land.

Despite their superordinate status as *tene*, Hiwa (population 5) and Dugube (population 37) are numerically weaker than their subordinate linked clans Koma (population 467) and Tobani (population 178).[3] Their title to Ialuba land is, in one sense, only nominal, an ideological argument mode giving speech-precedence in disputes. From the compositional figures presented in *Table 4* we may note the marked imbalance between the membership categories *tene : wali haga* of Koma (50 per cent: 9.8 per cent) and Tobani (25.6 per cent: 37.2 per cent). This may well reflect the latter's previous awareness of

Table 4   *Classification of adult Koma males*

	Mata	Ibu	Aguene	
Tene (Agnates)	8	0	48	56 (50%)
Yamuwini (Non-agnatic cognates)[4]	11	5	16	32 (28.6%)
Tene hamene (Quasi-agnates)	7	1	5	13 (11.6%)
Wali haga (Unrelated)	3	3	5	11 (9.8%)
Total	29	9	74	112 (100%)

Classification of adult Tobani males

	Habonema	Doyayu	Kiame	
Tene	3	6	2	11 (25.6%)
Yamuwini	9	4	1	14 (32.5%)
Tene hamene	0	2	0	2 (4.7%)
Wali haga	9	5	2	16 (37.2%)
Total	21	17	5	43 (100%)

unequal fighting strength between the clans. Koma interpret these and other population differentials as indicative of later settlement in Ialuba by Tobani. Tobani explain the same facts as evidence of constant attrition by Koma of land and people. Seventy-three per cent of *yamuwini* males tabulated above were born on their respective parish territories, which tends to confirm a trend for parental residence moves to be made before childbirth. A high level of uxorilocality – 53 per cent of all *yamuwini* are on their mother's land – is indexed by the fact that in over 60 per cent of these cases ego's father was influential in determining the birthplace (see Goldman 1981a : 453). The range of ties to the host parish were limited to M, FM, and MM which is in accordance with the normative expectations and obligations attendant on the *aba* complex (described in Chapter 3). Significantly, 41 per cent of all residence moves relating to any *yamuwini* of Koma or Tobani occurred as a direct result of some conflict. This situation parallels the patterns elicited for Melpa (see A. Strathern 1972 : 113) settlement changes. Warfare inside clan parishes was also a significant factor in residence moves, and both Miau and Mbalo segments (see *Diagram 3*) fled after intra-parish wars.

Diagram 1   Dugube and Tobani ancestral genealogy

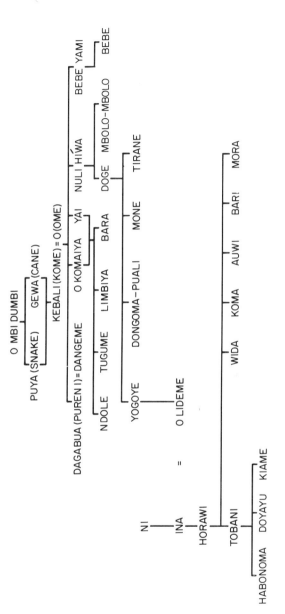

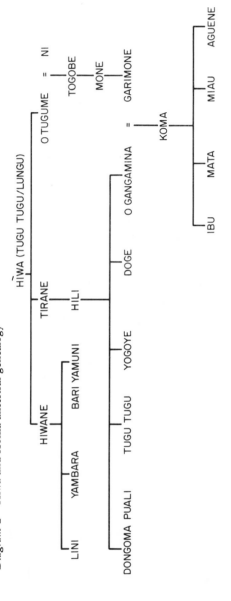

Diagram 2   Hiẁa and Koma ancestral genealogy

Diagram 3   Koma genealogy

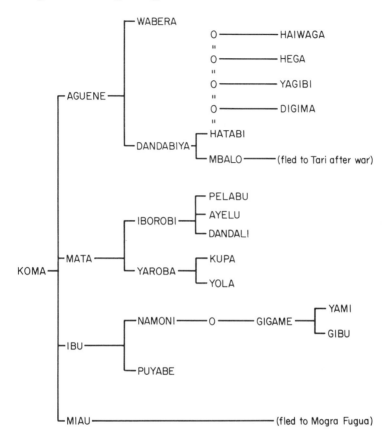

Unlike many other Highlands systems, inter-clan relationships in Huli do not exhibit complex enemy-ally ties, paired fighting units, or interconnected structures of war and feasting. Nevertheless, enduring lines of hostility can often be detected. An idea of enmity relationships among Ialuba clans, most particularly between Koma and Tobani, is provided by archive material concerning events that occurred at the time of initial contact. The first government patrol into the area was led by Assistant District Officer B. Murdoch from Tari in 1953, followed two years later by the patrol of Trollope and Sinclair: 'We were met by a large crowd of friendly natives of the Koma group . . . the people were friendly but heavily armed and few women seen' (Sinclair 1955). On a subsequent patrol to Ialuba in 1957 Sinclair's party was attacked and forced to shoot two men – Aluari (Muguni clan) and Agira (Garua clan). This incident in Wabu (see *Map 2*) has since gained notoriety through the published reports of Sinclair himself (1966 : 174–86; 1973 : 60–61). Informant accounts accord well with Sinclair's (1957b) perceptions of the events. The attackers were indeed largely from the Koma sub-clan Aguene to which the then headman (Gurubugu, father of Gangaro) belonged. Koma had resented and feared the presence of local Huli patrol guides for two reasons: (1) they anticipated a forceful seizure of pigs due to rumours of previous actions by the patrol south of Koroba; (2) they believed that Piru (a Huli patrol aide) would use Sinclair to force Koma men (in particular a man called Hebale) to pay compensation to his Yetamali friends in connection with a previous dispute involving people from Mogra Fugua (see *Map 1*). The accounts I collected relate that Koma, as *wai tene* ('source of the war'), paid out 195 pigs each for the two dead men shot by the patrol (see Appendix 2 : 2). In 1957 Sinclair again visited the area to re-establish contact with Koma and his remarks have direct relevance to the situation as I found it in March 1977:

'Diary entry: Friday 6th December 1957
In the early afternoon some 45 young Tobani men, all fully armed, arrived in camp. They said they had been out trying to pursuade the Koma to come into camp. My own idea is that they were seizing the psychological moment to declare an ''open season'' on the Koma.'

(Patrol Report No. 4; 1957–58)

These observations give historical depth to the current hostilities between Koma and Tobani. In December 1976 (three months before my arrival) war again erupted over ownership of those land boundaries marked out in *Map 2*. The area is important on account of size (twenty-five square acres, approximately), rich groves of pandanus and banana at Tanili, its potential for swamp-gardens and pig-foraging, and traditional ritual sites. The dispute is some thirteen years old, and during this time both clans had informally agreed not to use the territory west of Kemo and north of Garai river. When Gangaro (headman of Koma) attempted to assert his clan's rights by erecting a house at Tanili, Tobani responded with violence. The Koroba police were alerted and arrested several of the warring participants. The resultant public presentation of claims is indigenously recognized to have been the most important dispute, at this level, to

Map 2 Ialuba

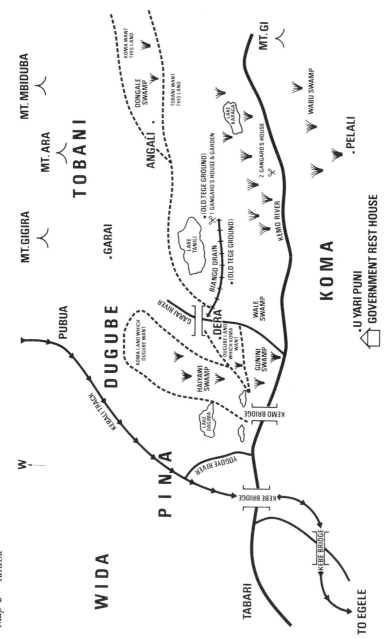

have occurred during my fieldwork period. In this one case I was fortuitously presented with the formal performances of all four clan origin myths detailing kinship interrelationships and modes of land residence and distribution. More than any abstracted or curtailed description could,[5] the text permits a detailed insight into the way inter-clan land disputes are debated in Huli. Of central importance is the speech genre *Malu* (see *Table 2*) which only headmen have the right to use in public.

Dispute 1

Issue: Land.
Disputants: Irugua – headman of Dugube
                Landa – headman of Tobani
                Pogoye – headman of Hiwa
                Gangaro – headman of Koma.
Land Mediators: Officials Muguye and Luni.
Others: Hiwa Tege – headman of Pina
            Kumuria – agnate of Dugube.
Date: 25 April 1977.
Location: Ialuba, cleared ground (*hama*) outside government rest-house.
Outcome: The initial hearing of the conflict in 1975 (D.1 : 263) ruled that
     Tobani should pay Koma 150 pigs for the land. This was never
     implemented as Koma refused to accept the pigs which were considered
     too small in size. At the conclusion of the present hearing Tobani stated
     their intention of carrying the matter to Koroba in the hope of reversing
     the decision. The land remained in a mutually acknowledged state of
     'taboo' until my departure in July 1978. There was no compulsion on
     either party to accept the mediators' judgment.
(Note: The opening address to the participants by Muguye is cited and
     treated separately in Chapter 5.)

1   GANGARO: The boundary of Pina, Koma and Dugu Yawini (Dugube) is Mt
      Abago.
      The people on this side of Mt Wiaga say they are Nuli Hiwa (Hiwa).
      Mirila (Duna), his mountain is up there;
      Hela Obena (Enga), his mountain is over there;
      Hulu Gomaiya (Huli), we are sleeping in the middle land.
      This is Tugu Tugu and Nuli Hiwa's land we are talking about.
      Dugube is saying it is his fathers' land, all the land on the other side of
      Kemo river he is saying it is his. We are going to talk on this. If people
      come from over the mountains and see we are talking about land that has
      only grass and ferns they might become angry with us.
      No. Hiwa divided this land and told us 'Stay on this swamp'. Where he
      named the lands I have been staying.
      I am going to pull out the *mana* that has been given to us, I am saying.

Dugube is Kebali's son and we have talked before with them. He says the land belongs to Kebali – Kebali is like the ridge-pole of a house and what travels along that track is the source.

I am saying this valley is Nuli Hiwa's and the Hiwa man [i.e. Pogaye] will talk from here.

POGAYE: The man that was there first,

20 O (it was) Tugu Tugu

The boundary between Dugu Yawini and Nuli Hiwa is

Mt Gigi Nawi

Mt Haliaga

Mt Uruaga

Mt Mbidubani

that is how it was done.

Dugu Yawini used to make *manda mbu* [decoration for *dindi pongo*] of this

I know nothing. I am Nuli Hiwa and this land is mine.

The marriage rites and spells (*ndi tingi gamu*)

The Haroli rites and spells (*dagia gamu*)

The war rites and spells (*danda gamu*)

The sexual intercourse rites and spells (*wali tabira gamu*)

The sorcery rites and spells (*hambu gamu*)

all of these have gone inside that man there [i.e. Gangaro]

it was done like that.

Hiwa Hili gave all of these talks

Also for Uru Kamia Hangalu (Tege rite) and Dawe Tege, these *mana* have gone inside there (*anda peadagoni*).

Hiwa, O there is only one Hiwa and I am here.

40 Some went to sleep on the other side to their mothers' land, to Mt Yubi.

Tugu Yambara is on Mt Yubi

Tugu Lini's sons are on Mt Gigi Nawi

Hiwa Hiwane is me and I am here

Bari Yumuni is over there

My clan is four [i.e. made up of four sub-clans]

that's how they have stayed.

Three sub-clans have gone to different places I am saying

the fourth, I am staying.

Kome is *yamuwini*, he is big [i.e. many] here

I am small [i.e. have few members]

The *mana* have gone to him alone

that is how it was done.

For the land,

O Tugu Tugu's land is there

that is how it is.

O the *mana* I am saying is like this:

First generation was Tugu Tugu	(*daba mbira* O Tugu Tugu)
Second generation was Tugu Hawa	(*daba mende* O Tugu Hawa)
Third generation was Tugu Hubi	(*daba tebone* O Tugu Hubi)
Fourth generation was Tugu Dabia	(*daba mane* O Tugu Dabia)

Fifth generation was Tugu Manda   (*daba dauni* O Tugu Manda)
Sixth generation was Tugu Pogea   (*daba waragane* O Tugu Pogea)
Seventh generation was Tugu Damura   (*daba kane* O Tugu Damura)
Eighth generation was Tugu Gawira   (*daba halini* O Tugu Gawira)
Ninth generation was Tugu Urugu   (*daba dini* O Tugu Urugu)
Tenth generation was Tugu, me   (O *i pini*)
Eleventh generation is my son   (*daba beane* O *i igini*)
For eleven generations
that is all (*o ogoni*)
My fathers were
Tugu Tirane
Tugu Hili
Tugu Hiwane
So Hili will talk from there.
GANGARO: The land of Hiwa has been said.
Tugu Doge is over there
Tugu Dongoma Puali is over there
Tugu Yogoye is over there
Tugu Mone is over there
80 Hiwa Hili is over there
it is like that.
I am here and I am born from Hiwa
From here I am going to talk.
The generations from the ancestors have been counted
The *mana* from Tugu Tugu
⎡ Do like this   (*ogo dagua biabe*)
⎢ Stay like this   (*ogo dagua habe*)
⎢ Say like this   (*ogo dagua labe*)
⎣ Eat like this   (*ogo dagua nabe*)
Those that have been said are in me.
That man [i.e. Pogaye] has counted from there
This Ni and Hiwa were exchanging women (*wali tobo bini*) on the banks of
the river Emema (in Levani valley). That is my land there where the nut
trees are.
Hubi Miau used to eat there
Hubi Ibu used to eat there
Hubi Mata used to eat there
Hubi Aguene is me, I never used to go there.
I am Huli Gomaiya and I stayed on this side [i.e. never go to Duna side].
100 Mt Ara is there and that belongs to Hiwa Koma.
O this Hiwa women, O from when they had exchanged women, O she was
led here, O and Hiwa went to Pabu (Wabia) and bore children.
The head of my land is at Guru Kabugua (Mogra Fugua) and some land
there belongs to Mogorali (Ialuba clans) and Yugu Bari. When we came to
this side we were called Hiwa Koma.
It was like that.
From the women that Hiwa and Abuarago (Ni) exchanged were born
O Hubi Taboba

Second was O Hubi Mone
Third was O Hubi Garimone
These three I am throwing down are not men
They are *dama*.
This Hubi Garimone he got one women from Amida Wanda, from the
other side of the Hanimu river (in Wabia). From Wambi Tabaya came this
women Gangamina and she was met by one man who was going to take
her to a man called Birini. 'My mother is down there so I will go and fetch
this woman', it was said, and he went and got this lady from Hiwa. He
came with her and they slept at Tobai which is behind this mountain [i.e.
west of Ialuba].
It was too big a mountain to climb.
120   'Shall we go through this mountain?' (the man said)
'Where are you from?' (Gangamina answered)
'I am from here. Along this road my father and myself used to stay.
This is where we used to hunt possum,
collect nuts
gather Keromi fruit.
This is a short-cut so we will go this way where there is no bush',
it was said like that.
O they came up over there to Honogo cave where they ate nuts and fruit.
When they had climbed up there
O then they came to Pongone cave and to Wali cave.
O there they stayed for seven days.
O this is how Garimone and Gangamina came.
Then they came to Wai Hega (Tabari) and slept there. They ate the nuts
from Tabari, the Ugu Tigibi leaves and Keromi fruit.
O from there they came to Ago cave and they slept there.
They went to Yogoye cave and slept there.
They went across what is now Tobani but before was bush, and they stayed
at Yogoye cave, Garai, Gelo, and Gangamina Garimone cave. They hung
the nuts in the ceiling to dry there.
140   Six months had passed during this journey. On the seventh month they
came to Birini, Mora's father.
'O brother, I have a woman for you', Garimone said.
When Birini came out to see the girl she was pregnant.
'O brother, this woman is not mine, you have brought someone's wife.'
Garimone was ashamed and ran away to Kauwa Mabu. Here he got the
sweet-potato leaves and went to Tigu Te where Lake Karugua was.
Gangamina followed him and they both carried the sweet-potato leaves and
came through Gi. The eighth month passed and the woman bore a child.
'How can I go back?' (Garimone asked).
Hiwa Hili (her father) was down there and had not received any bride-
price.
He followed them to the places they had gone; where they slept he slept.
He came to where the nuts and marsupial were.
'They came and ate all my things' he said. He came to the place where the
river Kemo goes underground and saw

tobacco leaves
charred wood
Ganga Walu plants and
Wango leaves [used in cooking] going around in the water.
'A man has made a fire' he said, and went off in search of the people.
160   Smoke was coming from Mt Gi and he went there. He saw they had slept at
Yogoye cave, at Garai cave, at Gero cave and went to Wabu swamp.
While he was there he heard a baby crying.
'Who is crying?' he said.
'I am here' she (Gangamina) said.
'Who are you?'.
'It is me' said Gangamina.
'Who are you with Gangamina?'
'I am here with Koma' she said.
He went up to them crossing the river Kemo. He had thirteen pairs of
cowrie shells (*dange*).
'You went a long time ago and you have born this child. I have seen the
road you have taken and you have done a good thing.'
He told her to turn her back and he shot the *haluma* arrow into
Gangamina's back.
O from there

the arrow spells	(*timu gamuru*)
the sexual intercourse spells	(*ndi tingi gamuru*)
the bow spells	(*danda gamuru*)
the marriage spells	(*wali dagiaru*)
180 the incest spells	(*wali tagini gamuru*)
the Haroli spells	(*Iba Giya gamuru*)

these were made into the wound.
When he had made them he broke the cowrie-shells into half and gave
them to Garimone and Gangamina.
They told
Tugu Doge,
Tugu Dongoma Puali
Tugu Tirane
Hiwa Hili
Tugu Mone
Tugu Yogoye
'Do what Gangamina says to do'.
Nogo Hangu Nana [pigs for male *dama*], kill
Nogo Hana Wali [pigs for female *dama*], kill
Ega [a Tege rite], plant
Himugu [a Tege rite] plant
Kebe Pobo [child-birth rite], do
'She will come back and I am going over there' he said.
He came and made a drain around that place and Hili slept there.
200   From Koma there is
Hubi Ibu
Hubi Mata

Hubi Aguene
Hubi Miau
it was done like that (*ani binigo*).
Now, Aguene is me and I am here.
A second thing I am saying (*mende laro*).
Hiwa Hili made a drain while he was at Tanili. While he was making this
Ewangwali and Papa Dawila (from Enga) came to him there. This is a talk
said by Dugube and I am telling it out now. Hiwa Hili gave them both
land. Papa Dawila made a drain there. This drain is at Biango Anda so we
can see it later. While Papa Dawila was making a drain this Ewangwali (a
dog) went to Hiwa Hili's house and looked inside. Hiwa Hili saw this dog
outside, not a dog but with long legs. He gave the dog some sweet-potato.
The dog ate some and carried some to his owner. Hili came to where the
man was digging drains,
'What are you doing?' he said.
'I am digging a drain so the water can go through'. Thus it was said.
Papa Dawila had nearly finished and was going to complete it the next day
220 so he went to sleep. Hili arose early and went again to see the man. 'The
river has been stopped by a stone. You go and sleep up there' he said. Papa
Dawila went up there and they made a Tege clearing on Tanili side. Ni's
friends Ewangwali and Papa Dawila came and made that drain at Tanili and
that is for me I am saying. When that had been done they cooked sweet-
potato in Hiwa Hili's house.
That is how it was done.
Now I am going to talk about men.
I have told you where I came from and about the sweet-potato leaves.
No man gave us these sweet-potato leaves; thus it has been said I am saying.
There was no other person there I am saying.
All this land belongs to Hiwa
it is like this.
Over there Koma was born first.
Koma's sons are Aguene, Ibu, Mata and Miau.
Garimone was the first to carry the sweet-potato vines

Garimone was the first	(Garimone *O mbira*)
Koma was second	(Koma *mende*)
Aguene was third	(Aguene *tebone*)
Wabera was fourth	(Wabera *mane*)
240 Wabera's son O Langua was fifth	(Wabera *igini O Langua O dauni*)
Sixth O Tiaburia	(*waragane* O Tiaburia)
Seventh O Urubuga	(*kane* O Urubuga)
Eighth O Tebela	(*halini* O Tebela)
Ninth O Wiliya	(*dini* O Wiliya)
Tenth O my father Gurubugu	(*pini O i hame* Gurubugu)
Eleventh I am here	(*beane O i kogoni*)
Twelfth is my son	(*hombene O i honowini*)
Thirteenth is his son	(*haleria O ibu honowini*)

The land has been divided there. Hubi Mata is over there where the Bauwa
tree is; he is on the mountain side.

Hubi Ibu, he is on the hill over there, his tail part is up there.
Hubi Aguene, myself, I am here.
Hubi Miau, he is at Mogra Fugua.
When the land was divided we didn't see any other clan (*wali haga*), it was done like that.
Wataga Pina's land was given by Tugu Yogoye
and Hiwa gave to Tugu Yogoye
thus I am saying (*ani laro*)
Hiwa also gave land to Wida
260 I thought Tobani was given land by Tugu Mone, but you are saying 'No, I was given by Kebali.'
Kebali? I am saying I am Hiwa. Before two white men came and divided this land [i.e. two Kiaps] and told Tobani to give 150 pigs. 'You will pay for the land' it was said. That's how it was done.
Hubi Tirane is sleeping over there.
Hiwa Hili is sleeping over there (at Tanili)
Hona Ni in that place.
One Tege clearing is over there
Another in that direction
A third across Kemo
A fourth where Hubi Tirane was.
Where Tugu Doge slept is over there
Where Tugu Dongoma Puali slept is over there
Where Tugu Mone was is there
O I am saying
This is all the land of Hiwa
Tobani, you were given only the mountain side, the swamp is mine so I am not going to climb the mountain side.
Where my fathers made a Tege clearing I am taking it
280 If I take all this land and Tanili it will give me pain
Why are we talking? My drains are up there at Tanili
We have left the land because we have been fighting for it.
That's all (*ogoni*).
MUGUYE: Is that all, or is there some more?
GANGARO: What can I add? The ones who slept on the other side of the mountains are *dama* I have said. No other clans can eat the Tia Yunida (possum), only Hiwa's sons. That's how it was. The incestuous pair [*wali tagini*: i.e. Garimone and Gangamina as classificatory cross-cousins] came and were told not to share the possums with anybody else. The Gurugu nuts, possum and nuts are over there across the swamp. Now anybody eats those; before it was forbidden (*illili*). That is the way it was. You have been saying that land belongs to Kebe (Kebali). No, we say the ridge-pole [i.e. the main track along which Kebali travelled] goes that way.
MUGUYE: While you [i.e. your ancestors] were there did anyone else come and make gardens?
GANGARO: No. Nobody came and planted there. Only now have they come.
MUGUYE: Can you remember whether you gave this land to Tobani?
GANGARO: The land he is on? Tobani is saying Hiwa didn't give it but

300   Dugube. Hiwa divided and gave that land I am saying. Hiwa gave to Pina
      and Tobani. His (Tobani) fathers' *mana* only he knows that. Dugube is
      their (Tobani) *tene*. Only now he has made gardens there, at first there was
      nobody there, that is what we are saying.
      MUGUYE: Did you see when his father came or not?
      GANGARO: My father didn't see it.
      MUGUYE: Did your father meet him somewhere or not?
      GANGARO: He didn't meet him.
      The names are there.
      O the clan Nuli Hiwa (Dugube)
      O that is Dugu Yawini (Dugube).

      (The following refer to ritual acts associated with *dindi pongo*)

      You cut the Balimu leaves
      You are making Dawe Gereya
      You are going straight to Bebenete
      You are going to Ira Gelo (Kelote)
      O Homa
      O Pela
      O Tiri
      O Mora
320   O Emabu
      O Koma
      O Pina
      O Tobani
      'You (Dugube) go straight' we (clans) used to say.
      There is no land of his up there, he (Dugube) just used to come through
      here [when performing *dindi pongo*].
      Dugube, you should have told this and said you had no land there.
      MUGUYE: Did you see whether, when Tobani came, it was man or *dama*
      first?
      GANGARO: That was man.
      MUGUYE: I am not talking only of the garden. Did you see Tobani anywhere?
      GANGARO: Tobani came and stayed where Tugu Mone gave him land, on
      the other side at Garai.
      MUGUYE: How many generations had passed from Tugu Mone and his
      fathers until Tobani came in? You think of it.
      GANGARO: It was not man who gave the land but *dama*. Hiwa Hili divided
      the land: the mountain side was given to Tobani and the swamp side
      (Ialuba) was given to me. That is how it has been said (*au lalu*). Tobani
      came from over that way (Garai). They were first at Wabia, they were born
      there. Tobani you are Walu Pubu [praise synonym: see Chapter 5], and
340   then you came here. This is what I am saying.
      'No' (Tobani are saying). He came from Guru Kabugua (Mogra Fugua) and
      made a bridge across the Kemo, and went to Tanili side. They have said like
      that. We have fought with the talk (*bi gungu*) then, and we came. You,
      Tobani, came from Yangoma and settled at Pongoli first; from Pongoli you

went to Pubua; from there to Garai and Arugu. In Garai you came to where
Tugu Mone was and he gave you land. It was done like that (*ani biyagoni*).
If you climb down to the swamp side, that is mine. The mountain side was
divided by Hiwa.
'No. That is Kebali's track' he (Tobani) has said (*au lene*).
MUGUYE: You are Hiwa Koma and he is Walu Pubu (Tobani)?
GANGARO: He is Walu Pubu (Tobani).
MUGUYE: When you count from Koma you are twelve generations?
GANGARO: Thirteen.
MUGUYE: When you count from Walu Pubu (Tobani)?
GANGARO: He too is like this. He has the same generations.
MUGUYE: Tobani, are you going to talk or have you some more talk to say
Gangaro?
GANGARO: Am I going to talk for him?
Where I have been I have said.
360   Where the boundaries are I have said.
The Tege grounds are in the places I have mentioned. Koma came and has
continued to stay here. Tobani came and planted sweet-potato on my land,
they climbed down to the gardens that are mine.
The guraya trees are there
The pandanus trees are there
The ancestral spirits are there
Koma divided these things as they are his.
You (Tobani) were given by Hiwa and I am Hiwa Koma
Tugu Mone gave you Garai but you are saying 'Dugube gave me'
You are going on the Humbirini road [i.e. wrong track, literally the 'road of
death'].
If you were here first then you would have given me the sweet-potato vines,
you would have given me fire.
You didn't give these I am saying.
Dugube, you came from the land of sago; you have your fathers' *mana* –
Dugu Yawini's (Dugube) *mana* is there. You have brought that *mana* and
have talked on my land.
MUGUYE: If you have finished let them speak (*ibugua lelo*).
LANDA: Dugube will speak first and Tobani later.
380   IRUGUA: Koma has said he was born from Hona Ni
He has talked about the land he is on.
Ai I am going to talk on how Dugu Yawini was born.
We are from the land up there
One (issue) we are fighting for the land   (*dindi garerebi*)
We are fighting for the ancestral spirits   (*homa dinini garerebi*)
We are fighting for the ancestral drains   (*homa gana garerebi*)
We are fighting for the old house sites   (*anda gumu garerebi*)
These are what we are going to talk on
We are sitting to talk on these
Where I went I will say
Those dead spirits
Those drains

Those drains up there
Just those we are talking on, what Gangaro has said is the same here
From your minds, us men who are here, let us share the talk
He has said he is Nuli Hiwa
I am Dugu Yawini
O Nuli Hiwa was born first by *dama* Kebali
When Nuli Hiwa was born then Hiwa was cut down, by Kebali and
400 Nuli Yai and Komaiya [types of sago] were born. These Hiwa were food.
Nuli Hiwa Mbolo Mbolo was born by Kebali
And then Hiwa Doge was born.
When the first Hiwa was cut down then Mt. Abago also fell.
Nuli Yai and Komaiya were felled
One fell in Umi (Strickland) and one this side where the river
Dogayu comes out.
Hiwa Ndole
Hiwa Tuguma
Hiwa Limbiya
Hiwa Barara
These were told to go to Mt Yagi, Mt Uruaga, and Mt Mbidubani to eat the
marsupial.
It was forbidden to eat the Horia, Haguanda and Yunida.
Hiwa Doge was told to go and stay there at U Yari Puni (Ialuba).
Before he was at Gambogoba and there he bore Hiliwa Yogoye and
Hiliwa Mone.
We are fighting for these dead spirits I have said
Hiliwa Tirane was born after these; where he was I am staying
420 Hiliwa Yogoye was up there
Hiliwa Mone was up there
Then Dugu Yawini himself came here
Dugube came and built houses here
The land was full with our houses
The boundary with Mirila (Duna) is Mt Gibu
The boundary with Pura Mogora is Mt Kebugu, Mt Kelango.
That is how it was done (*ani binigo*)
O then Hona Ni's sons (i.e. Koma) came here
With their big net-bags (*nu timbu heba*)
With their big axes (*ayu timbuni yi*)
With their big penes (*pindu timbuni*)
Then Walu Pubu came and married Lideme (Dugube lady). He came to
this side.
When it was like that my father gave him land.
Lake Karagua is there.
The good grass
The aprons
The fire sticks
These are from my father.
Cane (*tigi dobo*)
440 Oil (*amunami*)

These things are ours.
'Tobani you hold these things', it was said,
'You stay', it was said.
Then Wataga Pina came with thirteen pairs of shells (*dange*)
When he had come O Hiliwa Yogoye gave him land
'Stay over there', it was said.
Bauwaya (Wida) came and we gave him axe
'Stay at Deberebe and Karabaya', it was said.
'Carry the shells and stay', it was said.
I am Dugu Yawini (I will do these things for *dindi pongo*)
Oil (*amunami*)
Rope (*tigi dobo*)
Fish (*weneme*)
Tree grubs (*ira pubu*)
[these were previously collected and carried down to Kelote for the main earth rituals].
You will give pig and cowrie-shells [as payment for our ritual services]
You are Hona Ni's sons
Hona Ni and Dindi Hunabe have eaten us [i.e. taken our lands]
460   My fathers Dagibe and Egabe have said like this
Thus it has been said.
Bauwaya (Wida) was given that piece of land and Walu Pubu (Tobani) was given this swamp and mountain side. In the middle land are the nut trees where Hiwa Tirane sat. My father brought those trees and planted them. He brought the friction cane [i.e. he gave the knowledge for fire] and gave fire to
Those Walu Pubu (Tobani)
Those Hubi Miau
Those Wataga Pina
It was done like that.
The Harege tree [used in *dindi pongo*] was given to Walu Pubu [i.e. the rite itself]
Ega Pudu land was given to Wataga Pina, where the river Yogoye is sitting
Bauwaya (Wida) was given the axe (for Ega Kamia rites in *dindi pongo*)
He stays near the lakes Deberebe and Karabaya
It was done like that (*ani bini*)
When Koma came we gave him nothing [i.e. any rites to perform for *dindi pongo*]. We gave him land on the other side of Kemo; Kemo is the boundary that was put by my father. It's been said that land is mine I am
480   saying. Now I am going to say my *malu*. I have told you from Kebali and Hiwa, so the first generation I am counting from is me:
O the first generation is me
The second generation O Halimbo and Halembo
The third generation O Huni
The fourth generation O Handalu
The fifth generation O Warahi
The sixth generation O Balu and Wole
The seventh generation O Elabe and Dagibe

The eighth generation O Kobe and Ayango
The ninth generation Higi and Pole Wabu
The tenth generation O Koma and Nadele
The eleventh generation O Dabagua and Kehara
The twelfth generation O Mugu and Himugu
The thirteenth generation O Hiliwa and Yaliwa
The fourteenth generation O Pa and Mbele
The fifthteenth generation O Birini
The sixteenth generation O Hiluwi.
Why are we arguing? This is my land and my father has told me. There
were three wars and Koma took my land. Koma and Tobani had a fight
500 over one of our clan's women at Dera. Her name was Teme Leme. This girl
was making a garden up there and my father was having a Kaiya Tege (Tege
for dry seasons). There was a Guraya tree and a pig with two tails there. A
drain was made where that garden was and a tree was planted when it was
small. When the Kaiya Tege was being done a Hubi Gele came from Koma
and a man Hubi Agali (from Tobani). They came and fought over this
woman at the Kaiya Tege. We were all chased away by Koma but we came
back and stayed. That is one war.
Then there was a second war and a man was killed and we made Toro
Halaga (divination) with his bones. We were chased away by Koma again
but we came back and stayed.
There was a third war when my father was a young man and Koma chased
us to Garai, to Pubua, to Levani.
When that had been done (*ani biyagola howa*)
My father made a house up there and he pulled out the sweet potatoes from
the gardens, all the pitpit, killed a pig and took the jaw bone to the banks
of the Kemo and planted the jaw bone on a stick there [i.e. a sign of
intention to stay].
'You go' (I said to Koma).
'I am Dugu Yawini and I am staying here' it was said.
520 Thus it was said (*ani lene*).
I have said my *malu*. The land was done like that and the boundary is river
Kemo.
The penes (figurative) of the girls were cut
The penes of the boys were cut
The breasts of the girls were cut
[i.e. Koma have 'cut' us off from the land, our 'vital parts'].
The river Kemo is there I have said.
'Your fathers' spirits are there' Koma has said.
'Your gardens are here'
'Your ancestors have slept there' it has been said.
O The men that are here with our tail parts we are moving around and with
the head part we can see and walk around. You have cut off the head part
and our tail you are cutting now [i.e. the land].
The trouble (*daraboli*: pidgin) between us is like this we have seen.
That's all (*ai ogoni*)
LANDA: Ai now Tobani I will say.

My father was at Guru Kabugua (Mogra Fugua)
Aubi Pini's sons [i.e. Ni's sons] were Hubi Hubi [see Figure 5]
One is Yugu Bari
540   Two is Hiwa Koma
Three is Walu Pubu
Four is Hubi Bauwaya (Wida)
Five is Wataga Pina
Six is Yali Mora.
O there was one nut tree over there; while they were making drains they left
that nut tree it was said. Auwi's father and Himiya's father ate the nuts
while the others were making drains. Hubi Ina (Tobani) hit Hubi Gomiya
and he went to his mother's land. Hubi Ina climbed Mt Gi and came to this
side (Ialuba). He came and sat at Pelali. While he was sitting at Pelali he
saw some smoke coming from the other side of Kemo. 'My father is up
there, let's go to the other side' (his wife said). Ina and his wife made a
bridge with a Garere tree and crossed to the other side of Kemo. They came
to
Lake Tanili
Mugu Tai
Iba Ti
Iba Hini
Lake Tanili was small like a pool for tadpoles then. Dugube was there,
'You have come' he said.
560   'We saw the smoke and we came'. This was Lideme and Ina.
When they had stayed there Dugube gave some land.
While they had been at Pelali Koma's father had come from Mogra Fugua.
'My brother you have come so we will stay together' Ina said to him.
At Pelali there is a drain of Pina clan,
that is one drain
A second drain is for Wida and Tobani
that is a second drain
A third drain is for Koma
These three drains are at Pelali.
Then Ina went to the other side of Tanili where Iba Hini was and there he
bore Hubi Horawi. He climbed up to Iya and sat at Iya. There he bore Hubi
Tobani and Hubi Wida. Tobani married a woman from Dugube and they
gave us this land.
'I have put Dera and Dagi Anda for myself' he (Dugube) said.
'Koma, you stay on the other side of the river
Pina, you stay on the other side of the mountain.'
Tobani is born from Hubi Horawi and is staying there. The land was
divided and given; it is Dugube's land.
I am not going to say a lie to you.
580   Hubi Hubi is me. My father is Auwi Pini (Ni) at Guru Kabugua. My land
stretches to Mt Mbidubani. The boundary is Mt Gi. I am saying where the
dead spirits are.
First generation O Hubi Ina
Second generation O Hubi Horawi

Third generation O Hubi Tobani
Fourth generation O Doyayu, Kiame, Habonoma
Fifth generation O Angura
Sixth generation O Hogabe
Seventh generation O Yagalawura
Eighth generation O Nigale
Ninth generation O Wabila
Tenth generation O Hama
Eleventh generation O Haluya
Twelfth generation O Urulu
Thirteenth generation O Eganda
That's how it was done (*au binigo*).
There have been two wars it is true.
Hubi Gele and Hubi Agali had a fight for this woman Tege Leme. It was
done over there. This woman is from Hiliya and Yiliya, a Dugube woman.
600   This was the first war. They had a fight while they were making this Kaiya
Tege. Then we had a second war and we got the bones and made Toro
divination. We had a fight at Pelangua, Tobani killed thirteen from Koma.
Koma, they killed fourteen from Tobani. Four were also killed at Naira
Anga Anda.
O Wai Bali's son
Tugu Hili's son
Huli Wabaga's sons
Huli Pagana's sons
Nogo Yomo and Lebere's sons were killed
O Dogo Mura
Dogo Tunugua
Auwi
these betrayed us and killed two from Wagira clan.
When that had been done Tobani went and sat at Pubua (west of Ialuba)
While we were at Pubua they (Koma) came and fought us.
Then Tobani went to Wagina and they came again and fought us.
Koma kept planting sweet potato and we kept pulling them out.

. . .

That's how it was (*au bini*).
That's all (*ai ogoni*).
620   MUGUYE: Koma is one, that is Hiwa. Second is Hubi. So which one did your
father meet?
IRUGUA: He didn't meet him.
MUGUYE: The boundary is Iba Kemo?
IRUGUA: Walu Pubu (Tobani) he came down from Mt Gi. He married
Lideme and came. Wataga Pina, he is staying where Hiliwa Yogoye was.
Where Koma came from I don't know. . . .
MUGUYE: What I am saying you are not saying. There was Hubi and there
was Hiwa so which did your fathers meet? Hiwa's land I'm throwing down
what you said in your *malu*. You were talking of Hiwa, and Koma too was
talking of Hiwa. Do your fathers meet at Hiwa? The boundaries were made

by two men; your father stepped on one side and his father stepped on the other side. The boundary between you is down there, so now you tell me that your father and his father meet somewhere or tell me the generations at which his father came in. We will say this talk we are saying (*bi ogoni lole laramagoni*).

GANGARO: That is true.

MUGUYE: You tell everybody. This land has been divided by man, by *dama*, by our father Hona Ni. That is how it was done. . . . Which person, did you see? Did you see Koma's father or Koma's mother's relations, you say. I am talking so you can reply.

(Section inaudible due to adverse recording conditions)

IRUGUA: Koma came to his mother's land so how can I jump onto it?

MUGUYE: I am saying you get all of this land? I am going to ask you others here so you all think of it. These two didn't divide the land so Dugube will get it all, I am saying.

'I came to my mother's land' he (Koma) has said. He should have stayed on the other side of the mountain (at Mogra Fugua).

All right (*ogonigo*)

I have said

This land is a little bad it is like a quarter of a possum

One man or two men can't divide this land

Dama and man made the boundary.

The truth, how your father and his father met when the land was first divided

This man stayed here first

There was a garden over there

There was a house over there

My father told me to take them out

He was sent to this side

Not like a brother

Not like a father

A friend

A different one came and stayed

A step-relative (*yagini*) or brother-in-law (these should be said)

While he was staying did you divide the land?

Since that was said I am saying a talk so say 'Say a true talk'

(*au lalu i bi henemane labe lo bi larogoni*)

Not to say 'Wait to talk (*bi la habe lo ndo*)'

I will tell you to say 'Say a true talk'

(*bi henemane labe lo langulebero*).

LUNI: He is showing you the track for your talk to go on.

MUGUYE: You should make the talk on the mark ('foot-print': *ge nu wiyagoria*)

I have made.

(Repetition of Landa's speech by Kumuria)

MUGUYE: Are Dugube and Koma related (*bai ledabe*)?

660

KUMURIA: Koma is not related to us. Tobani is related, he married a Dugube woman and came inside.

MUGUYE: How was this land divided?

KUMURIA: Koma followed after Tobani and came and stayed here.

MUGUYE: Which woman?

KUMURIA: Hili's daughter. Tobani came from Kotabi (Mogra Fugua) to his
680   mother's land and sat at Tanili, Hini, Pelali. Then he went to the other side.

MUGUYE: Before, whose bone land (*dindi kuni*) was this?

KUMURIA: The bone is on that side, it is Dugube's land.

MUGUYE: Did Tugu Doge give birth to Hiwa?

KUMURIA: Kebali bore him. He bore Hiwa first for eating and then he bore Hiwa the man.

MUGUYE: Did these two divide the land?

KUMURIA: Hiwa and Dugube divided the land and waters.

LUNI: Before he asks a question I will say something. Koma and Tobani listen to me. The lies will be finished, the talk will be found out. We will continue to ask questions and you will be like a possum with nowhere to hide. Then you will feel like the possum who is going to be killed. The man will be found and he will die; the land will also die from this talk. That is the talk I have said.

MUGUYE: O Pina

Tobani

Koma

You are all Hubi Hubi. All of you came and sat at Pelali. Tobani you followed to your mother's land. He (Koma) followed to his mother's land
700   and came inside here. We will hear from all the men here
   There will be one man from Pina and we will hear his talk
   There will be one man from Wida and we will hear his talk
   There will be one man from Yugu and we will hear his talk
   There will be one man from Garua and we will hear his talk
   There will be men from Homa and Pela and we will ask them
When we have finished asking all these we will see who falls down
We will do like that
We are saying the talk to make it go on the main track (*haria tene*)
We will do like that (*ani buleberemago*)
We should say first who divided the land
To say that we are saying.

(It then rained heavily and the dispute continued inside the government rest-house)

GANGARO: You have said Hiliwa Tirane. It is not this name but Tugu Tirane and I have made the *pureremo* already. [Gangaro then proceeded to relate a further *mana* about the *dama* Irari Baloba detailing events, journeys and land marks associated with this deity.] The second *mana* is this. Anga Alua (pandanus species used in *dindi pongo*) was there; you have said this name because you want to steal my land. Anga Alua was over there (at Dera) and Bai (Dagabua) used to come for it. We used to give fire too. You

said you had the friction-cane but you are saying the *mana* that was put by
720   Hiwa and Ni. You used to collect the water from Lake Kupame and
Emberame (for *dindi pongo*), you collected the Andaya possum. ''You stole
my *mana*'' you have said. It is true, my brother Hubi Miau used the
friction-cane, he carried it (for *dindi pongo*) but he is not your brother.
Gangamina and Garimone were on this land and they bore Miau. I am
Koma and I am here. ''You stole my *mana*'' you have said, and we are
getting pain from this. The Hiwa Hariage (tree for *dindi pongo*) that was there
you have said is Hiliwa. For that one you have lied. That is Hiwa and that is
the talk that we used to say. Now you are conspiring, lying and fighting.
You have made up your *pureremo* and keep changing it. Where the river
Dongale is, there is the Hariage. Ni and Hiwa separated so that Dugube
could go straight to Bebenete (for *dindi pongo*) and perform Dawe. You
said you gave all of this to Miau, so Miau is whose son? We gave you space
to go to Bebenete; you were going to climb
Mt Gigi Nawi
Mt Gigira
Mt Mima
Mt Kebu and pass
Pela clan
Emabu clan
740   Homa clan
Hiwa Koma
Walu Pubu
Bauwaya
We gave you a space to go straight
Where you passed, 'That is my land' you have said
'That is Hiliwa Doge' you said
'That is Hiliwa Yogoye' you have said. This is because when the rain comes
(while you are performing *dindi pongo* on our land) you want to stop on
these lands.
What is Tugu Tirane's 'Hiliwa Tirane' you are saying
What is Tugu Yogoye, 'Hiliwa' you are saying
'Tugu Mone gave the land to Tobani' I have said. 'No! He is born from
Lideme and I gave him land' you have said.
The *mana* that was put for Ni and Hiwa you are taking it. When you count
the generations then it is true you have brought the *mana* from Dugube.
My father's *mana* I have told out. The dead ashes I have put everywhere. I
am Ni's son and I came to my mother's land; Hiwa is *tene*. I used to make
Tege at Tanili, I used to kill pig for *dama* where Tugu Tirane sat.
I am continuing to stay I am saying
760   We didn't divide this land.
'A war was made' you said.
'I killed seven of your people' you have said
I am saying we never had a war.
You fought other people
Gini
Tigi

Abu Higi
Giri Waga
Homa Yagua
Auwi
'You killed some of my men' you have said. You name them. I will say you
are saying lies.
When we used to have a war my father would have a *pureremo* for that.
There isn't one for you. We shouldn't talk on Hiwa and Kebali (it is
dangerous to even invoke their names) but you are claiming all the land.

. . .

MUGUYE: Did you see Tobani or Dugube?
GANGARO: I didn't see Dugube. I am Garimone. There were three women.
One was the woman that was exchanged (between Ni and Hiwa). Another
was the one who had incestuous relations.
780   The sexual intercourse spells
The war spells
The marriage spells
these were made into her back.
Because of this incest you Hubi are small (in number)
Hiwa is big.
'The possum and the nuts you eat by yourselves' Mone said.
Tobani came and sat at Pongoli first, he was from Yangoma (Tari). Then he
went to Pubua and got land there. From Pubua he went to Garai and got
land from Tugu Mone.

. . .

LANDA: Koma are saying, 'Tugu Mone gave you land'. No. Dugu Yawini
divided the land and gave us the first sweet-potato vines. The Dugube go
through Kebe Haria (Kebali tracks); they go where the snake (*puya*) is going
and make Dawe Peda . . . Irugua and Kumuria their fathers did this. It was
like that and they gave us these things to do. When the hole is made in the
ground [for *dindi pongo*] this is done at Dendepe (Pubua); from there Baya
Baya comes [i.e. making the earth good]. Kebali's daughter went that way
to marry with Dagabua clan.
Dugube gave us Hariage and we did it
They gave us *manda mbu* [hair-style for *dindi pongo*] and we did it
800   They gave us Dawe Peda and we did it
He gave us all these *mana* and divided the land. Kemo is the boundary so
why are we fighting?
MUGUYE: I am saying something (*ina mbira laro*)
Pina, when you go to Koma, and if Koma get the land, you will say 'I was
going to say that this land belongs to you. The other side were lying.' You
will say like this when they are cooking pig (so that you may eat some). You
must tell us the truth about this land.
Say one important talk.
HIWA TEGE: I am not going to say a talk for one side or the other. I did not
see who was here first; my fathers' *mana* does not say like this.

In the absence of any other headmen willing to talk, the parties returned to their respective homes. There were no further formal talks and the mediators returned to Koroba having informed Gangaro and Landa that they thought the land belonged to Koma. No further action was taken by either party, who both acknowledge an informal taboo on use of the land.

Contrary to accepted generalizations for New Guinea Highlands societies, the Huli neither forget names of remoter patrilineal ancestors, nor are they poor oral historians. This, as I have previously indicated, is consistent with the epistemological status of inherited *mana* and a logical system of explanation founded on the doctrine of *tene* ('first causes'). Moreover, the speech contexts in which such knowledge is declared may well account for the atypical length of Huli genealogies in the absence of high population density, recurrent land disputes, or a pattern of land devolution determined solely by a dogma of agnatic descent. The retention and periodic expansion of ancestral charters, which can vary here from twelve to twenty generations, is a response to the framework of anticipations about how litigants will establish primacy of tenure. To the extent that Huli genealogies approximate to African-type schemes, they do so partly as a product of the organizational structure of conversation in which they are discussed. The resumé of the dispute offered by Gangaro (lines 712–75) crystallizes the issues relating to historical personages and to correct patronymic prefixes:

'You have said Hiliwa Tirane. It is not this name but Tugu Tirane'   (712–13)
'What is Tugu Yogoye, "Hiliwa" you are saying.'   (751)
' "This is Hiliwa Doge", you said.'   (746)

ritual practices associated with previous performances of *dindi pongo*:

'The Hiwa Hariage that was there you have said Hiliwa . . . that is Hiwa and that is the talk we used to say.'   (726–27)
'Anga Alua was over there [i.e. in Koma land] . . . you have said this name.'
  (716)

and 'talk':

'you are saying the *mana* that was put there by Hiwa and Ni.'   (720)
' "You stole my *mana*", you have said.'   (725)
'You have made up your *pureremo* and keep changing it.'   (729)

The ritual ecology and economy of each clan is defined as a permanent record of land ownership; a challenge to the substantive nature of any clan *mana* is construed as an attack on that unit's identity base.

Whilst the attendance of official land mediators and the consequent scheduling of the dispute constitute introduced factors, the replication of speech order and topic syntax throughout the debate is in accordance with traditional processes and precepts. The pattern of turn-taking in the initial declaratory phase of the dispute (i.e. lines 1–619), and indeed the participant status of the speakers, does not reflect any officially imposed restriction. The pre-allocation of turn order expresses the tacit agreements of members regarding speech precedence among clans related as *tene-yamuwini*. The sequential pattern realizes the schema (see also *Figure 3*).

A (Hiwa)   *tene*
B (Koma)   *yamuwini*
C (Dugube)   *tene*
D (Tobani)   *yamuwini*

It is the restricted availability for self-selection by others in these settings that differentiates verbal interaction in D.1 from that of D.2 or D.3. In respect of the prevalence of phonological patterning or parallel repetition (e.g. 86–9, 523–25), these are not distinctive features but are recurrent aspects of all Huli speech. Political leadership is defined in this society as the authoritative right to perform *malu* in contexts such as D.1. The office of 'headman' is noncompetitive, the incumbent is most typically the eldest son of a previous headman. Irugua, Pogaye, and Gangaro are thus all agnatic descendants. Rhetorical skills and willingness to participate in disputes often permit younger brothers to assume this status. Since the only tangible benefits of being a headman concern rights over *malu*, the office is not contested by other candidate brothers. In the case of Tobani, the previous headman's son is considered too young to participate in such disputes and Landa, by consensus, operates in his place. Importantly, Landa's speech is fashioned 'as if' he were an agnate of Tobani (though he is a *yamuwini*). It is thus not the knowledge itself that serves to distinguish headmen from others, but the acceptance that they hold the only 'correct' version which may be utilized in public debates. Possession validates status, performance communicates possession.

In line with the specification of speech order there is a marked absence of the repair or remedial sequences that typify talking in D.2 or D.3. In the initial phase of the dispute there is no competition for 'floor-taking' so that the type of turn-taking gambits listed in *Table 1* (4) are not here in evidence. Nevertheless, one can note the frequent use of parenthetic devices to mark the boundaries between topics (e.g. 26, 35, 52, 55), and the turn-completion 'that's all' (283, 535, 619). Clearly, D.1 represents one context where the consequences of any interruption are severe enough to preclude their occurrence. The lack of any self-correcting procedures testifies to the importance of verbal exactitude in presenting clan *mana*. A delivery punctuated by frequent mistakes, changes, or overlong gaps, may be construed as indicating a level of artificial construction.

The syntactic structure of all four main speeches (19–74; 75–283; 380–535; 536–619) shows the following sequential progression:

(1) *Mapping routines:* the location of ancestors within a temporally and spatially defined framework. Speakers avail themselves of the opportunity to 'set' the debate terms in respect to place and ancestral names (e.g. 19–25, 40–45; 75–81, 95–100; 400–27). Renditions of toponyms and clan/tribal appellations employ an aesthetic lexicon (*bi mone*: see Chapter 5) as an index of the speaker's control of oratory:

Hulu Gomaiya (Huli: 5, 99) – Mirila (Duna: 3, 425) – Dugu Yawini (Dugube: 1, 27, 397).
Walu Pubu (Tobani: 467) – Wataga Pina (Pina: 543) – Bauwaya (Wida: 542, 447).

The occurrence of the prefixes *Hubi* and *Tugu* in the accounts given by Hiwa and Koma is thus an attempt to reinforce the links these clans have to each other, and to the deity Ni (see *Figure 5*; *Diagram 2*). As noted above, the key transformations of this patronymic to *Hiliwa* or *Hiwa* by Irugua is part of the referring activity that occurs throughout all the speeches. There is no disagreement, then, concerning the identification of any place or cave, merely whether the ancestors who stayed there 'belong' to Koma or Dugube clans. The confusion of the mediators in this issue was confounded by the recurrence of the name *Hiwa* in all accounts. In the discourse of Irugua it is used to denote a specific deity Hiwa (398), as well as two species of sago (*hiwa*) (400): 'Kebali bore him (Hiwa). He bore Hiwa first for eating, and then he bore Hiwa the man' (685–86). The praise term for 'sago' is Nuli Hiwa and it is this form that is used to reference clan identity by Pogaye (28), Gangaro (6), and Irugua (398, 400, 401). These issues are further confused by the citation of the same ancestors – Doge, Tirane, Mone, and Yogoye – in the speeches of Koma and Dugube. An attempt is made to 'personalize' the uses of 'Hiwa' by an overlay of tone contrasts which distinguish Hiwa$_1$ from Hiwa$_2$ used by an opposing litigant. Notwithstanding such devices, the two factions accuse each other of 'stealing talk' (375–76; 394–99; 725–27). It is noticeable that direct charges of counter-normative behaviour are deferred until after the completion of all four speeches. The initial allusions to disagreement are no more than statements of difference: 'This is Tugu Tugu and Nuli Hiwa's land . . . Dugube is saying it is his fathers' land . . . we are going to talk on this (6–7; 14–19) I thought Tobani was given land . . . but you are saying "No, I was given by Kebali"' (261–63), which later are couched in the more explicit terms of 'Now you are conspiring, lying, and fighting' (728). This sensitivity to using a blunt, forward, or direct manner in relation to accusations or disagreements can be discovered from the position of such statements in the text. In the advanced stages of debate the issues will have emerged and opinions formed as to whether a favourable outcome requires one to cast doubt on an opponent's version. This is highlighted by the continued state of confusion with regard to Hiwa: 'You were talking of Hiwa and Koma too was talking of Hiwa. Do your fathers meet at Hiwa?' (629–30); and the presupposition that some of the parties are lying: 'The lies will be finished, the talk will be found out' (690).

(2) *Significant events relating to* dama/*men*. Validation of land rights proceeds in this environment by a ratification of 'primacy'. Events associated with focal progenitors are detailed to establish self-identity, and the segmentary structure of the clan.

'I am Nuli Hiwa and this land is mine	(28)
My clan is four.'	(45)
'I am here and I was born from Hiwa	(82)
Hubi Miau . . . Hubi Ibu . . . Hubi Mata.'	(95–98)
'I am Dugu Yawini.'	(397)

Tenurial precedence is thus partly justified by recounting the historical patterns of land distribution and boundary determination. The attribution of *tene* status to Dugube and Hiwa signifies the recognition that they were 'staying on the land' first. Clan-pairing resulted from the union of *dama* from different places and the granting of land by 'land-givers' (see *Figure 3*). The two clans are immutably linked as 'consanguineals':

Dugube, Koma ti   bai ledabe nale?
Dugube Koma they related   or not?   (673)
('Are Dugube and Koma consanguineally tied [see Chapter 3] or not?')

Rival claims about 'bone land' (682–83) and 'who was there first' fix on the same set of diacritical factors: (a) the derivation of sweet-potato vines (146; 228–29; 372–73; 791); (b) the friction-cane for fire (374; 397; 465–66; 718–20); (c) ancestral drains (268–71; 391–93); (d) ritual grounds (268–71; 498–510; 758). To some extent this shared orientation reflects an understanding of the bases on which mediators may come to a decision. Equally, however, the data indicates a prospective assessment of arguments likely to be advanced by opposing speakers (see also 384–88): 'No man gave us these sweet-potato leaves . . . I am saying' (229), or mediators: 'There was no other person there I am saying' (230).

Kinship relations are expressed in terms of the communication of 'talks', the enumeration of which provides speakers with a further opportunity to demonstrate rhetorical skills (29–33; 175–81; 435–40):

ogo dagua biabe
this like   do
ogo dagua habe
this like   stay
ogo dagua labe
this like   say
ogo dagua nabe
this like   eat   (86–89) (see also D.3 : 477–82)

Part of the transmission of *mana* concerns the assimilation and practice of *dindi pongo* rites. Tobani and Dugube cite the ritual directives as evidence of original occupation (790–801; 439–56). Gangaro counters this claim by suggesting that the ritual acts of Miau segment derived from Bai Dagabua clan (718), and that Koma simply allowed Dugube passage through their land to perform the fertility rites. Importantly, Huli rely on the 'formalized indexing' of historical events in speech forms as a record of fact or truth. Gangaro denies that Koma and Tobani had three wars by indicating the absence of any inherited 'talk'. 'When we used to have a war my father would have a *pureremo* for that. There isn't one for you' (773–74).

Decisions concerning those mythical events for public and private consumption have, as previously noted, been determined in accordance with the dangers attendant on 'saying out' sacred knowledge (774–75). Moreover, orators are well aware of the possibilities that information will be stolen and adapted for use against them at some future dispute, 'you are saying the *mana* that was put by Hiwa and

Ni (720) . . . You have made up your *pureremo* and keep changing
it' (729).

(3) Malu *recitation*. The presentation of clan genealogies is separated
from mapping routines and event descriptions so as to parallel the
distinction between the chronological periods relating to *dama* and
agali ('man') (111–12; 227; 328–29). The pedigrees typically commence from an apical 'man' through agnatic descendants belonging
to the speaker's sub-clan. Counting is slow and deliberate, and never
aided by prompting from clan members. The phrase denoting the
numerical order of generation is invariably followed by the voiced
pause which precedes the citation of ancestral names:

daba	*mbira O Tugu Tugu*	
generation one	o Tugu Tugu	(57)

The pause is here an intrinsic part of the performance and is not construed as 'hesitancy'; it does not invite censure as being evidence of
fabrication. The characteristic phasing of *malu* seems a response to the
functional importance of pauses for the production of clarity, comprehension, and audibility (see Atkinson and Drew 1979 : 198). An
audience's monitoring of *malu* is critical, so the information must be
presented in manageable portions. The division between the two parts
of the above statement, and an intonational contour that stresses the
second section, are adaptations to the significance such names often
assume in later discussion. Furthermore, the convention that a performer should deliver a mistake-free rendition is negotiated by pauses
that allow speakers time for thought and verbal planning. There does
appear to be a relationship here between the strategic placement of
pause, the need to eliminate misunderstandings, and the noticeable
absence of mistake. In this regard, the phonological patterning of
ancestral names – Halimbo Halembo, Mugu Himugu, Hiliwa Yaliwa
(483–97) – indicates a mnemonic device likely to operate in ancestral
lines depicting brothers, or where the genealogy exceeds a certain
generational depth. As yet, there is little comparative data on the
performative aspects and contexts of genealogical recitation among
New Guinea societies. Nevertheless, I would contend that the specific
format of pedigree production in Huli is a determinative factor on
genealogical length. They are functionally adapted to political situations such as D.1 in which the organization of talk is peculiarly con-
ducive to genealogical manipulation, tampering, and fictive addition.
Information has to be communicated in one uninterrupted speech

act; there is no later opportunity for correction or re-statement. Since speakers, on the basis of past experience, are aware of the relationship between generational depth and tenurial precedence, there is a premium on managing one's *malu* to reflect primal status. The speaker has prospectively to structure his *malu* in anticipation of 'changes' effected by an adversary. The subsequent attention to such issues by the mediators in D.1 (352–56) confirms that such inferences are justified.

When items are being listed, the voiced pause occurs when the speaker wishes to lend emphasis to a particular phrase (108–10; 316–23). A contrast can be drawn here between the mode of name-listing in *malu*, and that which is characteristic of *damba bi* ('closing down': see *Table 2*) speeches. In these latter genres, names are not themselves subject to open debate, and any serial order of appellations is delivered in a rapid staccato fashion. Each phrase is accompanied by a half-turn of the head. In many such speeches (see Appendix 2 : 2; 3–8, 27–32) names form part of a standard paradigmatic set. Enunciation of the first term determines the order of the following names; this pattern is so widely known that a partial monitoring failure would not impair understanding. This valued oratorical feature is evident in some of the nominal citations found in D.1 (186–91; 407–10; 665–72; 764–70), and displays an assured, self-confident manner. The distinctive characteristics of the two modes of enumeration seem responsive to different situational demands. The phrasal breaks of *malu* are designed so as to reduce the possibility that any item may be missed.

From an examination of the content of the four principal speeches we learn the extent to which speakers design their turns in regard to both an ongoing stream of talk, and the projected turns of others. In all three environments abstracted above, there is a degree of prospective structuring of argument. This is evident in mapping routines, the length of *malu*, and the depiction of mythical events: 'This is a talk said by Dugube and I am telling it out now' (209–10: the implication is that Dugube will later claim this myth to be part of his own *mana*). It is also the case that the subsistent structural parallels between the speeches reflect litigants' orientations to the framework of debate terms announced at the outset of D.1 (this is presented as Text A in Chapter 5). Formal openings are dependent on a degree of scheduling, numbers, and a level of unit opposition; they frequently form an institutionalized transition to the main presentation of claims.

Mediators use these locales for defining the sufficiency dimensions according to which talk is assessed as valid, appropriate, or acceptable. Such 'setting speeches' orient participants to a normative frame of reference terms; to the general goals and ideals of dispute talk, and to the specific factors of occasion and conflict aetiology. The dimensions of contrast that appear internally to structure these turns at talk, and that result in the prevalence of bipartite and quadripartite forms, are discussed later. At this juncture I am concerned with demonstrating (a) how such normative statements are reiterated at later stages in the dispute, and (b) how a set of linguistic options typifies Huli 'mediation'.

Huli mediators (*dombeni* – 'middle-men') operate with a code of circumscribed commitment in which the components of assertion and the modalities of tentativeness are differentially located in any utterance, and indeed in the constituent units of turns. Notwithstanding the points made in Chapter 2 concerning the unqualified and categorical 'I-say-so' (*laro*: the neustic) versus assertions of qualified factuality – the 'it-is-so' (tropic) – a detailed examination of Muguye's and Luni's talk in D.1 reveals a reticence in formulating a decision or opinion concerning the relative merits/demerits of the opposing claims. The mediating processes variously involve:

(i) interrogative procedures of clarification: 328–56; 620–23; 673–90;
(ii) the formulation of relevant issues and questions: 628–33; 637–39; 659–63.

This latter strategy is part of a wider concern of mediators to provide a 'plan' for debate. In three critical segments of discourse (Text A: Chapter 5; 642–69; 695–711) conversational aims are proposed to set the context for subsequent speech behaviour – by defining a normative schema for debate – and to elicit specific types of verbal response. That is, both in the opening speech and subsequently (most typically where some impasse has been reached through the intractable positions of litigants) mediators attempt to prestructure talk. Particularly noticeable is the persistent use of the evaluative dichotomy of truth:

'Now you should make a true talk . . .'	(Text A: 23–4; 27–8; 51)
'I will tell you to say "Say a true talk"'	(D.1: 652; 666; 668)

and lies:

'When we have seen the lies . . .'	(Text A: 1; 15–19; 55–60)
'The lies will be finished . . .'	(D.1: 689–93)

This provides an area for the display of rhetoric through synonym substitution in syntactically parallel statements:

TEXT A

12	*dindi o howa uru*	52	*ai uru mandabi*
	concerning land and cunning		those I know
	ke uru		*ke uru mandabi*
	lies		the lies I know
	haya uru		*nde uru mandabi*
	persistence		the betrayals I know
	tandaga uru		*agali naga bayeni mandabi*
	pain		men's ways I know

In addition to formulating expectations of mendacity, and exhorting litigants to tell the truth, mediators are also concerned with the precedural forms noted above. At the general level there is a commitment to a conventional corpus of speech norms that gives the turn-taker a certain security of tenure. What is asserted and rhetorically announced are 'safe' maxims, a range of relevant issues or questions for debate, and sets of options or paradigmatic answers. The commitment is to a 'plan for future talk', a communicative activity which can be identified on account of the presence of gambits subsumed under the rubric 'prospective strategies of action' in *Table 1*.

Within the category of Plan (*Table 1* : 3c) gambits, one may note the occurrence of 'saying to say' assertions (634–35; 640; 665–66; 711) and 'future action' proposals (707–09). Speech 'reciprocity' (*Table 1* : 3b), which is an invariant component of mediatory turns – the notion that talk must be shared – is formally stated in lines 700–05 which exhibit parallel repetition with a substitution of clan names. Clearly, the assertive and imperative modes are restricted to acts of question formulation, the presenting of option possibilities, and an appeal to conform to generalized notions of 'good talk' (either content or form).

'So you say the real talk'	(Text A: 95)
'Say a true talk' (D.1: 668) . . . 'Say one important talk'	(D.1: 808)

There is a deferred commitment to direct forms of blame imputation or decision-making in the form of specific directives to action. Mediators pose, present, and suggest in an assertive way; what is proposed, however, is an attenuation of such directness. The code of mediation locates personal involvement at the 'I-say-so' level; propositional content reveals diminished assurance and straightforwardness. The speakers seem committed only to the option frames they erect and the stereotype norm formulations. They detach themselves from involvement in selection processes by sequentially deferring decision-type statements. This preferred strategy shows a sensitivity to the interactive repercussions attendant on party or issue polarization. Within the parameters I have described, the mediator can function in a context of security and certainty that is unlikely to alienate him from either disputant once the debate is completed on that occasion. This explains the frequent use of choice gambits (*Table 1* : 3d). I shall have more to say about the nature of mediation processes in my analysis of D.2. For now, it is sufficient to have noted the sense in which a 'middle-man' can be defined in terms of a set of linguistic options. The standardized nature of the communicative routines here are discoverable from the presence of the routinized expressions considered above. They are tied to recurrent situational contexts and help to sustain the tenurial validity of any incumbent acting in a mediatory capacity.

The decrease in the infant mortality rate, and the provision of health care, has meant a steady increase in population over the last decade, resulting in greater pressure on land resources. This pressure is not uniform over the whole of Huli territory but corresponds to proximity to mission or government stations. In a border community such as Ialuba the situation seems little changed from that found by Glasse (1968) to prevail in the Tari region during the 1960s. This is perhaps reflected in the relative infrequency of land disputes. An examination of *Table A1* yields a figure of only 6 per cent for land claims during my fieldwork period; 25 per cent of these originated prior to my arrival. It is evident from the statistical data that inter-clan land disputes embody a degree of intractability. Even at the formal level of land mediation, unless decisions are ratified by a Land Court, they need not be accepted or implemented. Indeed, 25 per cent of such land claims in Ialuba are 'pending'. Despite the small number of cases computed, *Table A8* shows that over 58 per cent of all land claims recorded had an outcome of 'renouncement'. Two contributory factors in this picture are the multiple-claim nature of many disputes, and the mediatory technique of proposing that litigants may wish to consider the option of claim renouncement (*Table 1* : 3a).

D.2 exhibits a marked stylistic difference in the structure of argument between intra-clan and inter-clan land claims. The occasion here is spontaneous, few people were in attendance and there were no official mediators, nor any *agali haguene* (headmen). The case represents the essence of traditional Huli disputing wherein 'men with the talk' attempt to help disputants come to an arrangement. Importantly, there is no formal opening speech, and sometimes subsidiary conversations occur alongside the single sequence of turns. Opposing litigants occupy separate space facing each other. Maliyago had come to the *hama* (open clearing) at Ialuba to voice his anger at the actions of his brother, and Helago was called by means of the familiar announcement and summons routines.

Most men and boys employ yodelling styles when travelling to signal their approach, or to elicit a response from someone they anticipate to be there. Two examples of this instrumental speech device are as follows: (1) *he*: *go he*: *go* ('I'm here I'm coming': rapid movement from higher to lower pitch level); (2) *ya*: *o* or *u*: *ah* (to signal assent, or ask 'Are you there?': high pitch fluctuation). The forms used can be highly idiosyncratic and either declarative or interrogative in intention. They allow for a degree of personal recognition over long distances. This type of verbal 'calling card' is known as *agali Û₁*, and can be used to summons people to a dispute or alert the valley to some important news such as a death or war. The following text was shouted across the valley following one man's discovery that his garden had been damaged by some pigs:

1 *Nogo mabu nainyada   laro*
  pig   garden has been eaten I am saying
  (my garden has been eaten by a pig, I am saying)
  Nogo ainagadabe hondole ibidaba laro
5 pig   whose   to see   come   I am saying
  I   mabu bamba nalu hene
  my garden before has been eaten
  Nogo handa walia halu
  pig   has been found out before
10 *Muni yalu ibilimu   laro*
  money bring when you come I am saying

(Field data)

We may note the evidence suffix -*da* (line 1) to indicate that the statement is made on the basis of the 'visible' phenomena and the stylistic conclusion term *laro* as an explicit performative. Though tonally distinguished from *U₂* ('song': see Chapter 2), the semantic relatedness of the terms U_1 and U_2 is constituted by the marked stylistic similarities between the two genres. This text, as many others cited in the book, indicates a spontaneous patterning of utterances according to a 2 + 2 + 1 format:

$$\left[\begin{array}{l} \text{Pig garden has-been-eaten I-am-saying} \\ \text{Pig whose to-see come I-am-saying} \end{array} \right]$$

These lines announce the facts of the incident and both are terminated by the explicit performative *laro*.

$$\left[\begin{array}{l} \text{My garden before has-been-eaten} \\ \text{Pig has been-found-out} \end{array} \right]$$

Lines 7 and 9 add contextual information and noticeably omit *laro*. Line 11 represents a type of conclusion that bounds the schema of binary statements preceding it and which retains the sentence final *laro*. This progression of moves is one that is clearly typical of dispute related speeches (see especially Chapter 5).

Women's shouting is classified separately and is termed *Wali Alo* (*alo* being onomatopoeic). This most often takes the form of invective and is terminated by a slow rise from low to high pitch over the vowel pattern *ah: u*:

Hebale O
Your lips are like the black dog's lips
So what are you doing down there I am saying
Run and carry your big lips here I am saying
ah: u

(Field data)

Diagram 4   Relations between Helago and Maliyago

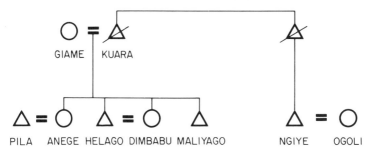

Dispute 2

Issue: Land at Wali Wano.
Disputants: Maliyago,
                     Helago.
Others: Koma clan – Ago, Egari, Timuria, Egele, Hayabe, Ugubugu;
               Pina clan – Kabo.
Date: 13 October 1977.
Location: Ialuba, clearing at U Yari Puni.
Outcome: Helago renounced claims on the site.

The argument between these brothers concerned the attempts of Helago to make a garden in Wali Wano which, five years previously, had been used by Maliyago. Maliyago is now claiming 10 Kina on account of the tree he had planted there and an old house he had built on the land. There is a history of bad relations between the two and Maliyago had preferred to stay in the next valley (Wabia) where he had been given land by a friend.

1   MALIYAGO: Why are you here Helago? I made the house over there so how old were you when I made that house? Our father made the garden so only you and Ngiya plant. I am throwing away that garden. I haven't any gardens and drains there. So how old were you when I built that house? You have done a good thing now [sarcastic comment].
     You will give me 40 Kina.
     My casuarina there you pay for that
     My house there you pay for that
     Why am I angry?
     I am talking straight (*tiga tiga larogoni*).
     I planted that casuarina there.
     AGO: Not like that (*agueni ndo*).
     He wanted to plant himself. The house and the casuarina tree
     'I put those first' he said, I am saying.
     'The old house
     The casuarina
     The tree medicine [pidgin: awareness of its agronomic value in soil fertility]
     Those I put.
     I wanted to plant and now you have come to plant
20   You throw it away.'
     He has said like that (*au layagoni*).
     HELAGO: Did you say you are angry?
     Or 'I planted it now you plant' you talked to say like that?
     I have said, 'Say a straight talk'
     So where can I plant?
     MALIYAGO: The land is there and placed
     From Wali Wano over there
     For planting coffee there is a place
     For planting casuarina there is a place
     For planting pandanus there is a place
     HELAGO: Are you making *mana* to me?
     MALIYAGO: We will keep saying the *mana*.

The nuts that you planted you keep taking and then there won't be any.
The casuarina that you planted, that too will be finished. When you try to
wind yourself around me then I am going to jump into the Kemo
[i.e. commit suicide]. If you hold onto my trees then truly (I will do that) I
am saying
. . .

MALIYAGO: That's what has been done. That house that has been made, on
40   my father's land, you are there now. The coffee that is planted I wanted to
plant. 'I want to plant' you have said. . . . The argument that has been said
(*lai lowa*) we are not going to make a fight talk. Truly we are both born
from one man and from one women. We have been broken off (*gai bini*)
from one bood. That's how it was done. I am saying how the old house site
was done. It was done when Helago was still a small boy.
HELAGO: 'I am going to plant' for that talk a talk has been made.
'We are both the eldest
We are both the youngest'
You have said this talk
I am not a small boy
You are not a small boy
How will we stay?
A second man can't say 'go'.
. . .

AGO: Maliyago, he (Helago) planted in that garden, so why has this made
you angry?
MALIYAGO: What are you saying?
If Ago clears a place and builds a house will Kauni (Ago's B) come and
make gardens there?
If Gangaro makes a garden there will Hirugu come and make gardens
60   there?
I am going to plant that garden so you go.
HELAGO: The youngest and the eldest they insulted me (two friends of
Maliyago)
You wanted to insult me
I am with shame here brother (*hambi*).
You will plant,
Like that it has been said.
I want to plant so I will find where my mother's and father's old house sites
are.
MALIYAGO: Dera is where the youngest will plant
Dera is where the youngest will plant
Dera is where the youngest will plant
The clan is broken off from one blood
We are going to divide the land
We will see we are broken off from one blood
We will divide the pandanus
We will divide the old house sites
You will see your old house site is at Dera.
. . .

MALIYAGO: His old house site is at Dera I am saying
I myself am going to plant here.
80   Throw it away   I am saying.
HELAGO: There used to be a person who went around the talk
While we are there he used to fight
With a stick
With a stone
With a bow
With an axe
You are strong (*hongo hea*) like that.
That is how the *mana* is [i.e. that Maliyago is showing excessive zeal].
MALIYAGO: The *mana* is like that? You will be doing like that. If you fight
and kill me who will get pig? If I kill you who will get pig?
HELAGO: I am not frightened of you, I am here.
MALIYAGO: I am not frightened of you, I am here.
AGO: This is what we used to do.
Now you two are arguing
'You are at Dera' you (Maliyago) have said
That is a bad talk.
At Dera Helago's mother and father's spirits didn't stay.
The place for the mother's and father's spirits is up there.
100   HELAGO: Our mother's and father's spirits are up at Galoma Balu, a second
is at Wali Wano and a third is at Daiyabi. That's all (*ogoni hangu*).
MALIYAGO: At Galoma Balu Helago and Kenobi built a house and they are
down there. Ngiya too, they built their houses there =

(Helago, who lives at Dera, harbours considerable resentment towards
Maliyago because he allowed a friend (Kakaye) to use the land at Galoma
Balu and Daiyebi)

HELAGO: = On this side or that side is where our father has been.
AGO: If he is staying on that side then you are staying on this side.
EGARI: *Agali dombenime lagabe be libinime laga?*   (*Table 1* : 2d)
Did the middle-men used to speak or did just two people speak?
O libinime laga ndo
Not that just two people spoke.
agali ogo howa yagini ndo
You are not from a step-father
i howa yagini ndo
you are not from a step-father
libu howa agali mbira igini
you two are the sons of one man
wali mbira igini
the sons of one woman
ogo dagua ogo   (*Table 1* : 1c)
it is just this.
120   *ai anga irane bi*
The trunks of the pandanus
tamu gumu bi

the old garden sites
e emberabi
the fallow garden plots
ai agua keba i ogo ha harudagoni
how you have stayed you should stay
ina agali maru kemaru agua laga
we men who are here used to say like this.   (*Table 1* : 2d)
*Amugua mbirago ibu anga amugua mbirali ibu gini bialu holebira ani bialu
e o biagoni ha bialu holebira*
Over there where the nuts are when he has cleared it he will stay
anda gumu nu biagoni wa bialu holebira
on that old house site he will dig and stay
O agi mbirago ibu amu haruagoni?
why has he been staying there?
ogo dagua bialu lalu piaga kama   (*Table 1* : 1c)
to say it has been done like this we are staying.
ai libugua howa laribigo lalu ogo hangu lalu hebi
140   What you two have been talking on is only this
laribigo lalu
what you have said, it is said
anga irane bi
⎡ the trunk of the pandanus   ⎤
  e embera ogobi
  this fallow site
  mabu gumuni bi
  on the garden spaces
  tamu gumuni bi
⎣ the old house sites   ⎦
libugua lai bi ogo dagua hangu lalu hebi   (*Table 1* : 1c)
you two have made an argument like this
ogo dagua hangu lalu hebigo howa kagua laribi ayu ogo
From when it was said like this you said bad things like it is now.
. . .

MALIYAGO: The coffee that you have planted over there you are not going to
plant. You are ⎡ not going to plant.
KABO: ⎣ I am saying a little something (*ina mbira emene larogo*),
listen. That is where Ngiya's father has been staying. You two have been
staying there. Now one of you wants to plant coffee. 'Throw it away' you
160   (Maliyago) have said like that. How did you get the land on that side?
MALIYAGO: Over there my father and myself we stayed. Now Kakaye and
myself have made a garden at Gambogoba. Ngiya, he has got gardens and
born children there, that is his old site over there. . . . Where our father
and mother were is at Daiyebi. You wanted to take Kakaye's house out and
stay on the land yourself, you said. You have said Galoma Balu, but you are
not going to talk for that one; Kakaye is staying there with his wife and
children. You plant your garden at Daiyebi where there is pitpit. I am
staying at Wali Wano brother (*hambi*).
HELAGO: Brother, I am staying at Wali Wano.

MALIYAGO: I am staying at Wali Wano =
HELAGO: = No, I am staying there.
MALIYAGO: If it is like that then the coffee that you have planted, and the
water you have carried for that, and the casuarina that is there – the day
after tomorrow I will cut them.
HELAGO: When you say like that brother (*hambi*) I am happy [the
implication is that his brother's tendency to violence will be displayed for all
to see].
AGO: Who planted the tree?
HELAGO: Maliyago.
TIMURIA: Men, in your hearts and mind the anger will persist
180   'How will it be done' you are saying?
You are talking for the casuarina tree?
'Our father's garden I planted
with this casuarina and this flower'
'Pay me' are you talking to say that?
On what do you keep talking?
bi ogoni tiga tiga laga bulene ngagoni
the doing of a straight talk that we used to say is there.
(i.e. we can make a good talk on these)
HELAGO: Where our mother and father sat you have cut yourself off and gone
⌈ the garden sites you have thrown away ⌉
| the nuts you have thrown away |
| the old house sites you have thrown away |
⌊ everything you have thrown away ⌋
you shouldn't jump into Kemo [i.e. commit suicide].
Brother (*hambi*), you say a different thing.
MALIYAGO: Our mother and father sat over there.
Over there 'You sit Kakaye' I said.
For Ngiya his land is on that side at Daiyebi.
'I am going to cut Kakaye's house' you said.

. . .

200   You were throwing all the lands away.
If you make a fence where our father has been and want to stay with
another there, then stay.
If I hold it and then make a fence I will stay with the person I want.
MALIYAGO: If you say like that then you give it all to another's son, cut the
casuarina there, make a drain for your sister's sons, plant your own
casuarina trees =
HELAGO: You listen, you think of what I am saying, ⌈ your mother's
MALIYAGO: ⌊ Casuarina, you ⌈ will
HELAGO: ⌊ No,
wait, you are interrupting =
MALIYAGO: = The casuarina, the nuts ⌈ where your feet have been
HELAGO: ⌊ Ai you are Iba Tiri, you wait.
MALIYAGO: You saw the nuts and the casuarina but you will stay at Dera
brother (*hambi*).

UGUBUGU: A man's talk ⌈won't
HELAGO: ⌊I am saying something, you listen. We have been
pointing our fingers like the cassowary's claws, brother (*hambi*). Where you
have been cooking I won't see. I never think to go back to my mother's
land. I am staying here. Another man will be staying there. Now you are
220   talking for how it will be in the afternoon. You say for how it will be later.
MALIYAGO: I don't know.
HELAGO: You are holding it in.
MALIYAGO: You are holding it in.
TIMURIA: All these talks you are making, here, there, over there they are
clearing everything away
those ones you have said, leave them.
'Brother, you have planted the coffee' for that one and who will plant, you
talk.
All the talks you have made, it is like a flame burning everything
When you have done all these things then
'Brother, did I plant where you had planted? You can't take the tree out
and sell it for money, so I will give a little money' (you should say
something like this).
MALIYAGO: That casuarina is there so you are not just going to plant.
TIMURIA: 'Pay some' it has been said like that.
HELAGO: You should show me where I can plant, I am saying. I am carrying
coffee seeds.
MALIYAGO: I planted the medicine (*marasin*: pidgin) for the land I am
saying.
HELAGO: You show me the old house sites where I can plant.
240   MALIYAGO: Which house site? The one you have stayed on.
HELAGO: Where you have stayed, that one.
MALIYAGO: Where you have stayed.
TIMURIA: 'How about you, how about you'; that has been said. When you
two talk like this you are making the situation bad. You talk on what you
should do now. 'I'll plant the coffee' or 'for that tree I'll give a little
money' or 'we will do it like this'.
HELAGO: I haven't got money like him. He walks around Komo and
Kundu, I am a poor man.
MALIYAGO: We are from one man and from one woman.
We have made an enormous quarrel here.
You will plant on that land so give me 10 Kina for the garden medicine and
I will just come to pick the nuts.
KABO: Helago, you give 6 Kina or 8 Kina for the casuarina I am saying.
This is not for the land I am saying.
The casuarina that he planted it can't be cut down.
HELAGO: On land man used to stay and I have been staying. If I was staying
at all the places then you would see some money. Where my mother and
father have been staying there my navel cord is buried. You can't throw
that one away. While I have been there he has made it bad.

. . .

260   HELAGO: It is like that. When one man is angry there then the talk will be said I am saying.

UGUBUGU: What anger?

Now you two have been talking about nothing.

But you two keep on tying it up there.

Are you two doing this to have a talk about some secret debt?

We are looking carefully here (*de pea ho bedama*).

It is not for the casuarina over there.

There is one issue (*te*) there.

There is one bone (*kuni*) being held there.

You are talking on some debt from before, we are saying (*larama*).

MALIYAGO: All right (*ogoni*), for planting ⌈coffee

HELAGO: ⌊When I was up there they insulted (*mege*) me, I went out onto the public space (*nomani*). Those things should be said now. It is sleeping in his heart. I threw it away and went. They were testing me to see if I had money or pigs. They insulted me like that. 'Give', he is saying. Why is he making that talk? He should throw it away. I am not going to get sore from this (*i dere nabule*). This is what we will do. For throwing the matter away it is fine (*karulape*). I am finding a land to plant coffee. To say truthfully I should pay 10 Kina for this did you

280   make a talk? Are you insulting me like the others did? Did you talk to insult me (*i mege bulenaga lowa laribe*)?

MALIYAGO: I planted that casuarina up there. The coffee that people plant does it ever just grow up by itself? It never does this. People plant Tabaya trees or casuarina trees as a medicine for the coffee. I made a drain there, I made a house there.

KABO: 'For planting the coffee which you have done I didn't hear you ask me. Why have you planted?' he has said.

Can you throw it away? I have said once already.

MALIYAGO: I am not going to throw it away. You pay for the old house site and the gardens. If you want to plant the coffee then pay or else throw it away and go.

        . . .

KABO: Helago, you make only one talk and go away. We middle-men who are here are going to say the talk.

Did you plant the coffee?

Did you make the garden?

We are here.

When you plant coffee in your own garden sometimes accidentally (*mememe*) it will grow . . .

'You go and plant coffee in your own garden', that is the source of this war

300   (*wai tene*).

'You throw it away' we are going to say like this.

No.

Maliyago, did you throw it away? . . .

Your brother is going to fetch firewood for you when you are sick

You will see your brother's face

Let him plant the coffee there
Can you throw it away we are saying?
MALIYAGO: We are sitting in Ialuba and there won't be a landslide [i.e. the talks won't wash things away].
That sister over there and that man, when they die I won't see their graves.
Those two will poison me, I should say like that.
EGARI: Maliyago up there has said he is the eldest
'I am the head'
Homa's other son you are the tail.
Anege over there, 'You are the tail' he has said
he is saying like that I am saying.
No, when you two are talking you are saying only this the whole time.
One small thing is a male pig there which in your heart you are covering
320   over (*dambia kego*)
That one tell him, we are saying.
It is like this in his mind
money, male pig or money, 'You give me'
something like this you have done
he is finding something there.

⎡ On his nuts ⎤
⎢ On his trees ⎥
⎢ On his figs ⎥
⎣ On his gardens ⎦

When it is like this then he will hit you
thus it has been said (*ani lene*).
In his mind the talk is sitting there
from one mother, from one women, the oldest and the youngest are both children.
On the old house site you are not going to jump (take over)
On the pandanus you are not going to jump
On the gardens you are not going to jump
the source (*tene*) like this we are saying.
'You are the youngest', are you saying like this?
340   'You are another woman's son' are you saying this?
No, in his heart a little anger is sleeping?
Why it is there we will see?
To see you choose, we men are here.
You two talk.
UGUBUGU: You are saying truly (*henene lare*).
TIMURIA: You say it out. You are a little angry it has been said. Say it out.

(Maliyago expounds the bad relations between himself and Anege, Ngiya and Helago)

. . .

EGARI: If you have done like that then I have talked so you may share the talk.
Why are you holding the talks?
Do you want to eat man's bones?
One source (*tene*) is they made you angry up there [i.e. before]

Your ribs were hit [i.e. you were made angry].
The source that was done, how was it done?
We are now talking from there.
Like those talks you should have talked.
Why are you wrapping it up?
Did you want to make us talk or why are you talking?
You are not holding any talk.
You are like an Iba Tiri.
Did you think like that or what?
360   You should have said 'Let's talk'
'The old garden and house site I am having myself'
'It is not nothing I am doing' [i.e. I am doing something with it]
'That is the reason I am doing the garden' (you should have said these).
We are not talking for whether your mothers were sisters or your fathers
were brothers.
You two are from one women and man.
So how did you do what you have done?
When you have said 'I was angry because of that' then you have made one
talk
Like that to say I have said (*au lowa laru*).
MALIYAGO: I planted the casuarina like a medicine. You plant the coffee
and pay me for the casuarina.
EGELE: We used to share the talks. We middle men used to speak.
The first time there 'I am going (you said). When you two (Anege and
Helago) are dying I won't see your face.'
You two did that and scattered.
One source like that you have talked on.
Truly we are the middle men so
We have said like that, let's talk to say it.

. . .

HAYABE: One pig has been eaten and gone up there
380   It has been looked after and then eaten [this statement is based on
knowledge of a previous argument between Maliyago and Helago].
Pila, was it you?
Anege, was it you?
Helago, was it you?
They haven't chosen (*daba*) now
These talks choose!
When you have chosen then with pigs or money we will see.
HELAGO: We are saying for those ones make a straight talk.
You are hiding these talks.
HAYABE: We are saying a straight talk. There was some money up there,
and you have eaten it. There was a pig there and you have eaten it. The
ones that are born here are going to stay on these lands. Anege has married
and borne children; you have married and borne children; Nigiya has
married too. All these will stay on the land. From the coffee that you
planted trouble [*daraboli*: pidgin] is coming out here. What is the source?

In your heart there is a pig which has been looked after and eaten; or there is some money which has been used. You choose the sources (*tene ogo daba daba*). To do like that I am saying.

KABO: *Ai ore baya gibi laya haria tai bialu wirimago uduguni*

400   He has said a very good talk, the track (for the talk) we are searching for is there.

MALIYAGO: Our mother's and father's land boundary is up there at Wali Wano.

'You pay for my casuarina' I have said, then you can plant the coffee.
Anege planted a nut there and that is where you have made a garden.
I am not going to 'Go'. Helago has come there; Ngiya too he had planted at Wali Wano. I was going to plant there but I saw you two had made a garden.
Where Helago's garden is O I am staying
Where Ngiya's garden is I am staying
Where Helago is and my casuarina I am staying
On Ngiya's side I am staying where I have nut trees
The casuarina trees are mine
The pandanus are mine
Our father's fig trees are there.

HELAGO: Are you making *malu* to us?

MALIYAGO: The old garden is there so if you want to plant coffee you plant it. Pay for my casuarina. Give me 10 Kina for the work that I have done.

(Egari then introduces the topic, already alluded to previously, of Maliyago's pigs. These were received from a bride-wealth and given to Anege to look after for him. Anege and Pila then used these for a further transaction of their own which angered Maliyago. His claim is that one of these had been pregnant and he had never received due restitution. He implicates Helago in the conspiracy)

MALIYAGO: You men have heard that Pila made a business [pidgin] out of my two pigs. I was at Wabia and I came so that you could share the pigs for

420   Yalibi's marriage. I had two pigs up there. What did you do with the two pigs? Did you use it in some marriage? I said like that and I went.

KABO: Those two pigs he has talked on, I know about them. You all haven't heard the talk. Those two pigs were given from Yalibi's marriage. When he came to get them, after they had been looked after for him, he saw they had been used. 'We have left two others' Pila said like that. One of those you carried off and sold for money, and another you sold for money.

MALIYAGO: For one pig he gave me 20 Kina; the other pig had piglets and it is up there.

haru ibalimu cope ti hongole
bring the pig if you want to plant the coffee
naibiriyagua hendeni i naibulebere
if it doesn't come then you won't come
larogoni hangu
that is all I am saying.

(Pause of two seconds)

Who used to marry with my pigs?
You are covering over my pigs.
We have talked for you to talk.
Truly, for the coffee you pay 10 Kina I have said.

    (Helago then gives an explanation of the events surrounding these pigs
    and his non-involvement in the decisions concerning them)
    . . .

HELAGO: You are making the talk come out onto the public space and are
440   carrying it everywhere
You are not going to say 'No' to a friend who is staying there
You are not going to say 'Go'
All the children are down there
Your sister is down there
You have talked on the public space so with whom are you arguing?
One of your pigs is there and another I will go and see about
You have been scattering the talks on the public space.
You wait (*hondo habe*).
Brother (*hambi*), I am giving you 20 Kina.
One pig I am looking after for you, I am saying.
'You are betraying me' you have said.
You are lying.
MALIYAGO: ⌈ *i mbalinigo libu libu* ⌉
      | my sister and those two |
      | *i mbalinigo ila libu* |
      ⌊ your sister and yourself ⌋
      Debene eda ka
      ⌈ Debene is staying there ⌉
      ⌊ *Dabeda ede ka* ⌋
460   Dabeda is staying there
      i ke hongoria holebira
      ⌈ You will stay where you have been planting ⌉
      | *i ko hengoria naholebira* |
      ⌊ Where I have been planting you won't stay ⌋
      ogoni hangu
      that's all.
HELAGO: I'm staying over there at Embo [land occupied by Maliyago's
friends].
MALIYAGO: You won't stay at Embo.
HELAGO: I will stay at Embo.
MALIYAGO: You won't stay there.
HAYABE: What was in Maliyago's heart he has said out. When Pila comes
we can straighten it out.
KABO: The talk we men have been saying
One track is the coffee and the casuarina tree.
The pigs, they are one track
The pig debts (*nogo kango*) the piglets and how you have looked after them,
with your affines (*imane balibu*) and your agnates (*aba hamene*: fathers and

brothers), those should be chosen. The pigs are one track. The ones we have talked on, the coffee, then you, Helago and us, we are here. We will ask
480   how the pigs were looked after and what you did. Let us talk for the coffee now.
'For the coffee, you plant' (are you saying that?)
'No, we will choose the pigs first so leave the issue of the planting'
Say a clear talk (*i bi mbira minibi la handa*).
EGARI: No, Homa's son you share the talk (*tale bia*).
It is getting dark now.
For the tree give 8 Kina or something; or
No, 'I am throwing it away, I will plant on my own land' (say this) it has been said like that (*ani lalu*).
Homa igini ini i habane ha tagira porago tale bia laro
Homa's son, what is in your heart is coming out, share it I am saying.
. . .

HELAGO: Two days ago a talk was said on boys and girls, *tene* and *yamuwini* [refers to an incident in which Kakaye and others made remarks about the land ownership status of Helago].
They will make an insult and that is what was done
When that talk had been made we said 'You come, let's talk' (about the insult).
When that had been said then boys and girls, *tene* and *yamuwini* went outside [i.e. wasn't discussed]
For the insult that was done we are talking. . . .

> (The final fifteen minutes reverted back to the issue of Helago's payment to Maliyago for use of the land. Helago kept insisting that Maliyago indicate the places where he could plant his coffee. The final exchange was as follows)

HELAGO: Where my father's spirit is, Kakaye is staying I am saying.
500   When I think of it my heart is not clear.
MALIYAGO: I am going
The day after tomorrow the coffee will be planted
'So what are you going to do' we are saying?

D.2 contrasts with D.1 with regard to the organization of talk, theme, and structure of claim presentation. This difference in expectations about appropriate speech, which recognizes *malu* to be contextually circumscribed to disputes between sub-clans or clans, underlies the censorial responses of Helago: 'Are you making *mana* to me?' (31); 'Are you making *malu* to us?' (415). Importantly, the Huli talk about land less in terms of an abstract concept of 'ownership' (-*naga*), than residence mode – where people have been 'staying' (*hene*): 'How will we stay?' (52); 'Over there my father and myself we stayed' (161). This reflects the discretionary areas of property division whereby an inheritance is for the communal use of descendants. The claims of

D.2 are less about land ownership than land use, grants of land use, and land improvement associated with trees (7), houses (285), and drains (285). Disputes arise between agnates on account of the ill-defined nature of the tenurial system in respect of procedures for equitable division. Maliyago's citation of parallel brother-sets – an analogy for a *modus vivendi* in D.2 (57–60) – stresses the notion that claims to land are based on patterns of use. Nevertheless, where a person is perceived to have 'thrown away' (90–93) land, others may activate their corporate rights to use. Divisions of land employment and residence do not entail an alienation or abrogation of the claims of others. In this respect, appeals to the norms governing kin relations do not impinge on the specific issues relating to usufruct. The recurrent motif of shared substance between the brothers (i.e. 'one blood': see Chapter 3) that typifies the speeches of litigants (42–4; 46–51; 249) and mediators (109–17; 364–67), is oriented towards the general maxims that 'brothers should stay on the land together', and 'brothers should not fight'. While defining the situation in such terms may function to delimit and de-escalate the repercussions of the argument, or indeed to urge the disputants to come to an amicable agreement, they do not provide a clearly defined set of rules concerning the justifiability of any claim for a situation such as D.2. In addition to the more explicit formulations, such as 'We are from one woman and one man / We have made an enormous quarrel here' (249–50), oblique allusions to the above norms are communicated through the rhetorical switching from the kin term *hamene* (B) to the alternative form *hambi / hambiya* (64; 168; 175; 214; 449). *Hambi* has a greater degree of affective import than *hamene* and is thus particularly suited to conveying sarcasm. Uses of the term in D.2 imply a hiatus between ideal and actual behaviour associated with people in the relationship of 'brother'.

In line with the differences in unit opposition between D.1 and D.2, the order of turn-taking is not governed by pre-allocational rules about the relative status of opposing litigants. The selection of speakers is ordered on a turn-by-turn basis which, for the most part, involves self-selection procedures. This system is characterized here by the presence of some of those turn-taking gambits delineated in *Table 1* : 4a–e (which are noticeably absent from D.1). We may note here, and elsewhere[6], the recurrence of such stereotype claiming devices as:

(I want / am taking this turn: first starter)
Ina mbira emene larogo
I am saying a little something   (157)

and the frequent occurrence of interruption and repair sequences as found in lines 209–12. These support observations made in Chapter 2 regarding the applicability of the conversational maxim of 'one speaker at a time' in Huli debates. While this system theoretically maximizes participant opportunity (in contrast to the 'closed' nature of D.1), the dispute transcripts show that talking tends to be restricted to a sub-set of speakers from a potential pool that may often number twenty or more. Given the axiomatic norm of 'sharing the talk' and an impersonally constituted participant category of 'middle-man', this feature of dispute talk is problematic. Moreover, the operational bias that the previous speaker is likely to be the next speaker in multi-party situations (see Sacks, Schegloff, and Jefferson 1974) is unlikely to apply over the whole of any talk where, as one observes, the close ordering mechanisms of question-answer etc. have limited occurrence. Part of the solution lies in the organizational tasks of dispute talk as clarified and announced by participants. As I shall show below, the commitment code of mediators is structured around the presentation of options and possible outcomes, which are directed back to the litigants for consideration and selection. The objectives are to persuade disputants to engineer an outcome by themselves. The corollary of this is that D.2 appears to divide into units of interchange between Helago-Maliyago which are bounded and interspersed (in ways defined later) by third-party contributions. This triadic model of talk appears to limit turn incumbents to particular points in a stream of talk. Importantly, this model is one that participants are continually orienting to, and displaying to each other, in their verbal interaction: 'Did the middle-men used to speak or did just you two speak?/Not that just two people spoke' (106–07).

Although the order of turns in D.2 and most other Huli disputes is not preset for the whole debate, there is a high probability that third parties will identify themselves as 'middle-men' when taking a turn, either explicitly or implicitly through the design of their turns. In doing this, speakers achieve a measure of immunity to accusations of bias, because the code of mediation delimits areas of personal commitment. That is, for a speech to communicate its character as 'mediatory' it has to be structured in accordance with the expectations of participants. The function of gambits in this process is, as noted previously, to frame semantically the component propositions so that this information is conveyed. Since gambits are responses to the recurrent problems of certain speech situations, and have conventional and routinized status, an inventory of such devices in any situation is likely to reveal the essence of the dispute-settlement process. In addition to the structural arguments forwarded concerning the relation between the semantic weighting of claims and their positional incidence, attention to talk in disputes can provide important insights into how language behaviour affects outcomes.

In relating the above observations to the text under discussion, one major contrast between Huli arbitrators and Western court 'examiners' is the way in which the former compound formulated questions in one turn. Instead of small dialogic units of question-response, speeches are delivered for attention as complete packages. This is consistent with a marked tendency to avoid claim decisions or blame allocation:

'Pila, was it you?	'What is the source?
Anege, was it you?	. . . there is a pig . . .
Helago, was it you? . . .	. . . or there is some money . . .
These talks choose' (382–85)	*You choose the sources*' (395–97)

$$\begin{bmatrix} \text{Plan for Future Talk} \\ \text{Choice: } Table\ 1 : 3d. \end{bmatrix}$$

In these two selections, which are a typical component of mediators' turns (see also 361–63; 180–84; 230–32; 132–38; 339–42), we see again how questions are posed and options presented as a suggested plan for talk; a prestructuring of topic direction. In each case these units are finalized by a verbally signalled Plan or Choice gambit (366; 185; 233; 344). The imperative is invariably used to exhort litigants to 'speak' according to a proposed range of issues, rather than an attempt to impose single option decisions. It is in this environment that speakers are most likely to state that they are issuing the command:

'To do like that I am saying.' (398) ⎫
'Like that to say I have said.' (369) ⎬ *Table 1* : 3c

Oratorical prestige is thus gained through skill at composing the paradigmatic option sets; the assertion that a Huli mediator makes is, from an etic standpoint, one of qualified commitment to judgment.

This circumscription of 'I-speech' can be set against a tendency to use the impersonal 'we' in gambits that have a retrospective character.

'The talk we men have been saying.' (473) ⎫
'To say it has been done like this we are saying.' (138) ⎬ *Table 1* : 1c

or where mediation is defined as that which was customarily said or done:

'We men who are here used to say like this.' (129)
'We used to share the talks
We middle-men used to speak . . .   } *Table 1* : 2d'
Truly we are the middle-men
We have said like that.' (372–78; see also 186–87)

This is one aspect of the security offered by the mediation code. The occurrence of impersonal pronouns is particularly evident in the gambits listed under 1c; 2d; 3a, b, c in *Table 1*. Significantly, where outcome proposals (rather than plans for future talk) are crystallized, speakers can diminish personal responsibility by reporting the suggested options as the talk of a collective and impersonal body. There is a referential indeterminancy concerning the outcome proposer:

'For the tree give 8 Kina or something; or
No, "I am throwing it away, I will plant on my own land"
It has been said like that (*ani lalu*).' (487–89)

Egari's speech (106–54) is a good example of how many of these features cohere in a text that is patterned by parallel repetition, and that displays a topic syntax consistent with structures elicited in Chapters 2 and 5. The prefacing statements (106–09) identify the capacity in which the speech is made (see also 372) using a confrontative rhetorical question. This is followed by a statement of relationship that invokes the morality of 'one substance' people (110–17) which, in turn, is followed by an oblique reference to residence patterns (120–27). A set of possible 'talks' is formulated (130–38) that gives way to a pronouncement of the bases of the dispute. Each topic is bounded and separated from the next by a gambit that provides a gloss on the preceding statements, and communicates the sense in which they are to be understood. As with many of the mediation speeches examined in this book, there is a noticeable prevalence of binary or quadripartite structures (110–17; 143–50; 190–93; 126–29) that can be accounted for in terms of embedded contrasts:

'You two are the sons of one man   'Debene is staying there
the sons of one woman.' (114–17)   Dabeda is staying there.' (457–60)

the practice of counter-balancing some statement by a negative:

'You will stay where you have been planting
Where I have been planting you won't stay.'   (461–64)

the tendency to pair names that have a similar sound (a marked feature of enumerative lists in Huli):

mabu gumuni bi
tamu gumuni bi   (147–50)

and the context-specific factors such as the need to present alternatives and to address oneself to the 'two sources' of any dispute:

'You are not from a step-father
You are not from a step-father.'   (110–13)

What is evident from the above data is the sense in which the gambit framework outlined in Chapter 2 functions to structure the flow of any mediation performance. These types of parenthetic modulation mark the interfaces between topic formulations in a way that is 'recipiently designed' (Atkinson and Drew 1979 : 92) for participants to acknowledge and accept the speech as one of mediation.[8]

In so far as we may talk then of mediation routines, there does appear to be some correlation between the occurrence of specific types of anger / insult exchanges, and the intervention of middle-men. That is, mediation speeches tend to occur where litigants have just previously been involved in some verbal duel. One characteristic of such exchanges is the repetition by both parties of the same statement, but redirected back to the opponent:

'HELAGO: Where you have stayed
MALIYAGO: Where you have stayed.'   (241–42)

One notices that after each occurrence of this in D.2 (92–3; 69–71; 169–171; 222–23; 241–42; 467–70) third parties take a turn, in recognition of the litigants' intractable positions. Moreover, an intervention that formulates a plan for future talk frequently engenders an increased activity of mediation by other candidate middle-men so that it is not uncommon for several such speeches to be made close to each other. Talking in disputes is too flexible to admit of an invariable structural pattern, but these tendencies do reflect the competition for prestige and renown that 'good talking' can bestow on an individual.

When we examine the derivation of those outcome options presented to Maliyago and Helago – that some payment is made for the agronomic value of the casuarina, or that Maliyago will take the land for himself – it is clear that they merely reiterate the announcements and intentions of Maliyago. They do not appear to come from norms or rules, but are oriented to litigants' interests. In those instances where a plan of action is precisely stated in terms of a single act (e.g. Kabo: 253–55), the low level of decision commitment is evident from the vacillation back towards a choice-presenting frame:

'You threw it away, we are going to say like this.
No.
Maliyago, did you throw it away?
Let him plant the coffee there
Can you throw it away we are saying?'   (300–07; see also 480–84)

This further option of 'throwing away' – of claim renouncement – is one of the most persistently used strategies in Huli disputes. Its status as a recognizable and distinctive gambit (see *Table 1* : 3a; 277–78; 288; 307) reflects a social system in which such actions are valued for their tendency to inhibit protracted talk and possible violence. Litigants may refer to past acts of renouncement as a form of self-crediting: 'I threw it away and went' (274). I shall return to this type of outcome plan in my discussion of D.3, so that it is sufficient here for me to indicate that in domestic disputes option sets always include claim renouncement.

The development of claims in D.2 directly reflects the dispute-resolution model described in my introduction, whereby 'ultimate sources, reasons, or responsible parties' (*tene*) are sought. Mediators are aware that disputants often manipulate claims in their profiles so as to allow more deep-seated grievances to emerge slowly once a 'state of play' has been reached. The activity of identifying *tene* is frequently indexed by the utilization of locative terms (see Chapter 5) which are used to place claims in a rank order according to their degree of causal primacy. Mediators expect disputants to 'hide talk' and thus exhort them to 'say it out' (346). Ugubugu's contribution (262–70) gives an indication of how such verbal routines tend to occur following the full airing of the initial claims. There is a presupposition that talk is held back: 'Why are you holding these talks? Why are you wrapping it up?' (348–55). These types of speech are marked by topic evaluation gambits (*Table 1* : 1e: 300; 338; 269). The subsequent development of claims surrounding various transfers of pigs confirms the routine's applicability in the case. Where the web of multiple-claims inhibits the resolution of any one issue, mediators will attempt to separate and sift 'real' from 'superficial' claims. It is highly significant, in the context of hypotheses forwarded in this book, that a claim of insult (*mege*) has priority in the profile of Helago. The first allusion to a normative breach (62–3) is perhaps no more than a passing reference. As the conversation progresses, an explicit claim is made (272–81) that is ratified by Egari as a relevant issue: 'One source (*tene*) is that they made you angry up there/Your ribs were hit / The source that was done, how was it done?' (350–52).

The issue of how and why insult claims are central to an understanding of all Huli disputes is one that I attend to in my analysis of D.3. But there are two other themes relating to D.2 that deserve comment. First, it is evident that the language for evaluating, reporting, and talking about talk is firmly fixed on the substantive discriminations of *bi* (talk). One notices the absence of confrontational categories associated with Western incriminatory procedures. What was said is given in the direct object position. There are no metalinguistic lexemes referring to the interactional moves of defence, examination, or judgement. Second, Helago's criticism of Maliyago in lines 439–45 highlights an earlier argument concerning matters appropriate for 'public' and 'private' spaces. This environmental categorization is a central feature of D.3.⁹ While it is not a land dispute, I have chosen to incorporate this case because it illuminates the themes discussed above and allows us to concentrate more specifically on how litigants handle themselves in situations of blame allocation. The talking occurred immediately following the incident of insult.

Dispute 3

Issue: Claim arising from 'insult' (*mege*) when Walumbu laughed behind the back of her brother Egeria.
Disputants: Walumbu,
          Egeria (both of Koma clan).
Others: Hega, Kabo – Pina clan
          Egari, Dalu – Koma clan.
Date: May 1977.
Location: Ialuba.
Outcome: Claim for compensation renounced by Egeria.

1   HEGA: The talk was spread on the road and that is why he became angry and hit you.
In the middle of the road over there.
It was like that and he hit you [*bayadagonigo*: visible evidence suffix (*da*) + intensifier (*gonigo*)].
          ⌈It was done like that
WALUMBU: ⌊Yes, it was done like that =
HEGA: (inaudible utterance) =
WALUMBU: I don't want to talk on this. The man is here and he will do it.

I am throwing it away and going off.
This is what I am saying. Did I used to say bad things?
HEGA: Concerning the hitting =
WALUMBU: The hitting has been done. I am alone.
My breast has been eaten by a dog. My son is dead.
HEGA: O, no. You didn't hear my talk and you are talking on.
Are you going to give shame compensation (*taga abi muleberebe?*)
WALUMBU: If he asks for it then I'll give it.
If he wants it he will say.
20   The other women were behind me so if he asks for it we will all give pig.
HEGA: If these other women are going to give pig then you will give
If they don't give (statement not completed: two-second pause) a *mana* has
been said and he hit you. Egeria is over there.
'Throw it away?' Shall we say that (*wa ha loleberemebe?*)?
Will you throw it away?
EGERIA: If they say they laughed and tell us the reason (*tene*), then we will
say 'throw it away'.
HEGA: O wait. The *mana* that was said in the morning, ⌈O
EGERIA: ⌊There was one woman
at first, and then many women went that way. They laughed and I went
where there was no track, I have said. You think of that.
WALUMBU: They were laughing, it was not my mind (*i mini nawi*). I was
going straight home but they came and laughed. This is why we are having
this   ⌈talk.
HEGA: | No
KABO: ⌊Aba, to let me speak you wait.
The source Ibai's father (Hega) has said.
When someone makes a joke and you laugh like a frog, as has happened,
then there is the source of the talk =
40   WALUMBU: = Those other women were behind me =
KABO: = Those people laughed at what you were saying.
The source was from what you said, and they laughed.
The ones that were behind him they laughed (*-da*: we can see)
That is how it was done
That man, when they had laughed,
'What did I say? Not knowing I went where there was no track' he is saying
(*-rua*: we can hear).
They were talking about the flood and then they laughed.
The sister wanted to make a joke and they ⌈laughed.
WALUMBU: ⌊Yes. I was making a small joke
about nothing (*yamo tabirene*), but they came behind me and laughed.
KABO: ⌈Laugh . . .
HELAGO: ⌊An important talk was told to you this morning. There were
many of you on that track and he was telling a *mana* [i.e. what to do with
the pigs when a flood comes to Ialuba].
WALUMBU: He was telling a *mana* about the pigs.
HEGA: Yes, you talked like that. He was angry and he hit you. If someone
hits you they mean to kill you.

WALUMBU: He felt sympathy (o *are laya*).

60 HEGA: You are his sister and he felt sympathy for you.

KABO: O, well then (*O karulape*)

The village court and others that are down there, they are not going to say (talk on this dispute).

We are here now [i.e. we are going to talk about this issue].

'The ones that were behind laughed and I ate shame (*taga pani nedo*)

For that you pay.

I am angry.'

For the anger, for the talk, we are here to talk.

EGERIA: When all the women that were behind come we will talk about the daughter and how I got sore (*dere*). It is said you can't laugh. No, it is not as if I was a bad and smelly man. When you have told why you laughed then I will throw it away.

KABO: I'm saying what I have said. This is what you have said – 'The source (*tene*) is the sister.' They laughed and you were on the shame (*tagani*), came back, and hit your sister.

Can you throw it away?

Nothing has happened?

For saying like that we are talking (*au lole naga laramagoni*).

EGERIA: You say ⌈I

80 KABO: ⌊Wait (*hondo habe*), there is a small space (*are emene*) and we can settle this. The women are there and they know the reason for laughing and can tell ⌈us

WALUMBU: ⌊I was just coming (*yamo ebere*) and they laughed, so if you want it carried [if you want compensation], if you want to throw it away, we will see.

KABO: 'The sister is the source of this' he has said. 'The others laughed at what she said.' If you say 'Pay' then do we collect from your sister or all the ones that laughed?

EGERIA: I had no track to go on and I made my own. They must say the reason they laughed. Tell the others to come here.

HEGA: No. For laughing a *mana* has been placed (*oba naga mana wiyadagoni*) and is there. Ibili's son (Egeria), 'Your leg will be cut off' (the flood will injure you) he said.

O bi oba ti oba ha : : *yada*

O they laughed at that talk [*da*: evidence suffix]

bi tene ni biagoria howa wali naigo ba : : *yadago*

the source was from there and he hit that woman

O wa hamabe au lowa larama

we said 'Can we throw it away?' we are saying.

100 EGERIA: You can't laugh. If they say throw it away then we are going to throw it away. When that is said where will you go?

HEGA: Now you two are arguing (*lai*) there. But there is something that can finish this off =

WALUMBU: = Nothing, throw it away. You are staying amongst the pitpit (*i gambe te ha*: you are confused). You are saying a little and leaving some of the talk for later.

EGERIA: The women that laughed behind you have gone now. The argument =

WALUMBU: = They are not my friends (*ina nenege ndo*). They are your brothers and sisters, your mothers, your sister-in-law =

HEGA: = No, the source (*tene*) of the laughing, ⌈you

WALUMBU: ⌊I was talking and they started to

HEGA: On that one, is that what you were talking about, or were you thinking of the *mana*?

WALUMBU: That is what I was saying and the ones behind me laughed.

EGERIA: It was said like that. I had no track and I broke through. They continued to laugh and only stopped when they came to Waiyabe's fence. I bent down, held my neck, and went into the pitpit.

HEGA: Did they talk about something, or what is the reason they laughed?

120 EGERIA: They just kept laughing and I went.

WALUMBU: That is what I said. They were behind and ⌈laughing

HEGA: ⌊No. The start was like this. 'When the flood comes it is going to cut off your legs'; you were saying this?

WALUMBU: That is true. We were talking about the leg being cut off [i.e. flood damage]. We weren't talking about a second or third thing. I was talking near my home and they came and laughed.

EGERIA: Enough. There were seven women there. I am throwing it away. We will see if there is a *mana* for this laughing [implied threat to go to an official court in Koroba].

EGARI: All of you pay 50 toya each and give it to him.

WALUMBU: Not 50 toya. We will pay 2 Kina!

HEGA: It doesn't matter if you give 10 Kina, there is a big *mana* there for laughing.

WALUMBU: All the talk is on the side of the man (*uruni agali naga dege la haga*).

KUMURIA: You are making a bad talk, throw it away.

WALUMBU: It is not me, it is you making a bad talk. The source is being covered (*mo yi hama*). We didn't insult (*la hirama*) you.

140 HEGA: No. Which is the source we are covering? The source we have talked on. Did another women talk there then? 'The legs will be cut off, the pigs will be led away' you said these things and we have seen this. We say *mana* and *gamu* for wild pigs and that man said this.

WALUMBU: Yes things were said like ⌈that

HEGA: ⌊The ropes ⌈and

WALUMBU: ⌊I am saying something, you wait and don't all talk at once, wait. He married two wives and one of them is there. His *kiane* (WZ) is there. 'The flood will cut off your legs' you said. My son is like dead, he has gone to coast. I was going to give sweet-potato to the pigs and I left my bag in the house. I called for the pigs and went.

HEGA: You have spread the talk on the road and it is not like water which can return and wash everything away =

WALUMBU: = There were many of us on the road. How could we insult

(*mege*) him? His female relatives (*ibu aninya mbalini damene*) were there I
am saying.

HEGA: This is now bad [-*rua*: sense perception suffix]
You brought the talk out from home (*andaga*) onto the cleared place
(*hamani*); for that *mana* that was said.
He should have hit you like that we have said
it was done like that (*au biyadago*).

160   When it was done then (*o biyadagonigo*).
'Will you throw it away?' No, we are saying
Will you give some money with these other women?
Your talk is still making it sore (*dere*).
Which track (direction) it will go, to say I am saying.

WALUMBU: If he asks to give then we will give.

EGERIA: We never used to just steal the things of people. For insult, 'Carry'
(have compensation) it is said. To rub on the sore (*i dere biago domole
naga*) I am going to carry. I am going to hear if you will give or not.

UGUBUGU: Those women and your sister they all laughed.

EGERIA: All seven of them laughed.

WALUMBU: You (Egeria) think you are in your house and you are insulting
me (*mege mege bi ale*) like you always used to do as if I was a lazy person.

EGERIA: ⌈The insult
KABO: | (inaudible start)
HEGA: ⌊Now I am saying something important, I'm saying an important
thing
With a sister or male relative (*aba hamene la*) we used to say bad words.
The talk is sleeping inside you

180   Not that it is not sleeping there.
It will come like water
Now you are tricking yourselves we have said
You both think of it.

EGERIA: She said 'You used to insult me', so what did I used to insult her
about?

HEGA: It will come like water. When it has come, the talk that is on this
track will be washed away like the things carried by a flood. When it is in
the middle of the water how can you retrieve it?

WALUMBU: Now I am ⌈saying
190   HEGA: ⌊You can't =

WALUMBU: = Stop, listen to me. Now I am saying how we came. When he
came we were talking about one pig given to me. That is a pig from
Degondo's daughter's marriage. You were looking for pig, you were
masturbating [*gida hinage*: idiomatic for 'searching for a pig']. My pig was
killed and given to them two days ago. He was looking for a pig for
homenego (funeral rites). 'I haven't any pig in my house so you go and look
in your own house' I said.

EGERIA: The pig which you gave half of to me I gave you 10 Kina for that.

KUMURIA: The talk you have said, this is the source (*bi ayu lenedago, tene
200   ogoni*). This is the source between you?

WALUMBU: When we talked of this, he hit me I have said.

KUMURIA: Can you understand this is like a war (*wai*)?
UGUBUGU: We are saying you can't say this.

(Several people start to talk at this point)

WALUMBU: If he asks then we will give. I won't have to look for this, I will
gave it.
OTHERS: ⌈(inaudible)
KUMURIA: ⌊(Wait (*hondo ha*)
Two or three people are there
We'll see those who laughed and why they laughed
What did that women say?
What did that man say?
What was the reason (*tene*) they laughed?
You'll see the women and then finish off on the laughing and then the
pigs.
Those two have argued (*lai*)
Don't talk too much (*bi anda habe naheago*)
We'll wait for the others to come outside
Throw it away.
EGERIA: Then tell those women to come.
220 EGARI: ⌈*O ala wali o ibini onebi*
First, that (one of the other women) woman is his wife
ibini onego labobi
there are two of his wives
wali ligubi
that women there (Egeria's sister)
ai ibini damene damene naigua biruagobi
⌊those are his relatives there
ai you didn't think of tying your pigs
we stayed so can you see the water coming now?
It is not good to ask only one woman for compensation.
WALUMBU: It is all of us =
EGARI: = Those women are at home and he told a *mana* there . . . the
mana has been said for all the women. He was talking about the water
coming when she made a joke.
WALUMBU: I was just joking =
EGARI: = You should go! What are you doing? Carry your pigs away, tie up
your chickens. He made a *mana* for women it has been said. He was just
walking and they were talking like this, I am saying. The ones behind there
put it into their minds and laughed.
240 WALUMBU: I was talking and this made them laugh =
EGARI: = When they laughed he got shame and went away.
WALUMBU: Then he returned and hit the mother of the dog [i.e. her son].
HEGA: We'll wait and hear why those three women laughed.
Did they laugh at that talk up there?
Or did they laugh at some other talk?
That is what we are saying.
EGARI: When Dalu comes and the other women have come then let's talk.

WALUMBU: Why should we go to court [i.e. in Koroba]? Those women were behind me and laughed at what I said.

EGARI: You won't give compensation by yourself
Your mouth is not their mouth
All of you will give 50 toya each

(Simultaneous conversations occur which are too indistinct on the tape-recorder to separate)

WALUMBU: (Probably in response to some comment by Egeria)
You are not an old rotten tree you are a young man
Now your skin is wrinkled a bit, tomorrow you will be an old man.

KABO: Rubbish is coming out of your ⌈mouth

WALUMBU: ⌊The young boys too are becoming like dust from an old tree =

KABO: = Listen (*o hale ha*) I am saying

⌈ We men here are not going to think about being men =

260   WALUMBU: │ = ⌈The men
       KABO: │   ⌊O wait (*hondo habe*)
                │   The women that are here are not going to think about being women
                │   The boys that are here are not going to think about being boys
                │   The girls that are here are not going to think about being girls ⌋ .

The talk that is coming out of your mouth (*hambu hege la*)
You are saying 'The skin is wrinkled up into a ball'
You are saying 'The eyes are close together'
You are saying 'That one is not well built (*ako hea lareru*)'
From this talk and that talk you will have a second court
This is the talk now going out from your mouths.
Not like this.
The source, Ibili's son (Egeria), 'The water will cut your leg off' he said like that
The others laughed at what was said
That is what we are saying [*au laruagoni*: -*rua*: sense perception evidence suffix].

WALUMBU: They laughed and he got shame and ran away.

KABO: No, what has been said I have said.
O that which was done, the source, they laughed at what you said?

280   Did you say something different and then they laughed?

WALUMBU: I don't know about any other talk.

DALU: Ai many talks have been said
I want to go but I'll make a little talk first
You are both with shame here
making sorrow (*darabi*)
You are one women
Second is you

A third is over there
You three laughed?
WALUMBU: One girl is here, one is not here, and one is Tomiabe's wife.
They were coming straight but when they saw this man's face, and we were
talking about the leg being cut off they laughed.
EGERIA: There were seven women there. They were laughing and I broke
into the pitpit and came to the road outside there.
WALUMBU: When women come then men used to leave the road. We saw
Egeria doing that I am saying.
DALU: You were talking about the flood and climbing the mountain, and
you said 'Man too will have their legs cut off'. Did you say this then?
Were the women talking to the man or the man to the women?
300   TANDAIYA: (One of the other women implicated by Egeria)
When the first flood came he said 'Go and make pig rope, make the pigs
calm'. Behind the house he was telling those women that the pigs and
children will have their legs cut off from the flood. All of us would see our
legs cut off. This was the first time he talked about the flood. I have
married his two wives. His mother Ogoda, his daughter and his sister-in-
law, I am not going to talk on these. I carried the sweet-potato for the pigs
in the morning and tied the pig up. Then I went down the mountain. I saw
these women and that man. 'The flood will cut off your legs', he said.
'Let's look after the pigs', I said. Then they laughed.
EGERIA: Those seven women laughed so was it because I had a sore (*dere*), or
I was smelly? You come and tell me, I am saying.
WALUMBU: They were the ones that laughed, we are saying (*au larama*).
DALU: When we think of it
agali naigumabi
that man there
ibu ainya mbalini labi
with his mother and his sister
ibu onebi
with his wife
320   *bi mbira laigume tagira pialu nalaga*
he never used to bring an argument talk outside
be laraliya?
(on previous evidence) did he ever use to do this?
(Several speakers in unison): *nalaga*
                            He never used to say these things.
DALU: People, does he ever make any small talk?
(Several speakers): He never speaks like that.
DALU: Never.
Now this one has come outside
You think about it all
'Now they have laughed' that is what has been said
O ibini wane biago O mbira la dai bialu
O his own daughter, O when she has replied first
O ibini mbalini O mende la dai bialu
O his own sister, O when she has replied second

Then all those that have been said
'He is talking truthfully'
'No'
'He is lying'
340   They will be thinking of these
He is going to get money, not from different people, but from his sister and
his daughter. They are going to mix their money together.
He has got shame from this.
WALUMBU: He got shame from the laughing but I don't know why.
KAKAYE: He got shame so you all go and give money to him
WALUMBU: I stayed behind I am saying. There are many others there. We
came on one bridge and joined up. That's all.
EGERIA: For stealing (taking compensation for no reason) I don't know
If they did like that, and laughing, then we should say
'We go to court'.
If they didn't do it then they are not going to give anything.
For laughing a *mana* is there
We'll see if a *mana* isn't there or not
When that was done, 'Let's go to court' I am saying.
There were seven women there.
DALU: For stealing, O I am saying
That man there they know him
wali ina agalibi bibahende mbira kobi
with woman and man he never makes a bad talk
360   *lai gungubi*
an argument or a fight
ibu one labi
with his wife
ibu mbalini labi
with his sister
ibu aba hamene labi
with his father and brothers [i.e. male relatives]
he never used to carry it outside.
'Give me money' (he is saying),
'Why did you all laugh?'
It is not a different woman, that is his sister
When she has replied, when the daughter has replied,
then that is what we'll do [i.e. wait for them to speak].
Why did they laugh?
'Let's go to court' it has been said.
KAKAYE: If you want to go to court then truly you will go.
WALUMBU: Why should we go to court. He wants the money so we will
give.
KAKAYE: You all give 10 toya each.

    (Overlapping talk at this point)

380   DALU: No, wait.
If one of you gives then you will carry heavy [i.e. be angry].

If it is said 'Give 10 Kina' you will carry heavy I am saying.
If it is said 'Give 12 Kina' you will carry heavy I am saying.
No, let's give 10 toya each.
'Only I will give', if you say like that then you will tie a knot there [i.e. make trouble for the future].
What did the man do down there? When the flood first came he talked so what did the sister say? The talk was pulled out again. The flood came to the houses and gardens and to everyone. The talk was pulled up and it returned [i.e. the same subject was mentioned]. The ones behind laughed like frogs. From there he got shame.
Aguene biyadabe?
was it done like that?
WALUMBU: It was done like that. What was in his mind went like that.
EGERIA: While these seven women were going they laughed and I broke into where there was no track.
WALUMBU: The shameful things and others I have thrown away. The *mana* says, 'Give'.
EGERIA: Those who laughed bring the money here tomorrow.
400 WALUMBU: Tomorrow, no. I am not like you with many gardens. I am in the bush and mountain side. No man came to my leg (I don't have a husband). Only myself am left and I am dying. 'I'll give it now' did you say?
EGERIA: It is for the laugh. There is no sore there from anger.
WALUMBU: Myself I have 2 Kina so I'm giving it to him (2 Kina are handed to Kabo to give to Egeria).
DALU: This is what I have said
What I said I am saying
It is not just for you
It is for all of the Ialubans
You have been here a long time so did this man used to say something bad or not?
(UNIDENTIFIED): He never used to say.
DALU: So that is what I said.
He never used to say these things.
Now he has gone outside with the talk.
With his sister and his wife, they have laughed.
EGERIA: When there are many men and only one woman do we ever make a joke or laugh?
KABO: We never used to do that.
420 EGERIA: Those seven women laughed and I broke into the pitpit. There was no track there. You think on it.
WALUMBU: You hit me so I'll give you this money and then you give me.
DALU: Did he hit you?
WALUMBU: Yes.
DALU: With a stick or weeds?
WALUMBU: He hit me with his hands and I fell in the gardens.
DALU: Did blood come?
WALUMBU: Blood? No.

DALU: No blood, then throw it away. Just give him to eat [compensation]. That is what has been said.

EGERIA: Why did you laugh? I didn't have any sore, that is what I am saying.

DALU: I know this man and he never makes a bad talk. If he had done like this it would be in me. Let's throw it away.

WALUMBU: He never makes such a talk except when at home where he makes a selfish talk (*bi mbuni mbuni*). When he is outside are you saying he never makes such a talk?

DALU: This is how it will be done. Who are the women that laughed?

WALUMBU: They are not here.

EGERIA: Tomorrow you must all meet and give me for the laughing.

440   DALU: O this is what we'll do. The women who laughed we will count them.

EGERIA: One is Walumbu, two is Haguene, three is Anagani, fourth is Horia's mother, fifth is Tomiabe's wife, sixth is Habo's daughter. There were many there and I couldn't see the seventh.

KABO: Wait, don't interrupt the mind
we are giving you.
O throw it away
We are going to talk on those things
One person will hold 10 toya
One person will hold 20 toya
We'll give you 1 Kina (= 100 toya)
No, we'll give 10 Kina
We will talk on this.

EGERIA: 'For the laughter give', this one I am now throwing away.
If you laugh later then we are not going to throw it away.
I didn't have a sore I am saying.

WALUMBU: You carry (take the money)!

EGERIA: We go to court.

(Overlapping talk at this point)

WALUMBU: We are giving you the money so what are you saying?

KABO: We are giving you 2 Kina so can you hear?

460   WALUMBU: You hit me and I am paying so will you pay me?
We are underneath the legs of men (*ge pouni ha*) and I am thus paying you.

DALU: You said something and he got shame. If he says this to you, you will get shame; it won't be pulled out. The pigs are there forever; where the footprint is you can't step on it [this statement appears to mean that people should avoid shameful contact with sisters].

(Concurrent conversations begin here and continue for some time. The feeling was that the matter had been 'thrown away' by Egeria. Nevertheless several speakers continued to address the participants sporadically)

KABO: In the *dawe* house (courting house) there will be one nice girl and there will be one smelly [*ngubi*: i.e. a sister who is thus tainted and forbidden].

EGERIA: Don't laugh again or you will kill pig or give money. I am not
going to take your money now. We have shown you whether there is a *mana*
or not.
(o *mana winidabe nawidabe ayu o walia harimagoni*).
KABO: I am saying a little something.
This is how it is when someone or a relative says something and you laugh.
Then we are not going to laugh. That man is there. When someone is not
wearing his apron properly, don't laugh otherwise you will kill pig [give
compensation].
ogoni dagua nabibe
don't do like this
ogoni dagua nalabe
don't say like this
480
manali layagoni
the men with the *mana* have said.

This dispute presents a microcosmic representation of many of the
models and analytical frames discussed previously. More so than
either D.1 or D.2, it is specifically concerned with problems of blame
(*dibade*: 'to cut') attribution, and thus the workings of the Huli
doctrine of *tene*. In the following analysis I focus my attention on
aspects of claim presentation and litigants' responses to actualized or
anticipated fault imputations. In these respects, I shall argue that
despite the manifest differences in sociocultural contexts between
Huli moots and Western courts, and indeed in the conception and
taxonomy of paradigmatic options, there nevertheless appear to be a
number of important structural parallels between the way blame is
handled in the two settings. From a cross-cultural standpoint, we may
specifically note that third parties sequentially defer a direct blame
attribution until later in the talk, while litigants faced with an
ascription of blame design their turns to orient talk towards blame
deflection. Although from an emic perspective the systems of cultural
meaning surrounding blame are defined quite differently, verbal
interaction in such environments is patterned along very similar lines
as a response to the avoidance of self-blame.

Atkinson and Drew (1979), in their analysis of court-talk, depicted
the paradigmatic options for a response to blame imputations as
falling into two contrasting sets: (1) that class of acknowledgement
moves, such as admissions or apologies, that accept blame; and (2)
that set of disavowal acts that include denials, justifications, excuses,
and counter-accusations. These categories do not have lexical representation in the Huli folk-system, but the conceptual contrast is one
that is nevertheless fundamental to the discursive frame of 'talk that is

hidden or covered' versus 'talk that is said out'. This semantic opposition is dealt with more fully in the next chapter. Importantly, as noted previously, dispute talking is not perceived in terms of confrontational verbal acts. The response options listed above are neither undifferentiated nor equivalent; 'some of the alternative available actions are *preferred*, while others are *dispreferred* actions' (Atkinson and Drew 1979 : 57). The Huli analogues, it should be emphasized, are not subject to any constraints of obligation or prohibition in dispute contexts. In any 'blaming' situation, actions that disavow a fault imputation – and that may, though not necessarily, consist of passing the buck – have positional priority over actions that acknowledge blame. That is, given that a litigant has equal access to both kinds of move, dispreferred status is evident from (a) the design features and sequential properties of the turns in which such actions are declared, and (b) the statistical prevalence of disavowal forms. Through choice of component defence mechanisms, and their sequential placement, recipients of blame display a predisposition to blame-deflection. The non-equivalent status of the options can thus be determined, as in the case of claims within a profile, from the parameter of positional incidence.

In all 'court' settings, blamings are managed within a milieu of culturally defined expectations about how people will respond. In this regard, ideas of concealment and mendacity are recurrent motifs in Huli. Most typically, one finds ritualized references in the early phases of mediation – and especially in setting speeches such as Text A in Chapter 5 – to the notion that 'you will be / are lying and I know that you are lying, but don't' (e.g. D.1 : 689–91). The Huli attitude to duplicity parallels that of the Burundi (Albert 1972) in so far as there is an explicit acknowledgement of the survival value of discretion and falsehood: 'In your mind you can't say out what you have done . . . this is like stealing pig and sweet potato. When we do that we never say out that we stole' (field data). As amongst the Burundi, the truth is good, but not all that is true is good to say. Interactional consequences vary from one dispute to another, depending on the information to be avoided. In compensation disputes concerned with deaths or injuries resulting from war, participants are invariably urged to 'name names'. For any potential speaker these injunctions present an implicit dilemma (Constructive (complex)) that we might formulate as follows:

if p then q
(p) If I / we tell out the names, then

(q) the identified person may get angry with me or criticize/ complain that I 'gave the source of the trouble'. I might be censored for my attribution of *tene*.

If not-p then r

(not-p) if I/we don't tell out the names, then

(r) I breach the norms of speech reciprocity and am accused of 'hiding the talk'.

A person will sometimes negotiate these multiple constraints by deliberately not attending the public dispute. This absence is not necessarily construed as 'negative' behaviour. In other disputes such as D.3, the reluctance to implicate others is mediated by employing vague subject identifications. I would argue that it is the way people define and contend with these conflicting sets of constraints that is likely to prove the most important dimension of contrast between dispute-settlement systems. Most notably in the New Guinea Highlands, the theme of covertness is endemic. However, there are very real differences among the member cultures as to how, when, and in what form the talk should be 'said out'. The available evidence indicates that among the Melpa (M. Strathern 1972) and Wahgi (*yu ne penem kesem*: 'they put the talk into the open': O'Hanlon n.d.), for example, a form of institutionalized confession or self-blame acceptance operates. Litigants are here exhorted to 'come clean' – a phrase that aptly conveys personal states of impurity – by publicly announcing admissions. This seems to correlate with a greater stress on the threat of concealed talk to group solidarity and cohesiveness. By contrast, among the Huli (where the above characteristics are absent) there is a very low incidence of behaviour that might be interpreted as apology, confession, or admission. Despite the fact that these actions have no labels in Huli, in certain situations people may behave in a manner that signifies an acceptance of responsibility. Since no positive value or credit attaches to 'owning up', the dispreferred status of blame acceptance is evident from the observation that this option is likely to be declared in private and direct actions of compensation. Behaviour is removed from the realm of public scrutiny. In the same vein, blame-deflection in Huli is an attempt to remove public registrability of a private state of pollution.

One of the striking aspects of D.3 is the importance attached to the element of 'publicity'. The distinction between private/domestic zones (*anda*) and public/epideictic zones (*hama/noma*) separates matters that should and should not be voiced in public. By establishing boundaries between the acceptable and unacceptable, mediators are able to confine and de-escalate the possible repercussions of conflict. Only issues of political consequence (i.e. involving unit opposition), or those that are likely seriously to affect current pig stocks or exchange relations, should be aired on *hama*. The disapprobation shown to breaches of this ground rule by litigants or mediators forms the subject of Helago's comments (1–2; 151): 'You brought the talk out from home (*andaga*) onto the cleared place (*hamani*) . . . it was done like that.' (156–59). Conformity to the implicit prohibition on washing dirty linen in public may equally be used as a character testimonial (320–21; 368). To repeat a previous observation, verbal censure in these types of dispute takes the form of 'argue at home' rather than 'don't argue'. The Huli conceive disputes to be an inevitable consequence of relationships; their concern is with containment and purification of *hama*. Techniques of minimization and neutralization of conflict frequently make reference to the common occurrence of familial arguments: 'With a sister or male relative we used to say bad words' (177–78). To the extent that these environmental categories are also predicated on the male/female distinction, one notes the sense in which Egeria rationalizes his anger/shame by repeated statements of his incapacitated state when attempting to walk on the 'public' road (31; 89; 116; 294; 396; 420–21). This kind of behaviour is associated with females. Women should step aside or 'go into the pitpit' when men approach and not the converse (see 295 for an opposing interpretation).

One of the consequences of the interactional sensitivity discussed above is that blame rebuttals have to be made in priority locales in any debate. Deferment of certain defence components may be interpreted as types of weaker strategies (see Atkinson and Drew 1979). It can be seen from the above summary of response postures that Walumbu is quick to shift blame from herself and attribute a fault to others at the beginning of the dispute. The important point, then, is not simply that Huli are practised buck-passers, but that turn design and sequential structure realize the culturally formulated orientations and sensitivities under which participants act. Focusing on the verbal contributions of third parties, the data suggest that there is a low level of commitment in the early phases to a direct identification of responsible parties. While speakers may thus be adjusting in advance to the possibility of denials, it is also the case that the tendency to avoid

Turn no.	Response postures: *Walumbu*
1 (17–20)	*subject-transformation:* blame apportioned to as yet unspecified 'others'; agreement to compensate
2 (32–4)	*event-transformation:* temporal sequence of actions established; denial of responsibility
3 (40)	repeat of 1.
4 (50–51)	actions referenced to self are mitigated by the diminisher *yamo* (nothing / small / inconsequential) *tabirene* (joke)
5 (83–5)	repeat of 4; agreement to compensate
6 (104–06)	accusation of "covering / concealing" talk
7 (108–09)	partial identification of others as Egeria's relatives
8 (115)	repeat of 1 and 2
9 (115–18)	temporal sequence of events elaborated
10 (132)	agreement to compensate on a higher than suggested figure
11 (135–36)	accusation of male bias amongst the mediators
12 (138–39)	accusation of male obfuscation; denial of "insult" act
13 (146–50)	elaboration on events
14 (153–54)	rhetorical questions: relatives don't insult; indirect self-accreditation as a "good woman"
15 (165)	agreement to compensate
16 (172)	*counter-claim* of "insults" by Egeria – refers to present and past behaviour
17 (191–97)	explanation of Egeria's actions
18 (201)	*counter-claim of violence*
19 (205–06)	agreement to compensate
20 (235)	repeat of 4
21 (242)	repeat of 18
22 (290)	partial identification of others
23 (378)	agreement to compensate
24 (397–98)	self-accreditation; shows understanding of *mana*
25 (400–02)	sympathy evoking statements
26 (404)	agreement to compensate
27 (422)	*counter-claim* for compensation for 'hitting'
28 (460–62)	repeat of 27; statement of male-female relationship

blame identification is a corollary of the code of circumscribed commitment previously described. The early speeches by Hega and Kabo are cautious recountings of facts and incidents out of which the serious state of 'shame' arose, and from which a positive inference of blame can be made. The task of identifying *tene* is prospectively structured. In this phase of fact-checking there is a marked presence of evidential suffixes that convey qualified factuality (4–5; 41–9), and that can often be manipulated for rhetorical effect:

'. . . *ti oba ha* : : *yada*
wali naigo ba : : *yadago*'   (94–6)

Following on from observations made about reports in Chapter 2, the mediator further distances himself from a direct commitment to *tene* identification by presenting potentially implicating statements as direct speech of another person:

'The ones that were behind laughed and I ate shame . . .
For that you pay
I am angry.'   (65–7)
'This is what you have said, ''The source is the sister''.'   (73–4)
' ''The sister is the source of this'', he has said.'   (86)

The level of personal involvement attaches to the assertion, not to the implications of its content. Blame imputations by third parties are thus likely to be delayed until later turns, when the chain of events has revealed itself. We see here how the structural properties of Huli language in respect of reporting reports and objectively modalized utterances affect language behaviour in disputes. That is, the system of unqualified categorical assertion and qualified factuality described in Chapter 2 is functionally adapted to the pragmatic requirements of maintaining one's neutrality of position when giving reports. This is emphasized by the importance attached to words in Huli and the norm that one 'shouldn't put words into other people's mouths'. Through direct quotation, a speaker is able to detach and disaffiliate him- or herself from what is said by another. It is presented so that others may draw their own inferences. The Huli are sensitive to the social consequences of the polarization of parties, alienation of any one litigant, and the dangers of 'naming names'. Research into two-party exchanges involving blamings (see Pomerantz 1978a) has revealed the same feature of blame postponement.

The question directed to Walumbu in line 17 is not in itself a blaming. Rather, it seeks tentatively to clarify Walumbu's defence position regarding the events that have occurred as well as forwarding a possible option for resolution. Throughout the case, the issue of shame and anger is a principal constituent of mediators' arguments. Significantly, these states are never contested by Walumbu. As anomalous psychological conditions, the Huli regard their existence as sufficient justification for indemnity (65–8): 'They are going to mix their money/He has got shame from this' (342–43). This, then, is the basis of Helago's question. The semantic dimensions of anger and shame are explored more fully in the next chapter. At this juncture we may, however, note the manner in which the injuries of insult, anger, and shame are metaphorically phrased. Particularly noticeable is the recurrence of the term *dere* ('sore': 70; 163; 166–69; 310). The demand for compensation is a demand for some medicinal substance to 'rub on the sore' (1967). The necessity for compensation derives from axioms regulating the treatment of sickness. As stated in the Introduction, the Huli conceive a structural homology between

dispute : compensation
'sickness / injury' : 'healing rites'

which semantically structures the language of dispute settlement. While the validity of my hypothesis is not dependent on it, the term for compensation – *abi* – may be a contracted form of *dabi*: 'to get well'. The giving of compensation is thus a recognition of the need to provide 'cures' and to inhibit the harmful action of 'bad thoughts'. *Agreements to pay compensation do not provide inference warrants or entitlements to impute an acceptance of blame.*

In the context of these observations, the repeated 'agreements to compensate' that characterize the postures adopted by Walumbu in D.3 do not imply blame acceptance. Her reply – 'If he asks for it then I'll give it' – reflects an appreciation of *mana* (397) relating to sickness conditions. Hega's question (line 17) is not treated as a directed blame attribution. In the second part of that same turn (17–20), Walumbu provides a defence component that is designed in accordance with a projected and anticipated move by mediators. Hega's utterance is construed as (a) making a presupposition of blame, and (b) prefacing a sequence that will attempt to identify *tene*. The turn is designed partially to pre-empt expected moves by others and thus to delay the opportionment of blame. Her implication of 'others' displays an understanding that prior questions and comments are designed to provide a basis for inferring blame.

How then is the preference for disavowal of blame managed? The most commonly employed techniques are to perform transformations on actor/agent referenced, and on the action referent relative to other events. As part of the process of blame deflection, Walumbu transforms the *subject* of the insult action (i.e. herself) to 'the other women' (20) at the earliest opportunity. It is evident that, in line with Hega's own sensitivity towards blame attribution, he immediately changes his previous referent of 'you' (16) to 'the other women' (21–2). Walumbu then disaffiliates herself from implication by temporally relocating her own actions. The insult to Egeria is turned into an event that followed the actions of 'other women' (*event-transformation*). An analysis of these postures begins to reveal a discernible sequential move from one type of defence mode to another at specific points in the case. This is a corollary of participants' attempts to exert a measure of control over projected blame sequences, as well as their appreciation of the strategic value of turn locales for initiating blame deflection. A subject-transformation that is left until the closing stages of any talk is likely to be less effective or acceptable. In so far as Walumbu is similarly reticent about naming names, the indeterminancy of 'the other women' is adapted to a strategy of slow identification. It is not until turn no. 22 that some more definite specification of 'others' is given. By postponing such information the speaker is able to forestall blame.

Focusing on the syntax of Walumbu's defence we may distinguish three separate strategies that occupy distinct dispute phases. Initially, following a blaming, litigants are attentive to the importance of managing blame-deflection at important stages in the dispute. Positional incidence is thus a reflection of efficacy. Speakers design their turns here in anticipation of projected sequences concerning *tene* by means of subject/event transformations. Overlapping with these mechanisms are components of self-accreditation and mitigation of actions referenced to self. The possibility of accusation is dissipated by the use of 'diminishers'. What is referred to by others as a 'joke' is attenuated by Walumbu to a 'small joke'. In this second phase certain stereotype counters may be used. In D.3, as in most disputes that involve women, accusations of male bias and obfuscation occur. Furthermore, the data indicate that these accusations and counter-claims tend to follow on from turns in which an agreement to compensate has been announced. Positions are not consistently maintained in Huli disputes. In the third phase (turn nos 16–27) there is a predominance of counter-claims. These tend to cluster at those points in any talk where a disputant perceives a consensus of opinion about the payment of compensation. This explains why Huli indemnity payments tend to have the format of bilateral exchange since they operate to subsume a range of claims between the parties.

Critically, the *profile* of Walumbu incorporates claims relating to insult and violence:

'You think you are in your house and you are insulting me like you always used to do.'   (172–73)
'She said "You used to insult me", so what did I used to insult her about?'
                                                                                                                                                (184–85)

The serial ordering of these reflects their non-equivalent status as profile options; they are not interchangeable in terms of their relative semantic efficacy. The parallels between D.3 and D.2 in respect of the positional incidence of insult claims, in conjunction with the statistical trends stated earlier, tend to validate the hypothesis forwarded, and the methodology chosen to demonstrate it. The structure isolated here holds over a considerable range of cases I collected (see Goldman 1981a). The frequency of the occurrence of insult claims at the head of profiles indicates that insult is peculiarly responsive to strategies that defer more 'important', or 'potentially difficult', claims until later. Its power to evoke immediate reactions of disapproval and sympathy are useful for initiating a basis for future talk. All of this is part of the shared knowledge of participants in any dispute. This 'masking function' of insult claims provides mediators with the impetus to re-locate *tene* ('origin, source, causes, reasons') in other latent grievances between the parties:

'The pig which you gave half of to me, I gave you 10 Kina for that.'
'The talk you have said, this is the source
This is the source between you.' (198–200)   *Table 1* : 1e

The evaluation of topics is performed with the appropriate gambit. The search for *tene* is an attempt to locate the original motive or intention. It is a process that may, through ramification, implicate others according to notions of culpable negligence, mistake, or presumption of contributory guilt. The identification of *tene* acts to define and delimit areas of responsibility for compensation.

The mediatory speeches of D.3 are in both content and form similar to those analysed for D.2. The option pronouncements again emphasize the conflict minimization value of 'claim renouncement' (24–5; 199; 76–8):

'Can you throw it away?
Nothing has happened.
For saying like that we are talking.'   (76–8)

One further aspect of the commitment code is the steadfast refusal of people to make a prediction about what someone might say, or to make a talk for another (see especially Text 5; Chapter 3):

'When Pila comes we can straighten it out.'   (D.2 : 471)
'We'll wait and hear why those three women laughed.'   (D.3 : 243)
'We'll wait for the others to come outside.'   (D.3 : 217)

In similar fashion, the evaluative contrast between truth (*henene*) and lies (*tindule*) is one that is left for others to decide:

'He is talking truthfully.
No.
He is lying.
They will be thinking of these.'   (337–40)

'Puma will say it is a bad thing you have been doing.
No.
You have been doing a bad work.'   (Text 5, Chapter 3)

The disjunctive format is commonly marked by the negative (D.2: 301–3; 340–41) in Huli. Talk is the expression of a person's essence, his mind (*mini*) and soul (*bu*). A man is measured in Huli by his words, so that to state the talk of another is to encroach upon his rights to self presentation.

It is evident from Appendix 5, *Table A1* that insult claims are the third most frequent category of case, accounting for 9 per cent of all the claims I recorded. This same percentage applies to figures presented in *Table A10* for one village court. Importantly, 83 per cent of these cases occurred during my fieldwork period, which suggests how they tend not to persist as profile possibilities for any substantial length of time. *Table A2* shows that 67 per cent of insult claims occupied an initial position in any profile. This reflects the relationship between the semantic weighting of such claims, in any system of claims, and the sequential and strategic properties of profiles. From Appendix 5, *Table A8* we learn that, despite the power of words in Huli culture, 83 per cent of all insult claims have an outcome of renouncement. This is accounted for by the function that such claims perform in case presentations to delay more deeply rooted grievances. Once debate is engaged, other claims emerge and the insult is unilaterally (or bilaterally) renounced as an issue. We may note further the fact that 27 per cent (*Table A8*) of all such claims were made between litigants related as affines.[10] This is (see Chapter 3) precisely the area of kinship where avoidance taboos are strongly stated, and thus any normative breach would perhaps be likely to be felt and argued vehemently.[11]

Whilst many of the observations made above indicate a level of continuity between blame responses in courts and moots, the different patterns of verbal interaction in these settings impose distinct constraints. In courts, defendants have to present their responses and accusations within a restricted format of question-answer. This limits their opportunities to avail themselves of a range of defence postures. In Huli moots, these close-ordering mechanisms are less in evidence, and participants can space their arguments over a period of time, knowing that there will be no lack of opportunity to express them. The search for sequential patterns here provides, then, common ground between anthropological studies of disputes and socio-legal approaches to Western courts.

Notes

1 From the accounts I received in the field, it would appear that the large-scale *dindi pongo* rites occurred perhaps once in every twenty years. While I was only able to gather detailed material on practices conducted by clans who inhabit the region from Ialuba south to Pureni (see *Map 1*), the data suggest that almost all clans were noted for some specific contributory rite. For example, certain clans were relied upon to provide the 'posts' for ritual houses (see Goldman 1979) erected at Kelote. This is formalized in the following well known *pureremo*:
Informant: Dai (Dagabua clan)

'Kokoma clan will cut the Hangabo tree
Padiame will cut Nguai Mano tree
Kiame (Tobani clan) will cut Harege
Huri will cut Dewane.'

Other clans would collect their totems and transport them to Kelote for ritual sacrifice:

Pi clan   we say *Urubungawe* (Lorikeet)
Kailu   we say *Uru Kamia* (Black Palm Cockatoo)
Muguni we say *Biango* (Dog)
Yugu   we say *Nogo* (Pig)
Tani   we say *Yari* (Cassowary)

The significance of this system of identifications based upon specific 'talk' and 'doings' can be appreciated from a reading of D.1. *Dindi pongo* served to place a multitude of clans within an overall schema that extends to Duna and Enga clans. To the extent that rituals were firmly linked to corporately owned clan lands, *dindi pongo* as an historical charter remains politically crucial to an understanding of Huli land disputes. In this brief account I have focussed on presenting what is commonly acknowledged to be the core of this belief system as evidenced by the degree of formalization given to information in specific speech forms. It would be extremely hazardous to claim that any account of *dindi pongo* is *the* correct one. Not only do different informants link central deities and places in different ways, but there is evidence to suggest that certain myths have been influenced by attempts to make them conform to events depicted in the Bible.

2 I have used the term rhyme in a special sense (but in accord with Huli aesthetics) for words that display assonance or alliteration. Where lexemes are manifestly paired on account of these properties, I have referred to the resultant syntagm as a 'minimal-pair'.

3 A full presentation of population figures, clan segment composition and other related statistical data, is given in Goldman (1981a).

4 I have used this gloss in the specific sense of cognates related to an agnatic core through a female agnate.

5 I should also point out that the decision to present transcript case-material is as much a response to the demands of students involved in Law and Society courses, as the methodological arguments presented in my introduction. A frequently voiced criticism in seminars I have conducted concerns the fact that one is rarely able to assess how an outcome is arrived at in any moot. While the answers to such questions are no doubt problematic, they are less so in the degree to which the discipline is a 'working' one. That is, provides a data-base from which analysts may suggest answers in respect to culture-specific cases.

6 The reader may also peruse D.3 for the operation of similar devices. I have not sought to exhaustively document every occurrence when giving text locations as this would have unnecessarily replicated analytical points.

7 In that this type of opening is a recurrent one in dispute talk I have treated it as a variant surface form of 'norm reference' gambits. As stated before, my list is a preliminary one only and could no doubt be refined in respect to different types of norm reference. I recognise that this type of opening also functions to claim a turn which emphasizes the point made in Chapter 2 that such routine expressions can serve a variety of functions in conversation.

8 Though space has precluded a detailed analysis of litigant speeches, various techniques of emphasis etc. can be discerned from a reading of D.2. For example, Maliyago declares the alternative actions for Helago with a turn-completion gambit (*Table 1* : 4e) to indicate finality: 'Bring the pig if you want to plant the coffee / If it doesn't come then you won't come / That is all I am saying' (428–34; see also 461–66).

9 In previous citations of this dispute (see Goldman 1980, 1981b) I have been guilty of not paying sufficient attention to the sequential order of speeches. Whilst the arguments forwarded in these articles are not affected, the opportunity to present the whole transcript here validates claims made in the Introduction concerning the analytical potential of full texts.

10 In contrast, 50 per cent (*Table A8*) of all land claims occurred between agnates. This may well reflect an opposing tendency whereby an increase in areas of discretionary action give rise to quantitatively higher disputes.

11 It should be understood that the descriptor 'renouncement' refers to the native categorization of outcomes as 'throwing away'. In D.3 it is only the element of compensation which is waived not the claim that there is a *mana* for laughing. The persisting attitudes of any litigant to the justifiability of a case does not impinge on the categorization of the outcome as one of renouncement.

5

Talking about talk

'It is not enough to know what to say, we must also say it in the right way.'
Aristotle (Rhetoric xii)

Part 1

In this chapter I concern myself primarily with certain terminological systems associated with talk in disputes. I outline the verbal frameworks of speech assessment in regard to both stylistic properties and thematic perspectives. This involves a consideration of the semantic axes on which the above lexical domains are based and organized. Furthermore, I have broadened the inquiry to include the manner in which the negative and positive polarities of talk are represented by stereotype figures constantly alluded to in 'talking about talk'. In attempting to explain the relationships between lexicalization principles, processes, and habits of conceptualization, it is necessary to interpret ethno-poetic notions in terms of phonological, lexical, and other stylistic options. To comprehend what making good speech or bad speech is in Huli requires an appreciation of the degree to which style is a matter of words (*bi*). In accordance with this observation the latter part of the chapter provides a detailed exposition of Huli vocabulary levels and specialized lexicons in their performative contexts. Two particular problems dominate the analysis:

(1) To what extent is speech determined in disputes and other related contexts by aesthetic and rhetorical norms, and what implications does this have for the relationship between form and meaning in Huli?

(2) How far are the inherent and related set of semantic dimensions specific to speech in disputes, or common to other behavioural domains (e.g. decoration or pig-exchange) involving processes of situational interpretation, definition, and negotiation?

There has been an implicit acceptance throughout much of the dispute literature that verbal conflicts represent 'fields of argument' in which norms are at some stage relied upon as devices to guide inference from facts to judgments. The corollary has been that notions of rationality and validity within this field have been demonstrated to be 'field dependent'. This dependence manifests itself in two forms. First, in the rules governing what is acceptable and unacceptable in behaviour and argument. Second, in the speech forms and patterns used to verbalize valuation processes. There are a number of foci within the sphere of 'talking about talk' that I am initially concerned to explicate and that are related to this latter form of dependence. These are:

(a) the phraseology used to express the nature of talk and trouble with particular reference to the conceptual 'effects' of talk – what Austin termed the 'perlocutionary' (1962 : 101) aspect of speech acts;

(b) the verbal repertoire and associated imagery used in the enactment and description of assessment routines during disputes;

(c) the set of lexical items employed to locate a stretch of speech or topic within the historical aetiology or causal framework of a dispute itself;

(d) the kinds of semantic dimensions that the above embody, and the degree to which they organize speech and behaviour in other related social contexts of display.

These foci constitute the language co-ordinates, the ground rules that determine the competent exercise of speech evaluation. They structure and organize the area of discretionary speech use called 'performance', by embodying fundamental norms and expectations relevant to interaction in disputes.

The Huli are, like many of the neighbouring Highlands peoples (e.g. the Melpa and Enga), both litigious and loquacious. They employ a number of terms to convey and define the speech situation 'dispute'. The superordinate descriptive labels are:

A.1. *bi* – 'talk, speech'   B.1. *lai*   – 'argument'
  2. *te* – 'discussion'   2. *genamo* – 'vituperative'.

Given that the Huli concept of language and speech is elaborated in terms of 'langue' (i.e. the systematic form of language), these lexemes are substantive specifications of the more inclusive category *bi* ('speech situations, acts, and events'). They can all be compounded with *lā* ('act of saying') in the way described in Chapter 2. The terms do not exhibit quite the complex set of inclusion and exclusion relations noted by Frake (1969) for the Yakan in terms of focus, purpose, and role. Rather, they exemplify contrasting or alternative types of speech action that relate directly to ideas about the proper conduct and organization of talk in disputes. Their semantic features segment a dispute – 'state of talk about claims' – into 'ordered' (A.1–2) and 'disordered' (B.1–2) conditions. These dimensions of meaning appear, significantly, to be terminologically marked for the respective labels. Choice of a particular descriptor reflects an individual's inferences concerning the state and development of any talk in progress.

A.1. *bi*. This is the most frequently utilized situational category. In common with the general import of 'talk' itself, *bi* signifies a sharing of discourse, a conformity to the axiomatic norm of speech reciprocity. Moreover, applications of *bi* acknowledge the turn-taking organization for verbal interaction and those mechanisms for co-ordination of speaker transfers. These produce order in the recognisable guise of 'talking in turn'.

A.2. *té*. In accordance with occurrences of *té* to denote myths, folk legends, and etiological narratives, the term here indicates topic development and control. *Té* implies an element of thematic continuity in discussion which is perhaps best glossed as 'debate'.

B.1. *lai*. This is a contracted form of *lai ha* ('to finish saying/ talking'). Disordered talk begins then when orderly speech ceases. *Lai* reflects the component of deviance (in the disordered condition of dispute) by further alluding to the point that when talking ends non-verbal actions may be resorted to. In contrast to A.1–2, both *lai* and *genamo* can refer to the culturally dispreferred actions of disputing without words. Situations described as *lai*, most typically, are characterized by persistent violation of speech norms such as occur in heated exchanges of abuse.

B.2. *genamo*. While sharing 'family resemblances' with the lexeme *lai*, *genamo* tends to be employed in the environment of talk about familial or limited party conflicts. The level of contrast with A.1–2 is between ratified multi-party discussions and essentially bilateral pursuance of claims; that is, between communal consumption and private gratification.

The implicit semantic distinctions of *bi* and *lai*, as modal conditions of 'dispute', contrast sequenced exchange behaviour with ego-centred appropriation of action – 'talking in turn and talking out of turn'. The publicly endorsed model of talk is an exchange structure based on equal distribution (*tale/yalu*); talk as an item of wealth should, in these circumstances, parallel the movement of pigs. The above categorizations further oppose the exclusively verbal against non-verbal confrontation, and the public presentation of claims against the private usurpation of settlement procedures. These features of meaning are critical facets of participants' models of ordered dispute. They determine the use of such labels in accordance with the situational definition the actor feels is most appropriate. In all respects, the categories indicate a fundamental division between ratified participation and actions subject to censure.

Further specificity regarding any stretch of discourse (within a dispute) can be generated by employing a format of *bi* + modifier: C.1. *bi gungu* (talk + fight) – 'arguing, fighting with talk'; 2. *bi gare* (talk + cut) – 'angry, painful talk'; 3. *bi bili bale* (talk + action of tree climbing) – 'talk which evades consequences'; 4. *bi pubi gi* (talk + house-surround) – 'one-sided talk'; 5. *bi gini* (talk + play) – 'verbal gymnastics or verbal back and forth'. The position and use of the term *bi* in Huli is thus similar to the Tzeltal lexeme *k'op* reported by Stross (1974 : 215). It denotes a wide range of speech genres and situations, while acting in a highly specific way in combination. The meanings of the compound terms cannot in all cases be gauged by the meanings of the component modifiers.

All the interactionally relevant categorizations of speech behaviour in disputes are shaped by phrasal lexemes centred on the substantive domain of *bi*. The design of debate, its reference terms and 'moves', are coded in the discriminative repertoires considered below. A dispute is not lexically segmented into sequentially discrete stages, there are no episodic phases of examination, cross-examination, or summing-up. The Huli system is generally lacking in specific confrontative notions such as defendant, plaintiff, or witness. As a corollary of this, overall strategies are similarly not characterized as defence, accusation, pleading, or other types of quasi-legal actions.

The majority of the compound phrases used in descriptive or evaluative routines, and especially those with pejorative connotations, usually occur in rhetoric as reduplicative transformations. Thus the form A.2. becomes *ti té*, B.1. *li lai* or C.2. *giri gare*. Reduplication is present with either partial phonemic variation on the word stem, or more simply exact duplication as in *bi daliga daliga* (talk + above) – 'the talk which is on top, superficial talk'. Reduplication is considered an aesthetic elaboration of standard forms, not a lack of fluency in speech.[1] A triad of metalinguistic terms express both aesthetic concepts and notions of symbolic content:

D.1. *bi mone/monehe* (talk + wasp) is used in a general sense for ethno-poetic devices of reduplication, assonance, alliteration, and other stylistic elements detailed in this chapter. The phrase also specifically denotes a valued lexicon that serves as a resource for creative 'good speech'. The wasp is an aesthetic symbol for Huli, valued for its properties of flight, sound, and rotundity. It is a recurring metaphorical motif in *gamu* associated with child-rearing rites.

D.2. *bi mabura* (talk + to go around) refers to standard turns of phrase, adages, proverbs and maxims 'roundabout expressions'.

D.3. *bi yobage* (talk + mark/sign/tattoo (*bage*)) signifies an action or speech which is 'veiled' (see Strathern 1975 : 189) in meaning. The phrase further implies a hidden symbolic element, as when a man overturns a bridge to state his intent or accomplishment of murder.

The importance of these indigenous aesthetic terms as markers of particular speech genres and concepts of speech evaluation is discussed in this chapter.

The inventory of metaphorical idioms expressing concepts of 'talk' provide an important source of insight into how the Huli view disputes as verbal encounters. Most commonly, talk may be depicted as species of cane and vine as in the lament cited in Appendix 4 (ref. C : 79–94): *Diwi* (*Wikstremis androsaemifolia, fam. Thymeliaceae*), *Gondele* (*Urena lobata fam. Tiliaceae*), *Dabale* (*Xanthomyrtus, fam. Myrtaceae*), *Gombabu* (*Cuperus melanospermus, fam. Cyperaceae*) and *Nabiya* (?). In conformity with such images, the action of speech is figuratively spoken of as 'cutting strings' (*di bia*) in the same text. Talk is like rope because it can be used to 'bind' things together, it has relational properties as a substance which can mediate between two spheres or persons. Accounts of the historical transference of 'talk' frequently utilize the *pureremo* form

> *gi hubua / gau hubua*
> *emene hubua / timbuni hubua*
> *limbu hubua / waiyambu hubua*

in which the rhyming couplets successively repeat the basic statement of 'a small talk is wrapped up / a big talk is wrapped up'; talk is conceived of as a 'bundle' (*hubua*). Talk is corporeal property which is held (*yi*), carried (*hono kogo*), given (*mia*), placed (*wia*) and capable of being stolen (*page*).

The natural environment, in both its animal and agricultural forms, provides a further source of metaphorical abstraction for cultural notions about talk. In the first instance, the man-bird motif (a dominant theme in Huli decoration) permeates speech conceptualizations. A man who talks without thinking is *agali kudaga* (man (*agali*) + Helmeted Friar bird (*Philemon novaeguineae*)) – a reference to the loud repetitive raucous call of this honeyeater. The parallel of human talk / bird talk is invoked, somewhat differently, in *ma hiriya* child rites. The speech of various lorikeets indexes increments of power, productivity, and strength which, through the medium of *gamu*, are instilled into children to make them 'strong talkers' (*bi kuni*). These same valued properties explain the use of Blue Bird of Paradise (*Paradisaea rudolphi*) feathers which are burnt into drums during their construction to imbue the instrument with the 'talk' of this bird. Such wild and aggressive qualities are further manifested by the predominantly male associated idioms for talk: 'bow' (*danda*: ref. Appendix 3 : A2), 'arrow' (*timu*: ref. Appendix 3 : A3), and 'drum' (*tabage*) as in the rhetorical question:

Hungi   *tabage yu   kebe?*
Wood (*Piper fam. Piperaceae*) drum   hold are you?
(Are you holding a soft talk? – i.e. a drum made from this pliable climber)

Cultural notions concerning the behaviour of birds thus abstract, from a pool of potential symbols, qualities which can enhance human speech and which are fundamental to representations of 'truth' discussed later.

In addition to the dominant themes of 'connection' and 'strength', idioms of talk that I collected reflect a preoccupation with concepts of growth and fertility. Talk is like grass, or sweet-potato which, if left or cut, will simply 'grow again'. Talk develops from 'pimples to boils', it 'grows' (*de lara*) or 'bears fruit'. The natural models of maturity provide parallels to states of dispute as situations displaying progressive development and traceable origins to first 'seeds'. These conceptions generate a related field of imagery and phraseology pertaining to dispute and dispute settlement. The stream of talk about events must be 'cut' (*pugua*) at some stage for the purpose of resolution. Issues have to be 'dug up' and 'pulled out by the roots'.

Further examples of semantically related language about dispute processes can be found in the schema presented in *Table 5*. Moreover, just as the range of possible agricultural tasks is bounded by limitations of material and medium, what can and can't be done in dispute resolution is analogously phrased through the conventional repertoire of *bi mabura* (proverb, maxim, or adage). In the following corpus of sayings (considered with respect only to content) it is evident that notions of *action* relate directly to the suggestive models of plant fertility and the manner in which man *interacts* with his natural environment. Consistent with these observations, Huli proverbs have their impersonal, familiar tone linguistically marked by prevalent use of the past customary mood suffix – *ga* – that which is 'customarily' the case. Generally, these aphorisms fall into the following classes:

(1) Turns of phrase that indicate that an action or event in the past cannot now be altered. The force of these precepts derives from standard allusions to the natural and immutable order of things similar to the Western adage 'what is done is done'.

  (a) The banana tree never bears fruit in the same spot twice: *hai halu mende do dai nabiaga*.

  (b) You can't dig up sweet-potato from an old garden: *hina walini ha puni i wa dai nabiaga*.

  (c) The pandanus tree never bears fruit twice in the same season: *anga dene ungua dai nabiaga / anga du pene do dai nabiaga*.

    (d) Where a Bai tree stands a Bauwa tree won't grow: *bai heneni bauwa naholebira.*

    (e) The arrow came after the bird had flown: *ega biralu pea timu ariba kago* (compare our 'locking the stable door after the horse has bolted').

(2) Sayings that urge immediate action rather than undue deliberation.

    (a) While you are saying men and Dama are there, women won't be able to eat: *dama ka agali ka lalu keria wali iba nane polebira.*

    (b) Your sweet-potato won't grow in clay: *hina dongomane hengene anda naholebirago* (i.e. this situation doesn't promote your aims).

    (c) Why look for sugar-cane when water is at hand: *iba hambu ngelalu du natogo biaga* (compare our 'don't look a gift horse in the mouth').

    (d) The dog and the marsupial are there, we never used to say the dog is going or the marsupial is going: *biango biango tia tia, biango pora tia pora nalagago* (they are both man's friend and we should give compensation for both men). These animals figure in two other related idioms:

        (i) As many as the hairs on a dog: *biango homa mbira iri ale nga* (used in reference to a multitude of things)

        (ii) Let us choose the hair of the dog and the hair of the marsupial: *biango iri tia iri dabamiya* (i.e. we'll share the talk and then choose the issues or culprits. This concept parallels our own notion of 'splitting hairs').

    (e) The pitpit stick and the pig's arse go together: *gambe hongo nogo yabunila palu palu* (a cooking analogy used as for 2d above).

    (f) Don't let the bitter taste of taro go away: *ma tumbu bi naraore kau biaga* (compare our 'strike while the iron is hot').

(3) Sayings that indicate a degree of deviance in speech behaviour.

    (a) When I was talking about sugar-cane did you talk about bananas?: *du larogola hai laribe?*

    (b) He is like the light coloured pig among the black ones: *nogo mindi dege kaga pagabua pea haridago* (similar to our use of 'black sheep' to denote the exception).

    (c) Have you been tying up the sugar-cane?: *du mbu lalu*

haribe? (i.e. have you confined your mind so that you do not listen to our talk?).

(4) Traditional sayings that stress, importantly, that actions have *tene* ('sources, causes, reasons, or motives').

    (a) The pandanus bears the seed before the fruit: *ina pundini anga tole ende hene biago.*

    (b) Men do not customarily kill for cold marsupial: *tia tambe naga agali nabaga.*

    (c) You saw the tail of the marsupial and you went ahead: *tia pongorali manene honowa pu pea larigobe* (similar in meaning to 'counting one's chickens before they are hatched').

These sayings have great significance in that they make explicit the dimensions of action that Huli consider important in talk about claims. Moreover, they reveal that analogic processes in this culture are based on event/action-dominated themes – as opposed to object-oriented abstractions. It is not simply a pandanus tree (4a above), but aspects of development that constitute the proverb. Stylistically, approximately 30 per cent rhyme, with partial syntactic symmetry in the two halves of the distich (2d, 2d(ii), 3a). I recorded a number of other sayings from natural conversation which, in contrast to the above, show object focus and provide apt analogies for situations past, present, and future. For example:

The Tagari river is short (by comparison) for we will stay long
(*Gutagali tumagi lowa habiya*);
or
The Areca palm tree is short for we will stay long
(*Bibi Ayege tumagi lowa habiya*).

Taxonomically the Huli regard these traditional sayings as indirect modes of speech, and, as such, part of good rhetoric. Their circumlocutory nature is semantically reflected in the lexical descriptor *bi mabura* ('talk + to go around' (*mabu (bi) ra*)) – literally, 'roundabout expressions'.

Within the sphere of 'talking about talk', the Huli employ a range of phrases to express the effects of speech, the 'perlocutionary' aspects of any speech act. E.1. *bi bara* – 'the talk hits, strikes, kills'; 2. *bi para* – 'the talk sticks or adheres'; 3. *bi habane pele* – 'the talk pokes the heart'; 4. *bi kodo/bi giabu* – 'the talk pricks or penetrates'; 5. *bi dibulebira* – 'the talk will cut you'; 6. *bi timu ale ho wiabo* – 'the talk stays like an arrow'; 7. *bi ka hara* – 'the talk spears'. When these expressions are employed in rhetoric there is a marked prevalence of reduplication: E.1. *bi boga baga*; E.3. *bi pili pele*; E.4. *bi kidi kodo/bi gibi giabu*. The degree to which these phrases describe talk as a form of physical action reveals a fundamental metaphoric and semantic mode. There is an indigenously conceived structural homology between the pathology and treatment of sickness and speech. The term *bi* in E.1–7 is interchangeable with the word *tandaga* ('pain'), and the form *bi tandaga* – 'painful talk' is a recurrent construct in discourse. We can relate this metaphoric code to the fact that talk, like illness, is a major concern of the Huli. The pathological metaphor is a metalinguistic statement about the range of shared features of meaning between speech and sickness. Through metaphoric extension, many of the terms listed in *Table 5* to connote the settlement of a dispute are also used in talk about treatment of illness. Pain, like bad talk, must be 'pulled out' (*dugua*) or 'made to die' (*mo homole*), and both may be attributed to the work of the same supernatural agents.

The systematic interrelations between talk and sickness, a dominant theme of this chapter, can be further analysed through attention to patterns of language use. Both talk and illness are said to 'strike' people, and the former may cause the latter. Among the lexical items employed to describe the action of illness two forms are prevalent: (1) *bara* ('hitting, striking, beating') as in *hagua bara* ('headache') and (2) *nara* ('eating, consuming') as in *ne nara* ('toothache'), *hale nara* ('earache'), *pu nara* ('suicide': literally 'eaten by rope'), or compounded with any anatomical noun to specify localized pain. The concept of *nara* in these contexts suggests the manner in which pain is consumed, ingested, or absorbed inside. Moreover, in addition to the general term *tandaga*, Huli distinguish between different modes of pain: *pele* ('pricking'), *nimu* ('throbbing'), *diri* ('stinging'), *tenge* ('piercing'), and *kabu* ('enveloping'). From the above terms relating to pain and indeed talk (E.1–7), it is clear that the semantic dimension of *inside/outside* is fundamental to the way in which talk and pain affects people.

There are a number of continuities and discontinuities between the Haya (Seitel 1974 : 57) and Huli concepts of inside/outside. Along the socially defined axis, *anda/hama* relates (as we have seen) to spatial divisions of private/public spaces, and conceptual distinctions between 'matters of the house or home and matters of public importance'. This is a critical grid for processes of dispute settlement. In respect of the personal domain, the inside/outside dichotomy in Huli does not parallel Haya notions. The concept of 'hitting inside', in Huli, implies effectiveness of speech through penetration rather than any transgression of boundaries:

ibunaga bime   ina habane be ka   larugo
her   with talk our inside   hit there I have said
(she has hit us inside with the talk I have said)

(Field data)

To 'hit inside' is akin to the Western notion of 'hitting home'; the inside/outside dimension is here referenced by the opposed terms *anda*: *tagira*. In this context *anda* signifies the affective states of *bu* ('life force'), *mini* ('mind'), and *dinini* ('spirit'). These are all held to reflect, as well as constitute, emotional dispositions. Bad talk, like pain and sickness, are conditions of these 'internal' physical or conceptual forces:

Agali bu   mini   keba haga bulebira
Men emotional base consciousness anger will continue to be
(In men's emotional base and consciousness anger will persist)

(D.2: 179)

Discrepant speech and behaviour may be attributed to situations where the spirit is 'outside'

I   ndo i   dinini tagira pene harua
You no your spirit outside went
(Not you, your spirit has left you)

(Field data)

Speech is assessed as the product of internal harmony and balance among the above three organs which represent the loci for most effectively influencing, by abuse or illness, the persona. This explains the frequent occurrence of statements which refer to talk 'going inside'[2] in contrast to ineffective talk which is superficial:

DALU: *Bi   ogoni ngubigo wa ha*
        Talk this   smelly   throw away
(This talk is smelly throw it away)
Bi   ngubi ore ayu laragoni
Talk smelly very now are saying
(That talk they are saying is very smelly now)
Bi   ina larugo ogo lalu mbira naleagoria
Talk I said   this said one   not said here
(A talk hasn't been said like the one I made)

Bi   ebere   larigo   ngubi larigo
Talk coming you said smelly you said
(The talk you have said is smelly)
GANGARO: *Bi   ngubi ndo*
          Talk smelly no
(It is not a smelly talk)
Bi   unugula   alego amugo alego ibu anda   polebira
Talk that one there like   there   like   her inside will go
(A talk like that one there will go inside her)

(Field data)

The concept of 'inside' (*anda*) in relation to individuals has broader cultural implications associated with processes of maturity and control. To 'grow up' is literally to 'come inside' (*anda ha*) through stabilization of life forces.

The manner in which the Huli utilize metaphoric expressions to translate speech into action in their verbal evaluation system can again be contrasted with Haya notions of speech effectiveness. Among the Haya, speech is conceived as relatively insubstantial by comparison with action, and there is diminished responsibility resulting from talk as opposed to other behavioural forms. The Haya proverb ' "May you be slaughtered", doesn't kill a cow' (Seitel 1974 : 53) (compare our 'Sticks and stones will break my bones but words can never hurt me') reflects the relative nature of actions and talk along the axis of substantiality. Among the Huli there is no such discontinuity between talk and action, and the prevalence of insult and resultant disputes attest to the seriousness attached to verbal utterances. This is an aspect of the way in which 'talk about talk' is couched in material terms. Moreover, the same dimension of effectiveness is employed to contrast speech with speech, rather than speech with action. This is reflected in the Huli proverb *nogombi po napole, yamo hege tomia bere* – 'the snake puts out its tongue but does not always bite'.

The discussion thus far has prepared the ground for examining a little more closely how a situation of dispute is conceptualized and verbalized in Huli. On one level is that cluster of ideas relating to female sexuality (heat, contamination, and anger) which can engender conflict as expressed by the terms *galo* and *anguatole* – something which is 'stepped over'. This has been detailed in Chapter 3. On a second level, and related to idioms of talk as 'cane/strings/connecting ropes', disputes are conceived of as deviations from the straight (*tiga*), something 'knotted' (*pongo*), 'crossed' (*banga*), or 'tied up' (*hubua*). Further examples are given in *Table 5*, especially

F.2 'twisted' (*nde*) and F.3 'entangled' (*lungu*). In most cases these descriptive constructs have reduplicative analogues, as in *pingi pongo*, *hibi hubua* ('tied up'), *lingi lungu* and *ndi nde* (see *Table 5*).[3] I would argue that the concept of 'knot' (*pongo*) is central to Huli ideas and expressions of 'deviance', and repeatedly occurs in the dispute texts given in this book. It is consistent with dispute settlement phraseology which stresses 'untying/unravelling' (see *Table 5*). Furthermore, as the dominant negative idiom, it is semantically and terminologically fundamental to sorcery forms such as *Dangi Pongo* ('knotting the grass' – after theft), *Yári Mabu Pongo* ('knotting the cassowary's claw' – love magic) and *Hubi Bi* (from *hubua* – to bind: 'to knot the talk'). Both verbally and non-verbally, 'knots' are associated with the presence and promotion of disorder. Most injurious *gamu* include this lexical item as a performative for causing distress.

Disputes are also negatively expressed in terms of increments of 'heat'; they 'burn like fires' (D.2: 229) or 'burn lungs'.

DALU: She said she will return so let's make it die [i.e. settle it]
We'll throw out the talk and this will be settled
One talk that mother said down there
You made a fire under that man Gangaro
You made a fire under me with those pigs
You made a fire under Ago.

(Field data)

This extract illustrates the metaphorical equation of conflict and 'fires'. The oppositions that Dalu emphasizes centre on the correlative notions of 'fire making' and 'making die' (*homa*), 'throwing away' (*wa ha*), or 'pulling out' (*dugua*). These images are given rhetorical force through the phonological patterning of parallel repetition (that is, repeated syntax with minimal variation). Conflict heat has to be 'extinguished' (*hundia*: see *Table 5*), for situations of 'inflammation' cause land to 'burn', 'die' (D.1: 693), or make pigs and women 'bad'. To comprehend how Huli conceive disputes we must attend to such verbal formulations, and indeed to levels of congruity between idioms of dispute and resolution.

Phrases expressing the nature and effects of talk or dispute constitute only part of the speech framework in which argument is conducted. Equally significant is the verbal repertoire associated with the evaluation of accounts. *Table 5* sets out the terms commonly used in the negative evaluation of speech and the lexical items connoting

Table 5 Talking about talk

	Negative evaluation terms		
	Standard form	Rhetorical form	Settlement phraseology
F.	1. *Bi Pongo* (knot)	*Bi Pingi Pongo*	*Hadole* – to untie
	2. *Bi Nde* (twisted)	*Bi Ndi Nde* (betrays)	*Mo tiga* – to make straight/*gini bia* – to rectify
	3. *Bi Lungu* (entangled)	*Bi Lingi Lungu* (confused/entwined)	*Tabama* – to settle (root Taba meaning to unravel,
	4. *Bi Golia* (walls of pig house)	*Bi Gili Golia* (closed in)	as in *Tababima* – to untie)
	5. *Bi Mo yi/mo dambia*	– (covered over/pressed in)	*Dugua* – to open/*Ali* – to dig up
	6. *Bi Gare* (cut off)	*Bi Giriya Gareya* (piecemeal/incomplete)	*Goda* – extract/*Haiya* – scatter
G.	1. *Bi Ke* (hard/heavy)	*Bi Ki Ke* (angry talk)	*Hi la/Hili Holi* – to sweep away
	2. *Bi Dere* (alive)	*Bi Diri Dere* (talk made alive again)	*Mo Yabia* – to make light
	3. *Bi Paro* (to ring-bark)	*Bi Paro Paro* (ceaseless/circular)	*Mo Homole* – to make die
	4. *Bi Gili la* (to pull)	*Bi Gili Gili* (fighting talk)	*Tongo/Tingi Tongo* – to finish off
	5. *Bi Tulira* (tailless)	– (without a finish)	(*tongo* = expire)
	6. *Bi Kiau* (infertile)	*Bi Ki Kiau* (unproductive talk)	*Gurapea* – to leave something go
	7. *Bi Kara* (to scratch)	*Bi Kiri Kara* (aimless talk)	*Golapea* – released
H.	1. *Bi Kulu/Kili Kulu* (thunder)		
	2. *Bi Gili Galo* (crunching)		
	3. *Bi Gili Gala* (shower down)		
	4. *Bi Ti Te* (hissing of steam)		
	5. *Bi Tigi Tugu* (hissing of steam)	Futile, ineffectual speech, can be used to	*Hundia Hu* – to extinguish/put out/make die.
	6. *Bi Di De* (bird speech)	mean 'gossip'.	
	7. *Bi Tuga Tuga* (babble of water)		
	8. *Bi Gomo/Gimi Gomo* (murmur)		
	9. *Bi Diburibu* (cutting/radio)		
	10. *Bi Ki Ku* (idle chat)		
	11. *Bi Muli Muli* (hum)		

dispute settlement. A number of important points emerge. The transition from standard to reduplicative forms in rhetoric, typical also of the terms listed in A, B, C, and E above, represents the shaping of speech by a specific aesthetic device based on sound play. Furthermore, because these terms are figurative, we can perceive two levels of congruity: (1) that within the set of negative phrases – the lexemes embody two basic semantic axes given below; (2) that between the negative expressions and the terminology for conflict resolution – the figures derive from related domains of social action, e.g. 'knotted/entangled' talk and 'unravel/untie'. Despite the lack of comparative data, material on the Melpa (A. Strathern, personal communication) strongly suggests that occurrences of reduplicative transitions in negative speech evaluation may be common in the Highlands.[4] In Melpa 'talking about talk', the term *ik* (talk) is compounded in precisely the same way as the Huli word *bi*. Moreover, negative evaluation utilizes terms that reflect aspects of sound, *ik ngokor ngakor* (talk + creaking), *ik nilyim nalyim* (gossip); elements of direction, *ik mbukl mbakl* (talk + separate ways), *ik wurung arang* (talk + east–west) and covertness, *ik kroya meroya* (talk + crooked), *ik klorok marok* (talk + closed up). There are a number of English analogues, also reduplicative, that can be cited: 'phoney-boloney', 'mumbo-jumbo', 'prittle-prattle', 'chit-chat', 'tittle-tattle', and 'twiddle-twaddle'. These appear to parallel Huli usages for insubstantial, ineffective speech. Additionally, there are reduplicative forms which refer to heated argument or dispute: 'argy-bargy', 'argle-bargle', 'ding-dong', 'hoo-ha', 'higgle-haggle'. Such speech evaluation forms constitute emphatic expressions frequently associated with contexts (such as teacher-pupil situations) where rhetoric may be important.

Significantly, the Huli and Melpa terms delineated above embody a number of semantic dimensions. These are:

Dimension of covertness – 'hidden talk' as in F.1–5, *Table 5.*
Dimension of futility – through insubstantiality, ineffectiveness and impermanency as in G.3, 6, 7/H.1–11, *Table 5.*
Dimension of control – over knowledge and speech.

I develop my analysis by explaining how these dimensions are further reiterated in, as well as oriented to, speech during disputes. It is not analytically critical that no Huli term exists for these dimensions, nor that we fail to find a suitable gloss for the features of meaning conveyed by indigenous phrases embodying the abstracted dimensions.

What seems important is that we understand the idiomatic aspects of the contrasts along any one of the axes. For example, along the dimension of substantiality, Huli oppose talk like 'pain' with talk like 'smoke' (*bi hagua*) or any of the phrasal lexemes H.1–11 in *Table 5*.

At this juncture I shall follow the mode of explication set out in Seitel's (1974)[5] analysis of Haya metaphors for speech by considering those *bi mabura* ('proverbs') that relate to the description of verbal action. These constitute a separate class from those maxims detailed earlier.

5   (a)   The snake puts out its tongue but does not always bite: *nogombi po napole, yamo hege tomia bere.*
    (b)   Are you fetching water from the root of the Ere (*Octamyrtus pleiopetala fam. Myrtaceae*) tree?: *Ere pini iba duguarebe?* (implies that the talk is ever-flowing and ceaseless like water from these roots).
    (c)   The talk is like pouring water on the Marita nut: *abare iba ale odarego* (water is poured onto this nut and then squeezed out. The adage implies that the talk has, like the water, no permanence).
    (d)   Are you just masturbating?: *i wi gidaribe?* (indicates that talk is as wasteful and fruitless as the act of masturbation).
    (e)   The talk is like the nut falling on the Mandi (*Acalypha insulana fam. Euphorbiaceae*) shrub and scattering away: *mandi gene hiru hondone tu porebe* (that is, it has no lasting impression).

These turns of phrase precisely reflect the elements of meaning subsumed by the dimension of 'futility', and complement the set of negative evaluation terms listed in *Table 5*. Once again, these observations invite comparison with data available on the Haya, where object-oriented forms such as fire, sand, grass, tobacco, water, and mud occur as metaphorical predicates. The Huli material reveals a prevalence of *action-oriented* metaphors. It is the interaction with the environment, rather than purely an abstraction of objects, that constitutes the base for analogic processes of thought in Huli speech.

The way in which the dimension of effectiveness is referred to in rhetoric is best illustrated through an analysis of the following extract. It is the initial speech made by a land-mediator as a preface to D.1. and is here treated separately.

TEXT A Speaker: Muguye (Official land-mediator for Koroba).
1   Tindule *ogo handama pialu nai mondoni duguwuwa*
    When we have seen the lies they will be pulled out and left on the gardens
    nogo wi puni ale kau bidago lowa
    they were sour like the penes of pigs
5   *Dugubai howa kemagola howa ini* tandaga tago tago *i pelebame dibulebira*

While we are there pulling them out that man will have pain added and
will be cut with an axe
Bi ayu larogoni tandaga *o uru handamaro bulebero*   [1(d)]
The talk I am saying is that I will see an end to the pain
10   *handamaro ore buwa dindi aba ogo ha polebira*
      when I have done this the land will go the 'father' (owner)
      Dindi o howa uru
      Concerning land and cunning
      ke uru
15   lies
      haya uru
      persistence
      tandaga uru
      pain
20   *handalu handamaru*   [1(f)]
      I have seen all these things
      *Ayu bi heneneore loane mbira yamaga ho kebaria bi henene biago ala laba
      nale*
      Now you should make a true talk, when you hold it in now don't say later
      you should have said a true talk
25   *Tindule biagome dindi miya au labiya keba*
      We will say a lie gave the land
      Ai henene loane bauwaya ni hendedagome
      The truth should be seen on the Casuarina trees that are planted
      gana ni wa bidagome
30   on the drains that were dug
      anda ni bidagome
      on the houses that were built
      wandia agandiala li bidagome
      on the women's and men's houses that are there
35   *toro wale ni* hengedagome
      on the nut trees that were planted
      i yai kago
      these things are holding me
      Dindi kuni ibunaga lenego
40   It was said the 'bone land' (ancestral land) belongs to one
      i dugubai howa i berelabe hea bebe?
      when one is pulled out should the other stay?
      be ibu herelabe hea?
      or should the other one sit?
45   *Au laramago poro ayu mana ngagoni mendeligo gi ha mbira nayi pole
      ndo*   [1(c) / 2(d)]
      We are saying the *mana* is there, not that one should go without anything
      in his hand
      gi ha mbira yalu polane mana nga birua lareba
      he should go with something in his hand, the *mana* is like that
50   *O bi henemane labiya kaba au bi langero*
      We should say the truth that is the talk I am telling

Ai uru mandabi
those I know   [1(f)]
ke uru mandabi   [1(f)]
55   the lies I know   [1(f)]
nde uru mandabi   [1(f)]
the betrayals I know
agali naga bayeni mandabi
men's ways I know
60   *Ai ogo bi ore laragome ogoria dambi holobada*
With a talk like this we might be weighed down here
dindi mirago ibu nu hanalu holebira
then the land will be carried in one man's string bag
I nde Walu Pubu
65   You are Walu Pubu (Tobani)
ibu nde Hubi Koma
he is Hubi Koma
Hiwa Koma au leagome howa
that is Hiwa Koma it is said
70   *Hiwa la Dugube lame yeni hagaga bu kabira libuni*
Hiwa and Dugube keep on holding (disputing) each other
Bi ogoreni yeni howa lalu kabira mendeli tandaga mialu piaga wini lowa
When one holds onto the talk the other person will get pain
bi langiru
75   that is the talk I have told
*Emene mbira lolane nemandi ogoria nde lolene wauwa howa timbu ngaruni
ale homa habale homagago*
You should make a little talk and take a short road and then these big
things used to be settled quickly
80   *Agali bi tandaga wia wiabo hayagoni hameigini laya agini*
The painful talk that continues to stay there is within the clan
Wali haga la habale homolane
With another clan it will be settled quickly
Agali mo tudu wiale birago hameigini la
85   Within the clan it will be left like a scar
wali haga uru debenego
between clans it will be good
Koma labo labo laribiyagua tandagabi
If two men of Koma argue then that is painful talk
90   *Tobani labo labo laribiyagua tandagabi*
If two men of Tobani argue then that is painful talk
Wali haga la debene wai timbu ore biribi yaguabi yamo
Between clans it is good, if you make a big war it is nothing
Ogoni bi ibini ladeba
95   So you say the real talk   [3(c)]

The design features and components of turns reflect to a considerable extent the sequential position of these turns in a stream of talk.
As a result of a degree of formality and scheduling, prefatory speeches

such as the above alert participants to setting-specific injunctions and general conversational maxims. In functional terms, they embrace moves that set the context for subsequent speech behaviour by providing a schema of reference and debate terms, and moves intended to elicit specific types of verbal responses. These orations attempt to structure the 'talk' that is to follow. How this is done, and what mechanisms are used, is something that deserves close attention.

With respect to the interrelations between 'talk' and 'pain', the speech allows us to perceive, in a performative and rhetorical context, just how such metaphors permeate speech. The notion of *tandaga* ('pain') is repeated throughout the text and linked to negatively assessed talk such as 'lies' (line 1), 'hidden talk' (line 73), or 'sour' (line 4) speech. The concept of settlement – 'pulling out' (line 2) or 'making die' (*homa*: lines 76–83) – is phrased as the removal of 'pain': the restoration of order is a restoration of health. The implicit structure of the speech reveals marked lexical patterning based on a number of salient oppositions along the semantic axes delineated above. Along the dimension of covertness, Muguye contrasts actions of 'holding' talk in (lines 23; 73) with 'saying out' (line 23). Talk that is 'true' (*henene*: lines 22; 28; 51) is constantly opposed to 'lies' (*tindule*: lines 1; 15; 26; 55) and other forms of negative talk (lines 12–21; 52–9). The expectation of mendacity is couched in these oppositions to pre-empt what is understood as the inevitability of falsehood. In these respects, the speech re-orients people to the system of meanings embodied by conversational maxims. The dimension of futility is indexed by the contrasts between that which can be 'pulled out and left' and that which remains like a 'scar'; that which is 'within' clans and disputes 'between' clans; and that which can be settled 'quickly' and matters which can cause protracted debate. The substantial metaphor of 'pain' is located at the intra-clan level.

The speech is clearly both retrospective – in its references to the way things 'used to be done' (line 79) and concepts of 'hidden' talk – and prospective in anticipating the kinds of talk required. The underlying syntax of these perspectives conforms to the sufficiency dimensions defined in Chapter 3:

truth-sufficiency statements: context-dependent notions of evidence which Muguye defines as Casuarina trees, drains, houses and nut trees (lines 28–36);

role-sufficiency statements: reiteration of norms against withholding information and kinds of talk – cunning, betrays, lies or persistence (lines 12–20; 52–59) – which may 'weigh down' (*damba*) the debate. Speeches should reflect *mana* and the rule that a person who leaves the land should 'take something in his hand';

type-sufficiency statements: the implicit references to forthcoming citations of *Malu*, and the importance of making 'small' or 'short' (*emene*: line 76) speeches as situationally appropriate to dispute resolution.

These sufficiency axes form the basis for apportionment of credit or discredit in discourse. They reference speech norms and thus provide a choreographic frame for the 'dance in talk' (Goffman 1981 : 73).

From a stylistic viewpoint the speech exhibits marked phonological patterning throughout. This occurs both in the series of terms that share initial phonemes – *tindule* ('lies'), *tago tago* ('mixed'), and *tandaga* ('pain') – and in the repeated items where parallel syntax is used – the connective suffix *uru* (lines 12–19), the compound suffix *gome* (*go* (emphasis) + *me* (agentive: 'by means of'): lines 27–36), and the phrase 'I know' (*mandabi*: lines 52–9). Moreover, the parenthetic, opening and closing stereotype phrases built around 'saying' divide between references to *mana* ('we are saying': lines 46–7), and the individually formulated conceptions of pain and truth ('I am saying/telling': lines 9; 75).

The kind of expectations embodied in the above colloquy echo closely Melpa ideas that 'people don't reveal talk quickly, they deny and deny for a long time and only later do they reveal the facts' (Strathern 1975 : 196). Within this domain of hidden talk – of hugger-mugger – there are a number of proverbial sayings that parallel those given for the axis of futility:

6 (a) Women hide their breasts when men look on: *wali andu hendeore halu kema handagola ni yi halu kemi* (used to imply that a speaker is conducting his talk in an analogous manner).
   (b) Are you giving water to the snake/marsupial?: *puya/tia iba meregobe?* (A reference to the action of pouring water into the mouths of these animals before cooking them so as to cleanse the intestines. The implication is that there is an attempt to wash away or cover over the talk.)

These proverbs organize and structure interaction within a conflict by reference to background cultural expectations. In her analysis of Ilongot oratory, Rosaldo remarked that 'through talk about talking, speakers are able to orient themselves to assumptions about the relation of language and social context which are ordinarily left implicit' (1973 : 215). In precisely the same way as the idiomatic terms of G and H in *Table 5* and their associated traditional adages, the proverbs stand in relations of congruity and contrast with other speech patterns. On the level of congruity they embody the same semantic elements as in the terms listed in F.1–6 (*Table 5*). At the level of opposition, they fall at one end of the axis of covertness. Having examined negative speech, I now turn to look at the terminology of positive evaluation and its associated metaphors.

Many ethnographers of speech have noted the culturally defined importance of 'straight' speech (see Rosaldo 1973 : 197; Strathern 1975 : 189). This applies to the Huli. The five most common positive evaluation terms are: J.1. *bi kuni* (talk + bone) – 'strong/important/real talk'; 2. *bi ibini* (talk + itself) – 'real talk'; 3. *bi tigabi* (talk + right (direction)) – 'straight/true talk'; 4. *bi henene/ henemane* (talk + stayed (*hene*)) – 'true talk'; 5. *bi haruane* (talk + ridge-pole of house) – 'straight/true talk'; 6. *bi tombe hea* (talk + full stomach) – 'satisfying talk'. The significance of choosing an idiom such as *kuni* ('bone') in the vocabulary of speech assessment can best be appreciated from the contexts of use outlined in Chapter 3. The connotations of strength and permanency provide an important contrast with the 'insubstantial' aspects of those negative terms previously described. The association of straight and 'true' talk is best viewed from the perspective of the Huli emphasis on talk being 'open' and 'visible'. We have seen that the sphere of sense perception in terms of sight is linguistically marked in Huli as a critical dimension to the presentation of accounts and statements. Given the cultural salience of sight and truth, and the many modes in which their relationship is manifested, a more detailed exposition is separately presented below.

A further constituent of the map of linguistic co-ordinates is the set of locative terms. These function to place discourse within the historical aetiology of the conflict, or speaker's strategies. They locate talk within the structure of argument in progress. K.1. *bi tene* (talk + origin/source/base) – 'source of the talk'; 2. *bi irane* (talk + trunk/ stem of plant or tree) – 'important talk'; 3. *bi magane* (talk + branch) – 'part of the talk'; 4. *bi amane* (talk + base of the banana or sugar-cane plant) – 'main or first talk'; 5. *bi gane* (talk + splinter) – 'small piece of talk'; 6. *bi hanuni* (talk + middle) – 'compromise or unbiased talk'; 7. *bi kugi* (talk + rubbish/scraps of food) – 'talk remaining from before, unsettled matters'; 8. *bi daliga* (talk + above) – 'superficial talk only'; 9. *bi dindi ha* (talk + below) – 'talk secret to a group, or talk which is underneath as opposed to "above"'; 10. *bi haguene* (talk + head) – 'main talk or issue/introductory talk'; 11. *bi talini* (talk + threshold of house) – 'first talk or topic, as opposed to extraneous matters'. A number of comparative points can be made between Huli and Melpa systems. M. Strathern's study of official and unofficial courts among the Melpa (1972) called attention to the centrality of such phrases as *ik oki* – 'to dig out the talk' which are paralleled by the Huli terms *ali* ('dig') and *goda* ('extract') (see *Table 5*). Truth is something buried, hidden from sight, something that has to be made to come out into the open. The Huli concept of *tene* ('source'), like the Melpa notion of *pukl* ('base': *ik pukl* – 'base of the talk'), places events in a temporally bound causal sequence that also locates and identifies responsibility. Once again we can best comprehend the figurative import of *tene* from the social contexts in which it is embedded:

Tene ('origin')
$\left\{ \begin{array}{l} \textit{Wai tene} \text{ ('war sources'; see Glasse 1968 : 94)} \\ \textit{Tene te} \text{ ('source legends', oral history)} \\ \textit{Mànda tene} \text{ ('first hair of Haroli')} \\ \textit{Mabu tene} \text{ ('original garden')} \\ \textit{Bi tene} \text{ ('source of the talk')} \\ \textit{Tene} \text{ (i) agnates (ii) qualifies kin terms to distinguish close from classificatory kin} \end{array} \right.$

The way in which the lexeme *tene* is used to delimit areas of liability in any causal chain of conflict has been documented in my analyses of case material. The locative terms K.1–11, given above, express notions of permanency and importance, contrasting what is 'basic/fundamental' with matter that are 'superficial'. In dispute contexts, parallel oppositions formulated in terms of *haguene* ('head') – *herene* ('tail') (e.g. lines 8–10; 11–16 Text B) or *ala* ('before/first') – *mani* ('later/secondly': lines 1; 9) reveal an indigenous acknowledgement that people manipulate claims. In the presentation of a case individuals may change (*mo ariba*: line 8) the sequential structure of claims according to strategies explained elsewhere. This approximates to the analytical notion of 'positional incidence' forwarded in this book. In the following speech Dalu verbalizes such concepts by noting the way in which a wife presented

grievances about pigs, houses and other arguments with her husband
in a revised sequence:

TEXT B Speaker: Dalu
1   *Anda ogo ala gini bule nogo nigo labo mani tiga bulebiya*
    The house first will be straightened and the pigs later we
    will settle
    anda ala tiga bulebereba
5   the house first you two will straighten
    au lalu ogoni labo hondo bi ogoni dagua lo ngebibe
    like that it was said and for those two you are talking?
    Ai ina howa mo ariba halu bi udu layago mo herene ariba ho ngelowa
    from there you changed the talk and made it the tail
10 *Ai mo haguene anda ogonaga ala mo tiga ibiribe laro?*
    The house you made the head and came to straighten it I am saying?
    Bi layago mo herene ariba howa lo ngelowa
    The talk you said you have changed and made the tail
    Anda naga mo haguene ho yalu
15 the house you have carried and made the head
    I agalinila lai mo haguene yu ibiridagoria hale halo hendeni
    The argument with your husband has been made head and carried here, it
    has been heard and seen.

Dalu's speech stresses that the wife reversed the precedence of issues
from that which obtained at the outset of the dispute.

I turn now to an examination of the third semantic dimension
abstracted earlier, the axis of control. I am specifically concerned with
the types of status contrasts defined by the negative and positive
qualities I have been examining in respect of speech.

Iba Tiri, shame and duplicity

How then do the Huli idealize speech aberrations or other modes of
behavioural deviance? Despite a marked absence of any hierarchical
set of status denominations, the appellation Iba Tiri is frequently
employed in conversation to attribute negative qualities or assessments. In contrast with other members of the Huli pantheon, Iba Tiri
represents both a culture hero and trickster; he embodies characteristics of immense symbolic complexity. Unlike other *dama* he features
in many *bi té* ('folk-stories'), and is the only supernatural being to
have a recognizable and elaborately defined persona, all of which
signify the singular importance this spirit holds for the Huli. Given
that many of the thematic motifs associated with Iba Tiri show homologous relations with the mythic complex detailed by Wagner (1972)

for the Daribi hero Souw/Sido/Sau, it seems appropriate to analyse both the continuities and discontinuities in a comparative framework. I would argue that the striking resemblances between these culture heroes, shown by the data given below, suggests that the Huli Iba Tiri is perhaps part of the linked series of myths in the tradition of 'Papuan hero tales' (Wagner 1972 : 19).

In the aetiological narratives (*tene tē*) I collected, Iba Tiri was rarely included in overall schemata of *dama* genealogy. In some accounts he is portrayed as originating from Dubube, which is consistent with the Huli equation between deviance and 'outside' influences. An invariant element in all the texts concerned with Iba Tiri is the centrality of an illicit sexual act with the female progenitor Hona Hana (sometimes Dindi Ainya). In so far as this infidelity predates the birth of 'man' (*agali*), the relation between 'sexuality and fertility' (Wagner 1972 : 21) assumes critical importance. The myths detail five central components to the resulting events of this sexual act:

(i) the feeling of 'shame' (*taga*) experienced by Iba Tiri (see Wagner 1972 : 30–2 regarding the shame of Souw);

(ii) the birth of the mountains Hari Alua, Hari Ambua, and Hari Haliago on a land that was previously flat. This links Iba Tiri with certain features of the Huli landscape (Wagner 1972 : 20);

(iii) through the act of intercourse Iba Tiri had put out the fire in Hana's genitals and gave it to humans. This parallels the notion of a 'travelling creator' associated with Souw;

(iv) all the participants in the drama go off on a number of separate journeys through Huli land;

(v) Iba Tiri, following his shame, carved out fingers and feet from the amorphous flesh of Hana to create the 'roots' (*pini*) and 'dates' (*pongo*) for her progeny (i.e. Huli people). During this act he is said to have uttered the following *mana*:

Hugu   dugu bialu
Vaginal secretion pulled out
Hagua   dugu bialu
Red ochre pulled out
Baralamba la donge lalu
Baralamba plants prepare.

These actions relate to the conduct of *Ndi Tingi* ('marriage') rites and to the ritual of *Ma Hiriya* associated with child-growth. Iba Tiri thus appears as a moral benefactor, a 'law giver' creating order and linked to sexual reproduction. These themes, which parallel those noted by Wagner (1972) for Souw, are further culturally embedded in the system of relations between this spirit and agricultural fertility. Iba Tiri is variously invoked in garden magic:

Gamu (to increase size and number of bananas)
Informant: Anya (Tobani Clan)
Wanelabo   wane   andu mogobia logolabaro
Wanelabo's daughter's nipples   I am stretching
Iba   Teria Yagira angeneni   Iba Tiri   wi   logolabaro
Rivers Teria Yagira on their banks Iba Tiri's penis I am stretching
Iba Tiri   wi   hubua bero
Iba Tiri's penis I am wrapping.

The penis of Iba Tiri is a mediating element between man and good fortune (as above), as well as misfortune. Like Souw, the genitals of Iba Tiri are 'exaggerated' (Wagner 1972 : 33) and hot. Furthermore, the appearance of fruit from the Ficus tree (*poge*) after a drought is attributed to Iba Tiri as are the health of 'pig bristles' (see Wagner 1972 : 28).

Despite these important thematic replications between Souw and Iba Tiri, certain culture-specific transformations exist that perhaps constitute a mythic sub-tradition between Huli, Wiru, and Duna.[6] This concerns an inextricable link to 'water', for Iba Tiri is primarily conceived as a 'water spirit'. I have already commented in Chapter 4 that he is believed to cleanse all waters and thus provide the essential 'life-giving' fluid of water/rain (this explains the reference to 'banks' in the *gamu* cited above). Water also represents a sphere of danger, and drownings are often attributed to the malevolent work of Iba Tiri. In opposition to the explicit links of this spirit to human order, is a more pronounced emphasis on his trickster qualities.

Both the Duna designation Yu Tiri and the Huli title Iba Tiri literally translate as 'water (*iba/yu*) fool (*tiri*)'. The name is fused to an image of 'playfulness', and indeed two forms of cat's-cradle (*hawalanga*) are denoted by the phrases Iba Tiri *ti* ('Iba Tiri's excreta') and Iba Tiri *māli* ('Iba Tiri's dance'). Iba Tiri is held responsible for any unaccountable loss of an axe head. In response, people 'trick' (*hoge*) the spirit into returning the adze by first presenting pig meat and then withdrawing it when the lost item is recovered. Through such actions we can appreciate that Huli reciprocally interact with Iba Tiri along symmetrical lines of deceit. In accordance with the dominant motif of 'water', constipation, diarrhoea, and water-based illnesses are attributed to this jester. Traditionally, these were relieved by oblations of pig and performances of *Tiri Yagia* in which men, dressed in imitation of this spirit, fought over a male-transvestite. Significantly, this was the only occasion when any supernatural agent was an object of mimicry, thus indicating the degree to which Iba Tiri occupies a conceptual domain separate from other *dama*.

Iba Tiri is conceived as having a defined abode and mode of dress or decoration. The relevant characteristics are codified in the following *pureremo* which may be used as a narrative device to introduce Iba Tiri in *bi te*:

Iba Tiri Bembe *tigida* / Baralu *tigida* / Tuya *tigida* / Tumane *tigida* / Golia *tigida* / Ayele *tigida* / *dambale dene udugununugu lama* (or *dambale hegene* / *uluba wangaru udugununugu lama* / *elabe yangaru babagi hama* / *iba hanua nogo lama* / *iba mbereya nogo lama* / *guru wali nogo lama* / *guru kayele nogo lama* / *aleba hauwi nogo lama* / *iba ngele nogo lama*
Iba Tiri is along the banks of Bembe river / along the banks of Baralu / along the banks of Tuya / along the banks of Tumane / along the banks of Golia / along the banks of Ayele / the ends of his string-apron are uneven / the points of his three-pronged arrow are uneven / his Ribbon-tail feathers are all on one side / he makes a noise like a grass-skirt and we used to say (think) it was pig / he makes a noise like fish and we used to say it was pig / he makes a noise like a lizard and we used to say it was pig / he makes a noise like a Dugube rattle and we used to say it was pig / he makes a noise like a cricket and we used to say it was pig.

The text displays the stylistic patterning typical of this genre. Three basic statements about habitat, dress, and behaviour are repeated through the device of parallel syntax. Lexical substitutions form rhyming pairs: the alliterative forms *Bembe* / *Baralu* – *Tuya* / *Tumane*, and the phrasal lexemes *iba hanua* / *iba mbereya* – *guru wali* / *guru kayele*. These poetic features complement the dualistic facets of Iba Tiri.

References in the text to dress – unevenness – and trickster qualities reinforce the conclusion that Iba Tiri represents a form of institutionalized disorder. The name appears in jokes that negatively assess appearance, providing the level of contrast with Haroli (discussed in the next section): it is an opposition of uncontrolled and controlled decoration / deportment. An improperly attired person is an Iba Tiri, or, synonymously, *wali dali* (female) / *agali dali* (male). Moreover, the same designation is frequently used in speech assessments to signify 'meaningless' talk and lack of order:

HELAGO: . . . *la pugua bere ai Iba Tiri harago hondo ha*
     . . . you are interrupting, you are an Iba Tiri, wait.   (D.2: 209–12)

EGARI: *Bi uru ale lole larene*
    To say those talks you should have said
Ina udugua yu moga bigi berego i udugua agi?
Why are you wrapping/hiding it then?
Bi loane larebe be uru agi naga lare?
Did you want to make us talk or why did you talk?
ai libugua agi biribidago udugu bi nayi yene
you two have done this but you are not holding any talk
Dali yene
you are holding Iba Tiri (i.e. you are an Iba Tiri).   (D.2: 354–58)

A person who does not hold talk is an Iba Tiri. This status contrasts with *manali* ('men of *mana*'), *miniwi* ('mind (*mini*) + placed (*wi*)': wise men) and *biyi* ('holder of talk'). Importantly, Iba Tiri fuses deviant dress and speech in a manner that emphasizes the very real relationships between these modal forms of self-presentation. The censorial usages of this designation articulate concepts of disorder.

Like the Daribi images of Souw, Iba Tiri exemplifies 'contrasting or alternative qualities' (Wagner 1972 : 33) manifested by a dualism that pervades allusions to this spirit. The variant names of the hero occur, without exception, as minimally-distinct pairs (typical of verbal teasing games):

    Yuguale – Dabuale : Muguali – Dabuali : Elabe   – Helabe
    Kedo   – Gengedo : Mini   – Aminila : Wangoba – Memeba

These are the most commonly cited names of which Amini and Muguali also signify axes, a decorative accoutrement of Iba Tiri. These paired designations are understood to represent male and female counterparts. This dualism is further inherent in the cross-culturally valid semantic equation of duplicity and 'double-dealing'. In the *Tiri Yagia* rite, referred to above, there are *two* Iba Tiri and each performer wears *two* Ribbon-tail (*Astrapia mayeri*) feathers. This appears to symbolize decoratively the cultural notion that a liar (or Iba Tiri) is a person 'with two minds and two talk' (*mini kira bi kira*). The term *Elabe Yange* (Ribbon-tailed Bird of Paradise) contains the morph *ela* – 'to shake/move'. Movement of feathers in bird or human display has sexual connotations associated with courting behaviour. This 'sexual motif' is linguistically reflected in the optional line to the above *pureremo*: *Elabe yange pulu lungu bialu* ('With the Ribbon-tail feathers flapping').

In this latter regard, Iba Tiri (like Souw) is a cultural stereotype for representing 'shame', perhaps ultimately located in the historical 'shaming' episode mentioned above.

LANDA: *Aba wānekui ko hayadago*
    Aba on your forehead it is bad
Tagame Ialuba gai lalu
With the shame the Ialuba tree will be bent
Tagame Iba Tirime gai nalego
With shame and Iba Tiri you won't bend
ai mana lare
that is the mana *you* are saying (sarcastic remark).
EGELE: If he doesn't kill and give (pigs) the Ialuba tree will bend.
It will be like an Iba Tiri is there (i.e. with shame).
LANDA: If I am bent like a Ialuba tree I won't be a man, I'll be an Iba Tiri,
with shame (*tagame*).   (Field data)

Shame, like anger, is a state requiring compensation. As a form of
affliction or illness it necessitates something 'to rub on the sore' (ref.
D.3). To have shame is to be 'broken up' (*taga*: emphatic form *taga
tele*: 'spinning shame'), or 'bent' like the Ialuba tree which is the
straightest species of palm in Huli (see above). Anatomical concomitants of shame centre on the 'nose'; it will 'point down' (*ngui
dali ho ngegoni*) or 'break' (*mbiru ngui wanekuiru haga bule-
berema*). A person with shame is there 'with a nose like a person who
has had intercourse with his sister' (*ngui uru mbalini tangana mbalue
kego*). Shame is defined then with reference to illicit sexual relations,
and thus relates directly to concepts of Iba Tiri. The physiological
conditions of 'shame' expressed through the modal states of 'nose'
are consistent with the importance this anatomical part holds for
Huli. I explain this in more detail in Part 2 of this chapter. Equally
significant is the fact that shame also attaches to the 'forehead'
(*wānekui*) as do other negative states expressed in this conversational
extract: *i wānekui emene taga taga birago* ('there is a little shame on
your forehead') (field data). The forehead represents the most
important physiological index of moral and emotional dispositions.
As the locus of truth it can thus reflect states of 'shame' or 'lies'. Since
shame is also conceived in terms of a taint or contamination, it affects
the 'nose' in analogous fashion to female pollution.

    Indigenous statements about 'lies' show a high degree of corre-
spondence with notions of shame and anger. The anatomical indices
of lying are a 'swollen nose' (*ngui to ha*) and 'red eyes' (*de daramabi*).
Conversational idioms express the counter-normative status of lies as
'holding excreta', 'throwing excreta', or as something that 'comes out
the anus'. Such notions of 'waste' (i.e. futility) link very directly to
insult and anger as 'smelly' (*ngubi*: see Part 2) talk:

bi ti baga, bi ngubi magubiru ina haria ha bi la gimbu gimbu hame nalego.
the excreta talk, the smelly talk, the sick talk are joining together and I
don't like it.　　　　　　　　　　　　　　　　　　(Field data)

These connotations of taint and sickness provide a level of semantic
continuity with shame, anger, insult, swearing, and other speech
modes considered in this chapter. They are all deemed to be products
of 'two minds' rather than one.

Finally, lying is also considered by Huli to constitute a breach of
speech maxims. When asked to explain what lies are one of my
informants offered the following insights:

'He will talk like this. When someone sees he is lying he won't listen to
what I am saying. He will talk fast and will keep on talking. He doesn't hear
what I say and he is not going to share the talk (*bi mo tale bule ndo*). What
I say does not go inside but is left out (*ibu mo pea nahe ngelowa*).'

Conformity to the rules by which conversation proceeds symbolizes
ordered relationships. A liar, as the text makes clear, fails in such
interactions through defaults in respect of sharing talk, monitoring
the talk of others, comprehension (what goes inside/outside), and
obedience to the proper sequential order of turn-taking.

The above conceptions of Iba Tiri, shame and lies, define then the
negative pole of the dimension of control. I turn now to the contrasting and positive definitions of speech control.

Haroli, truth and knowledge

On one level, the Huli regard *manali* (*mana* + people (*li*)) as
opposed to individuals who display erratic or excessive tendencies.
The term does not denote a fixed position of authority in society, but
is used in general reference to people who hold knowledge and talk of
various kinds. The full implications of this concept have been detailed
before, but the following speech fragment fixes specifically on how
manali exhibit control, and what this is in any dispute:

TEXT C
1　This is the way it will be done, the *mana* men will share the talk
　on the garden you two have made when the *mana* men have seen then
　they will share the talk, those men there
　it won't be done in the corner
5　it will be done on their eyes
　When Habia's father comes the *mana* men will share the talk
　the *mana* men will share the talk
　'I'll eat you go!' don't say that
　don't you answer back like that
10　if you say 'I'll eat you go outside', you (he) will say 'go with him'

those two sources the *mana* men will share
the sources 'you go' and 'you go' (he says) that you two are saying
those *mana* men will say (i.e. that the sources are those)
when that is said then from there it will be shared
15 Now you two can't say 'You go', 'You go'
When we have seen if Habia's father's talk goes inside your talk
the *mana* men will share the talk
we'll see if this woman is going to pay this man
we'll see if this man is going to pay this woman
20 the *mana* men will share and give it, that is the talk being said.
(Field data: Egari)

In its performative context this speech constituted a soliloquy and thus contrasts markedly with the formality of Muguye's oration (Text A). Nevertheless, there is a high degree of correspondence between the two speeches in terms of implicit syntax, formulation and sequential structure. The overall design components and organizational devices are composed of statements standing in a balanced and structured relationship to each other. These are expressed in bipartite or quadripartite formulations. Typically, an idea is elaborated through a negative proposition followed by a positive delineation of characteristics. As a recurrent rhetorical device this represents a structural finding of immense importance. In part, this design feature is linked to speakers' orientations to the semantic and sufficiency dimensions I have described. These I have shown to be articulated through the presentation of contrasts along each axis. However, this conversational pattern occurs with such frequency and generality that it argues against the simplistic categorization of formal / everyday speech codes in favour of a wider appreciation of the 'structured' nature of naturally occurring talk. In so far as 'sharing the talk' appears then as one aspect of control, it represents a gambit that 'frames' the proposition / counter-propositions made in the above speech. In Text A the same function is performed by the repetition of gambits relating to truth, lies, and pain.

TEXT C
manali yabu lolebira
the mana men will share.
(lines 1, 3, 6, 7, 11, 13, 17, 20)
TEXT A
tindule . . . duguwuwa / handamaro
lies will be pulled out / see an end to (verb + *maro* = 'conclude')
(lines 1, 5, 8, 10, 20, 25)
tandaga
pain.
(lines 5, 8, 72, 80–90)

These reiterated norms, which occur in initial, medial, and final turn locations, provide a framework for the interspersed binary statements given below. They provide constant summations.

Speech injunctions – two things that must not be said:
TEXT C
  8 'I'll eat you go' don't say that
  9 Don't you answer back like that
    (also lines 12 and 15)
TEXT A
  81 The painful talk . . . is within the clan
  83 With another clan it will be settled quickly
  85 Within the clan it will be left like a scar
  87 Between clans it will be good
    (also lines 73, 78–9, 89–93)

These units display a binary structure which can be defined on both semantic and syntactic grounds.

Modes of resolution – paired negative and positive formulations:
TEXT C
  4 It won't be done in the corner
  5 It will be done on their eyes
TEXT A
  42 When one is pulled out should the other stay?
  44 Or should the other one sit?
    (Disjunctive rhetorical device)
  46 Not that . . . should go without anything . . .
  49 He should go with something . . .

The corresponding Huli lines are linguistically marked by the sentence final lexeme *ndo* ('no'). Unlike parallel Daribi (see Wagner 1972 : 34) patterns, in Huli speeches the negative frequently appears as the intitial, or heading, proposition preceding the positive:

It is not a smelly talk (*bi ngubi ndo*)
A talk like that will go inside her

That is not woman's talk (*wali ndo*)
That is the talk of Dama.   (Field data)
TEXT D
  2 You are not woman (*i wali ndo* (*go*))
    You have been eating and catching insects everywhere
TEXT E
  12 You are not like a man (*agali ale ndo*)
  14 You are an Iba Tiri.

The semantic contrasts need not always be expressed in terms of a single pair of statements. It is common for any one positive or negative proposition to be replicated by repeated syntax with one or two-word substitutions (for example, Text E or Text A: 13–20; 52–9). This embodies the cross-culturally prevalent proclivity for enumeration and types of repetition in rhetoric, and is evident in the texts cited in this book.

Final statements or conclusions – paired disjunctive / conditional propositions:
TEXT C
17 [The *mana* men will share the talk]   (gambit)
18 We'll see if . . . woman pays the man
19 We'll see if . . . man pays the woman
20 [The *mana* men will share the talk]   (gambit)
TEXT A
78 [You should . . . little talk . . . short road . . . settle quick]   (gambit)
89 If two men of Koma . . . that is painful talk
91 If two men of Tobani . . . that is painful talk
95 [So you say the real talk]   (gambit)
TEXT B
13 The talk . . . and made the tail
15 The house . . . and made the head
17 [The argument . . . has been heard and seen]   (gambit)

The implicit structural syntax of these speeches conforms to the schema abstracted in Chapter 2. There is a progression from statements about the *present state of play* (Text A: 11; Text C: 7), to things that *shouldn't be done / said*, and finally to *conclusions* about how things could be. The binary aspects of this framework of moves is paralleled by the binary presentation of statements for each move bounded by gambits that 'frame' propositions and provide links between topics. The structure provides a security for the contexts of insecurity and uncertainty about the effective up-take of suggestions or proposals. Each topic can be defined in retrospective or prospective terms and is frequently marked by lexical and syntactic repetition. The final disjunction of resolution possibilities reflects cultural orientations to consensus and parity.

Control of speech is thus inextricably linked to equal distribution of turns at talk. This axiomatic norm of speech reciprocity often functions to inhibit application of ideologies of dominance prevalent in other social contexts. In the same way as the dimensions of futility and covertness are expressed in distinct sets of proverbs about talk, so the axis of control is similarly defined. There are a number of traditional sayings that reverse or reiterate orders of primacy such as elder/younger or male/female, and that function to allow others to 'gain the floor' for speech. They thus emphasize the egalitarian nature of talking in Huli:

7 (a) He might still have some shoulder-bone (valued part of pig) in his bad string bag, so let him speak: *nu kuni payene la dibini hanaganego lelo waha* (implies that appearances can be deceptive, a counter to *ad hominem* arguments).
   (b) The smallest bird was the first: *ega Yuli Dimbi wahenego* (used to permit young children, or those who stand in relations of juniority to others, to speak).
   (c) He is like a rat trying to be the head: *hurume haguene harigo* (used to censure another who is getting 'above' his station).
   (d) He is like a banana trying to ripen from the bottom up first: *hai erene howa ibiru daga nahagago* (signifies an inversion of the natural sequence of maturity).
   (e) He is small trying to be the head of the sago: *emene hiwa haguene hariba* (similar to c and d above).
   (f) Women turned round the bow/struts of a house: *wali danda/anda maga beregeda*. (This is one of the most important proverbs relating to the male-female dichotomy. It associates females with the 'bow' – a salient symbol of manhood. The import of the saying is an implicit reference to the mythological primacy of woman who had to teach men to put the bow-string on the proper side, or to place the horizontal holding-struts of a house on the inside. The proverb is used in situations where attempts are made to dismiss female contributions on the basis of their politically marginal status.)

These *bi mabura* are aesthetically valued forms of circumlocution (*mabura* – 'to go around') which refer to cultural truths. Such tropes re-orient disputants to fundamental assumptions and presuppositions about the interrelations between speech, social transaction, and context. While people are enjoined in disputes to talk in 'straight', 'open' language, and not 'hidden' talk, *bi mabura* constitute a compromise between appropriate/inappropriate and direct/indirect speech. As conventional formulae signifying acknowledged truths, the censorial repercussions of their indirectness are mitigated. *Yobage*, by contrast, is individually formulated and thus not acceptable. This paradox of an acceptable level of veiled meaning is thus resolved through contextually circumscribing those occasions when it is permitted. *Yobage* is an inherent feature of the genres *Tamba bi* and *Wali O*; when divorced from these contexts it is counter-productive in the excavation of truth and thus subject to censure. Ego-centred displays of oratory should not tend towards excessive obscurity.

The notion of truth in Huli culture is very directly related to what is 'visible', just as lies express the covert, hidden, and unseen. This is explicit in both Muguye's and Egari's speeches:

TEXT A
2 When we have seen the lies . . .
22 I have seen all these things
28 The truth should be seen on the . . .
TEXT C
4 It won't be done in the corner
5 It will be done on their eyes.

The sphere of sense perception in respect of sight is linguistically marked in Huli. Statements based on direct perception carry the evidence suffix – *da*. Indeed, the concept of permanency is perhaps reflected in the lexeme *henene* ('truth': *hene* – 'stayed'). The indigenous parallels to the Western idea of a witness are expressed by the phrase *de hendene* – 'the ones who saw'. The figurative language of truth attempts then to express the intangible in terms of the tangible. In this respect the occurrences of the morpheme *mugu* are critical to the understanding of veracity. *Muguni* ('footprint') is used as a gloss for any kind of visible evidence. In the wailing text cited in Appendix 4, the impressions left behind by a deceased woman are metaphorically spoken of as 'footprints of the birds' (C: 57–70). The related lexeme *mugube* corresponds to the colloquial phrase 'it is just his way'; it signifies habit, custom, personal idiosyncrasies, a subjective perspective on truth.

The importance of seeing in the evaluation of veracity is further indexed by *bi mabura* such as the following:

8 (a) Did you actually see the ants coming down the tree branch?: *Bai magane ugurili daligago handaridago?* (Used as a challenge to an opponent to state what visible evidence he has for his claims.)

Significantly, truth is also mapped onto the anatomical landscape in the same way as lies, anger, and shame. The forehead is considered the locus where such moral and emotional concepts are visibly manifested for others to monitor. Its significance for understanding all aspects of Huli thought cannot be understated.

Aba, my forehead is getting dark (i.e. anger)
The talk you have made has no forehead (i.e. 'truth')
Agali wanekui dumbi yalugo napolanego
Man's forehead forehead   cannot be broken
When we have seen her mind and forehead we will divorce.   (Field data)

Truth is something visible and registrable on the forehead, situated between the organs that detect authenticity. Non-verbal attestations of validity are made by placing the index finger in ashes and pressing the tip to the forehead. This demonstrates a willingness to become dirty or burnt for the sake of acceptance. The lexical items which denote forehead reveal further sociocultural dimensions to truth. The conventional variants *wānekui/wānekuni* contain the morphemes 'bone' (*kui* or *kuni* both occur) and 'woman/daughter' (*wā* (female sex-specific marker e.g. *wali* – woman, *wandari* – girl, *wane* – daughter) + *ne* ('type of')). The term 'daughter's/woman's bone' encapsulates the relation between 'feminine priority' (see Gell 1975 : 172) and the concept of veracity or validity. Pressing the fingertip to the forehead has the force of 'on my daughter's/woman's bone'. The importance of this anatomical point is also marked by the existence of eulogistic synonyms (see Part 2) which figure prominently in rhetoric and 'high' speech:

> *Bi Mone* ('good talk')
> *Wānekui* ('forehead') → *Dumbi yalu, Ega Wagi, Homa embo,*
> *Gogobane, Wagobane*

Such praise terms may be placed adjacently to the conventional analogue as in the texts cited above. Importantly, the word *homa* (in *Homa embo*) means 'one', which precisely reflects the unity of truth in contrast to the 'duality' of lies. To recapitulate the main elements: *location* – the forehead is in the 'middle' (*hanuni*); *covertness* – the forehead is open and visible; *substantiality* – the forehead is bone and permanent.

The positional priority of 'forehead' has then the positive connotations of being in the 'middle', a real or conceptual location that expresses unbiased and sharing behaviour. Exemplification of these notions is found in the system of exchange and consanguinity embedded in *aba* kinship. *Aba* are construed as persons between whom reciprocal economic, ritual, and social obligations exist; this is, as I have shown, verbally realized in the *aba* pureremo (see Chapter 3). Conceptualizing this state in terms of intermediation (*hanuni*) conveys and captures fundamental truths about this kin relationship:

> *homa embo* hanuni
> forehead   middle
> (the *aba* are in the middle like one's forehead)

galu wabia   hanuni   *li*   *hengedagoni*
Lesser bird of paradise feathers middle up there are planted
(the *aba̅* will be planted in the middle like Lesser feathers on a
wig)

The force of these statements derives in part from their content, and
in part from the switching of vocabulary to the 'high' stylistic lexemes
of *bi mone* (see Part 2 below). *Galu Wabia* is substituted for the conventional term *Komia* (Lesser bird of paradise), and *homa embo* for
wa̅nekuni. The *aba̅* pureremo develops a metaphorical identity
between the actions of placing these kin in the 'middle' land and the
action of placing feathers in decoration. The semantics of *hanuni*
('middle') express mediation through the exchanged bridewealth
(*wariabu*) between patrilines, and the fact that *wariabu*$_2$ is an inter-
mediate category of bride-price (i.e. between *haguene* and *daga*: see
Chapter 3). Importantly, the forehead also constitutes a medial
element between talk and decoration. In displays of cultural truths
one wears one's words as one wears one's wigs – in the middle and on
the 'forehead'. Talk and decoration are modal aspects of a continuum
defining authenticity.

It is important to explore a little more deeply the centrality of forehead in decoration behaviour for it is here that we find a strategic
nucleus of rhetorical devices used in disputes. More so than *manali*
('*mana* men'), Haroli represent the essence of those qualities that
contrast, along the axis of control, with Iba Tiri – the 'good/excel-
lent' versus the 'bad/inept'. As stereotype embodiments of such
attributes, these appellations serve to define and communicate status.

Despite the virtual cessation of Huli bachelor cults, in which hair
and body were the foci of purificatory and cosmetic rituals, wigs are
still worn by most adult males as part of everyday adornment. They
have retained much of their traditional significance and constitute a
visual criterion for cultural differentiation of the Huli from their
neighbours. This is indigenously expressed in those *pureremo* cited in
Chapter 2. Explanations as to why hair is a medium for aesthetic
attention in Huli reside partly in the way hair seems cross-culturally to
reflect social motifs and movements, and partly in the specific set of
meanings inherent in the following linguistic parallels:
(1) *Ma̅nda* denotes hair of the head – in a particular style – or wig,
and is derivationally related to the prosodically distinguished lexeme
ma̅nda ('knowing/understanding'). The growth of hair symbolizes

an attainment of maturity, strength, and *mana*, representing a
Samson motif in the culture. Adult males could not marry until they
had grown a beard. This relatedness of meaning between the two
forms of *manda* illuminates the associations between concepts of
truth, authenticity ('knowledge'), and Haroli.

(2) The term *iri* is employed for both human strands of hair (*mànda
iri*) and bird feathers (*ega iri*). This underlines, perhaps, the semantic
analogies between man and bird that typifies the philosophies of all
Highlands cultures. Specifically, movement of *iri* is important as a
sign of vitality. Feathers used in decoration must shake (*bara*) in one
direction; those that lie to one side (*pu pagi*) or flock in different
directions (*ba tara ba tara*) are considered unaesthetic. This sense of
movement is captured and instilled into children through references
in *gamu* to 'flight' (*yaga*):

lu wuale ale pupu
go like the wind against the hair
yayu yamama ya pudu pudu
flap your wings

(3) Inseparable from the above equations is the ideological correspondence between the statements 'I am decorating' and 'I am
becoming/transforming myself into a cassowary'. This metaphoric
equivalence is reflected in the morphologically related terms *yàri*
('decorate/adorn') and *yári* ('cassowary'). The cassowary represents
something that is both wild and aggressive. Dispute opponents are
referenced as cassowaries: *yári gi hondone dolaga biba hendeni* ('the
cassowary's fingers have been pointed and seen') (D.2). Minor sorcery
is still practised to inhibit a protagonist's speech, action which is
expressed in *gamu* as 'knotting the hair of a cassowary'. These themes
provide a skeletal frame for understanding the senses in which Haroli
manifested truth and control in its quintessential forms.

The Haroli cult concerned only bachelors (from about the age of
sixteen) who would, for a period of two years or more, seclude themselves in the bush. There they underwent stringent ritual sanitization
– a cleansing of the body, eyes, and mind of female pollution.
Instruction was given by elders known as *mambo* or *igiri aba* ('boys'
father'). Each clan had at least one *tigi anda* ('cult house' – forbidden place) attended, predominantly, by males of the parish. Many
Koma men I interviewed had enrolled as *Iba Giya* (Haroli neophytes:
most likely a compound of *iba* (water) + *ngiya* (given)) in Pureni

(twelve miles away) on account of its reputation for producing the finest graduates. People who shared the same Haroli house often refer to themselves as *mànda mandagi* ('one-hair people').

While secluded in the bush, novices would cultivate their hair. This process was infrequently interrupted by public displays – perambulations from the 'wild' to 'domestic' domains. Such division of space is analogous to, and is understood to parallel, bird of paradise behaviour. The separation of home / nest grounds – *anda* – from public / display grounds – *hama* – underlies references to 'coming onto the cleared dancing ground' found in the *gamu* text cited in Appendix 3B, and discussed further below. Moreover, in so far as the dispute process is predicated on the 'inside / domestic versus outside / public' dichotomy, we can again appreciate the extent to which the models of talk and decoration are homologous.

Gradation of Haroli status was marked by the type of hair-shape grown, and the auxiliary and symbolic items of adornment. Initially novices would wear *mànda tene* ('source, origin, first hair': see *Diagram 6*, p. 241) using only charcoal (considered as aesthetically basic or crude) for facial decor, and carrying pan-pipes (signifying 'playfulness'). When the *coiffure* was fully fashioned, and the requisite ritual stages completed, the same hair would be turned upwards into the *mànda hare* ('red-hair': see *Diagram 5*, p. 240). Bows – connoting manhood, virility, and maturity – replaced pan-pipes, use of colour was permitted, and *gamu* communicated to enhance beauty. Conceptually, accession to *mànda hare* represented a status transition from immaturity to maturity, articulated by decorative icons. *Mànda* were not wigs but styled hair which was cut and made into wigs after renouncement of Haroli membership. We can account for both the colour and shape of *mànda* in terms of the following explanations.

The use of red ochre for the higher form of *mànda* seems to express an attainment of strength and power inherent in the life-blood of the cult. The wearers are imbued with the potency of the cult's progenitor – a woman (see Appendix 6). Power is acquired through ritual and the properties of 'heat' inherent in 'red / blood' (*darama* (*bi*)). The impotence of *mànda tene* is contrasted with the potency of *mànda hare* through the symbolic opposition of black and red respectively. The Haroli manifested the will of males to negotiate the primordial fecundity of females, through metaphoric assumption of cross-sex status. Initiates were known also as *igiri more* ('virgin boys'), and *more* is a term conventionally restricted to talk about girls.

The shapes of the two *mànda* are in positional contrast as 'down-turned' – *mànda tene* – and 'up-turned' – *mànda hare*. This reversal is terminologically expressed by the word *beregeda* ('turned around'), the same notion used to describe the relation between Mother of Life and Mother of Death in the myth cited in Chapter 3. I suggest the two shapes proclaim states of 'display' and 'non-display' encapsulating, as a metaphorical statement, the presentational modes of birds of paradise. Furthermore, in this imitative process, we can isolate the Superb bird of paradise (*Lophornia superba*) as the critical species. A number of related factors provide a degree of validation for the interpretative hypotheses I have adduced:

(a) feathers that ring the edge of *mànda hare* (collectively termed *gai gulu*[7]) should stand perpendicular to the rim on which they are placed, thus pointing outwards. This parallels the 'umbrella' fashion of feathers in the display mode.

(b) The distinctive cape (*dalu to* – 'umbrella') of the male Superb is positioned on wigs/hair-shapes at the 'forehead'. The significance of the symbolic statement expressed by such actions is 'visible' at the locus of truth. Feathers are placed in the 'middle' (*hanuni*) on both a horizontal and vertical axis (the forehead and vertex points).

(c) The Superb is denoted by the term *yagama*, the root of which means 'flying' (*yaga*) – an accentuation of this bird's value. The property of flight is extremely important in this ethno-ethology, and it is one that people attempt to instil into themselves and children. Metaphorical allusions to flight permeate many of the texts considered in this book: children are eulogized as Superb birds of paradise (see Appendix 2; 1 : 24); clouds too may be equated with these birds (Appendix 4; A : 15–20). In these rhetorical contexts *yagama* is a polysemous lexeme which, in its conventional usages, can signify both flight and the Superb. As a praise term (*kai*: see part 2), it can refer to clouds (Appendix 3; A : 4) or birds in general (Appendix 3; A : 3). In all cases the semantic component of 'flight' is expressed.

(d) The significance attached to the Superb bird of paradise may perhaps also reflect the fact that it constitutes, in Huli, the most numerous species of the family *Paradisaeidae*.

(e) In a way analogous to the inversion of *mànda* shapes, the Superb crest is also in reverse position on each wig. This intimates two separate levels of inversion realizing two distinct propositions.

The above iconographical collage reiterates that *mànda tene* are in the process of achieving power and knowledge; their attempts are

Decorative statements				
Composition	Mode	Medium of contrast	Mode	Composition
Mãnda Hare ↓	Display	Shape	Non-Display	*Mãnda Tene* ↓
Red ↓	Potency	Colour	Impotence	Black ↓
Superb crest	Non-display	Position	Display	Superb crest

indexed by the display mode of the Superb crest. In contrast, *mãnda hare* (both in shape and colour) represents successful attainment of these attributes. The reverse mode – non-display – of the Superb crest appears then to underplay this state of advancement, a restraint on excess. Themes of modesty are embodied in related ethnographic data:

(1) The Huli say that when the Lesser bird of paradise – whose display behaviour is imitated in a rite called *Tege Komia* says, 'I'm good, I'm good', then its performance will be bad; when it says, 'I'm bad, I'm bad' the display will be good. There is a need then for circumspection. Self-praise should not be directly stated. The importance of this cultural formulation is that it highlights the senses in which the non-display mode of the Superb crest is a 'downgrader' of self-given compliments.

(2) When placing the Superb crest on the *mãnda hare* (i.e. in its downgraded mode) Tobani Haroli articulated concepts of humility through the *gamu* that accompanied this act of adornment:

Informant: Landa (Tobani clan – former 'father' of Tobani Haroli)[8]
I am shy of seeing men like the sons of the dogs Wai and Wayeri
I am shy of seeing men like the sons of the dogs Pela and Pibi
I am shy of seeing men like the sons of the dogs Ogobi and Agabi.

Landa explained to me that one was shy of people when richly decorated, like dogs who slink away when men approach.

I cannot here do full justice to the complexity of Haroli and its decorative symbolism. However, with respect to speech and concepts of truth, certain arguments emerge that require attention. The progression to the high form of *mãnda* ('hair') was clearly also an attainment of *mãnda* ('knowledge'). In the overall schema of transition markers (*Figure 6*) the evolution from boy to man is conceptually

Figure 6   Haroli status transitions

Mànda Tene	Mànda Hare
pan-pipes	→ bows and arrows
charcoal	→ red and yellow ochres/use of oil on body
gamu not given	→ *gamu* given
prohibited entry to cult house	→ permitted entry

Mànda Hare

When wearing the *brown* feathers (*honagaga*) of the *immature* cassowary talking to the public prohibited
When wearing the *black* feathers (*yári mindi*) of the *mature* cassowary talking to the public permitted

equated with the developmental stages of cassowaries; this transition is decoratively affirmed in the division of brown/immature and black/mature feathers (see Wagner 1972 : 80 for a comparable Daribi dichotomy). Importantly, permission to speak is linked to maturity, knowledge, and aggressive qualities that are essential to epideictic contexts. One should preferably talk when one's mental and physical disposition is socially acceptable.

The hierarchical facets of *mànda* are retained outside the context of Haroli. The two hair-shapes were transformed into duplicate wigs.

Diagram 5   Mànda Hare

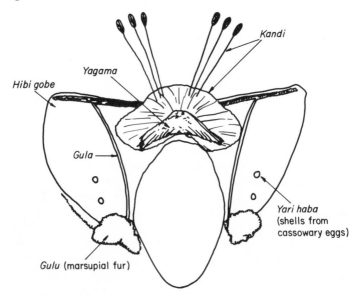

Diagram 6   Mǎnda Tene

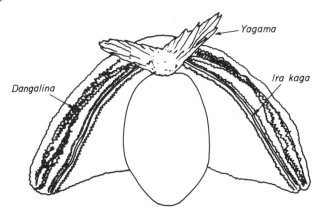

The *mǎnda tene* constitutes 'everyday' apparel which remains consistent with the non-display mode of its shape. The *mǎnda hare* marks 'ceremonial' attire. The semantic dimensions of public/private zones and display/non-display dovetail into each other here. This is indigenously declared in the parallels drawn between Haroli 'coming out into public view' and male birds of paradise displaying to females.

TEXT *Tagira pialu gamu* ('spell for coming outside')
Informant: Landa (Tobani)
Like the black six-wired bird of paradise (*Parotia lawesi*)
I am going
Like the brown Lawes' I am going
I am going to the cleared dancing ground at Igi
I am going to the cleared dancing ground at Babagi
(The rest of the spell repeats the above two lines substituting other ground names in the same rhyming-pair format)

The emergence of the initiate onto the display ground (*hama*) like this bird is again decoratively symbolized by the placement of its elongated shafts behind the Superb crest on the 'forehead'. A similar notion of birds flocking to dance areas is developed in poetic fashion by the *Mǎli gamu* given in Appendix 3B. The performer is there identified with the Lesser bird, and his performance metaphorically spoken of as 'fruit' ready for plucking. The audience descends onto the dance ground to 'pick the fruit' – that is, to give approbation and admiration.

These same oppositions and idioms pervade talk in disputes. On one level, this exposition provides for a better understanding of the cultural salience attached to 'forehead' in relation to truth and *mãnda* ('knowledge'). We can interpret the polarity of *tene* and *hare* as a manifestation of the male-female dichotomy. The duality of agnation and consanguinity is restated. Acknowledgement of the primordial fecundity of woman is proclaimed by symbolic manipulation of body and hair. On another level, as previously noted, the domain of decoration provides a strategic nucleus of rhetorical devices. Haroli contrast with Iba Tiri, they personify the quintessence of beauty and purity. The patent division between Haroli and 'ordinary people' is frequently utilized in disputes as an analogy for the behaviour of opponents. In the following extract the previous actions of disputants are explained in terms of the decorative constitution of Haroli. This is linked to mental dispositions of confidence, assertion, and over-eagerness.

Bi   tene   tai beramigo
Talk source you are finding
(You are looking for the source of this talk)
igiri ko   ale darua
boys bad like those
(you thought we were like bad boys there)
mãnda dania hea   uru
wigs   rope   there and
(with your wigs made with rope)
mãnda genduria   uru
wigs   string-pulls and
(with your wigs made with string pulls (these tighten the wigs onto heads))
dingi   denge (reduplicative) *uru*
fitting well   and
(fitting well on the head)
aulai   hewaila   uru
yellow flowers purple flowers and
(with yellow and purple flowers (*Helichrysum bracteatum*) in your wigs)
mãnda dania dege gidi gade leru   ogoria howa
wigs   rope   just yellow-painted face here   from
(with your wigs and yellow-painted face, then)
pongorali erene-manane hondowa   gu ke   larigo
possum's tail -top   having seen big-head you got
(you saw the possum's tail (see 4c above) and became big-headed)
'Koma ti   ndo' loliya naga larimibe?
'Koma them no ' to say this   did you talk?
(Did you talk so that we can say Koma didn't do it? (rhetorical))
(Field data)

What is significant about such analogies is the implicit association between decorative states and tendencies towards conceit ('big-head') and over-confidence ('you saw the tail of the possum . . .'). The underlying norm requires that these attitudes be tempered by modesty. In this latter regard, there is clearly a potential conflict between the need to avoid self-praise and the need to declare one's worth. These behavioural constraints apply to both verbal and non-verbal actions so that the parallels between speech and decoration go further than the reservoires of rhetorical and figurative analogies. Assessments of speech and attire are assessments of persona, and the individual must present himself in a manner that is sensitive to possible censure or criticism such as are expressed in the above extract. In naturally occurring conversation, sociolinguists (e.g. Pomerantz 1978b) have shown that with respect to compliment responses one solution to the conflict between self-praise and self-praise avoidance is the employment of 'downgrades'. In response to a praise utterance such as 'Isn't that *fantastic*' a recipient may reply with a scaled-down moderate term such as 'Yes, it is quite *good*'. Such devices represent a compromise (incorporating elements of both agreement and disagreement) between incompatible sets of constraints.

Patterns of behaviour in response to praise are a cross-culturally interesting area for study. My analysis of Haroli data reveals how solutions to the 'co-operation of conflicting preferences' (Pomerantz 1978b : 81) – to declare / accept compliments (self-accreditation) and to avoid self-praise (self-effacement) – can be embodied in manipulations of decoration. On one level there are parallels here between speech and decoration behaviour in Huli. On another level the implications appear to be that conversational structures provide models for cross-cultural testing even in non-verbal domains. The materials presented above clearly articulate a system of constraints relating to modesty and self-praise avoidance. The wig wearer is involved in a private conversation acting as both praise profferer and praise recipient. His response strategy to 'compliments' – given by himself or anticipated from others before public presentation – is to utilize 'downgrades'. This is initially achieved by reversal of the Superb crest defining his mode of presentation along the display / non-display axis. Furthermore, the assumption of modesty and shyness is achieved through *gamu*. To praise oneself verbally, or act in a manner that others interpret as self-praising, has a violative status. This is indexed by verbal censure, examined above, stressing 'over-confidence', and also 'performance' which, like that of the Lesser bird, will be bad. For both speech and decor the Huli have defined notions concerning acceptable and non-acceptable display which can be 'overdone or over the top'. Wigs and feathers constitute metaphorical turns at talking, while their shape, colour, and decorative modes are turn-units making statements of credit (↑) or scaled-down agreement (↓ downgrades).

Self-praise   *Mànda Hare*
Wig-shape   : ↑ 'I'm flying, displaying'
Colour   : ↑ 'I'm powerful'
Feathers   : ↑ 'I'm mature with knowledge'
Superb crest : ↓ 'I'm not displaying'

These statements are sequentially organized in terms of status progression in the cult, and between wig and Superb crest. This latter item is thus a kind of second-assessment which makes a scaled-down agreement with the 'tone' of the rest of the decor. Moreover, the units that signify credits and downgrades can be said to inhabit differently shaped turns in a relation of opposition between *mànda tene* and *mànda hare*. The rhetoric of decoration, and the embodied dimensions of meaning, indicate the senses in which certain 'doings' are a kind of 'saying'.

All the above themes are reflected in speech where self-advancement through rhetoric and oratory must be balanced by being seen to 'share the talk'. One solution is to adopt the syntactic and stylistic elements of lexicalized genres while not seeming to duplicate these speech forms exactly. Excess entails possible rejection through censorial applications of terms like *tambi bi*, *dawe*, *malu* and *gamu* detailed in Chapter 2. In other speech environments, solutions to the conflict between being direct, and yet sensitive to the possibilities of giving offense, entail manipulating the sequential position of moves. Different conversational routines exhibit varied types of compromise to the constraints of direct confrontation and avoidance of a blunt, abrupt posture. A number of conventional response formulae are associated with recurrent and standardized communicative contexts. While these were mostly collected from interviews with informants, rather than gleaned from extemporaneous speech, the expressions were clearly conceived of as components in two-part exchanges. The format of these corresponds, in most cases, to a request/demand (verbally or non-verbally signalled) followed by a response. The sequential nature of these utterances as 'reactive speech acts' (Coulmas 1981 : 71) shows again that we cannot divorce a consideration of the verbal from non-verbal domains.

The expressions cited below are routines of denial, rejection, and licensed abuse. It is a presupposition of their use that offensiveness is mitigated; they are not 'discrediting to the speaker' (Coulmas 1981 : 90) because as conventional responses they come under the auspices of what are acceptable and appropriate linguistic options. The speaker, as with *bi mabura* ('proverbs'), appeals to the impersonal authority of *mana*. He thereby establishes his detachment from responsibility for his talk and thus from the social consequences of denial or abuse that can obtain in other situations. These stereotype formulae enable one to say 'no' (or make apt comment) in an indirect way that is also, importantly, tinged with humour. Successful denial of requests is dependent on the ability to respond in an approved manner that does not give offence.

The expressions of 8(a)–(f) occur only in exchanges between males, while those of (g)–(i) are not tied to the sex of either participant (signified by the letters A and B) in any encounter.

8 (a) A. Request/demand for smoke leaves (*mundu*: *Nicotiana tabacum* fam. *Solanaceae*)
     B. Have you been hunting with an Obena woman for marsupial and exhausted all your tobacco?: *Obena wali haru howa tia kaba tombe lalu henebe?* (Obena women are believed, unlike Huli women, to continually smoke)

 (b) A. Request/demand for tobacco while another person is still engaged in its preparation
     B. Have you come to my arse like the butterfly before the excreta has come?: *ti na dedo ore yabunini pongonia biraribe?* (A variant of this is used in disputes to force another speaker to wait his turn)

 (c) A. Repeated requests for tobacco
     B. You have smoked so much your nose is broken?: *ngui polo piyane nenebe?* (The phrase 'broken nose' reiterates the important dimensions this anatomical part has in insults)

 (d) A. Failure to respond to a question
     B. Have you eaten fruit like the *Malibu* bird and got diarrhoea?: *Malibu dumbi li nenego naga ti pole biyane bedebe?*

 (e) A. A situation where a person is thought to have hidden the fire-tongs
     B. Did you hide the tongs to masturbate your penis?: *wi gidule pero mo do haribe?* (This is an oblique reference to the origin myth of tongs used initially by women to masturbate their husbands' penes)

(f)   A. A situation where a person remains, uncomfortably, in the path of smoke from à fire without palpable reason

      B. Have you eaten a Dugube woman's vagina? / Have you eaten what the Dugube woman stepped over?: *Dugube wali kalaba nenego hiyu hau ngebe? / Dugube wali galo nenebe?* (The expression implies that the man's mind is confused through female contamination, especially potent in the case of 'foreign' women)

(g)   A. Request/demand for sweet-potato (as for h and i below)

      B. Is your mother caught in my cassowary trap?: *I ainya i yári kono ha denebe?*

(h)   B. Has your mother been feeding twelve pigs and finished all her sweet-potato?: *I ainya nogo homberia bari binibe?*

(i)   B. Has your mother jumped onto the pigs' fence and sat there?: *I ainya nogo goleni iraga ho berenebe?*

A number of observations can be made in respect of the above data. Excessive currency of such expressions does in some sense diminish their literal meanings and force. Propositional content is thus secondary to illocutionary force in these indirect procedures of denial. This function is primarily related to their conditions of use. In this respect, these formulae are quite distinct as a category of verbal routine from a class of Huli adages that are altogether less challenging in their implications. These maxims tend to be phrased as conditional propositions of the form 'if p then q'. For example:

Wandari dengui handaya honiyagua mamu   dolebira.
Girls   faces   if you stare at   pimples will grow.
Iralu   delariyagua hamburi   habale ibulebira.
Fungus if you burn moustache quickly will come.

In contrast to these, the verbal strategies of 8(a)–(i) are constituted as 'confrontative rhetorical questions' (Schieffelin 1979 : 95). They tease, shame, and abuse by often indicating the inadequacies of the person addressed as a self-sufficient individual. They emphasize intemperance by redirecting the question or demand back to the questioner. Moreover, there is some indication in 8(g)–(i) that many of these routines are more frequently utilized by adolescents. In these latter three cases reference is made to the obligations attendant on mothers to provide young children with food. Through the routines children gain understanding of the sequential properties of conversation important to all verbal encounters.

Clearly, these speech forms are direct and forthright and yet still achieve some diminution of threat and offense. A balance is struck between rejection and challenge by transposing what is local and specific about the event – aspects of speaker, situation, and utterance – to a recurrent and general situation. Disagreement with these conventional responses is ruled out for 'one cannot disagree with the right order' (Bloch 1975 : 16). Such routines pre-empt and pre-structure what may appropriately follow.

Part 2

In so far as we understand talking in disputes to realize and embody a number of rhetorical strategies, it is important that an analysis of speakers' attempts to persuade and attract attention untangles the intricate meshing of form and substance. Form has lexical, syntactic, intonational, and phonological parameters. I am concerned in this section with how the Huli construe and manipulate these dimensions as aspects of their verbal aesthetics – that which is pleasing in discourse. In my previous consideration of kinship and cosmology I emphasized that the articulation of ideas and norms assumes a very definite stylistic guise. To engage in verbalizing shared values and conventions is thus often to adopt a mode of speech that conforms to a set of restraints defined in terms of the four parameters listed above. A foray into speech poetics is a natural outcome of an interest that fixes on performance phenomena when norms are invoked and utilized. If it is the case that an audience is indeed 'drawn to the form' of rhetoric (Burke 1969 : 58), then clearly it is also the case that the shape of the message can in many instances be exploited for its own sake. Furthermore, there is a real need systematically to relate stylistic devices that identify differently named verbal genres with patterns of 'good speech' in naturally occurring discourse.

Much of the stylistic patterning of speech in disputes results from attempts to display valued eloquence. This normally falls short of invoking or replicating speech forms that might occasion censure and ridicule of the type examined previously. Formalization, in the sense then of manipulating creatively the poetic resources of the language, is not an *a priori* given constraining speech production, but a negotiated state. The conceptual distinction here is that between determinative rules, and strategies of interpretation and selection (see Lyons 1977 : 549). Where talk exhibits stylistic similarities to the poetic verse structures of *gamu* or *pureremo*, it is an outcome of verbal artistry not restricted to incumbents of particular roles or authority / power statuses.

Speech play

The most pervasive facet of Huli speech practices is the attention to, and exploitation of, the phonic medium. Sound play – alliteration, assonance, reduplication, rhyme, collocation of lexemes which repeat or modify a fixed sequence of sounds – is the verbal artifice that most typifies the taxonomic forms given in *Table 2*. The constituent design and cohesiveness of many of the texts examined below derives from the fact that the utterance segments relate through similarities in their phonological shape. Sound play permeates through the multiple vocabulary sets – the lexical dimension of form – crucial to an understanding of Huli rhetoric. The lexical item used to refer abstractly to this phenomenon is *bi mone* ('good talk': *bi* (talk) + *mone* (wasp)), but in various contexts of occurrence may be described by terms which reflect the semantic or functional import of the total speech act.

In cases of dialogue or play between children in which verbal gymnastics is an essential component, the phrase *bi gini* ('talk playing') is used to refer to the linguistic action and its phonological concomitants. In these situations, sound play fosters and solidifies the awareness of metalinguistic dimensions to communication. More especially, it promotes understanding of the cultural values placed on phonic engineering with reference to aesthetics and sound-symbolism. As a facet of the development of communicative competence, the importance of sound play is reinforced through all stages of the learning process. It is an inherent feature of the educational mediums *bi te*, *gamu*, and *pureremo*. In addition to the auditory appeal of sound repetition (a basis for many modern media advertisements), word play does appear to have important mnemonic functions in the transmission of knowledge and information. It is culturally rooted in all speech patterns associated with Huli *mana*.

Verbal teasing among children is one socialization context in which a pre-structured type of speech play, as opposed to more spontaneously produced sequences, occurs. Joke sequences approximate to our own games of 'now you see it, now you don't'. In the example cited below utterances are often co-ordinated with non-verbal gestures which make an offer and then retract it. A clenched fist is produced while stating one of the positive terms; following a short pause the hand is opened to reveal an empty palm, an act appropriately signalled by an opposing term. Semantic opposition is indicated by antonymous forms that show only slight changes in the sequence of sounds:

Ogolabo	*Tegelabo*
these two	not these two
Ogoda	*Nogoda*
this one	not this one
Mba	*Mba tau*
let us go	let us not go
Au	*Hau*
here it is	nothing here
Bole laya	*Ega bole laya*
I'll hit you	I'll hit a bird.

Contrasts of meaning based on negation, normally signalled by the addition of the prefix *na-*, are here marked by changes to the phonemic content. In Huli, this manner of indicating opposition – whereby contrastive terms display a similarity of phonological shape – is highly prevalent. Throughout the presentation of data relating to joking, naming, insults, and toponyms, I have stressed that the verbal marking of contrast is not completely arbitrary in the language. This sound-symbolism partakes of the functional significance and aesthetic resonances of sound play. In some other Highlands cultures this phenomenon would appear to have only random occurrence; there are, for example, the Fore (Lindenbaum 1976 : 55) terms *oka* ('testes') and *ako* ('vagina'), and the Daribi (Wagner 1967 : 255) lexical pair *duare* ('bad') and *duagi* ('good'). What is noticeable in the Huli case is how pervasive this particular exploitation of sound is throughout the speech economy.

   The rhetorical and mnemonic effectiveness of such devices as sound play, in framing statements of cultural importance, is similarly evident in many of the *pureremo* that occur in disputes. The following normative formula is invariably invoked in cases of illicit sexual intercourse.

Hina	*mbira*
Take care of (pigs)	first
(The first possibility is to look after pigs now and transfer bride-price later when there are sufficient pigs)	
Hende	*mende*
Bride-price pigs	second
(The second possibility is to pay bride-price now)	
Tauwa	*tebone*
Compensation pigs	third
(The third possibility is to pay compensation for illicit sex)	

The statements present the blamed party with three choices after being charged with a sexual offence. They again emphasize the importance of disjunctive formulations in speeches oriented to dispute settlement. Rather than confronting a person with only one proposed course of action – do this/do that – the *pureremo* is option-presenting in terms of an 'either/or' format.

The constituent design of the norm centres on assonance and alliteration between the words collocated with the numerical terms *mbira*, *mende*, and *tebone*. The substantive nature of the options themselves are framed using the familiar technique of listing with numerical indicators. The rhetorical efficacy of this device is enhanced through contiguous placement of words that phonemically echo each other.

A more complex extension of the above principle of collocation is manifested in the following *pureremo* text. Syntagmatically, the parts are connected through isolation of lexemes whose phonological shape is identical with the initially positioned sounds of the first-part number terms. In its performative mode, each part is divided from the adjacent phrase by a caesura. The *pureremo* states the sanctions involved when a person breaches norms regarding the stipulated times for licit sexual intercourse. The first four days of a month are excluded, as this is ideally the period of menstruation when sexual activity is prohibited. The basic morphs of the counting system are given first though they form no part of the *pureremo* itself. Following the terms for the relevant days of a month, the respective sanctions associated with intercourse on these days are cited:

Number morph	Day term	Sanction phrase
dau (5)	*dauningi*	*da lole*
	on the fifth day	he will be burnt
waraga (6)	*waraganengi*	*warago hole*
	on the sixth day	he will get malaria
ka (7)	*kanengi*	*ka lole*
	on the seventh day	his skin will peel
hali (8)	*haliningi*	*haiya lole*
	on the eighth day	he will be scattered
di (9)	*diningi*	*di lole*
	on the ninth day	he will be flying around
pi (10)	*piningi*	*pi lole*
	on the tenth day	he will fall down
bea (11)	*beanengi*	*bea lole*
	on the eleventh day	he will be broken

Intercourse should therefore ideally begin on the twelfth day of the month and continue for four days. There is no derivational relationship between the number-morphs and the initial lexemes of the sanction phrase. Structurally, each statement is composed of phonological similarities in the constituent elements. This aesthetic device clearly determines the conceptual design of the *pureremo*. The instrumental significance of this genre in didactic situations is reinforced by the mnemonic values of such stylistic structures.

This same organizational principle structures a wide range of pre-patterned forms relating to conventional knowledge. The text given below expresses the notion of time with reference to the moon (*ega*); it is anthropomorphized in parallel fashion to our own concepts of the 'man in the moon':

Hombene angi   hombene   ibule
On the twelfth day (out) on top it will come
Halene angi   hale howa hama   ibule
On the thirteenth day listening   silently it will come
Dene angi⁹   de howa yalu   ibule
On the fourteenth day having opened its eyes it will come
Nguini angi   ngui higi bu yalu   ibule
On the fifteenth day (with) squinted nose it will come
(Counting starts again from 1–9)
Pini angi   pi lole
On the tenth day it will fall down
Beane angi   bea lole
On the eleventh day it will break
Hombene angi   homolebira
On the twelfth day it will die

Despite the prevalence of gestural counting systems in New Guinea, there is no clear evidence for the Huli that the lexemes relating to number and the associated characteristics given in the adjoining segments indicate some historical semantic connection. We may note from the manner in which *hombene* ('twelfth') is tied to both *hombene* ('top') and *homolebira* ('will die') that the constitutive principle is replication of sequences of sounds.

Artifices of sound represent an aesthetic preference and predisposition that is at the foundation of both rhetoric and play. The unexpected frequency of sound play in the recorded text materials, comprising both pre-formulated and conversational speech, isolates it as a critical resource for artistic endeavour in Huli.

All the texts considered so far in this section have two further common structural features: (1) pronounced rhythmic and pitch patterns, and (2) bipartite design. For the most part they all exhibit parallel syntax in which the initially enunciated segments relate to each other as members of the same semantic field. There is repetition in the form of enumeration that may encompass numbers, places, body-parts, etc. In this respect the initially positioned components parallel the conversational formulae, considered for talk in disputes, that frame the semantic information to follow. The enumerated items provide a structured frame for introducing statements or aspects of a topic to be emphasized. The two component segments are divided by a caesura, such that in performance these texts have a cadence reminiscent of the pattern of generation designation in *malu*. The intonational contour of these rhythmically phrased utterances is low-rising (over the first phrase) to falling (on the second part). This tonic movement is consistent with the sense in which the enumerated units are incomplete utterances. As with the numerical index of *malu*, the initial phrases provide a reference map for plotting culturally acknowledged responses. The format is similar to question-answer frames and they share the normal question intonation. The fall in contour over the second parts correlates with a focus on its message content; it is stressed as the main information to be imparted. This dyadic structure of reference and response is a syntactic feature that is common to conversation in disputes and has been commented upon elsewhere in this book. Significantly, the use of these tones to indicate a distinction between the framing segment and that which is framed, has been noted for fixed expressions in English such as '*In my opinion*, he is wrong' or '*In any event*, that is not what I said' (see Keller 1981 : 107). There is, then, a degree of relation between the function of these semantic framings in talk and the first parts of the texts considered above.

In considering how linguistic form and cultural function interrelate with regard to sound play, these same artifices are also employed to enhance the visual imagery of mythical beings depicted in *bi tē*. In addition to the formulaic characterization of Iba Tiri, the only other recurrent narrative figure to have a distinctly developed representation is *Baya Horo*. This character is invariably linked with themes of death and cannibalism which are reinforced in a dramatic way when, after the introduction of his name, the following statements are rhythmically uttered:

Tombene   *tangi*
Stomach (he wears as a) cap

Ayuni   *ayu yi*
Spleen (as an) axe he holds
Nuni[10]   *nu   hene*
Omentum (as a) net-bag carried
Yabuni   *yandare yi*
Anal passage (as a) spear   he holds
Gibuni   *gi   hondole*
Adam's-apple (he wears as an) arm bracelet

The text manifests the same structural principles; second parts repeat partial sequences of sounds from adjacent lexemes. There is also internal vertical rhyming as most terms for body parts or numbers end in *-ni* or *-ne*, depending on the preceding vowel, and in accordance with vowel harmony rules. With other types of enumeration there is a likelihood that items will share final vowel phonemes (given that all words end in a vowel in Huli), which results in a high degree of assonance in speech. An important facet of the achievement of artistic effect in speech, then, is cultural awareness of the poetic potential and resources of the phonic medium. It may be that the marked frequency of types of phonological patterning in prestructured and naturally occurring talk in Huli can be accounted for in terms not only of the importance of speaking well, but perhaps also the learning load of an average individual for competent interaction. While this is a difficult concept to quantify for cross-cultural comparison, it does correlate with the mnemonic functions we know such linguistic forms embody. In addition, such highly recurrent devices index the sociocultural value of, and attitudes to, talk in the transmission of knowledge.

Vocabulary levels and vocabulary sets

Repetition and metamorphoses of sound shape are a prominent feature of the uniformity of style that characterizes Huli speech forms. Though many verbs related to specific sounds have onomatopoetic force – e.g. *ti te* ('cackle') – mimetic play with sounds is generally less prevalent than the structures described in the last section. While it is the case that these phonological principles underlie and pattern the multiple vocabulary sets distinguished by Huli, at the rank level of words these same lexicons constitute an axis along which speech genres and events are indigenously differentiated. The Huli display an unremitting attention to synonyms, which again registers the high degree of verbal consciousness in the culture. The existence of so large a number of distinct lexicons is attributable to (a) the prevalence of contexts and themes of concealment relating to speech disguise in secular and sacred pursuits; and (b) an aesthetic indulgence in exploiting form. The distinct vocabulary sets are cross-cut by the phenomena of vocabulary levels whereby words fall into the following three categories.

Bi 'words'

(i)   *Bi illili* ('forbidden words': encompasses sacred terms)
      Bi tu ha ('boundary (*tu*) words': prohibited language)
(ii) *Hége* (low-valued words and expressions considered abusive; profane terms common in angry speech or used as expletives)
(iii) *Kai mini* ('praise names': high-valued words used to extol and eulogize)
      Mini mende ('second names': synonyms that are generally exalted forms, though the spectrum includes both neutral and derogatory lexemes)
      Bi mone ('good words': in this specialized sense refers to dignified expressions; high-valued words)

Synonyms are thus differentiated by distinctions in ranking that are not applicable to the elegant or inelegant use of everyday language. Reference to *Table 3* indicates clearly that alternative terms may be lexical replacements or simply conventional words whose connotations emphasize some aspect of the neutral phrase. In either case we can observe the manner in which these substitutions morphologically mark the derogatory or uncomplimentary features of meaning central to *hége*. Where neutral terms, through context and appropriate stress or intonational patterns, approximate to the attitudinal import of the low-valued synonyms, they may be referred to as *bi ko* ('bad talk') but not *hége*.

Bi illili / tu ha

There are four principal contexts where use of everyday vocabulary is prohibited and employment of specialized cant or argot is culturally required.
(1) When entering primary forest for the purposes of hunting, collecting pandanus, or travel, Huli adopt the lexicon referred to as *tayenda tu ha illili* ('bush (*tayenda*) divide (*tu ha*) taboo (*illili*)'). The

normal Huli verb suffixes and grammatical structure remain un-
changed. The vocabulary is understood and explained as an attempt
to evade or trick bush-spirits, rendering them unable to cause harm
through anticipation of human intentions. The 'private' language
cannot be understood by harmful supernatural agents. The complex
series of rites and spells performed both prior to and during one's
sojourn in forest areas are similarly oriented to the creation of effective
boundaries (*tu*). I recorded some 300 lexemes in Ialuba of which 25
per cent were clearly Duna terms incorporated as substitute words,
but bereft of their conventional Duna meanings. Other *tayenda*
words are related to their normal Huli equivalents as minimally-
distinct forms:

Huli:	*bemo*	ashes	Tayenda:	*emo*
	bamba	before		*yamba*
	darama	blood		*yarama*
	dombeni	middle		*yombeni*[11]

We can again observe how minimal pairing appears to emphasize the
manner in which the relevant terms are different, and yet retain an
element of similarity. A small proportion of Tayenda analogues are
homonymous with ordinary lexemes: e.g. *erene* ('tail/back-bone'),
in *tayenda*, denotes all types of liquid- or water-associated nouns and
verbs. Indeed, what is striking about *tayenda* terms is that, in the
interests of economy, they reduce a multitude of normally differentiated words to one term by virtue of an attributed common semantic
base. Thus the *tayenda* construct *hambu ha* connotes the idea of 'consumption' implicit in a range of ordinary Huli terms,

hambu {
  pain (*tandaga*)
  swallow (*embedogo*)
  eat (*na*)
  chew (*dange*)
  teeth (*ne*)
  tongue (*hege*)
}

hangarine {
  carefully (*bayua*)
  correct (*tigabi*)
  good (*bayele*)
  eye (*de*)
  sweet (*dendebi*)
  mind (*mini*)
}

in the same way in which *hangarine* expresses shared meanings among
a number of ordinarily distinct lexemes.

It seems important to also note that the forest lexicon retains the
agglutinative logic of everyday vocabulary. The conventional number
terms *haleria* (thirteen), *deria* (fourteen), and *nguira* (fifteen) contain
the morphemes *hale* (ear), *de* (eye) and *ngui* (nose), which is paralleled

homologously in *tayenda* vocabulary: i.e: *konone* (thirteen: *kono* ('ear')), *hangarabane* (fourteen: *hangarine* ('eye')) and *gumane* (fifteen: *guma* ('nose')). While in everyday language cardinal numbers end in -*ra* or -*ria*, the *tayenda* substitutions consistently have a final suffix of -*ne*, a quite typical feature of enumerations in Huli. In many instances, then, the conventional and *tayenda* words retain the same intension/extension features within their respective language environments, in addition to compounding with other terms in structurally similar ways. For example,

Huli	Tayenda
agali miniwi ('knowledgeable')	*amona hangarine*
man mind (*mini*) + placed (*wi*)	man eye/good/mind
agali haguene ('headman')	*amona lobane*
man head	man top/head/above
de iba ('tears')	*hangarine erene*
eye water	eye water/liquids

(2) Haroli *mǎnda hare* initiates would be taught a sacred vocabulary for use when entering cult areas (*tigi anda*). This lexicon functioned to discriminate these higher ranked novices from the low-valued *mǎnda tene* members. Despite minor regional differences certain transformations seem invariant:

Huli	Haroli
mundu be (bamboo pipe)	*gamba dagua*
iba (water)	*gudu*
agali (man)	*hirali*
wali (woman)	*gayalu*
bi (talk)	*guyu*

The vocabulary set is not as extensive as *tayenda* and these two lexicons are not totally discrete in that some borrowing of terms occurs between them.

(3) A third situation in which word change is the norm concerns the performance of rites in the sacred sites of Lidu and Kebe. Ritual experts protect themselves from danger of contact with the spirits they invoke through speech disguise. In that the rituals of Kebali are also associated with ancestral behaviour a further rationale for the lexicon (given to me in the field) was that this was the language of the first Dama. In essence, the lexical replacements I recorded reflected similar transformations as for *tayenda* and Haroli.

(4) The final area in which word change is institutionalized is the transmission of *mana* during the *rites de passage* of Tege. A specialized lexicon formed part of the teasing and degradation practices to which young initiates were subjected. Lexical change was here, as in the other contexts described previously, central to strategies of deception. Many of the Tege terms appear semantically to reflect aspects of their conventional analogues:

Huli	Tege
agali (man)	*tegene* ('those of Tege')
wali (woman)	*endeli* ('handle/strap' (*ende*) + 'person' (*li*): those at the end of the pigs)
iba (water)	*puya* ('snake': reiterates the association of these two elements in dogmas of mortality)

In addition to these situated usages there are two further contexts where *bi tu ha/illili* prevail. The first concerns name invocation and is dealt with fully in the section below. The Huli also prohibit certain words in talk about illness. Specifically, chronic bronchitis must be referred to as *bu burayu* or *amuali*, and leprosy as *ge hamua* ('marsupials' feet': the term is based on the visual similarities with the deformities of leprosy) or *gambe te* ('clump/grove of pitpit'). These are understood as synonyms for *hagara* and *kudugu* respectively, which are avoided in conversation as part of a more general reluctance to invoke dangerous names.[12]

Separate from these are the generally high-valued lexemes of *mini mende*, *kai*, and *bi mone*. The boundaries of these three lexicons are not tightly demarcated and there is indeed some overlap of forms. Nevertheless, they are all related to conceptual fields where the display of verbal art is paramount. In this regard they serve to index, as well as to distinguish, levels of competence in performers and audiences.

Mini Mende

These synonyms occur both in the various genres given in *Table 2* and in everyday speech where rhetorical or slangy effect is desired. The lexicon is extensive only over material objects and retains genus and species differentiations.

Conventional term	*Mini mende*
du (sugar-cane)*	*hiwa tege**
nogo (pig)*	*mindi**
tia (marsupial)	*dulu baya*
anda (house)*	*tamu**
komia (Lesser Bird of Paradise:	*galu wabia*
Paradisea minor)	
andaya (Doria's tree-kangaroo:	*homai*
Dendrolagus dorianus)	
dalu (rain)*	*ginane**
wānekui (forehead)	*homa embo*
ma (taro)	*hubi gaiya*
ayu (axe)	*gamiago*
* (names discussed below)	

For the most part, *mini mende* are lexical replacements that, within
the context of graded levels of usage, are predominantly 'high' forms.
Many of the terms are composed of forms that occur in everyday
speech, and are marked by discriminable semantic features; for
example, *homa embo* ('one (*homa*) + head (*embo*)'), expressing the
unity of truth visible on the forehead. *Mini mende* are prevalent in
gamu, *tamba bi*, and *pureremo*. Their oratorical force can best be
gauged from the occurrence of *homa embo* and *galu wabia* in the *aba*
text cited in Chapter 3. Unrelated to this aesthetic function, these
synonyms also act to provide veiled references. Names of dead relatives or slain enemies are never mentioned for fear that such invocation may impel spirits to act in a hostile manner. However, through
the circumlocution of *mini mende*, disguised reference to dead
individuals is possible; the relationship between the two lexicons is
here reciprocal. Where a Huli proper name has the same form as a
term in either lexicon then substitution of the alternative equivalent
is required in the contexts specified above. In the case of a man called
Dalu, *ginane* is substituted as both terms signify 'rain'; for the name
Andaya (conceived as composed of the morpheme *anda* ('house')),
tamu would apply. Equally, the names Hiwa Tege or Mindi would be
substituted by the conventional words *du* and *nogo* respectively.

Bi Mone

These lexemes occur in precisely the same speech environments as
mini mende, but differ structurally from the latter in that the

substitutions are morphologically related to their conventional
analogues. Most typically, though not invariably, transformations of
neutral words are effected by compounding the same terms with a
lexically discrete prefix which, in many instances demarcates a
semantic field. The essential contrast between *mini mende* and *bi
mone* is that of replacement in opposition to word elaboration.

Conventional term	*Mini mende*	*Bi mone*
wali (woman)	*bai yamo / gau welo*	*mandi wali*
bauwa (Casuarina)	*yauwale*	*hobe bauwa*
lai (*Dodonaea viscosa* fam. *Sapindaceae*)	*puruma*	*tege lai*
keba (digging-stick)	*nama*	*dabali keba*
agali (man)	*hirale*	*hulu agali*

The appended lexemes do not appear simply as aesthetic adornment, but substantially qualify the amended terms through the
addition of meaning. The component *hulu*, as a form of *'huli'*,
emphatically marks tribal identity and collocates with terms denoting
people. In this context it parallels the use of Hela in Hela Dugube or
Hela Duna, by reiterating shared sociocultural history. It is thus common in the high-speech forms to find occurrences of *hulu wane*
('girl'), *hulu igiri / hulu yawi* ('boy'), or *hulu gomaiya* ('Huli': see
Appendix 2; 2 : 38). In the case of trees, or material culture, the prefixing term either indicates the context of use, or names the species
from which an object was made. Thus we may decipher the *bi mone*
construct *dabali keba* as *debali* (shrub: *Xanthomyrtus fam. Myrtaceae*) + *keba* ('stick'), or *tege lai* as *tege* (rites in which the *lai* tree is
used) + *lai* (tree). Names of places and clans are particularly subject to
bi mone transformations where again the initial terms (as for example
hubi discussed in Chapter 4) may circumscribe a discrete area of
meaning. Notwithstanding the prevalence of these semantic qualifiers, *bi mone* forms are also characterized by the types of stylistic
devices examined earlier. Most notably in the field of kin terms there
is reduplication – *imane* ('affines') may be rendered as *imalu imane*
– and slight modifications to the phonological shape of such lexemes
as *ainya* ('mother') – *ainyali* (Appendix 4; C: 1), *ama* (Appendix 4;
C: 11), *amale* (Appendix 4; C: 11), *amu* (Appendix 4; C: 29) *amai*
(Appendix 4; C: 41), and *amuli* (Appendix 4; C: 95). Often the conventional term and *bi mone* equivalent are paired as minimally

distinct forms and simply chanted as a form of word play. For example,

wali (woman)   – *warili*
lembo (anger) – *lewale*
manga (refusal) – *mangale*
nogo (pig)   – *nogoli*
yama (heart)   – *yamali*

Micro-analysis of *bi mone* vocabulary illustrates how in the Huli data repetition of a sequence of phonemes in adjacently placed words can mark synonymity. Moreover, the slight modification of phonological shape signifies the discrete domains, or usage levels, of the two continuously located terms. In the following *pureremo* text, which codifies the decorative accoutrements of war, the *bi mone* lexemes manifest the range of stylistic principles – the assonance of *waya-ayu-alu* prefixing *humbi* ('shield'), or the species denominations of *wagaba* and *ayege* (black palm) – described above; they prefix conventional terms.

waya humbi/ayu humbi/alu humbi/honagaga/
shield   shield   shield   cassowary feathers
melabe dindi/   wagaba hibuni/hula pungua/daiya dongoma/
red clay on body bow-string   charcoal   white clay on shield
dumbi du/ayege yandare
red leaves spear

Kai

In focusing on the cultural contexts of performance, we can better appreciate that the linguistic correlates of high-style for Huli are firmly located at the level of words. *Kai* terms may occur in any one text together with both *mini mende* and *bi mone*, but are distinguished from these latter categories in two vital respects: (1) for each conventional lexeme there may be as many as seven equivalent *kai* terms; and (2) these enumerative sets are structurally determinative of the genre design. In the *kai* lexicon there is no differentiation of genus and species as all terms are generic. While it is common to find conventional forms occurring as *kai*, hyponyms undergo semantic transformation by assuming superordinate status. Thus *abuage* (sulphur-crested cockatoo), *ubiya* (Count Raggi's bird of paradise), and *yagama* (Superb bird of paradise) are synonyms for 'bird' (*ega*) in the paradigmatic *kai* set given in Apendix 3; A: 3.

The distinguishing feature of this eulogistic vocabulary then is the production of similar-sounding synonyms that, from the Huli viewpoint, constitutes poetic verse form rather than any type of redundancy. Examples of *kai* usage found within texts cited in this book are as follows:

Conventional term	*Kai* analogue
pig (*nogo*)	*ibuna*: *awaiya*/*parila*: *paiyabe*/*nali*: *hinali* (Appendix 3; A: 1) *bene*: *hendene*/*tambugua*: *pagabua*/ *hone*: *gebe* (field-notes)
bird (*ega*)	*abuage*: *aiwaye*/*bidagua*: *bareagua*/ *yagama*: *yamalu* (Appendix 3; A: 3)
cowrie-shell (*dange*)	*puluni*: *pulumagi*/*ilini*: *gilini*/*dodone*: *dagini* (field notes)
children (*wāneigini*)	*gili*: *gawali*/*barina*: *bangale* (Appendix 2; 1 : 4–7)
cloud (*bereliba*)	*yuguai*: *yagama*/*pogo*: *pogale*/*lungi*: *alungi* (Appendix 3; A: 4)
bag (*nu*)	*ayeri*: *angai*/*mindili*: *mamai* (Appendix 4; C: 95–100)
wig (*mãnda*)	*gombe godale*/*daiya dabura*/*abu abai*/ *mbiri bayeri* (field-notes: *mãnda gamu*)
rain-cape (*to*)	*abale*: *ayago*/*laboni*: *labali*.

(Field data)

In their performative contexts *kai* words form bound sets that have both a predetermined and sequential character. Choice of the first member dictates the order of the following terms that allows an audience, or co-participants, to predict content and form. The *kai* lexicon is inextricably related to the design format of the genres in which they occur. *Dawe* verses most typically have a structure of six lines. There is pronounced syntactic and semantic parallelism such that the component utterances differ in the respect of having oneword synonym substitutions. The idea stated in the first line is repeated with identical metre and grammatical structure; the substitution of *kai* terms aesthetically enhances, as well as intensifies, the semantic import of the verse. Parallel repetition, as one 'important axis of stylistic variation' (Gossen 1974 : 76) in Huli oral tradition, pervades *dawe* (see Appendix 3; A), *gamu* (see Appendix 3; B), *wali-o* (see Appendix 4; A–C) and *damba bi* (see Appendix 2; 1–2), all contexts in which *kai* lexemes figure prominently. While saying the same thing in a slightly different way is an explicitly recognized stylistic mode, the couplet formation of terms in any *kai* set reaffirms the significance of name-pairing in Huli speech.

Examination of *kai* analogues reveals the prevalence of minimally-distinct pairs or contrastive sets that does not, in any obvious manner, reflect dualistic facets of the genres themselves. In addition to paired assonant or alliterative terms, it is common for *kai* sets also to manifest an overall rhyming pattern of *-ni, -ini, -ali, -ene* or some other consonant-vowel/vowel-consonant-vowel final syllable (see Pugh-Kitigan 1975 : 45). The collocation of similar sounding words is most prominent in citations of place names:

> *Igi*: *Babagi/Nedo*: *Nedolo/Gauwi*: *Gambolo* (Appendix 3; B)
> *Ibiya*: *Haluya/Hagai*: *Garai/Baya*: *Tabaya* (Appendix 4; A)
> *Hayere*: *Hedawi*: *Dibawi* (Appendix 4; A)
> *Gurugu*: *Gamiabe*: *Ganana* (Appendix 4; C)
> *Ora*: *Orabi/Aya*: *Anda* (Appendix 4; C)
> *Wabu*: *Wale/Wale*: *Dongale/Dongale*: *Dandabua/Igiya*: *Tigiya/Ibi*: *Yaribi Ialuba*: *Ialaba/Hungibia*: *Hiyabe/Hewe*: *Hogore* (Appendix 3; C)

Kai terms are the unit of variation in a fixed supra-structure. As an encompassing framework, semantic and syntactic parallels organize the sequential incidence of praise terms.

In many respects the formal rigidity of a *kai* paradigm manifests the 'listing/enumerative' proclivity typical of both naturally occurring and prestructured speech. In the latter contexts repeated syntax with one- and two-word substitutions can be effected with normal vocabulary utilizing place names (e.g. lines 3–5, Appendix 2; 2), or animal and plant species terms. These may even fall into distinct rhyming groups as in *godane*: *galuni*: *tirane*: *hengedane* (lines 15–18 Appendix 2; 2) which share the *-ne/-ni* final syllable. Nevertheless, the distinguishing feature of *kai* is that the syntagms are constituted of synonyms that follow each other in a predicted sequence. Moreover, the composite *kai* forms appear in many instances to lexically reflect semantic aspects of their conventional analogues. The praise words for drum (*tabage*) – *dua laya*: *ibi laya*: *hiru laya*: *lau laya* – all contain '*laya*' meaning 'has spoken'; the *kai* words *bene*: *hendene*: *dawene*, signifying 'pig' (*nogo*), respectively mean 'hit': 'seen': 'cooked' (see Pugh-Kitigan 1975 : 43). Similarly, the *kai* term for stomach (*tombe*) – *himu mbagua* – may metaphorically reflect the notion of a waste (*himu*: 'sand') and container (*mbagua*: 'gourds' (*Lagenaria siceraria fam. Cucurbitaceae*)), just as the *kai* form *hiliwa*, meaning 'bone' (*kuni*), is a common ancestral name reinforcing the symbolic association of bone and patrilineal descent. In other composite *kai* terms certain lexemes delimit fields of reference. This is particularly exemplified in the initial word *bai* – as in *bai mope*: *bai hinini*: *bai nana*: *bai hinana* (see Appendix 3; B) and *urubu* – *urubu gela*: *urubu hegele*: *urubu urulu*: *urubu ngawe* (ref. Appendix 3; B) – that occur only in the context of bird enumeration. The extent to which performances of these speech genres are experienced as ordered phenomena is thus partly dependent on relations that lexical items contract with similar units in any given lexicon, as well as the kinds of relationships between vocabulary systems.

Hége lā

In contrast to the variable forms of 'good words' (*bi baya*) are a number of distinct categories of 'bad words' (*bi ko*) which, while not finely discriminated into separate vernaculars, retain stylistic continuities with the vocabulary sets discussed above. Offensive language is metaphorically linked to conditions of 'heat'. The Huli have defined notions concerning the pathology of states of shame and anger that engender vulgar speech. Such intangible ideas are indexed on an anatomical landscape that provides a visual map for reading off an individual's emotional and 'inner moral condition' (O'Hanlon n.d.). The body, skin, hair, and nose assume central significance as members of a 'body lexicon' used in the making of uncomplimentary references. They feature prominently in the enactment of insult routines and as lexical items in the description of these same speech acts.

Huli imbue the organs of speech with precisely the same derogatory and metonymic properties associated with them in such Western phrases as 'watch your *tongue*', 'I want no more *lip* from you', or 'don't give me any of your *mouth*'. The constructions *ne haria* ('teeth track'), *hámbu hège la* ('lips and tongue'), or *ne hámbu la* ('teeth and lips'), can all signify talk in reference to distasteful speech. The power invested in various products of the articulatory process derives from associated concepts of anal imagery. From the mouth comes 'smelly talk' (*bi ngubi*), 'shit talk' (*bi ti baga*) and 'sick talk' (*bi magubi*). Conceptually linked to these idioms of dangerous waste-products are ideas concerning insult and bad words as damaging material. This cluster of associations constitute principles of the lexicalization of negative talk.

The power of words is transmitted to objects through the medium of 'breath' (*bu he*), the constituent phrases of a *gamu* are punctuated by short expirations. Similarly, words may be carried in saliva, and spitting is routine after use of *hège* (swearing) or forms of dangerous talk. These semantic associations are lexically marked in the term for spitting (*hamaga tola*) which literally means 'to emit death'. The tongue also serves to index increments of force as in the children's teasing game of tongue-poking, appropriately termed 'poison tongue' (*hège tomia*). More importantly, the figurative extensions of these anatomical terms are often given separate lexical status in the language. The label *hège*, as a descriptive term for abusive words, is best understood in the context of the pairs

hège (tongue) : *hége*   (swearing)
hãmbu (lips)   : *hãmbu* (sorcery)

That the Huli recognize a semantic connection between the tonally distinguished forms perhaps justifies a supposition of a single poly-semous lexeme in each case. The relatedness of meaning between the words again indicates that pitch is not here semantically critical; within the language system tonal contrasts appear generally, though not invariably, to indicate shades of meaning. The cognitive status of 'bad words' and their anatomical associations seem marked by a lexicalization principle which emphasizes continuities as well as contrasts in meaning.

The sphere of negatively valued talk is both verbally elaborate and determined by aesthetic norms such as reduplication. Consistent with a cultural emphasis on negative concepts, we find that relations of meaning are intimately bound to ethno-poetic manipulations of devices such as minimally-distinct forms. This constitutes a stylistic continuum that cross-cuts both vocabulary sets and levels. In addition to the highly important pair *hége* ('swearing'): *mege* ('insult') similar phonemic principles pervade the terminology of anger. Feelings of animosity may be referred to by any of the terms in the contrastive set (initial consonant): *hembo*: *lembo*: *gembo*. All the variant terms for states of anger manifest similar sequences of sound registering the cultural importance of this state:

lembo: *lomba* ('break'): *lewale* (see Appendix 3; A: 5)
higi ('scowl'): *higili* (see Appendix 3; A: 5): *hagai* ('blocked')
manga ('refusal'): *mangale*
amba: *tambo* (see Appendix 2; 1 : 8)

To be angry is to be 'cut up', figuratively signified by such terms as *gai* ('broken'), *gare* ('slice': *giri gare* a reduplicative form), or *diba* ('cut/chop'). The concepts of accusation and blame (*dibade*) are thus also couched in idioms of 'cutting up' another. Anger, as stressed throughout this book, is something that 'sleeps' (*pada*) inside; it is an internal state of *bu* ('emotion') that is all-consuming. This 'inside' dimension is graphically expressed in the idiomatic phrases *hina linguria* ('mouldy/rotten parts of sweet-potato'), and *gambe poboraya* ('insect in the pitpit') used to signify a literal state of 'being eaten up inside'.

From the lexical items which the Huli language provides for referring to anger (and the products of this state), four properties recur. These are (a) *heaviness* (*genda*), in the figurative sense of something burdensome which must be 'made light' (*mo yabia*); (b) *heat* (*pobo*), conceptually related to the uncontrolled aspects of female sexuality (discussed in Chapter 3) the effects of which are said to 'hit the ribs' or 'burn the heart'; (c) *frustration*, that appears common to the tonally contrasted words *kēba* ('anger') and *kéba* ('digging-stick'); and (d) *entanglement*, described by the term *pongo* ('knot/tied') which we have seen to be the most central idiom of deviance in the language. The ethno-pathology of anger stresses that the mind (*mini*) and heart (*bu*) are 'tied', and only through the medium of compensation can anger be relieved.

These are part of a more enduring and embracing metaphor of illness which expresses ordered/disordered relationships and states of mental or physical well-being. Compensation is the mandatory 'medicinal' antidote to anger precisely because it represents a type of 'curing' rite (see Strathern 1981 : 10 and Goldman 1981b : 58). Notwithstanding decisions relating to blame or liability, illness must always be positively counteracted. To a person who continually displays anger the refrain 'have you got leprosy?' (*ge hamua harebe?*), or 'have you got respiratory ailments?' (*bu burayu harebe?*), may be addressed.[13] It is in the context then of this preoccupation with health and sickness that we must understand four distinct sets of *hége* expletives used to express anger towards:

  (i) children: *hangabuge*, *poromali* (*poro*: to break), *homabe* ('die')
 (ii) pigs: *yani* ('swollen'), *ambua dindi* ('yellow clay': used to rub on the body during sickness), *pe to* ('puffed up/swollen'), *ma to* ('mumps/glandular conditions'), *ngue kagira* ('worms'), *daraga iba* ('water has climbed inside' i.e. sickness)
(iii) dogs: *dondogoli* ('nasal mucus'), *ngui iba* ('nose water': mucus), *bandagoli*, *habogumbi*, *habidogo*
 (iv) adult (child speaking)
      puya ('snake': if told to fetch water)
      mambu (if told to fetch sweet-potato).

These exclamatives of reproach and rebuke are conceived as forming distinct lexical sets. Children, pigs and dogs are equated on account of a tendency to exhibit wayward behaviour held to be typical of sickness states. The vocabulary of illness provides the descriptive terms for expressing low-valued behavioural and physiological conditions. To use *hége* is to engage in negatively valued talk. In accordance with male ideology relating to uncontrolled or excessive actions, only women are said to employ these expletives; this kind of talk displays a lack of regard for *mana*.

Insult

The cultural motif of illness dominates language used to describe and express anger. In this regard, what counts as *hége* (swearing) can also be categorized as *mege* (insult) – descriptors which, I have argued, may well be derivationally related. It is pertinent in the general context of my discussion of what constitutes deprecatory speech briefly to survey the field of insult. Examination of the relevant data reveals a continuum of semantic and stylistic principles fundamental to the lexicalization process and general patterning of speech in these contexts. It is the very nature of pejorative talk in Huli to be inextricably tied to certain significant promontories in an anatomically constituted landscape.

To explore the field of insult is thus to enquire into the way people's physical appearances tend to influence, fundamentally, the way in which they think about themselves and the way they perceive others. Assessments, for praise or invective, are generally classifiable under the binary contrast of good (*baya*) or bad (*ko*), depending on certain positively delineated qualities. As previously indicated, these antonyms are not gradable opposites but signify absolute properties. In respect of the physiological axes of skin, hair, body, and nose, evaluations are made in the context of talk concerning decoration, illness, or insult. In situations where these physical parts become a focus for attention, the commendatory/derogatory polarity is subject to detailed specification discussed more fully below. However, there is no comparable lexical indexing of the normal or everyday condition of skin or hair – the Huli verbalize states of ill-health but not the converse conditions of health or well-being. Specifically, the good/bad dichotomy operates as an equipollent opposition denoting positive properties in respective domains of discourse. Consistent with this feature, we find no lexically marked contrastive relation between 'health' and 'sickness' in Huli. Rather, they seem part of a privative opposition, conceptually but not lexically defined, of states of sickness and non-sickness; one is not more or less sick, but simply ill or not-ill. Conditions of absence from illness are thus not verbally expressed in Huli because they appear not to be cognitively salient in the culture as worthy matters of comment.

In respect of these observations, statements concerning physiological evaluations proceed by positive specification of attributes which, for the most part, relate to nose, skin, hair, and body. Whilst these attributes are not defined in consistent pairs of opposites (divided between censure or praise), at a general level certain contrasts do emerge. The prevalence of allusions to 'nose' in insults can be attributed to the recurrent reference to bad words as 'smelly talk'. This idiom is, importantly, realized morphemically in the related lexemes *ngui* ('nose'): *ngu* ('taint'): *ngubi* ('smelly'). The modal states of the nose are a grid for expressing death (*ngui ti tau*: 'exploded nose'), shame (*ngui dali ho ngegoni*: 'nose points down'), greed ('flared nostrils'), and lies (*ngui to ha*: 'swollen nose'). An 'open' nose permits one to smell pig and thus avail oneself of economically advantageous opportunities. Contrastingly, a 'closed' nose results from female contamination. The open/closed axis is embodied in the forms cited below. An excessively open nose is, however, a sign of greed, envy, and damaging desire characteristic of the cravings of *dama*. The commonest insult forms pertaining to nose and skin which I recorded in dispute texts are as follows:

Nose (*ngui*) +		Skin (*dongone*) +	
yanga (flared)			
pongobi (tied)		*hagere* (wrinkled)	
mugule (crushed)		*mberabi* (rolled up)	
mbala (flattened)		*pedegele* (folded)	
lalua pea (spread)		*gabu* (dry)	
pole pea (nosey)		*kumbururu* (scaly)	
higi (scowling)		*ka* (peeling)	
hagama (dirty/blocked)			
kaiabi (dry)			

In the context of assessments of decoration, the surface quality of the skin should have a glowing oiled sheen as denoted by the terms *dara* ('shine'), *kiau* ('bright'), *wã* ('glisten'), *migi mege* ('reflective') and many others. Skin should be tight and smooth. Insults, by contrast, emphasize the aged condition of skin as dry, dull, and crinkled. The vocabulary relating to the appearance of nose and skin is more elaborate than for other organs although eyes, forehead, and mouth may also be the subject of disparaging remarks. Similarly, abuse may focus on aspects of dress – *dambale pongo la hea* ('apron is too short'), *dambale doge/tegeda hea* ('torn/shredded apron') – deportment, or hair (*mãnda*). In this latter regard derogatory comments stress the unevenness of tuft, looseness of fitting (*gamu hea dagoni*), and generally, properties which are conceptualized as a loss of 'heat'. An old, neglected, and tattered wig is literally a 'cold wig' (*mãnda* (wig) *tambe* (cold)).

My concern here is specifically with certain semantic and stylistic dimensions to insult rather than the contextual and conversational features that are dealt with separately elsewhere in the book. *Mege*, as a categorization of speech acts, subsumes the verbal forms of *talia* ('rebuke/reproach'), *gurua* ('criticize') and *la hira* ('cooking talk'). These three lexemes imply a modulated or mitigated type of abuse but can be used synonymously for *mege* where (a) some reference is made to the material properties of words as inducing pain (*tandaga*) or sores (*dere*); and/or (b) there exists a possibility that the action can be made the subject of a claim for compensation. In the following dialogue these two conditions are determinative of the reference idioms used. We may further note the conceptual relations between insult and smelly talk as 'growing' and 'hitting' inside:

DALU: that smelly talk (*bi ngubi*) is growing inside man's heart.
DAIYA: you held a criticism (*gurari yago*) or you didn't hold a criticism. One day you two will come and then if you make a criticism you will bring compensation.
DALU: your talk will continue to stay inside like an arrow, it is rattling like trees in there (*ira dengero ogo ha*).
GARIBE: she made an insult (*mege*) and then she gave a pig, the first time. She made an insult and a second pig she gave, the second time. She will keep on making that insult.

(Field data)

Mege is not restricted or circumscribed to the same degree as *hège*. Abuse, as an actionable offence, depends on circumstances of the utterance and social relationships of the interactants. In disputes, the 'power' and 'illness' implications of insult may be less where 'woman's talk' is rhetorically stated as ineffective.

In addition to contexts where insults constitute legitimate claims, *mege* is also used to refer to types of venial abuse; the distinction between the two references is contextual not substantive. Invective is not an actionable offence in the degradation rites of Tege or the 'fight songs' of *Dawe* (see Appendix 3; A: 1–3). This licensed aggression represents a form of permitted ill-doing where there is acceptance of responsibility for talk and admission that it is 'bad words', but no consequent liability for indemnity. This implicit division between licit and illicit abuse is applicable to talk in disputes. Once an accredited state of debate is in progress, insults are conceived as an expected type of response to anger. They are not condoned but neither do they entail culpability in the sense of liability to compensation. *Mege*, as illicit insults, occur then outside the acknowledged forum for discussion, they are 'brought out onto the public place' in a manner described and detailed elsewhere in the book. Expressions of anger inside the dispute arena carry diminished responsibility. The ecological concepts of 'inside' (*anda*)/'outside' (*hama*) disputing space thus determine the indemnity implications of speech acts containing abuse.

There are two further significant dimensions to insult that deserve comment. First, there is the marked prevalence of formulations which deny status by implicit reference to stereotype attributes of 'manhood' or 'womanhood'. For example:

TEXT D
You are not woman
You have been eating and catching insects everywhere
You never carry intestines of pigs
You are like smelly.

(Field data)

The interlocutor implies the woman is lazy in pig husbandry and thus never tastes the fruits of her endeavours (women always receive pigs' intestines when any pig is killed). A parallel technique, aimed at denying conventionally defined human status, is to attribute 'larger than life' characteristics implied by the designations Iba Tiri or *dama*. *Dama* represent both uncontrolled behaviour and excessive greed (*humbirini* – which signifies avarice and the land where dead souls migrate to plague human descendants). Disparagement may thus focus on individuals' attitudes, desires, or, significantly, their verbal offerings. Talk classified as abnormal reflects a deviant personality. This may be associated with supernatural beings or possession:

wali ndo dama bi lenego
that is not woman's talk but the talk of dama
damame henge mulene ngago
the dama will get space inside there.

(Field data)

Equally, aberrant speech may be accounted for in terms of attributions of conventionally defined properties of cross-sex or immature persons. In the following extract, the ineffective nature of talk is stressed by alluding to its lack of direction and impermanency (i.e. it doesn't 'stay inside'):

bi ina larigo haria nawi
the talk you have made has no track
wane-igini emene bi laridagoni
you have talked like little children[14]
wali wane la bi o laridagoni
you have talked like a woman and a daughter
agali bi ndo laridagoni
you haven't talked like a man
hale haria unugu ha ti haria ha polalu piyadagoni
it has gone into your ears and come out of your arse.

(Field data)

Related to the above insult forms is the importance of the overall homology between sickness and speech as one semantic implication of the Huli concept of talk. This extends to the broader levels of causal aetiology and responsibility. Illness, like bad talk, is symptomatic of failure in a person's social and moral dealings with other individuals or *dama*. Types of sickness are the most prevalent sanctions attendant on breach of norms. Insults which focus on speech or physical disabilities are comments on the moral stature of people. For Huli, sickness is both the physical realization and index of social transgressions. The Huli are not reticent about relating aspects of health and appearance to status definitions. In the following tract a woman insults her husband's brother whose leprosy is commonly attributed to a previous incestuous (*tagini*) relationship:

TEXT E

1   *morowane duguinigo nigo*
     your thigh-bone has been pulled out down there
   ko ore nigo
     you are very bad down there
5   *magu ore nigo*
     you are very sick down there
   wali ale ni porego
     you are going like a woman there
   ngubi ni porego
10 you are going smelly there
   agali ale ndo
     you are not like a man
   Dali Iba Tiri
     you are an Iba Tiri
15 *ko ore amuali hea burayu amu ni pore*
     you are going bad, with bronchitis there
   wabene hugu bere ni porego
     you are going with pus in your hip there

(Field data)

The speech neatly encapsulates the range of negative attributes pertaining to smell, illness, Iba Tiri and 'manhood' that I have been discussing. This nexus of related concepts provides the synonym substitutions that are stylistically characteristic of incidences of repeated syntax found in the above text.

A full understanding of the relation between insults and 'body language' can be gained only in the light of how the Huli depict the polar physical representations of good and bad appearance. It is not simply a question of defining the stereotypes in terms of decoration or anatomy, but of comprehending the manner in which such fixed images are used to make inferences and assumptions about behaviour. This reiterates a central argument that the Huli perceive a common system of meanings between the manipulation of pigs, paint and parlance. They are modal forms of presentation of person. In the following speech the offender–offended contrast is framed in terms of the stereotypes of decorated–sick people. The opposition is developed in respect of mental dispositions whereby the decorated men act in a state of exhilaration, confidence, assertiveness and aggression:

gulu pobe ge laga yi dege dege ru
with pan-pipes and leg bands, just those
dumbi yalu da dege dege ru
with shining foreheads, just those
manda parebi dege dege ru
with decorated wigs, just those
bolangua harugula denge payabu handale hayeni howa
when you passed me you saw I wore a bad leaf-dress
(*Cordyline fruticosa fam. Liliaceae*)
nabolebero laribe?
'I won't kill pig!' did you say that?
luma bolebere . . .
the day after tomorrow you will kill pig
o hula pungua hiru ebere kegonigo
with decorative charcoal you are coming and are there
o agali i nigo bo ngulebere
o man my pig you will kill and give
o ko dambale uru galawangabi burayu bi o bedagome
o bad man, with uneven front-apron, with bronchitis, sitting there (you thought that was me)
dawaliya
nevertheless, we'll cook your pig

(Field data)

The rhetorical efficacy of this passage lies partly in the emotive resonances of standardized allusions to the decorated and the decrepit. Contrast of dress and mental attitude is that of Haroli and Iba Tiri, symbolizing in the above speech the respective positions of the dispute participants. The metaphorical power of these images is also partly attributable to the orator's understanding and display that talk about decoration is one context where vocabulary switching is a prerequisite for 'good speech'. This is evident from both the data cited in the previous sections dealing with *bi mone* and *kai*, and in the above occurrences of the eulogistic terms *hula pungua* ('charcoal') and *dumbi yalu* ('forehead': *wānekui*).

The causal relationship between the utterance of bad words and illness is further realized in a condition known as *hale o* ('ringing in the ears'). This results from insulting someone in their absence, and the blighted person must recite names of candidate enemies in order to clear their malignant influence. Insults may also be expressed non-verbally. Gestural abuse is overtly sexual and takes one of three distinct forms: (1) *gi dombo*: the second and fourth fingers are raised and bent so as to flank an outstretched middle finger. This is understood to represent a penis and testicles; (2) the hand is shaped into a claw, signifying a vagina, and an opponent is exhorted to consume his 'mother's/sister's vagina'; or (3) *wea*: anal exposure (the import of which accords with notions of excreta detailed earlier in reference to lies).

These non-verbal proclamations are often figuratively alluded to in speech concerned to stress the counter-normative aspects of behaviour. The speaker may juxtapose a number of terms which repeat a single idea and which will rhyme on account of the addition of the connective suffix *-ru*:

gunguru lairu   wearu
fighting, arguing, anal exposure.

The lexical items that describe such non-verbal routines can thus be employed metaphorically, as rhetorical devices, to express the cultural implications of insult. They function to define excessive behaviour in the same way as the lexicalized genre terms are used as a grid for discriminating aberrant speech, or assessments of appearance differentiate between mental dispositions. These points are explicitly formulated in the following homily:

Ayu kàbu bedago
Now you are sitting there decorated
ndo, nigua pu dali haregola gende tagira puwa
no, when you go down there anger will come out
o kemago mege timbuni bima
you will be making a big insult to us men
o wea la dali holebere
you will expose your arse down there
gi dombo nigua biai holebere
you will rudely gesticulate down there
i hangu ndo larama
it is not just you we are saying
wali agali la mana wiyago ogo
for man and woman a *mana* has been placed there

hamani lo yu tagira pobe hea ndo
on the public space it shouldn't be said and carried outside.

(Field data)

In the above text we can again glimpse the types of models of order and disorder that the Huli use in disputes. The contrast between 'decorated' (and therefore 'well-behaved') people and those given to 'insult' is clearly defined. Moreover, the spatial distinction between *anda* ('home'/'inside') and *hama* ('outside'/'public') is stated in reference to norms (*mana*) that insults should not be made public knowledge. Insults are 'smelly talk' (*bi ngubi*) and should not contaminate *hama*; they are produced by uncontrolled speakers.

Paralleling the restricted sets of anger terms for children, pigs, and dogs, one may insult a relative in Huli by uttering the deviant form of the conventional kin address term. This is vocalized either by itself, or as a minimally-distinct pair:

ainya (mother)	:	*kainya*
mama (father; male cognate)	:	*mame*
aba (father)	:	*kaba*
hame (father)	:	*kame*
imane (affine)	:	*kimane*

We may note, once again, that antonymy is here marked by morphologically related lexemes manifesting initial or final position variations. Furthermore, in a pair format these terms assume a distinct prosodic pattern such that the second element shows a fall in intonation. This is consistent with its semantic status as the stressed insult component. As with many of the linguistic expressions of *mege*, the above lexemes can be used to make metaphorical references to, or talk about, behaviour. Disordered talk is a model of disordered relationships. The opposition of a daughter to her parents is rhetorically formulated in terms of the conventional insult routine:

ainya – kainya, mama – mame	
mother	father

The deviant forms *kainya* and *mame* also signify 'vagina' and 'penis' respectively. Again, linguistic violation of a conventional form here generates a semantically debased, but related, image (analogous to colloquialisms such as 'money – shmoney'). The polysemous and assonant factors provide then further scope for variety of expression. Abuse is predicated on culturally given values, morality, definitions, and descriptions of what is deviant. It requires 'linguistic knowledge of proper verbal forms of insulting' (Gumperz 1975 : xix) which can in turn be structured by stylistic patterns.

I have sought in this chapter to explicate the degree to which aesthetic and rhetorical norms determine speech both within and outside the context of disputes. Furthermore, I have defined those inherent semantic axes and features that organize various lexical domains. The delineation of a number of verbal repertoires – positive and negative evaluation terms, locative and perlocutionary expressions – within the field of 'talking about talk', revealed a complex metaphoric code drawn from speech patterns prevalent in social contexts associated with disputes. The components of meaning that constitute the metaphors express levels of congruity and contrast along a number of semantic dimensions. The axis of futility is characterized by the contrast of talk which 'hits' inside or outside, or talk which is like 'pain' or 'bone' (substantial idioms) against those lexemes listed in *Table 5*, H.1–11 (all insubstantial images). In the same way, along the dimension of control *manali* ('*mana* men') or Haroli are opposed to the meanings of disorder conveyed by the designation Iba Tiri. These in turn are spheres which subdivide along the same principles of opposition. With respect to the axis of covertness, 'straight' and 'true' talk are contrasted with talk which is 'covered over' or 'veiled'. Moreover, a homologous structure of contrast relations is found to typify the domain of proverb relating specifically to speech content and production. The results for the interpretation of talk reveal a balance of expectations concerning the appropriateness of direct and indirect patterns of speech.

The materials considered in this chapter indicate that the Huli appreciation of 'good usage' represents as much an interest in form as the content of words. Variety of expression is achieved at every level through mechanisms – such as synonym forms – which display rhyme. The unexpected degree of frequency of these artifices of sound elevates the sound-meaning relationship above the level of arbitrary connection. Specifically, in the lexicalization of antonyms and synonyms, minimally-distinct pairings and prosodic features such as tone contrasts, appear iconically to express parallels in semantic, syntactic and phonological structures. Throughout the data on insults, naming, and norm formulations, opposing elements appear as linked parts of a 'conceptual unity' (Pos 1938 : 245). The contrastive units imply each other and this association is frequently marked by a sharing of sounds. That certain phonic devices have been selected for their properties of sound-symbolism seems further evidenced by the occurrence and juxtaposition of morphologically unrelated assonant words like *danda* ('bow' signifying 'man') and *damba* ('bride-price' signifying 'woman') in pre-patterned speech. The prevalence of the sound patterns discussed in this chapter also reflect the small number of vowel and consonant phonemes in Huli, vowel-harmony rules and vowel-final word forms which all combine to produce constant assonance; rhyme is an almost inevitable by-product of talk in Huli.

Notes

1 Interestingly, stammering is denoted by the reduplicative terms *bi labo labo / libi libule / libi labale*, all derivationally related to *labo* ('twins') – that is, 'to talk in twins'. In Huli, this is separate from the perception of articulation problems signified by the term *hege tele* ('spinning tongue').

2 Talk is said to 'sleep inside' (*bi i ha pada*) people.

3 Two further examples are *bi gimbi gembo* (talk + wood that is not cut straight) – 'crooked talk', and *bi limi lama* (talk + intertwined roots) – 'tangled talk'.

4 The Daribi term for 'idle talk' is *dwaidwai po* (Wagner 1967 : 253).

5 Throughout this section I have used data from the Haya (Seitel 1974) for comparative purposes. There are no comparable materials as yet published on 'talking about talk' for New Guinea Highlands societies. The similarities and differences between Huli and Haya emphasize the extent to which we need to relate dominant cultural themes to other behavioural domains. Indeed, as I have shown, the way the inside / outside dimension is articulated in each of the two cultures can be accounted for in terms of the way 'pain' is conceived and expressed.

6 All three cultures appear to have a 'water-spirit' who is said, though not necessarily believed, to shoot arrows into people causing pain. In Huli, these are removed by a healing rite known as *Iba Tiri timu dugua* ('pulling out the arrow of Iba Tiri').

7 *Gulu* appears to be a praise term which, when occurring in compound lexemes, signifies an aesthetic facet: e.g. *gulu pobe* ('pan pipes'; *gulu wambia* (Komia Bird of Paradise), *gulu* (marsupial fur: see Diagram 5) and *gai gulu* (collective term for decorative feathers). This semantic marking is very common in the eulogistic lexicons of the Huli.

8 From a stylistic viewpoint we can again note the familiar name-pairing and repeated syntax that typifies *gamu* texts.

9 The number morphs of 13 / 14 / 15 also signify ears / eyes / nose respectively. In dogs these parts are believed to be formed at birth on these specific days.

10 I am grateful to S. Frankel (private communication) for identifying the anatomical parts denoted by *ayuni* and *nuni*.

11 I use the term Huli in my discussions of these specialized lexicons to signify the everyday, conventional terms.

12 There are other contexts in Huli culture where vocabulary switching occurs. Most notably, in cooking where the term *duni* ('leaf') – as in *hai duni* ('banana leaf') – is always replaced by *angi*. In the absence of any indigenous explanation for this behaviour, we may surmise that use of the term *angi* separates the context of cooking from other uses to which leaves are put (e.g. wrapping, thatching, dressing, or makeshift umbrellas). It seems to mark the fact that a multitude of different leaves are being used for a 'common' purpose.

13 This same question may, contrastingly, be directed towards a person who displays exceptional skills such as in the making of *mànda* (wigs). Clearly, illness is related to manifestations of 'odd' behaviour.

14 This is a frequently used censure form and in the following extract we may again note the association between ineffective talk, immaturity and states of the mind (*mini*):

mini ibule
the mind will come
ni igiri emene dege bi layago
down there you have talked like little boys
i nde mini ibule birago wàne auwe
your mind will come, later it will be clear
ayu igiri emene kego
now you are a small boy

(Field data)

6

Talking about outcomes

My intention in the preceding chapters has been to provide a sociolinguistically informed analysis of disputing among the Huli. As a
'plan for future talk', the study suggests the manner in which a focus
on the verbal interaction within disputes can promote understanding
of the relationships between claims, processes, and outcomes. In the
place of a comprehensive outline of conflict resolution mechanisms in
this society, a set of images, models, and conclusions has been developed from, and located within, transcript-based data. The *actes
juridiques* of the system are constituted by interpretative and evaluative processes that reaffirm the sociocultural framework of sense and
nonsense. Talk is both the topic of anomaly and the resource with
which people confront it. Much can be learned, then, from the terms in
which people categorize and construe their own verbal behaviour. This
analysis requires a consideration of the dimensions of meaning that
structure the apportionment of credit / discredit or praise / censure, and
an assessment of the significance of form to content. In these respects,
it seems to me, the study of disputes must embrace and be an aspect of
the study of conversation in culturally specific settings. To the extent
that the Huli forensic apparatus is predicated on discriminations of

talk, and the sense in which a dispute is defined indigenously as a 'talk situation', the approach adopted here is consonant with the place and value of verbal behaviour in this culture.

An overall identity between dispute-management and dirt-elimination is a corollary of the meanings attached to the discrete categories of 'private' (*anda*) and 'public' (*hama*). It serves as a grid for distinguishing matters which should, or should not, be discussed in moot situations. Dispute-settlement articulates how boundary maintenance involves linguistic rituals of separation and sanitization. The consciousness of pollution that pervades all forms of social behaviour, and that underlies the elaborate 'negative' vocabulary of the Huli, is an ideological framework built around the absolute pre-supposition of the sexual disjunction. The male/female dichotomy impinges upon the dispute system as a determinant of both media-tion strategies, and the stereotype responses of women to male control of 'talk': 'We are underneath the legs of men and I am thus paying you' (D.3: 461); 'All the talk is on the side of man' (D.3: 135). Language use and structure provides here diagnostic evidence for an uncompromising stigma philosophy. The incriminatory and defensive speech patterns, in so far as they express notions about anger, shame, sickness, and violence, reveal a consistent set of ideas about the nature and implications of female sexuality. In the hands of dispute participants, this language becomes a powerful medium for discrimination. The vocabulary of dispute interaction is thus replete with the semantics of female associated actions, products, and 'talk': *Wali wane la bi o laridagoni* ('You have talked like a woman and a daughter'); *Agali bi ndo laridagoni* ('You haven't talked like a man'). Such dimensions of inequity and imbalance are counterpoised by presuppositions relating specifically to talk about outcomes and the axiomatic norm of 'speech reciprocity'. A dispute is conceived of as a context for verbal exchange and display in which people should 'share the talk'. One does not request speaking rights in Huli; no perfunctory rituals of apology or excuse preface turns; space must be usurped through assertion but no specific categories of candidate speaker are necessarily excluded. The claims of women to have a say under the auspices of an egalitarian principle are ratified by proverb content and use (see Chapter 5). Male ideology that women have no *mana* must be set against those behavioural contexts where the ritual and chronological primacy of women is declared and deferred to.

Because so many Huli disputes take place on *hama* ('cleared open spaces') it appeared prudent to inquire how far interaction reflected the constraints and ethos of 'public' presentations. The imputed parallels between the manner in which actors utilize the substances of pigs, paint, and parlance manifest themselves in metaphor. They are conceptually interchangeable and equivalent modes of behaviour that are, in their transactional states, amenable to open and public assessment. One employs on *hama* one's best pigs, one's finest feathers, and one's 'good words'. Attributions of praise are informally registered on reputations. These, in turn, frequently provide mediators with the inferential bases for claim evaluation: 'You have been here a long time so did this man used to say something bad or not?' (D.3: 410). In the degree to which we may perceive actions on *hama* as types of display, as well as the very real sense in which words and decoration are symbolic vehicles for self-identity, some appreciation of ethno-ethological concepts was demanded. Specifically, the relationship between man and bird is a recurrent motif in this, and in many of the neighbouring, cultures. Bird behaviour represents a rich pool of attributes and properties that can be used as a model, or as an analogy for pre-existing models, on which to pattern human actions. The distinction between nest/display grounds, the pose of display, and the sanitization of display grounds – features recognized to typify bird of paradise behaviour – inform the cognitive frames used by dispute participants. Moreover, the cultural stereotypes of the 'good' and 'bad' against which disputants are measured, are defined in respect of both talk and dress. This complex set of meanings, interrelating birds, decoration, dress, and knowledge are encapsulated in the tonally contrasted lexical pairs:

mànda (hair/wig) : (knowledge) *mánda*
yári (cassowary) : (decoration) *yàri*.

Some attention to language use and structure is thus particularly critical for an interpretation of Huli behaviour and the production of meaning. There is a high correlation between certain prosodic and phonological patterns and the representation of synonymy and antonymy. What is noticeable about this matrix is indeed the relative frequency of occurrence over a wide range of data. It seems not unreasonable to assume that the presence of these lexical patterns expresses the cognitive status of the verbal behaviour with which they are associated. Whatever the principles of conceptualization, I would contend that these fields of meaning also manifest the workings of a cultural aesthetic.

One index of the cultural importance attached to talk in the realization of outcomes is, as I have previously noted, the prevalence of *gamu* ('spells') in all fields of action. The Huli philosophy of action is inextricably bound to an appreciation of the power of words and the need for correct performance of verbal formulae. While winning and losing are not lexically marked concepts in Huli, favourable outcomes to any dispute can be influenced by affecting the 'talk' of an opponent. While most of the traditional sorcery forms are no longer practised by the majority of Huli, that sub-class of spells within the category of minor sorcery known as Hubi Bi ('wrapping/binding' (*hubua*) + talk (*bi*)) – and which is concerned with 'binding the talk/mind' of a dispute antagonist – has persisted. These spells are frequently paired so that the first part enhances one's own speech, while the second aims to destroy that of an opposing litigant. The spell may be recited either before or during the dispute and is frequently accompanied by the tying of a knot in a piece of grass or string. The following text provides an insight into the symbols of aggression associated with 'dispute':

TEXT: Hubi Bi *gamu* (second part only)
Informant: Hagai (Tobani)
Bebalu   Bebe Yame la   /tane   u baro   /mabuni
Cassowary cassowary   both/hair of the armpit I'm hitting/cassowaries' claws
u baro   /pulali   u baro   /ma iri   u baro   /manda iri
I'm hitting/lip hair I'm hitting/neck hair I'm hitting/head hair
u baro   /de iri   u baro   /de panda iri u baro
I'm hitting/eyelashes I'm hitting/eyebrows   I'm hitting

The equation that is made here between dispute opponent: cassowary is consistent with the kinds of symbolic statement concerning 'aggression' that characterizes Haroli decoration. A similar identification is made by Helago in D.2: 'We have been pointing our fingers like the cassowary's claws, brother' (D.2: 216–217). Native exegesis of the spell fixes on the characteristic of immovability that these particular hairs have in common. An attempt is made to 'still' (*ema nabi*) the speech of a litigant. While the situation of settlement-directed talking is defined in triadic terms, from any litigant's perspective the outcome is dependent on the relative verbal performances of the two *tene*.

Notwithstanding the eventual states of agreement or disagreement following any occasion of talk, the Huli conceive these social encounters as displaying a Sisyphean aspect. The inevitability of recurrent and cyclic disputes within the community is attributed directly to the essentially incomplete nature of speech transactions. The deficiencies of the settlement process are reflected in the aphorism 'talk never dies'. In this context the term *bi kugi* ('talk' (*bi*) + 'left overs/ remains' (*kugi*)) refers to those issues which have remained unsettled from a previous dispute: 'There was some previous talk which had been left over and then you fought over this. Was this how it was?' (Field data (Goldman 1981a)). It is not that claims are never finally settled, but rather that the outcome of any dispute may not encapsulate the total range of claims being pursued. Impasses are here temporary adjournments of dialogue rather than statements of intractable position. Claims may be pending for years in Huli and it can be seen from Appendix 5 *Table A1* that on average most issues are debated on at least 2.2 occasions. Even with the cessation of warfare, claims arising out of past conflicts and injuries sustained are likely to persist well into the next decade.

It has become almost a cliché in the anthropological study of disputes to conclude that the function of the settlement system is to restore relationships, to maintain a balance or equality between the litigants. At the level of native explanation, this type of generalization does not faithfully represent the meanings embedded in the context-specific lexis of 'settlement'. The substantive metaphors relating to disorder, dispute, and normative breach are couched in the language of illness. The 'immaterial', or secondary, injury that accompanies any type of interpersonal conflict in Huli is expressed as one of 'sickness'. It is clear from my analyses that actors employ sequencing rules (be they implicit or explicit) in their behaviour so that, with respect to the claim order in any profile, actions conform to a conventionally defined pattern. In similar fashion, indemnity payments are made in conformity to an imperative inference structure that obligates a causal agent to ensure that types of sickness – of which anger and shame are but two different modal states – are eliminated. The objectives of the settlement system in Huli are, I shall argue, the restoration of a physical state free from afflicting illness.

Compensation

'Brothers, can you give me some pigs so I can close the wound.'

In order to comprehend the kind of rite which compensation represents it is necessary to remind ourselves of the structural homologies stated to exist between the pathology and treatment of sickness and speech in this society. In my analysis of 'talking about talk' I indicated the senses in which illness provided a source of metaphor used to articulate fundamental truths about the perlocutionary dimensions of speech. Moreover, the negative images that convey a state of dispute invariably turn on the central importance of 'pain' (*tandaga*). In accordance with these notions I suggested that compensation is here a symbolic application of 'medicine', a healing rite. An examination of the indemnity lexicon is particularly revealing in this regard. The term for any kind of compensation in Huli is *abi* which, I tentatively argued, may well be a contracted form of *dabi* meaning to 'heal, recover, get well'. *Abi* is most usually compounded in a format of adjectival qualifier + *abi*, the former constituent denoting the type of breach for which payment is made. For example: *taga abi* ('shame compensation': see D.3), *keba abi* ('anger compensation') or *mege abi* ('insult compensation'). Whatever the qualification of *abi*, the transfer is made to 'rub on sores' (D.3) or 'wounds'. A secondary mode of reference to the type of indemnity issue makes use of a terminological repertoire denoting the pigs involved. I have set these out, in addition to other closely related transfers, in *Table 6*. These expressions are shorthand normative formulations communicating who should give and receive *abi*. They both describe the 'topic' of payment as well as restate the function of the pigs in the healing process.

Importantly, then, the meanings of compensation as 'cure' are encoded in some of the descriptors used to talk about exchange routines. The phrase *nogo nigi*, for example, denotes a type of ally indemnity as well as reflecting the equivalence between pigs and healing leaves (*nigi*). The obligations concerning compensation are a corollary of the normative prohibition on causing sickness. Payments are made in conformity to axioms regulating individual health. The agreement of Walumbu to compensate her brother Egeria in D.3 was not an admission of guilt, but an expression of tenets pertaining to the mutual obligations of kin regarding sickness. The conceptual basis of Huli *abi* is a chain of imperative entailments, a set of elementary deontic propositions that may be phrased in the modality of obligation (O):

(O) reveal anger (illness) → (O) of offender to assuage (heal) → (O) of injured to publicly acknowledge assuagement.

Table 6 *The semantics of compensation*

Term	Meaning	Referent
NOGO MAGU	(*magu*: sick/vomit)	Pigs given as a loan to those unable to pay compensation to some third party; they are metaphorically 'sick'.
NOGO GIMA	(*gi* (hand) + *ma* (back))	Payment made to an ally for killing an enemy. His 'hand' is 'backed' by these pigs
NOGO NIGI/KAGA	(*nigi*: leaf – *Laportea, fam. urticaceae*; used to relieve pain)	Payment to an ally who has sustained injuries during fighting.
NOGO TAUWA	(*tauwa*: testicle is placed)	Payment to the kin of a girl with whom illicit sexual intercourse is held to have occurred.
NOGO DAMBA	(*damba*: to close down/cover over)	Pigs given to the kin of a murdered man. The term *damba* may also denote any large payment of pigs which 'close' the issue or transaction as for example in the purchase of land, or as denoting collectively 'bride-price'.
NOGO DAUBWA	(*dau*: five)	Payment which is an earnest for *damba*, in which each initial pig, or half of a pig, represents five pigs to be given later.
NOGO PALI PALO	(*pali palo*: reduplicative play on *palia*: to sleep)	Pigs which mark the cessation of hostilities. They figuratively make the conflict 'sleep'.
NOGO KANGO	(*kango*: killing stick)	Pigs given as restitution for a debt or pig that has been killed. The transaction 'kills' the debt.

This framework of directives provides a meta-statement of the moral dimensions behind giving *abi*. The sequencing rules define the *mana* referred to by Walumbu in D.3: 'If he asks for it then I'll give (18). . . . The *mana* says give (397)'. Breaches in the chain (defaults) such as omission (to assuage or recognize appeasement) are considered serious and can lead to fighting. For Huli, states of sickness or pain are explained as the results of the causative power of man or *dama*. A person can produce changes in the state of health of another either positively – by doing / saying X – or negatively, by forbearing to do / say X. The fundamental directive category of obligation – the ought, must, should, duty, or right of our own normative discourse – is inherent in applications of *abi* categorizations. The calculus of directives given above is not dependent for its ontological justification on linguistic promulgation, any more than a norm's existence is language-dependent. That members orient to such a model can be demonstrated from both verbal and non-verbal behaviour.

There is a dichotomous division of compensation pigs into *nogo haguene* ('head pigs') and *daga* (which we may gloss as 'others'). This separation is invariant regardless of issues. The *fundamentum divisionis* is that of size; the former category consists of the largest pigs which normally constitute one-third of the total number of pigs given over. In regard to *nogo haguene* the principle of equivalence obtains such that, in bilateral *abi* transfers, perceived inequalities between the exchanged pigs always result in an aborted transaction. The patterns of contribution and distribution regarding *abi* pigs are much the same as for bride-price. Individuals rely on a personal network of exchange which links debt and credit relations in the spheres of compensation, bride-price, mortuary donations, and, previously, ritual. The systems are mutually interchangeable inasmuch as debts created in one domain may be repaid with pigs from any of the other spheres of exchange. The parallels between bride-price and other indemnity forms are further exemplified by the terminological equivalence of *nogo haguene* and *wariabu*$_2$ (bride-price section: see Chapter 3), and the fact that *haguene* pigs must always be 'killed and consumed' by the complainants. This enforced consumption of 'head' pigs expresses an element of finality in any claim, an acknowledgement of assuagement which is said to 'make the trouble sleep'. The killing of *haguene* is a symbolic action which terminates hostility; omitting to perform this action may re-activate the conflict. The parties are *not* thereby reconciled, only the state of sickness of each litigant is construed to have been affected. In the case of war injuries, where pain recurs, or death is attributed to the injury, further *abi* may be demanded of the responsible parties notwithstanding any previous payments. Clearly, it is the relative balance of physical health in each individual that concerns the Huli, not necessarily any notion of restoration or reconciliation between the parties.

To examine the relative incidences of the various outcome options discriminated by Huli – pending (*wene*), compensation (*abi*), renounced (*wa haya*) – in relation to the positional incidence of claims and other social-structural parameters, it is necessary to focus on some of the statistical trends derived from Appendix 5, *Tables A1–A10*.

Pending

Pending claims are those which are either unilaterally or bilaterally regarded as unsettled, and which may be aired again on some future occasion (such as D.1). *Table A1* indicates that approximately one-third of the total number of claims recorded originated prior to my fieldwork period, and that 87 per cent of these had been debated twice or more. Approximately 17 per cent (*Table A9*) of computed claims were still 'pending' further talk. Moreover, these appear to occur proportionately more frequently where the case has been publicly (i.e. on *hama*) aired, and in inter-clan disputes. The next highest incidences occur between distant agnates and affines. The pattern that emerges, not surprisingly perhaps, is that with an order of increase in structural distance there is a corresponding rise in intractability; the explanations for this can be found in an examination of the issues underlying pending outcomes. *Tables A2, A4*, and *A6* show clearly that according to the positional incidence of a claim along the continuum from initial to tertiary, there is a proportional increase in the relative incidence percentages of pending outcomes: initial (12 per cent); secondary (20 per cent); tertiary (40 per cent). In other words, where the claim is made relative to other like (but contrasting) units in any profile – and perhaps relative to the intersections between the two profiles – can affect the outcome form. The critical relationship between positional frequency of occurrence and outcome seems, in my opinion, to provide an important new perspective on the nature of disputes and their settlements. It is one that I have argued must be articulated in respect to the semantic weighting that claims have both in themselves, and relative to any sequence of claims in a profile. Pending cases appear to be proportionately high in the following types of claim: attributed homicide (66 per cent), pig theft (57 per cent) and war compensation (50 per cent). We may note from *Table A8* that, overall, 75 per cent of the above three classes occur at the inter-clan level, and nearly half (43 per cent) of the claims made occur in secondary or tertiary locales. There is, then, a consistency here between positional incidence, type of issue, and the social range of the dispute. Furthermore, it is precisely in these types of claim that the largest number of pigs is most likely to be exchanged. One might expect here a co-variant order of increase in the incidence of counter-claims. In respect to war compensation (50 per cent) and pig theft (33 per cent) the overall figures show exactly this kind of pattern. With a perception of higher loss there is an increased likelihood of a counter-claim. The reasons for any pending matter are manifold but include denial of liability (11 per cent) – a characteristic of all pending attributed homicides – temporary withdrawal of a litigant (18 per cent), delayed settlement and counter-claims (25 per cent: this is an average figure for all pending claims and can be seen to be significantly smaller than the percentages recorded for war compensation and pig theft above). In fact, counter-claims may well account for nearly a third of all pending cases as many of the other reasons forwarded included this additional aspect. These results are consistent with the noticeable fact that large compensation payments tend to be more in the nature of bilateral exchanges than unilateral transfers.

Notwithstanding the high proportion of counter-claims, the basic determinant of pending outcomes does not lie in this factor. In over half of the disputes recorded, an agreement on the number of pigs had been reached; the problems arose in the transaction stage. That is, it is not the presence of counter-claims *per se* that is responsible for the large proportion of pending claims, but the discretionary areas surrounding the actual act of transfer/exchange. Most typically, perceived inequalities in the relative sizes of *haguene* pigs thwarts the transfer. In so far as all indemnity payments are subject to the same strains we can appreciate yet a further sense in which bride-price (*wari* ('woman') *ab[u]* ('compensation')) is considered as a sub-class of *abi* transfer. Whilst the occurrence of counter-claims can thus be interpreted as one index of case protraction, the problematic areas may in fact be in the stages of execution rather than in the negotiation of outcomes.

Renouncement

The abandonment of claims, or pursuance to the point of material recompense, represents the single highest category of dispute outcome (47 per cent). In some cases the statistical sample is too small to elicit significant trends, but renouncement appears to occur proportionately more frequently where claims are privately pursued, and where disputants are either parish co-residents or closely related (e.g. close agnates: 48 per cent; affines: 54 per cent). The positional incidence of claims does not seem to be critical in this outcome class. Computing across the dispute categories one is struck by the fact that renouncement is proportionately high where considerations of minimum / maximum outlay or return of pigs is most critical. For example, despite the importance of insult claims, no less than 83 per cent of such demands concluded with renouncement. The lowest percentages occur in those cases where the investment of talk and time is likely to yield a high pig return: war compensation (16 per cent), fighting (25 per cent), pig theft (28 per cent), premarital sex (22 per cent) and money debts (20 per cent). The picture is somewhat more complex than this, however, since other factors impinge on any situation. The relatively high figure of 45 per cent for adultery cases manifests the degree of difficulty in obtaining legitimate and acceptable evidence for one's claims. This applies equally to theft of garden stuff (36 per cent). In instances of damage by pigs to gardens (53 per cent), almost half the cases involved first-time offenders, while an overall one-fifth of renouncement outcomes are directly linked to denials of liability. *Tables A2, A4,* and *A6* reveal that many such disputes are not pursued on the grounds that these actions might induce shame / anger in either or both of the parties. Many of the cases of land dispute (58 per cent) were of this nature and indicate the efficacy of norms regulating land devolution to agnates and $\bar{aba}$.

The Huli talk of renouncement as 'throwing away' (D.3: 24); there is a diffuse recognition of the value of such actions to the maintenance of peace. Nevertheless, a distinction is made between those issues which can be thrown away and those which should be compensated. Although in D.3 mediators are able to suggest the option of renouncement to Egeria, in cases of ally compensation where physical injury is apparent, such an option is often explicitly rejected: 'The wound has been pressed in. We can't just break off the talk and press it back to him. We can't throw away the talk about Aumai's arrow [received during a previous war]' (field data).

Compensation

From *Table A9* we may note that compensation has an outcome incidence of 30 per cent, and is thus not the most common type of dispute conclusion. It occurs predominantly in the context of publicly aired grievances, a facet consistent with the ethos of *hama* and the rationality of pig production. Though the overall occurrence of compensation is significantly low at the inter-clan (26 per cent) and affinal (27 per cent) levels, an indication of the problems involved in pursuing claims between these parties, it appears somewhat higher (36 per cent) for disputes within the parish. The interpretation that the differential involved reflects stronger obligations between parish members is plausible. However, it is not in itself sufficient to explain the fact that across the dispute categories (*Table A8*) compensation outcomes are more frequent in precisely those types of issue that occur between clans and affines: fighting (68 per cent), money debts (80 per cent), war (33 per cent) and premarital sex (77 per cent). It would appear that compensation is related to the incidence of renouncement in inverse proportion such that, with the perception of high pig returns, compensation is more likely to obtain. Secondly, the incidence of compensation decreases (*Tables A2, A4, A6*) markedly according to the positional order of the claim: initial (36 per cent), tertiary (18 per cent). In this respect it is significant that over 50 per cent of all fighting, money debts, war, and premarital sex claims are presented in the initial position of any profile. As I have argued above, compensation represents a 'healing' of sickness and a material expression of the phase of speech reciprocity. There is no operative principle of equivalence between the destructive value of any delict and the value of any *abi* payment. The calculation of any *abi* is directly dependent on a figure given by the prospective recipient: 'What he asks for we give' (D.3: 17–18; 165; 205–06; 297). Both parties are sensitive to the possibility of inducing anger or shame in the other by stipulating too high or too low a figure. In this regard, as I noted previously, the amount of pigs is very rarely a problem for compensation talk. The roughly prescribed scale is set by convention and precedent in each geographical area and in response to the person: pig ratio in that area. Ialubans were well aware that Tari Huli utilize larger numbers of pigs in compensation payments.

It needs to be stressed that the transfer of *abi* is primarily a unilateral action, so that the principle of reciprocity cannot be immediately located through observable turns of gift and counter-gift. The workings of this principle are located at the level of obligation to signal acknowledgement through symbolic acts of pig killing. As among the Duna, 'One simply "gives *damba*" or "marries a woman with pigs"'; one does not enter into a consciously defined exchange of precisely defined values' (Modjeska 1977 : 276). The *abi* and *nogo* taxonomies are the linguistic instruments of the system which have a semantic capacity to convey 'ought' propositions. In this regard the relevant relationship sets: speaker (talk)/donor (pigs): hearer (talk)/recipient (pigs) define 'personal' interests (the rationale of display) and 'impersonal' interests (ratification of the moral order). The metaphorical equivalence of pigs, paint, and parlance in Huli reflects the ordering of behaviour in terms of the manifold contrasts and polarities explicated throughout this book. They are the prime substances with which a person can influence his standing and reputation in society. The production process relating to all three symbols are characterized by male exploitation. The domain of *hama* is controlled and appropriated by males – increments of prestige are here publicly logged. The homologies between interactions involving these primal substances derive from their value as alternative modes of self presentation. Open inquests into an individual's status are, additionally, a test of his network accountability.

As a result of developments in the understanding of conversational machinery, anthropologists now generally attest to the value of including attention to speech in approaching problems within the discipline. Discourse is a structured activity, and the study of disputes – in so far as its raw data is constituted (in no small part) by extended verbal interchanges – must accord dialogue its due importance. The methodology adopted here is an attempt to avoid the vacuity of theoretical propositions divorced from indigenous statements, or distanced from the experiential complexity of case material. I have attempted to explore some of the implications that a focus on speech, and more particularly the structural notion of sequentiality, have for the conception and analysis of disputes and their settlement. Moreover, I have suggested some of the models required for precision in the examination of confrontation episodes. These transformations in perspective and emphasis within our sub-discipline, make demands in two specific directions: namely, the careful collection and the presentation of verbatim transcripts. These precepts provide a firm foundation for a truly multi-disciplinary approach to the data which, in historical hindsight, is likely to be approved as having done least violence to the ethnographic material.

Appendix 1
Kinship terminology

Hame / Aba / Taribuni[1]	F; FB; relatives father calls brother
Ainya	M; MZ; relatives mother calls sister
Ama	MZ (*aea / amale* also used for female cognate. *Amani* can be used to signify 'relative')
Hanini / Yawa (ne)	Cross-cousin of either sex
Ababuni	
Magane	MB
Arabuni	FZ
Mbalini	Sibling of opposite sex; opposite sex parallel-cousin
Hamene[2] */ Hambi / Hambiya* (m)	B; same sex parallel-cousin
Hagibuni / Hagiya (f)	Z; same sex parallel-cousin
Igini	S; BS
Wane	D; BD
Aba	Cross-cousins' children; ego's non-agnatic cognates
Mama / Mamabuni[3]	All male cognates of +1/−2 generation
Baba	All female cognates of +1/−2 generation
Agua / Aguene / Aguabuni	Relative of +2/−2 generation
Aguenene / Aguaneli	Relative of +3/−3 generation

Aburi[4] / *Mama mamali*	Ancestor (genealogical distance unspecified)
Affinal kin terms	
One	Wife
Agalini	Husband (*agali* (man) + *ni* (noun specifier))
Hagalini[5]	Co-wife
*Kiane	HB; Husband's male parallel-cousin
*Aruni	HZ; Husband's female parallel-cousin
*Imane[6]	Affinal relatives
*Balibuni / *Mbalibuni*	Wife's sibling
Yagini[7]	Step-father (*yagi* (side))

* *reciprocal terms of address or reference*

Notes

1 The meaning of the morph *buni* is difficult to determine precisely as in word medial positions both the unvoiced /p/ and the voiced /b/ occur. The phonetic realization of the orthographic symbol 'b' can be either (b) or (p) in word medial positions. It is plausible to suggest that *buni* may be a compound of *bu* ('seat of emotion', metaphorically one's 'heart') + *ni* ('on'). *Buni* also refers to one's liver which itself has connotations of emotional attachment as in the phrases *buni ha* ('to be close to') or *i buni ore* ('my true friend'). In the context of kinship terminology *buni* functions as an intensifier and endearment suffix which may or may not be attached to such terms as *agua* or *mama*. It is in the light of such observations that we can understand the relationships, discussed in Chapter 3, between *aba* (cross-cousins' children) and *ababuni* (MB/ZS). Reference should also be made to Modjeska's (1977) work on the Duna in which he notes the ritual interdependence of agnates and non-agnatic cognates in *Kiria pulu* rites. The same term *apa* (Modjeska 1977 : 290) is used to gloss this relationship of reciprocity. The quoted texts are very reminiscent of those I have cited for *hanini* and *aba* in Chapter 3: 'Another kinsmen, an *apa*, will say, "we'll go inside together. If you die first, I'll cut off your head. If I die first you can cut off mine"' (Modjeska 1977 : 290).

2 *Ne* as a suffix of kin terms appears to function similarly to its role in 'rendering nouns specific' (Rule 1964 : 62); e.g. *iba* ('liquid') – *ibane* ('sap/semen'). *Ne* also marks generation levels as in *hame* (F) – *hamene* (B) and *aguene* (+2/–2 generation) – *aguenene* (+3/–3 generation) – *aguenenene* (+4/–4 generation). Vowel harmony rules sometimes render *ne* as *ni*.

3 Changes to those terms listed in Glasse (1968 : 148) occur in the words *hanini*, *hagibuni* and *mamabuni*. In the Huli phonetic system 'v' is not a phoneme but an allophone of the phoneme 'b'. I have orthographically transcribed '*mamavuni*' (Glasse 1968 : 148) as *mamabuni* which is consistent with observations about the morph *buni* made in Note 1 above.

Adyena (Glasse 1968 : 148) does not denote a specific kin type but is a general term signifying 'friend'.

4 I was unable to obtain any consistent applications of the terms *aburi*, *aguabuni* and *aguaneli* which are used as synonyms for any relative of +2/−2 generation.

5 A first wife is referred to as *berene* ('seated'), the second as *dombeni* ('middle') and a third as *heyogone* ('youngest').

6 As an emphatic form *imane* can be compounded with *balibu* to yield *imane balibu* denoting affines. The term itself is almost certainly related to the Duna morph *ima* ('woman': cf. Modjeska 1977 : 100) again reinforcing the sense in which affines are relatives through a female link.

7 Adopted children are referred to as *buyini*, a compound of *bu* ('heart')+*yini* ('held') – i.e. their heart is held by the foster parents.

Appendix 2 ———
Text: *Damba Bi*

1
TEXT *Damba Bi* This speech followed a spirit-killing ritual. It is a good
example of the adaptation of a conventional style to an unorthodox
context. The speech attempts to reassure a female that she would bear
many children in the future.
Informant: Tainya (Kane Clan – Mogra Fugua)

1   *Aba   ainya   la   udu   kago*
    Father mother both there are
    (His mother and father are both there)
    Wali   ibu aba   ainya   la   udu   kago
    Woman her father mother both there are
    (that woman's father and mother are both there)
    O ainya   layayagua
    O mother if you say
    (when one says mother, then)
    Gili   agua
    Children grandchild generation
    (children will be born down through the generations)
5   *Gawali   agua*
    Children grandchild generation
    (children will be born down through the generations)

Barina   agua
Children grandchild generation
(children will be born down through the generations)
Bangale agua
Children grandchild generation
(children will be born down through the generations)
Amba tambo   lawa
Anger displeasure when they have caused
(when they have caused anger and displeasure)
Hembo lembo   lawa
Anger displeasure when they have caused
(when they have caused anger and displeasure)
10 *Ti   waru la   lawa*
Excreta mud both when they have caused
(when they have caused trouble)
Gai   manga la   lawa
Anger refusal both when they have caused
(when they have caused anger and refusal)
Wa toa laragola   birai holane
Cries   when they have made sitting down completely
(when they have cried they should sit down)
Holebirago   ainya
They will stay mother
(they will stay for ever; all this is from the mother)
Hamehanda andagua   harua
Father   fruit (*Lithocarpus rufo-villosus fam. Fagaceae*) is there
(from the father one obtains this fruit and)
15 *Baralamba*
Baralamba leaf (*Euodia fam. Rutaceae*)
Hombedagua
Bower of Macgregor's Bowerbird (*Amblyornis macgregoriae*)
Ega Honagaga
Cassowary plumes
Dumbi yalu
Forehead (i.e. 'truth')
Hari Lidua holebirago
Mt. Lidua they will stay on
20 *Honebibi ru*
Like the White men (non-indigenous people)
Ira   puba ale
Tree grubs like
Iba   tibu ale
Morning mist like
Hari mandiga ale
Lightening   like
Yagama   ale
Superb Bird of Paradise like

25   *Anga lo   ale*
Pandanus like
Nano gage   ale
Mushrooms like
Ani   holebira
Thus they will stay

2
TEXT *Damba Bi* (Recognized as part of the speech made to Koma clan enjoining them to collect compensation for the two men shot by Sinclair in 1957)
Informant: Gurubugu (previous headman of Koma)

	Ira Keloni po pogoli wiagaru	We used to plant the Poge fruit (*Ficus copiosa*) at Kelote
	Kugunu taiyali wiagaru	We used to plant the Taiya fruit at Kelote
	Iba Tagali ange ange	On the banks of the Tagari river
	Iba Kapiago ange ange	On the banks of Lake Kopiago
5	*Iba Kiabo ange ange*	On the banks of Kiabo
	Dali Tele udu barogo	I'm killing Dali Tele marsupials
	Hea Hali udu barogo	I'm killing Hea Hali marsupials
	Huru Ngidi udu barogo	I'm killing Huru Ngidi marsupials
	Ogoni balu	Having killed these
10	*Hogai igini*	The sons of Hogai
	Dataligo igini	The sons of Datali
	Baro Baroaba igini	The sons of Baro Baroaba
	Uru igini mo mogo bule pu	Go and gather together
	Ina hanarogo	I am carrying (i.e. giving compensation)
15	*Iba godane aleru*	Like the young Godane bamboo
	Galuni aleru	Like the Galuni bamboo
	Tirane aleru	Like the Tirane bamboo
	Hengedane aleru	Like the Hengedane bamboo
	Hamberogo	I am collecting pigs
20	*Ibi Laya po bero*	With the Ibi Laya leaves (*fam. Orchidaceae*) I am making a lid
	Mayu Laya po bero	With the Mayu Laya leaves (*Solanum torvoideum fam. Solanaceae*) I am making a lid
	Gundu Walu po bero	With the Gundu Walu leaves (*Commelina*) I am making a lid
	Uru nalu udura hole pu lagago	When those have been eaten you will go and stay there
	Ha lareria bo ya dindi ha	While shouting 'ha' we used to kill and turn them over
25	*Ke lareria bo yaraga haga bialu*	While shouting 'ke' we used to kill and turn them over

	Te lareria bo yaraga haga bialu	While shouting 'te' we used to kill and turn them over
	Dali Tele bariba	You killed the Dali Tele marsupials
	Huru Ngidi bariba	You killed the Huru Ngidi marsupials
	Hea Hali bariba	You killed the Hea Hali marsupials
30	*Hari Arani iba Wabu hambiabe*	On Mt. Ara fetch the water of Wabu
	Pogo mundia unguabe	Pick the pandanus nuts
	Iba Wabu tole duguabe	Pull the stones from Wabu lake
	I Mirila hendeni	I have seen the Duna
	Tumbudu tangi biruli	With their head caps
35	*Anga ba dambaleru*	With an apron of pandanus leaves
	Mbagua yoleru	With their bodies rubbed in oil
	Ega malunguru	With their cassowary feathers
	I unu Huli Gomaiya	I am Huli
	Bauwa payabu bidago	With Bauwa leaves (*Casuarina*) as a tangett
40	*Bai tola payabu bidago*	With Bai leaves (*Castanopsis acuminatissima*) as a tangett
	Aulai do mànda deneru henedago	With yellow flowers (*Helichrysum bracteatum*) in the hair
	I mini tiga tiga	My mind is straight
	Ira Habono pu larogoli	I used to plant the Habono tree (*Rapanea fam. Myrsinaceae*)

Appendix 3 ——————————
Text: *Dawe*

A
TEXT *Dawe* (courting songs)
Occasion: Pig killing at Wabu in July 1977

Specific sub-genre of Dawe: *Ū Wai* (song-fight)
1   Like his wrinkled hands, he won't have any 'pigs'
    Gimbuni hagareya ogo aleme 'nogobi' napaluenego
    Gimbuni hagareya ogo aleme 'ibuna' napaluenego
    Gimbuni hagareya ogo aleme 'awaiya' napaluenego
    Gimbuni hagareya ogo aleme 'parila' napaluenego
    Gimbuni hagareya ogo aleme 'paiyabe' napaluenego
    'Nali' nde
    'Hinali' uru napaluenego
2   Your bow (idiom for 'song') is like a mother's-daughter's vagina, I am
    planting a boundary in Ibiya land and I will stay on this side
    I ainya wane hamba dandayi Ibiya *ira wadali holebero*
    I ainya wane hamba dandayi Haluya *ira wadali holebero*
    I ainya wane hamba dandayi Hagai *ira wadali holebero*
    I ainya wane hamba dandayi Garai *ira wadali holebero*
    Baya *nde*
    Tabaya *ira wadali holebero*
3   Boys, your arrows (idiom for 'song') will not go inside us for we are many
    here like the 'birds'

Igiri emene padale timu 'ega' lele bidabagoria da holebere
Igiri emene padale timu 'ubiya' lele bidabagoria da holebere
Igiri emene padale timu 'abuage' lele bidabagoria da holebere
Igiri emene padale timu 'aiwaye' lele bidabagoria da holebere
'Bidagua' nde I 'Yagama' nde
'Bareagua' I 'Yamalu' lele bidabagoria da holebere
Specific sub-genre of Dawe: *Wali Ibilo* (to make the woman come)

4   Girl, don't sit and stare but come quickly
Lawini yamali wa hondo bira nabi ala ibu
Lawini yamali wariame hondo bira nabiabe ala ibu
Girl don't sit and watch the 'clouds' but come quickly
Lawini yamali 'yuguai' hondo bira nabiabe ala ibu
Lawini yamali 'yagama' hondo bira nabiabe ala ibu
'Pogo' nde
'Pogale' hondo bira nabiabe ala ibu

5   The song that we have made is in your 'heart' and making you jump onto
this place
Lima ogo larimadagua 'yama' ogo ha pogo larago
Alima ogo larimadagua 'yamali' ogo ha pogo larago
Alima ogo larimadagua 'higili' ogo ha pogo larago
Alima ogo larimadagua 'hagai' ogo ha pogo larago
'Lembo' nde
'Lewale' ogo ha pogo larago

B
TEXT *Mâli Dagia Gamu* Spell made to increase the brightness (*kiau*) of
decoration.
Informant: Hebale (Koma clan)
Occasion: Prior to performance of *Mâli* in Ialuba, July 1978

The Lesser Bird of Paradise (*Paradisea minor*) is coming down onto the
cleared dancing ground at Iri
Gulu Wambia Iri yamo yamo li dalinigome
It is coming down onto the cleared dancing ground at Irai
Irai i yamo yamo li dalinigome
It is coming down onto the cleared dancing ground at Wambo Waralo
Wambo Waralo yamo yamo li dalinigome
It is coming down onto the cleared dancing ground at Haroli Hanai
Haroli Hanai yamo yamo li dalinigome

5   The Lesser Bird is coming onto the cleared dancing ground at Igi
Gulu Wambia Igi hama
They have said it is me
I dege lea
It is coming onto the cleared dancing ground at Babagi
Babagi hama
They have said it is me
I dege lea

It is coming onto the cleared dancing ground at Nedo
Nedo hama
10   They have said it is me
I dege lea
It is coming onto the cleared dancing ground at Nedolo
Nedolo hama
They have said it is me
I dege lea
It is coming onto the cleared dancing ground at Gauwi
Gauwi hama
They have said it is me
I dege lea
15   It is coming onto the cleared dancing ground at Gambolo
Gambolo hama
They have said it is me
I dege lea
For the Urubu bird (Lorikeet) the Bara tree is bearing fruit in Bai
Ega Urulu Urubu ti naga Bai Bara darua
The Bara tree is bearing fruit in Barabia
Barabia Bara darua
The Bara tree is bearing fruit in Tiyua
Tiyua Bara darua
20   The Bara tree is bearing fruit in Tamaru
Tamaru Bara darua
For the Urubu birds the Habia tree (*Schefflera fam. Araliaceae*) is bearing
fruit, it has borne fruit down there
Ega Urulu Urubu ti naga Bai hegogo, Habiago ni uli uli darua
The Bara tree (*Eudia fam. Rutaceae*) is bearing fruit, it has borne fruit down
there
Barago, Barogo ni uli uli darua
The Bai Mope (Lorikeets) and Bai Hinini (Lorikeets)
Bai Mope ega Bai Hinini ega
They have made a secret talk and will come to pick the fruit
Urume kui ndi lo podolebira
25   The Urubu Gela (Lorikeet) and Urubu Hegele (Lorikeet)
Urubu Gela ega Urubu Hegele ega
They have made a secret talk and will come to pick the fruit
Urume kui ndi lo podolebira
The Ndi Ndu (Swifts) and Ndi Ndalu (Swifts)
Ndi Ndu ega Ndi Ndalu ega
They have made a secret talk and will come to pick the fruit
Urume kui ndi lo podolebira
The Bai Nana (Papuan King Parrot: *Alisterus Chloropteris*) and Bai Hinana
Bai Nana ega Bai Hinana ega
30   They have made a secret talk and will come to pick the fruit
Urume kui ndi lo podolebira
The Habia tree is bearing fruit
Hego daro

The Bara tree is bearing fruit
Bara daro
The Pandanus tree is bearing fruit
Londo daro
The Lamba tree is bearing fruit
Lamba daro

C
TEXT *Dawe Bilagu* Traditionally performed as part of a series of rites to ward
off ancestral spirits deemed to be causing sickness. The song (*nere*) traces
land sites throughout Huli. The brief section below refers to locations in
Ialuba.
Informant: Pina (Pina clan)
Occasion: Festivities following the opening of Egele school 1978

In Wabu and Wale the Hornbill (*Aceros Plicatus*) has broken the fruit of
the Bai tree
Wabu Wale Bai pogole Abuayale
In Wale and Dongale the Hornbill has broken the fruit of the Bai tree
Wale Dongale Bai pogole Abuayale
In Dongale and Dandabua the Hornbill has broken the fruit of the Bai tree
Dongale Dandabua Bai pogole Abuayale
In Igiya and Tigiya the Hornbill has broken the fruit of the Bai tree
Igiya Tigiya Bai pogole Abuayale
5   Hornbill, Hornbill
Ega Abuale, Waleya
The Hornbill is in the places Ibi and Yaribi
Wabula Ibi Yaribi Wabula
The Hornbill is in the places Wale and Dongale
Wabula Wale Dongale Wabula
Shout
Alo
Howl
Baya
10 They have shouted Ialuba, Ialaba
Ialuba Ialaba ole laya
They have shouted Hungibia, Hiyabe
Hungibia Hiyabe ole laya
They have shouted Hewe, Hogore
Hewe Hogore ole laya

Appendix 4 ———————
Text: *Wali O*

A

TEXT *Wali O* (lament)

Occasion: Death of a young boy away from home, December 22nd 1977

Don't let the side of your 'hair' go bad in the foreign land O I'm
saying
Pupai wane urume 'bayeri' lene inaga giru buleni o laro-o
O child don't let the side of your 'hair' go bad O I'm saying
Wane igini-o 'mbalupa' lene inaga giru buleni o laro-o
Those things given by the Hela and Dugube hold them in your right hand
I'm saying
Hela Helabe Dugube Dibaiya wane urume ngiyadago gi tiga ya laro-o
When the aeroplane has broken through the mist come O I'm saying
Ega Digai walai ginu gandalalu ibu o laro-o
5   Daughters of Tuyawi and Walawi, they are shaking hands in Iba Gigi I'm
saying
Iba Gigi Tuyawi Walawi wane labo uru dabiame lama laro-o
O bird's child, the hair will be pulled up mother I'm saying
Ega igini naga bayeri gungu yaraga ama laro-o
The 'clouds' are not enormous so when we have cried we will break through
I'm saying
'Alungi' udugo gibi ndogo iwa lalu pudamiyago laro-o

The 'clouds' are not enormous so when we have cried we will break through I'm saying
'Yuguai' udugo gibi ndogo iwa lalu pudamiyago laro-o
The 'clouds' are not enormous so when we have cried we will break through I'm saying
'Yagoma' udugo gibi ndogo iwa lalu pudamiyago laro-o
10   Son of Gai-o, when you have broken through the mist at Mende Mendeli Magali come O I'm saying
Gai igini-o Mende Mendeli Magali ginu gandalalu ibu o laro-o
Father I am saying
Aba laro
When you have brought those clothes you will come you said
Abai ina uru balu hanalu ibule larigola
I am going to marry with these men Hariabu Hurawi I am saying
Hariabu Hurawi danda poledago laro-o
I am going to marry with these men Gayawi Egawi I am saying
Gayawi Egawi danda poledago laro-o
15   'Cloud', when you have changed stay as a Superb Bird of Paradise I'm saying
'Lungi' budalu Ega Yagama habe
'Cloud', when you have changed stay as a Superb Bird of Paradise
'Alungi' budalu Ega Yagama habe
'Cloud', when you have changed stay as a Superb Bird of Paradise I am saying
'Bembeli' budalu Ega Yagama habe laro-o
Daughter of the Bai (*fam. Fagaceae*) fruit in Hayere I'm saying
Hayere ginda gilupaya wane
Daughter of the Bai fruit in Hedawi
Hedawi ginda gilupaya wane
20   Daughter of the Bai fruit in Dibawi I am saying
Dibawi ginda gilupaya wane laro-o
Daughter of the water source in Hayere I'm saying
Hayere dugu pele wane
Daughter of the water source in Hedawi
Hedawi dugu pele wane
Daughter of the water source in Dibawi I am saying
Dibawi dugu pele wane laro-o
Daughter of the mushrooms in Hayere I'm saying
Hayere nano ombe wane
25   Daughter of the mushrooms in Hedawi
Hedawi nano ombe wane
Daughter of the mushrooms in Dibawi I am saying
Dibawi nano ombe wane laro-o

B
TEXT *Wali O*
Occasion: Lament for a son who died in Hagen, March 1977

Those things given by Digawi and Walawi hold in your right hand O
Digawi Walawi urume ngiyadago gi tiga yagi yabe o
Those things given by others in Ega Wadaga hold in your right hand O
Pupai wane Ega Wadaga labo urume ngiyadago gi tiga yabe o
Don't let your 'hair' go bad O
'Bayeri' naga giru buleni o
Don't let your 'hair' go bad O
'Hurube Gurube' naga giru buleni o
5   Clouds bring the cut 'hair' O
'Abai' pudini alungi urume yalu ibu o
'Clouds' bring those things O
'yuguai' urume yalu ibu o
'Clouds' bring those things O
'Ibalu Yagoma' yalu ibu o
Bring the cut 'hair' I am saying O
'Bayeri' pudini yalu ibu larogo o
Bring the cut 'hair' I am saying O
'Abai' pudini yalu ibu larogo o
10   Bring the cut 'hair' I am saying O
'Aluba' pudini yalu ibu larogo o
Clouds bring those things I am saying O
Alungi urume yalu ibu larogo o

C
TEXT *Wali O*
Occasion: Lament by a daughter for a dying mother, Mogra Fugua 1977

Mother
Ainyali ainya
Mother daughter of possums, mother I am saying
Ama ere wango wane ainya laro
Mother daughter of possums, mother I am saying
Ama ere waru wane ainya laro
There won't be any making of pigs' fences in Mimalia, mother I am saying
Mimalia nogo hagira nabulene ainya laro
5   There won't be any making of pigs' fences in Yagama, mother I am saying
Yagama nogo hagira nabulene ainya laro
Mother daughter of Gigira, Gilambi, Hibagi, Lango Mimabe I am saying
Ama Gigira Gilambi Hibagi Lango Mimabe wane laro
Mother daughter of Wabu Wagalu, Wahabale, Guba Dagare my mother I
am saying
Ama Wabu Wagalu wane, Wahabale wane, Guba Dagare wane i ainya laro
Mother, you grew up at Tanili, daughter
Ama Tanili biru nehanda wane
You grew up at Tegiya (Ialuba) daughter I am saying
Tegiya biru nehanda wane laro
10   Mother-O mother I am saying
Ama-o amale laro-o

Mother-o

Ainyali ainya-o

Those babies asked what has happened to their mother; you crossed from the tail to the head part of Gurugu, Gamiabe and Ganana (Mogra Fugua) I said

Wali ainya ambolo urume ainya abiyabe layadagua Gurugu, Gamiabe, Ganana mane tene domara lawa

Mother-o, those babies asked what has happened to their mother; you crossed from the tail to the head part of Ora Orabi and Aya Anda I said

Ama-o ambolo urume ainya abiyabe layadagua Ora Orabi Aya Anda mane tene domara lawa

Mother-o, those babies asked what has happened to their mother; you crossed from the tail to the head part of Hari Ibini and Hayere I said

Ama-o ambolo urume ainya abiyabe layadagua Hari Ibini Hayere mane tene domara lawa

15 Mother I said I didn't know you crossed from the tail to the head parts I am saying

Ama Ainyali ainyago mane tene domarago tobara lawa laro-o

Mother-o

Ainyali ainya-o

Mother daughter from Paia I am saying

Ainyali ainya Paia wane laro

Daughter from Panigu I am saying

Panigu wane laro

Daughter from Pabula I am saying

Pabula wane laro

20 Daughter from Ama Gora I am saying

Ama Gora wane laro

Daughter from Hare

Hare wane laro

Daughter from Gora I am saying

Gora wane laro

Mother, daughter from Dibawi where the mushrooms grow I am saying

Ama Dibawi nano ombe wane laro

Daughter from Hedawi where the mushrooms grow I am saying

Hedawi nano ombe wane laro

25 Daughter from Hayere where the mushrooms grow I am saying

Hayere nano ombe wane laro

Mother, daughter from Iba Nagabi (Duna) where the water flows out I am saying

Ama Iba Nagabi dugu baya wane laro

Daughter from Aba Warabe where the water flows out I am saying

Aba Warabe dugu baya wane laro

Daughter from Ali Agabe Ayege where the water flows out I am saying

Ali Agabe Ayege dugu baya wane laro

Mother, mother I am saying

Amu ama laro-o

30   Mother mother mother I'm saying
    Ainyali ainya ama laro
    Mother-o, daughter from Wali where the ripe figs grow mother I am saying
    Ama-o Wali ibiri wane ama laro
    Mother, daughter from Bayeri where the ripe figs grow mother I am saying
    Ama Bayeri ibiri wane ama laro
    Mother, daughter from Gula Gigimi Gugara (Pureni) where the ripe figs grow I am saying
    Ama Gula Gigimi Gugara ibiri wane ama laro
    Daughter from Yuli Gili mother I am saying
    Yuli Gili wane ama laro
35   Daughter from Agau Gili
    Agau Gili wane
    Daughter from Ogo Gili
    Ogo Gili wane
    Daughter from Yuli Higi mother I am saying
    Yuli Higi wane ama laro
    Mother daughter from Dambale Ala Gilibu where you slept mother I am saying
    Ama Dambale Ala Gilibu paluene wane ama laro
    Daughter from Yuli Gai mother I am saying
    Yuli Gai wane ama laro
40   Daughter from Agai Igi mother I am saying
    Agai Igi wane ama laro
    Mother I am saying mother
    Amu laro amai

    Mother mother I am saying
    Ainyali ainya laro
    Mother-o, those babies asked what has happened to their mother; you were sitting with your girl-friends at Ayenda I said
    Ainyali-o ambolo urume ainya abiyabe layadagua Ayenda wandari yango bedabe lawa
    Mother-o, those babies asked what has happened to their mother; you were sitting with your girl-friends at Orabi I said
    Ama-o ambolo urume ainya abiyabe layadagua Orabi wandari yango bedabe lawa
45   You were sitting with your girl-friends at Tewabi I said
    Tewabi wandari yango bedabe lawa
    Mother, those babies asked what has happened to their mother; you were sitting with your girl-friends at Gurugu Ganana Gamiabe I said
    Ama ambolo urume ainya abiyabe layadagua Gurugu Ganana Gamiabe wandari yango bedabe lawa
    Mother, those babies asked what has happened to their mother; you were sitting with your girl-friends at Ora Ayenda I said
    Ama ambolo urume ainya abiyabe layadagua Ora Ayenda wandari yango bedabe lawa

Mother mother I am saying
Ainyali ainya laro-o
Mother mother mother I am saying
Ainyali ainya ama laro
50 I tricked those babies in Yabera Yawane, say this
Ambolo iya naga Yabera Yawane lalu lubia haro labe
I tricked those babies in Gamara Yagueni, say this
Ambolo iya naga Gamara Yagueni lalu lubia haro labe
I tricked those babies in the swamp gardens of Erebi Iga Ibau Angabe, say
this
Ambolo iya naga Erebi Iga Ibau Angabe gi lara lubia haro labe
I tricked them in the swamp gardens of Harigi Hayago Hengebe, say this
Harigi Hayago Hengebe gi lara lalu lubia haro labe
I tricked those babies in the mud at Yagira Dabo Daralu, say this
Ambolo iya naga Yagira Dabo Daralu waru lalu lubia haro labe
55 Mother mother I am saying
Ama amu laro-o

Mother
Ama
Those 'birds' have put their footprints where you used to step mother what
will I do?
Ge wiaga ogoria 'gogoma' urume ge wiyadagua ainya abiauwa?
Mother, those 'birds' have put their footprints where you used to step
mother what will I do?
Ama ge wiaga ogoria 'abiya' urume ge wiyadagua ainya abiauwa?
Those 'birds' have put their footprints there mother what will I do?
'Abale' urume ge wiyadagua ainya abiauwa?
60 Those 'birds' have put their footprints there mother what will I do?
'Diribi' urume ge wiyadagua ainya abiauwa?
Those 'birds' have put their footprints there mother what will I do I am
saying?
'Bauwiya' urume ge wiyadagua ainya abiauwa laro?
Mother mother
Amuli ainya
Where you used to put your digging-stick there was a bird's footprint there
yesterday
Ayari ina kebaya laroli biagoria abe gogoma ge nde wiagayago
Where you held your digging-stick there was a bird's footprint there
Dabali keba ina ya la hene o biagoria ega abiya ge nde wiagayago
65 Mother, where you held your digging-stick there was a bird's footprint there
I am saying
*Amaleo dabali keba ina ya la hene o biagoria ega nguariya ge nde
wiagayago laro*
Mother what will I do?
Ama i abiauwabe?

Mother when the dry season comes
Amale kaiya biru birua

Only myself will feel lonely and bitter like the taste of 'taro' I am saying
'Ayago' kaubi ini hangu nawago laro
Mother when the dry season comes
Ama kaiya biru birua
70 Only myself will feel lonely and bitter like the taste of 'taro' I am saying
'Genoma' kaubi ini hangu nawago laro
Only myself will feel lonely and bitter like the taste of 'taro' I am saying
'Galiango' kaubi ini hangu nawago laro
Only myself will feel lonely and bitter like the taste of 'taro' I am saying
'Ibabu' kaubi ini hangu nawago laro
Mother when the dry season comes
Ama kaiya biru birua
Only myself will feel lonely and bitter like the taste of 'taro' I am saying
'Marali' kaubi ini hangu nawago laro
75 Only myself will feel lonely and bitter like the taste of 'taro' I am saying
'Mabuali' kaubi ini hangu nawago laro
Mother when the dry season comes
Amale kaiya biru birua
Only myself will feel lonely and bitter like the taste of 'taro' I am saying
'Gabuali' kaubi ini hangu nawago laro
Mother I am saying
Ama laro-o

Mother
Amaleo
80 Mother, yesterday in the dry season I told you to make some 'talk' while we
were sitting at Mogra Fugua
*Ama kaiya abe birua amu ina 'diwi' mbira di bia larugula Hayere gabanda
uruni birua*
Mother I told you to make some 'talk'
Ama ina 'diwi' mbira di bia larugula
'Do you want to make Toro Halaga on me?' you said
I nde Toro Halagabe lariya
'I have "talked" enough so are you going to make Toro Halaga on me?'
you said
'Dobai' haru dibaru i hondo Toro Halagabe lariya
Mother
Amaleo
85 Yesterday in the dry season I told you to make some 'talk'
Kaiya abe birua ina 'gondele' mbira di bia larugula
'Do you want to make Toro Halaga on me?' you said
I nde Toro Halagabe lariya
'I have "talked" enough so are you going to make Toro Halaga on me?'
you said
'Dobai' haru diburu i hondo Toro Halagabe lariya
Mother, yesterday in the dry season I told you to make some 'talk'
Amaleo kaiya abe birua ina 'gombabu' di bia larugula

'Do you want to make Toro Halaga on me?' you said
I hondo Toro Halagabe lariya
90   'I have "talked" enough so are you going to make Toro Halaga on me?'
you said
'Nabiya' ina haru diburugo i hondo Toro Halagabe lariya
Mother, yesterday in the dry season I told you to make some 'talk'
Ama kaiya abe birua ina 'dabale' mbira di bia larugula
"Do you want to make Toro Halaga on me?" you said
I hondo Toro Halagabe lariya
This bitter tasting taro is in me mother I am saying
Ayago kaubini ini ha winidago ama laro
Now I am seeing it I am saying
Ayu hendedogo larogo

95   Mother mother-o
Amuli ainya-o
You were pretending you had a new 'bag' and body
'Ayeri' gauni tingida hareliya
You were pretending you were a new young girl
Ibiri gauni tingida hareliya
Mother you were pretending you had a new 'umbrella'
Ama 'abale' gauni tingida hareliya
You were pretending you had a new 'bag'
'Angai' kauni tingida hareliya
100 Mother I am saying
Ama laro-o

Appendix 5
Claims: statistical data

Key to Tables A1–A10

P	pending
R	renounced
C	compensation: P (pigs), K (kina)
O	other
Pr	private hearing of case
Pb	public hearing of case
p	taken to police
k	taken to Koroba court
exch.	settlement involved exchange
Rf	refusal to settle
CC	counter-claim made
LD	Liability denied
NP/or P	claim not pursued
SH	claim renounced on account of shame
CU	culprit unidentified
DS	delayed settlement
Sub/s.i.c.	claim subsumed in another compensation
(:)	number of claims: total number of times issue debated/total number of pigs or kina given in settlement
A	agnate
NAC	non-agnatic cognate
NR	non-related member of parish
UD	unidentified
In. Clan	inter-clan

Table A1 *Inclusive totals*

Claim type	Total	'77–'78	Repeated	Pre-'78	Repeated	Public	Private
1 Damage by pigs							
(a) To gardens	32	31	(5:10)	1	(1:2)	9	23
(b) To livestock	3	3	(1:2)	—	—	1	2
2 Illicit sex							
(a) Premarital	9	5	(3:7)	4	(4:11)	8	1
(b) Adultery	11	9	(2:4)	2	(2:4)	7	4
3 Homicide							
(a) Attributed	3	1	—	2	(2:5)	3	—
(b) Attempted	4	3	(1:4)	1	(1:4)	3	1
4 Debts							
(a) Money	5	—	—	5	(4:8)	5	—
(b) Pigs	9	4	(1:2)	5	(2:4)	8	1
5 Theft							
(a) Pigs	7	4	(1:3)	3	(3:6)	7	—
(b) Garden stuff	11	8	(3:6)	3	(1:3)	9	2
(c) Other	4	3	(1:2)	1	(1:2)	3	1
6 Compensation							
(a) War	6	—	—	6	(5:12)	6	—
(b) Fighting	16	10	—	6	(6:12)	8	8
(c) Other	1	—	—	1	(1:2)	1	—
7 Land claims	12	9	(2:4)	3	(3:7)	8	4
8 Insult	18	15	(4:8)	3	(3:7)	15	3
9 Poisoning	2	1	—	1	(1:2)	2	—
10 Trespass	5	4	(2:4)	1	(1:2)	5	—
11 Bridewealth	32	19	(4:9)	13	(12:28)	21	11
12 Ownership	6	5	(1:2)	1	(1:3)	2	4
13 Custody	1	—	—	1	(1:2)	—	1
14 Sorcery	1	—	—	1	(1:2)	1	—
Total	198	134	(31:67)	64	(56:128)	132	66

Table A2 *Initial claims*

Claim type	Total	'77–'78'	Repeated Pre-'78	Repeated	Public	Private	Compensation	Other	Renounced	Pending	(Taped/transcribed)	Pending (reasons)	Renounced (reasons)
1 Damage by pigs													
(a) To gardens	30	30	—	(5:10)	7	23	13 (2:3P + 11:126K)	1 (Killed)	16	—	—	—	8 1st Time/4 LD (3 CC)/2 CU/1 Rf/1 NP (Trivial)
(b) To livestock	3	3	—	(1:2)	1	2	1 (1:2K)	—	2	—	1	—	1 1st Time/1 liability denied (no proof)
2 Illicit sex													
(a) Premarital	8	4	4	(2:5) (4:11)	7	1	6 (6:12P)	1 (Married)	1	—	2	—	1 Liability denied (no proof)
(b) Adultery	8	7	1	(2:4) (1:2)	5	3	5 (5:16P) 2:k/p	—	3 1:p	—	—	—	2 Liability denied (no proof)/ 1 Subsumed in compensation
3 Homicide													
(a) Attributed	1	1	—	(1:4)	1	—	—	—	1 1:k	—	1	—	1 Liability denied (no proof)
(b) Attempted	2	1	1	—	2	—	1 (1:1P)	—	1	—	1	—	1 Subsumed (given up)
4 Debts													
(a) Money	3	—	3	(1:2) (3:6)	3	—	3 (3:50K) 1:k	—	—	—	—	—	—
(b) Pigs	2	1	1	—	1	1	1 (1:1P)	—	1	—	—	—	1 Liability denied
5 Theft													
(a) Pigs	4	2	2	(1:3) (2:4)	4	—	1 (1:3P)	—	1	2 1:k	1	1 Rf (CC)/1 withdrew	1 Liability denied (no proof)
(b) Garden stuff	10	7	3	(3:6) (1:3)	8	2	4 (4:5P)	—	4	2 1:k	1	1 s.i.c./1 withdrew	1 Subsumed (given up)/ 1 Culprit unidentified
(c) Other	3	3	1	(1:2)	2	1	1 (1:10K) 1:p	—	2	—	—	—	1 Not pursued (trivial)
6 Compensation													
(a) War	4	—	—	(4:9)	4	—	2 (2:21P)	—	1	—	1	1 Refusal (counter claim)	1 Liability denied (no proof)
(b) Fighting	4	2	2	(2:4)	2	2	3 (3:14p + 20K exchange)	—	1	1 1:k	2	1 To be disputed	1 Not pursued (trivial)
(c) Other	1	—	—	(1:2)	—	3	1 (1:12K) 1:p	—	—	—	1	—	—
7 Land Claims	8	7	1	(2:4) (1:3)	5	3	1 (1:1P)	1 (Divided)	5	2 1:k	3	2 Awaiting government mediation	1 Rf/4 NP (2 given up: 1 shame: 1 trivial)
8 Insult	12	12	—	(4:8)	10	2	2 (2:2P)	—	10	—	9	—	4 Sub (2 given up: 2 s.i.c.)/1 LD/5 NP (4 trivial/ISH)
9 Poisoning	2	1	1	(1:2)	2	—	—	—	2 1:k	—	2	—	2 Liability denied (no proof: innovative defences)
10 Trespass	4	4	—	(2:4) (4:9)	—	7	2 (2:20K)	—	—	2	1	1 LD/1 withdrew	2 NP (trivial)/2 Sub (1 given up: 1 s.i.c.)/4P/2Rf (2CC)
11 Bridewealth*	17	13	4	(2:4) (3:7) (4:8)	10	7	1 (1:12P)	2 (Divorces)	4	4	7	2 DS/2 Rf (not enough pigs)	1 Sub (in compensation)/2 NP (2 trivial)
12 Ownership	5	5	—	(1:2)	1	4	—	1 (s.i.c.) 1:p	3	1	1	1 Withdrew	—
13 Custody	1	—	1	(1:2)	1	1	—	—	1	1	—	1 To be disputed	—
14 Sorcery	—	—	—	—	—	—	—	—	—	—	—	—	—
Total	132	103	29	(28:59) (26:60)	80	52	48	5	64	16	35		

* 2 cases of divorce

Table A3 *Social range of initial claims*

No.	In-clan	UD	A v NAC	NAC v NAC	NAC v NR	A v NR	Distant A v A	Close A v A	Other	Affinal	Maternal
1a)	4 (3R:Pr)(1C:Pb)	2 (2R:Pr)	12 (1C:Pb)(2R:Pb)(4R:Pr)(4C:Pr)(1o:Pr)	4 (1C:Pb)(1C:Pr)(2R:Pr)	2 (1C:Pr)(1R:Pr)	2 (2R:Pr)	1 (1C:Pb)	3 (2C:Pr)(1C:Pb)	—	—	—
1b)	—	—	1 (1C:Pr)	—	1 (1R:Pr)	—	1 (1R:Pb)	—	—	—	—
2a)	6 (4C:Pb)(1o:Pb)(1R:Pb)	—	—	—	1 (1C:Pb)	1 (1C:Pr)	—	—	—	—	—
2b)	1 (1C:Pb)	—	1 (1C:Pb)	—	—	—	1 (1R:Pb)	—	—	4 (2R:Pr)(2C:Pb)	1 (1C:Pr)
3a)	1 (1R:Pb)	—	—	—	—	—	—	—	—	2 (1C:Pb)(1R:Pb)	—
3b)	—	—	—	—	—	—	—	—	—	—	—
4a)	2 (2C:Pb)	—	—	—	—	—	1 (1C:Pb)	1 (1C:Pr)	—	—	—
4b)	—	—	—	—	—	—	—	1 (1C:Pb)	—	—	1 (1R:Pb)
5a)	2 (2P:Pb)	—	—	—	—	—	—	—	—	1 (1R:Pb)	—
5b)	3 (1R:Pb)(2C:Pb)	1 (1R:Pr)	2 (1C:Pb)(1P:Pb)	—	—	1 (1C:Pb)	—	3 (1P:Pb)(1R:Pb)(1R:Pb)	—	—	—
5c)	—	1 (1R:Pb)	—	—	—	—	1 (1P:Pb)	—	—	2 (1R:Pr)(1C:Pb)	—
6a)	3 (2C:Pb)(1R:Pb)	—	—	—	—	—	—	—	—	—	—
6b)	1 (c/P:Pb)	—	—	—	—	—	—	2 (1C:Pr)(1R:Pr)	—	1 (1C:Pb)	—
6c)	—	—	—	—	—	—	—	1 (1C:Pb)	—	—	—
7)	2 (2P:Pb)	—	2 (1R:Pr)(C/o:Pb)	—	—	—	2 (1R:Pb)(1R:Pr)	1 (1R:Pb)	—	1 (1R:Pr)	—

(continued)

Table A3—*continued*

No.	In-clan	UD	A v NAC	NAC v NAC	NAC v NR	A v NR	Distant A v A	Close A v A	Other	Affinal	Maternal	Total
8)	4 (3R:Pb)(1R:Pr)	3 (R:Pr)	1 (1R:Pb)	—	—	—	—	2 (1C:Pb)(1R:Pb)	2 (2R:Pb)	3 (1R:Pr)(1C:Pb)(1R:Pb)	—	33
9)	—	—	—	—	—	—	—	—	—	2 (2R:Pb)	—	34
10)	3 (2P:Pb)(1C:Pb)	1 (R:Pb)	—	—	—	—	—	—	1 (1C:Pb)	—	—	5
11)	2 (1P:Pb)(1R:Pb)	—	3 (2R:Pr)(1o:Pb)	—	—	1 (1R:Pr)	2 (1R:Pb)(1P:Pr)	2 (1R:Pb)(1P:Pr)	—	7 (2o:Pb)(3R:Pb)(1P:Pr)(1R:Pr)	—	31
												10
12)	—	1 (1P:Pr)	1 (1P:Pr)	—	—	—	2 (1o:Pb)(1R:Pr)	—	—	2 (2R:Pr)	—	5
13)	—	—	—	—	—	—	—	—	—	1 (1P:Pr)	—	13
14)	—	—	—	—	—	—	—	—	—	—	—	1
												132

Collation

	In-clan	UD	A v NAC	NAC v NAC	NAC v NR	A v NR	Distant A v A	Close A v A	Other	Affinal	Maternal	Total
	4 (R:Pr)	7 (R:Pr)	2 (R:Pr)	2 (R:Pr)	3 (R:Pr)	2 (R:Pr)	2 (R:Pr)	—	—	8 (R:Pr)	—	
	14 (C:Pb)	4 (C:Pb)	1 (C:Pb)	1 (C:Pb)	1 (C:Pb)	2 (C:Pb)	4 (C:Pb)	1 (C:Pb)	—	6 (C:Pb)	—	
	1 (o:Pb)	1 (o:Pb)	—	—	—	1 (o:Pb)	—	—	—	2 (o:Pb)	—	
	8 (R:Pb)	3 (R:Pb)	—	—	—	4 (R:Pb)	4 (R:Pb)	2 (R:Pb)	—	8 (R:Pb)	1 (R:Pb)	
	7 (P:Pb)	1 (P:Pb)	—	—	—	1 (P:Pb)	1 (P:Pb)	—	—	—	—	
	—	1 (P:Pr)	—	—	—	1 (P:Pr)	1 (P:Pr)	—	—	2 (P:Pr)	—	
	—	5 (C:Pr)	1 (C:Pr)	1 (C:Pr)	1 (C:Pr)	—	4 (C:Pr)	—	—	—	1 (C:Pr)	
	—	1 (o:Pr)	—	—	—	—	—	—	—	—	—	
Total	34	23	4	4	5	11	16*	3	—	26	2	132

* (50% involved real brothers)

Table A4 Secondary claims

Breach type	Total '77–'78	Repeated Pre-'78	Repeated '77–'78	Public	Private	Compensation	Other	Renounced	Pending	(Taped/ transcribed)	Pending (reasons)	Renounced (reasons)
						Settlement forms						
1 Damage by pigs												
(a) To gardens	2	1	—	(1:2) 2	—	1 (1:1P)	—	1	—	—	—	1 Refused (counter claim)
(b) To livestock	1	—	—	—	—	—	—	—	—	—	—	—
2 Illicit sex												
(a) Premarital	1	1	—	(1:2) 1	—	—	—	—	—	—	—	—
(b) Adultery	—	—	—	—	—	—	—	1	—	1	—	1 Liability denied (no proof)
3 Homicide												
(a) Attributed	1	—	—	—	—	—	—	1	—	—	—	1 Liability denied (no proof)
(b) Attempted	1	—	—	—	1	—	—	—	—	—	—	—
4 Debts												
(a) Money	—	—	—	—	—	—	—	—	—	—	—	—
(b) Pigs	2	2	—	(1:2) 2	—	1 (1:3P)	—	1	—	2	—	1 Subsumed (in compensation)
5 Theft												
(a) Pigs	2	1	—	(1:2) 2	—	—	—	1	1:k	1	1 Refusal (CC)	1 Liability denied (no proof)
(b) Garden stuff	—	—	—	(1:2) 1	—	—	—	1	—	—	—	1 Liability denied (no proof)
(c) Other	1	—	—	—	—	—	—	1:p	—	—	—	—
6 Compensation												
(a) War	2	2	—	(1:3) 2	—	6 (6:6P + 44K)	—	3	2 1:p	2	2 Refusal (2:CC)	1 Refusal (CC)/2 not pursued (2: trivial)
(b) Fighting	9	2	—	(2:4) 4	5	2 : 1p/1k	—	3	—	1	—	—
(c) Other	—	—	—	—	—	—	—	—	—	—	—	—
7 Land claims	3	1	—	(2:4) 2	1	—	1 (Claim agreed)	2 3	—	2	—	1 Not pursued (trivial)/1 withdrew/ 3 Subsumed (2: in compensation/ 1: given up)
8 Insult	3	1	—	(2:5) 2	1	—	—	3	—	2	—	—
9 Poisoning	1	—	—	—	—	—	—	—	—	—	—	—
10 Trespass	1	1	—	(1:2) 1	—	—	—	—	1	—	1 Withdrew	—
11 Bridewealth*	11	5	(1:2)	(5:13) 8	3	1 (1:1P)	3 (2 Divorce) (1 s.i.c.)	4	3 1:p	9	1 Withdrew/ 2 To be disputed	1 Subsumed (s.i.c.)/1 LD/2 NP (change of mind)
12 Ownership	1	1	—	(1:3) 1	—	—	—	—	1 1:k	1	1 To be disputed	—
13 Custody	—	—	—	—	—	—	—	—	—	—	—	—
14 Sorcery	—	—	—	—	—	—	—	—	—	—	—	—
Total	39	18	(1:2)	(19:44) 28	11	9 (11P + 44K)	4	18	8	21		

* 7 cases involved divorce

Table A5 Social range of secondary claims

No.	In-clan	UD	A v NAC	NAC v NAC	NAC v NR	A v NR	Distant A v A	Close A v A	Other	Affinal	Maternal
1a)	—	—	1 (1R:Pb)	—	—	—	—	—	—	1 (1C:Pb)	—
1b)	—	—	—	—	—	—	—	—	—	—	—
2a)	—	—	—	—	—	—	—	—	—	—	—
2b)	—	—	—	—	—	—	—	—	—	1 (1R:Pb)	—
3a)	—	—	—	—	—	—	—	—	—	—	—
3b)	—	—	—	—	—	—	—	1 (1R:Pr)	—	—	—
4a)	—	—	—	—	—	—	—	—	—	—	—
4b)	—	—	1 (1R:Pb)	—	—	—	—	—	—	1 (1C:Pb)	—
5a)	2 (1R:Pb)(1P:Pb)	—	—	—	—	—	—	—	—	—	—
5b)	—	—	—	—	—	—	1 (1R:Pb)	—	—	—	—
5c)	—	—	—	—	—	—	1 (1P:Pb)	—	—	—	—
6a)	1 (1P:Pb)	—	—	—	—	—	—	—	—	—	—
6b)	—	—	2 (2C:Pb)	—	—	—	—	3 (2C:Pr)(1R:Pb)	—	4 (2R:Pr)(1C:Pb/1C:Pb)	—
6c)	—	—	—	—	—	—	—	—	—	—	—
7)	—	—	—	—	1 (1R:Pr)	—	1 (1o:Pb)	1 (1R:Pb)	—	—	—
8)	1 (1R:Pb)	—	—	—	—	—	—	1 (1R:Pr)	—	1 (1R:Pb)	—
9)	—	—	—	—	—	—	—	—	—	—	—
10)	—	—	—	—	—	—	—	1 (1P:Pb)	—	—	—

											Total
11)	1 (1o:Pb)	—	2 (1o:Pb)(1R:Pb)	—	—	—	—	1 (1R:Pb)	7 (1C:Pb)(1R:Pb)(2P:Pr)(1o:Pb)(1R:Pr)(1P:Pb)	—	
12)	1 (1P:Pb)	—	—	—	—	—	—	—	—	—	
13)	—	—	—	—	—	—	—	—	—	—	
14)	—	—	—	—	—	—	—	—	—	—	
Collation											
	—	—	—	—	1 (R:Pr)	—	—	2 (R:Pr)	3 (R:Pr)	—	6
	—	—	2 (C:Pb)	—	—	—	—	—	3 (C:Pb)	—	5
	1 (o:Pb)	—	1 (o:Pb)	—	—	—	1 (o:Pb)	—	1 (o:Pb)	—	4
	2 (R:Pb)	—	3 (R:Pb)	—	—	—	1 (R:Pb)	3 (R:Pb)	4 (R:Pb)	—	13
	3 (P:Pb)	—	—	—	—	—	1 (P:Pb)	1 (P:Pb)	1 (P:Pb)	—	6
	—	—	—	—	—	—	—	—	2 (P:Pr)	—	2
	—	—	—	—	—	—	—	2 (C:Pr)	1 (C:Pr)	—	3
	6	0	6	0	1	0	3	8*	15	0	39

* (25% involved real brothers)

317

Table A6 *Tertiary claims*

Breach type	Total	'77–'78	Repeated	Pre-'78	Repeated	Public	Private	Pending (reasons)	Renounced (reasons)	Settlement forms — Compensation	Other	Re-nounced	Pending (Taped/transcribed)
1 Damage by pigs													
(a) To gardens	—	—	—	—	—	—	—	—	—	—	—	—	—
(b) To livestock	—	—	—	—	—	—	—	—	—	—	—	—	—
2 Illicit sex													
(a) Premarital	1	1	(1:2)	—	—	—	—	—	1 Not pursued (shame)	—	—	1 1:k	1
(b) Adultery	2	2	—	—	—	1	1	1 Subsumed (given up)	1 Liability denied (no proof)	—	—	1 1:k	2
3 Homicide													
(a) Attributed	2	—	—	2	(2:5)	2	—	2 Liability denied	1 Liability denied	—	—	1	2 1:p
(b) Attempted	1	1	(1:4)	—	—	1	—	—	—	—	—	1	1
4 Debts													
(a) Money	2	—	—	2	(1:2)	2	—	—	1 Not pursued (trivial)	1 (1:2K)	—	1	2
(b) Pigs	5	3	—	2	(1:2)	5	—	1 Refusal (CC)	1 Subsumed (in compensation)/ 1 Not pursued (shame)	2 (2:3P)	—	2	4 1:p
5 Theft													
(a) Pigs	1	1	—	—	—	1	—	1 Refusal (CC)	—	—	—	—	1 1:k
(b) Garden stuff	1	1	—	—	—	1	—	1 Subsumed (in compensation)	—	—	—	—	1 1:p
(c) Other	—	—	—	—	—	—	—	—	—	—	—	—	—
6 Compensation													
(a) War	3	3	—	—	—	2	1	—	—	—	—	—	—
(b) Fighting	3	1	—	2	(2:4)	2	1	1 Refusal (CC)	—	2 (2:17P)	—	—	1
(c) Other	1	1	—	—	—	1	—	—	—	—	—	—	1
7 Land Claims	1	—	—	1	(1:2)	1	—	1 To be disputed	—	—	—	—	1
8 Insult	3	2	—	1	(1:2)	3	—	1 Liability denied	1 Not pursued (trivial)/ 1 Subsumed (given up)	—	—	2	2 1:k
9 Poisoning	—	—	—	—	—	—	—	—	—	—	—	—	—
10 Trespass	—	—	—	—	—	—	—	—	—	—	—	—	—
11 Bridewealth*	4	—	—	4	(3:7)	3	1	1 Delayed settlement	2 Subsumed (in compensation)/ 1 NP (change of mind)	—	—	3	3
12 Ownership	—	—	—	—	—	—	—	—	—	—	—	—	—
13 Custody	—	—	—	—	—	—	—	—	—	—	—	—	—
14 Sorcery	1	—	—	1	(1:2)	1	—	1 Refusal (counter claim)	—	—	—	—	1 1:p
Total	27	13	(2:6)	14	(11:24)	24	3			5 (5:20P + 2K)	—	11	22

* 1 case involved divorce

Table A7 Social range of tertiary claims

No.	In-clan	UD	A v NAC	NAC v NAC	NAC v NR	A v NR	Distant A v A	Close A v A	Other	Affinal	Maternal
1a)	—	—	—	—	—	—	—	—	—	—	—
1b)	—	—	—	—	—	—	—	—	—	—	—
2a)	1 (1R:Pb)	—	—	—	—	—	—	—	—	—	—
2b)	2 (1P:Pb) (1R:Pr)	—	—	—	—	—	—	—	—	—	—
3a)	2 (2P:Pb)	—	—	—	—	—	—	—	—	—	—
3b)	—	—	—	—	—	—	—	1 (1R:Pb)	—	—	—
4a)	—	—	—	—	—	—	—	—	—	2 (1C:Pb) (1R:Pb)	—
4b)	2 (1P:Pb) (1R:Pb)	—	—	—	—	—	—	2 (1R:Pb) (1C:Pb)	—	1 (1C:Pb)	—
5a)	1 (1P:Pb)	—	—	—	—	—	—	—	—	—	—
5b)	1 (1P:Pb)	—	—	—	—	—	—	—	—	—	—
5c)	—	—	—	—	—	—	—	—	—	—	—
6a)	—	—	—	—	—	—	—	—	—	—	—
6b)	1 (1P:Pb)	—	1 (1C:Pb)	—	—	—	—	—	—	1 (1C:Pr)	—
6c)	—	—	—	—	—	—	—	—	—	—	—
7)	—	—	—	—	—	—	1 (1P:Pb)	—	—	—	—
8)	1 (1R:Pb)	—	—	—	—	—	1 (1P:Pb)	—	—	1 (1R:Pb)	—
9)	—	—	—	—	—	—	—	—	—	—	—
10)	—	—	—	—	—	—	—	—	—	—	—
11)	1 (1R:Pb)	—	1 (1R:Pb)	—	—	—	—	—	—	2 (1R:Pb) (1P:Pr)	—
12)	—	—	—	—	—	—	—	—	—	—	—
13)	—	—	—	—	—	—	—	—	—	—	—
14)	1 (1P:Pb)	—	—	—	—	—	—	—	—	—	—

(continued)

319

Table A7—continued

Collation	UD	A v NAC	NAC v NAC	NAC v NR	A v NR	Distant A v A	Close A v A	Other	Affinal	Maternal	Total
1 (R:Pr)	—	—	—	—	—	—	—	—	—	—	1
—	—	1 (C:Pb)	—	—	—	—	1 (C:Pb)	—	2 (C:Pb)	—	4
4 (R:Pb)	—	1 (R:Pb)	—	—	—	—	2 (R:Pb)	—	3 (R:Pb)	—	10
8 (P:Pb)	—	—	—	—	—	2 (P:Pb)	—	—	—	—	10
—	—	—	—	—	—	—	—	—	1 (P:Pr)	—	1
—	—	—	—	—	—	—	—	—	1 (C:Pr)	—	1
13	0	2	0	0	0	2	3*	0	7	0	27

* (100% involved real brothers)

320

Table A8 *Inclusive totals*

No.	In-clan	UD	A v NAC	NAC v NAC	NAC v NR	A v NR	Distant A v A	Close A v A	Other	Affinal	Maternal
1a)	4 (3R:Pr)(1C:Pb)	2 (2R:Pr)	13 (1C:Pb)(3R:Pb)(4R:Pr)(4C:Pr)(1o:Pr)	4 (1C:Pb)(1C:Pr)(2R:Pr)	2 (1C:Pr)(1R:Pr)	2 (2R:Pr)	1 (1C:Pb)	3 (2C:Pr)(1C:Pb)	—	1 (1C:Pb)	—
1b)	—	—	1 (1C:Pr)	—	1 (1R:Pr)	—	1 (1R:Pb)	—	—	—	—
2a)	7 (4C:Pb)(1o:Pb)(2R:Pb)	—	—	—	1 (1C:Pb)	1 (1C:Pr)	—	—	—	—	—
2b)	3 (1C:Pb)(1P:Pb)(1R:Pr)	—	1 (1C:Pb)	—	—	—	1 (1R:Pb)	—	—	5 (2R:Pr)(2C:Pb)(1R:Pb)	1 (1C:Pr)
3a)	3 (1R:Pb)(2P:Pb)	—	—	—	—	—	—	—	—	—	—
3b)	—	—	—	—	—	—	—	2 (1R:Pr)(1R:Pb)	—	2 (1C:Pb)(1R:Pb)	—
4a)	2 (2C:Pb)	—	—	—	—	—	1 (1C:Pb)	—	—	2 (1C:Pb)(1R:Pb)	—
4b)	2 (1P:Pb)(1R:Pb)	—	1 (1R:Pb)	—	—	—	—	3 (1C:Pr)(1C:Pb)(1R:Pb)	—	2 (2C:Pb)	1 (1R:Pb)
5a)	5 (4P:Pb)(1R:Pb)	—	—	—	—	—	—	1 (1C:Pb)	—	1 (1R:Pb)	—
5b)	4 (1R:Pb)(2C:Pb)(1P:Pb)	1 (1R:Pr)	2 (1C:Pb)(1P:Pb)	—	1 (1C:Pb)	—	—	3 (1P:Pb)(1R:Pb)(1R:Pr)	—	—	—

(continued)

321

Table A8—continued

No.	In-clan	UD	A v NAC	NAC v NAC	NAC v NR	A v NR	Distant A v A	Close A v A	Other	Affinal	Maternal
5c)	—	1 (1R:Pb)	—	—	—	—	1 (1R:Pb)	—	—	2 (1R:Pr)(1C:Pb)	—
6a)	4 (2C:Pb)(1R:Pb)(1P:Pb)	—	—	—	—	—	2 (2P:Pb)	—	—	—	—
6b)	2 (1C/P:Pb)	—	3 (3C:Pb)	—	—	—	—	5 (3C:Pr)(1R:Pb)(1R:Pr)	—	6 (2C:Pb)(2C:Pr)(2R:Pr)	—
6c)	—	—	—	—	—	—	—	1 (1C:Pb)	—	—	—
7)	2 (2P:Pb)	—	2 (1R:Pr)(1C/o:Pb)	—	1 (1R:Pr)	—	4 (1R:Pr)(1R:Pb)(1P:Pb)(1o:Pb)	2 (2R:Pb)	—	1 (1R:Pr)	—
8)	6 (5R:Pb)(1R:Pr)	—	1 (1R:Pb)	—	—	—	1 (1P:Pb)	3 (1C:Pb)(1R:Pb)(1R:Pr)	2 (2R:Pb)	5 (3R:Pb)(1C:Pb)(1R:Pr)	—
9)	—	—	—	—	—	—	—	—	—	2 (2R:Pb)	—
10)	3 (2P:Pb)(1C:Pb)	—	—	—	—	—	—	1 (1P:Pb)	1 (1C:Pb)	—	—
11)	4 (1o:Pb)(2R:Pb)(1P:Pb)	—	6 (2R:Pr)(2o:Pb)(2R:Pb)	—	—	1 (1R:Pr)	2 (1R:Pb)(1P:Pr)	3 (2R:Pb)(1P:Pr)	—	16 (5R:Pb)(3o:Pb)(4P:Pr)(2R:Pr)(1C:Pb)(1P:Pb)	—
12)	1 (1P:Pb)	—	1 (1P:Pr)	—	—	—	2 (1o:Pb)(1R:Pr)	—	—	2 (2R:Pr)	—
13)	—	—	—	—	—	—	—	—	—	1 (1P:Pr)	—
14)	1 (1P:Pb)	—	—	—	—	—	—	—	—	—	—

Table A9 Outcome forms and social-range characteristics

	Inter-clan	Unident-ified	Agnate v non-agnatic cognate	Non-agnatic cognate v non-agnatic cognate	Non-agnatic cognate v non-related member	Agnate v non-related member	Agnate v agnate (distant)	Agnate v agnate (close)	Other	Ego v affines	Ego v maternal relatives	Total
Compensation: public	14	—	7	1	1	1	2	5	1	10	—	42
Compensation: private	—	—	5	1	1	1	—	6	—	3	1	18
Renounced: public	14	1	7	—	—	—	5	9	2	16	1	55
Renounced: private	5	3	7	2	3	3	2	4	—	10	—	39
Pending: public	18	—	1	—	—	—	4	2	—	1	—	26
Pending: private	—	—	1	—	—	—	1	1	—	5	—	8
Other: public	2	—	2	—	—	—	2	—	—	3	—	9
Other: private	—	—	1	—	—	—	—	—	—	—	—	1
Total	53	4	31	4	5	5	16	27	3	48	2	198

Table A10 *Hiwanda village court statistics January 1977–May 1978*

	Damage by pigs	Theft	Sexual offences	Poisoning	Damage to property	Marriage/divorce	Insult	Fighting	Debts	Failure to work on roads	Playing cards in public	Disobeying court orders	Trespass
Orders issued	16	35	34	1	12	12	25	27	6	21	13	4	3
Settlement Order (Form F2)	6	14	3	0	5	5	3	2	3	5	2	0	0
Pigs paid: 1–5	0	2	2	0	0	2	0	0	2	0	0	0	0
over 5	0	7	0	0	1	2	0	1	0	0	0	0	0
Money: 5–20 kn	3	2	0	0	2	0	3	1	0	0	0	0	0
20–50 kn	2	3	0	0	2	0	0	0	1	0	0	0	0
50–100 kn	0	0	0	0	0	1	0	0	0	0	0	0	0
Community work (1 month)	1	0	1	0	0	0	0	0	0	5	2	0	0
Orders for imprisonment	1	0	0	0	0	1	0	0	0	0	0	0	0
Preventive Order (Form F4)	0	4	2	1	0	4	2	2	1	0	0	0	2
Order (Form F6)	10	21	31	0	7	7	22	25	3	16	11	4	3
Pigs paid: 1–5	1	1	1	0	0	2	0	0	0	0	0	0	0
over 5	0	1	3	0	0	6	0	4	1	0	0	0	0
Money: 5–20 kn	3	1	2	0	0	0	4	1	8	11	8	0	2
20–50 kn	3	3	3	0	1	0	4	4	0	1	0	0	0*
Over 50 kn	3	13	20	0	4	0	10	17	1	0	0	2	1
Orders for imprisonment	4	11	18	0	4	1	7	13	1	1	0	1	0
Community work (1 month)	0	2	2	0	0	0	3	0	0	3	0	0	0

Note: Sessions: 72
Unsettled: 7
Quashed: 3
Imprisoned: 37

Appendix 6 ———————
Text: *Tene Té* ('origin myth') of Haroli

Informant: Degondo (Koma Clan)
I collected several versions of this myth and while names and places often varied, theme and sequence of events remained constant.

There were two young girls from Bebogo called Pandime and Pandana. The former was the youngest of the two. There was also a young bachelor who left his garden and pigs to go to the father of these girls. The old man asked him, 'Boy, where have you been?' The boy replied, 'I am coming to stay with you.' After some time the boy eventually informed the father that he was returning home to his gardens and pigs. The old man remarked, 'You want to go but I have nothing to give you!' The boy told him that he should give something and at last the father gave him a pig. 'I don't want this pig, give me another.' The old man gave him cowrie shells (*dange*) but the boy refused these. 'Can I .give you my eldest daughter?' asked the man. Again the boy refused. The father then wrapped his youngest daughter into a parcel and gave it to the boy with these words: 'Carry this parcel in your bag, it is my *gubalini* (most prized possession). Don't lose this thing, don't leave it on the ground, don't undo it, don't take it out. When you go to the garden carry it with you; when you make house, cook food, chop wood or sleep, have it with you always.' The boy then returned home with the parcel. One day he went to the bush and saw his pigs. They had been digging-up his garden and eating his sweet-potatoes. He threw down the bag and went off to get his bow and arrows. He chased the pigs back to his garden where he had left the bag. As he arrived he saw a young girl sitting on his bag. 'What is this? You have jumped over (i.e. contaminated) my bag and sat on it. Where you are sitting I left my bag so is it there?' She didn't move or answer and he shot the girl with a *kopi* arrow. The girl then spoke, 'What my father told you not to do you have done. Now you have shot me. Cut some bamboo and fetch my blood. Plant it in the mud with a fence around it.'

We say from the blood of this woman is Haroli, Andaya Wiliaba, Iba Giya, Iba Wiliaba, Iba Dagia.[1] We say Hibu ti (small crystal carried by initiates) is her bone, the Wiliaba plant her lungs and heart, the Tia Telengau plant her vaginal blood. When we used to plant these we said *taga taga* ('shame shame').

Note

1 These terms denote both the cult itself and the plants which represent the life-force of Haroli initiates. The occurrence of the term *iba* ('water') in three of the above synonyms again emphasizes its purificatory and life-giving properties. The possible meanings of the word Haroli relate directly to competing symbolic interpretations of the cult itself. Two possibilities suggest themselves:

   (i) *haroli* – compounded of the morphemes *ha* (to stay) + *roli* (verb suffix: customary mood – 'used to'). The term would have the force of 'those who habitually stay in the bush'.

   (ii) *haroli* – compounded from *haro* (acorn: *Lithocarpus rufo-villosus, fam. Fagaceae*) + *li* (suffix for 'person'). The phallic connotations of 'acorn' are evident in joke formulations:

   inaga haro ebere golo ibira hara
   your acorn (i.e. penis) is broken off and falling down there

   Haroli in this second sense might signify 'the penis-men'. One might accordingly interpret the ritualized hair-behaviour as a form of symbolic interaction with displaced genitalia.

   The proper noun Haroli need not, of course, semantically reflect any of the above meanings though it is a consistent feature of this culture that labels do appear to carry morphemically that which they denote. The Huli do not, in their explanations or rationalizations of this cult recognize phallicism. Nevertheless, set against this is the fact that semen is located in the head. That complex of ideas explicated by Leach (1958) might thus be applied so as to propose the 'head' as a phallus, and the wig/hair a type of phallic covering. Whilst the data presented in Chapter 5 certainly supports the contention that for Huli hair represents 'personal power', it does not permit inferences of genital displacement *simpliciter*. *Mãnda* (hair/wig) is a collage of inconographical elements all of which can be explained in terms of the dominant symbolic association between man and bird. Rather than commencing with a psycho-analytic theory of castration and aggression, I have explored the interrelationships between shape, colour, position and adornment within a developmental sequence that parallels the growth stages of Cassowaries.

References

Albert, E. M. (1972) Culture Patterning of Speech Behaviour in Burundi. In J. Gumperz and D. Hymes (eds) *Directions in Sociolinguistics*. New York: Holt, Rinehart & Winston.

Aristotle (nd) *Rhetorica*. Trans W. Rhys Roberts (1924) Oxford: Clarendon Press.

Atkinson, J. M. and Drew, P. (1979) *Order in Court*. London: Macmillan Press.

Austin, J. (1962) *How To Do Things With Words*. Oxford: Clarendon Press.

Barnes, J. A. (1962) African Models in the New Guinea Highlands. *Man 62*: 5–9.

Bloch, M. (ed.) (1975) *Political Language and Oratory in Traditional Society*. London: Academic Press.

Brown, P. and Buchbinder, G. (eds) (1976) *Man and Woman in the New Guinea Highlands*. American Anthropological Association: Special publication No. 8.

Buchbinder, G. and Rappaport, R. (1976) Fertility and Death Among the Maring. In P. Brown and G. Buchbinder (eds) *Man and Women in the New Guinea Highlands*. American Anthropological Association: Special publication No. 8.

Burke, K. (1969) *A Rhetoric of Motives*. Berkeley: University of California Press.

Cheetham, B. (1977a) 'Huli Prosodic Vowels.' Unpublished manuscript.

—— (1977b) 'Counting and Number in Huli.' Unpublished manuscript.

Coulmas, F. (ed.) (1981) *Conversational Routine*. The Hague: Mouton.

Coulthard, M., Montgomery, M., and Brazil, D. (1981) Developing a description of spoken discourse. In M. Coulthard and M. Montgomery (eds) *Studies in Discourse Analysis*. London: Routledge & Kegan Paul.

DeLepervanche, M. (1967–1968) Descent, Residence and Leadership in the New Guinea Highlands. *Oceania* 38: 134–58; 163–89.

Douglas, M. (1966) *Purity and Danger*. London: Routledge & Kegan Paul.

Feld, S. and Schieffelin, B. B. (n.d.) 'Hard Words: A Functional Basis For Kaluli Discourse.' Unpublished manuscript.

Frake, C. O. (1969) Struck by Speech: The Yakan Concept of Litigation. In L. Nader (ed.) *Law In Culture and Society*. Chicago: Aldine.

Gell, A. (1975) *Metamorphosis of the Cassowaries: Umeda Society, Language and Ritual*. University of London Monographs of Social Anthropology No. 51: Athlone Press.

Glasse, R. M. (1959a) The Huli Descent System: A Preliminary Account. *Oceania* 29 (3): 171–83.

—— (1959b) Revenge and Redress among the Huli: A Preliminary Account. *Mankind* 5 (7): 273–89.

—— (1965) The Huli of the Southern Highlands. In P. Lawrence and M. Meggitt (eds) *Gods Ghosts and Men in Melanesia*. London: Oxford University Press.

—— (1968) *Huli of Papua: A Cognatic Descent System*. Paris: Mouton & Co.

Gluckman, M. (1973) Limitations of the Case Method in the Study of Tribal Law. *Law and Society Review* 7: 611–41.

Goffman, E. (1981) *Forms of Talk*. Oxford: Basil Blackwell.

Goldman, L. R. (1979) Kelote: An important Huli ritual ground. *Oral History* 7 (4): 14–18.

—— (1980) Speech Categories and the Study of Disputes: A New Guinea Example. *Oceania* 50 (3): 209–27.

—— (1981a) 'Talk Never Dies: An Analysis of Disputes among the Huli.' Unpublished doctoral thesis: London.

—— (1981b) Compensation and Disputes in Huli. In R. Scaglion (ed.) *Homicide Compensation in Papua New Guinea*. Law Reform Commission Monograph No. 1: Papua New Guinea LRC.

Gossen, G. H. (1974) *Chamulas in the World of the Sun*. Harvard, Mass.: Harvard University Press.

Gulliver, P. H. (1982) Review of J. Comaroff and S. Roberts, *Rules and Processes: The Cultural Logic of Dispute in an African Context*, Chicago, London: University of Chicago Press. *Man* (N.S.) 17 (3): 565–66.

Gumperz, J. (1975) Foreword. In M. Sanches and B. Blount (eds) *Sociocultural Dimensions of Language Use*. London: Academic Press.

Harris, R. (1981) Review of E. Goffman, *Forms of Talk*, Oxford: Basil Blackwell. *Times Literary Supplement* 18: 1455–456.

Hides, J. (1936) *Papuan Wonderland*. London: Blackie & Son.

Hoad, R. A. (1957) Patrol Report No. 10: Koroba Station.

Hymes, D. (1972) Models in the Interaction of Language and Social Life. In J. Gumperz and D. Hymes (eds) *Directions in Sociolinguistics*. New York: Holt, Rinehart & Winston.

Keenan, E. (1974) Norm-makers, Norm-breakers: Uses of Speech by Men and Women in a Malagasy Community. In R. Baumann and R. Sherzer (eds) *Explorations in the Ethnography of Speaking*. New York: Cambridge University Press.

Keesing, R. (1971) Descent, Residence and Cultural Codes. In L. R. Hiatt and C. Jayawardena (eds) *Anthropology in Oceania*. Sydney: Angus & Robertson.

Keller, E. (1981) Gambits: Conversational Strategy Signals. In F. Coulmas (ed.) *Conversational Routine*. The Hague: Mouton.

Leach, E. R. (1958) Magical Hair. *Journal of the Royal Anthropological Institute* **88** (2): 145–64.

Leech, G. (1974) *Semantics*. Harmondsworth: Penguin.

Lindenbaum, S. (1976) A Wife is the Hand of Man. In P. Brown and G. Buchbinder (eds) *Man and Women in the New Guinea Highlands*. American Anthropological Association: Special publication No. 8.

Llewellyn, K. and Hoebel, E. A. (1941) *The Cheyenne Way*. Norman: University of Oaklahoma Press.

Lyons, J. (1977) *Semantics*. Cambridge: Cambridge University Press.

Meggitt, M. J. (1964) The Kinship Terminology of the Mae Enga of New Guinea. *Oceania* **34**: 191–200.

Milner, G. B. (1971) The Quartered Shield: Outline of a Semantic Taxonomy. In E. Ardener (ed.) *Social Anthropology and Language*. Association of Social Anthropologists Monograph No. 10 London: Tavistock.

Modjeska, C. (1977) 'Production among the Duna.' Unpublished Ph.D. thesis: Australian National University.

O'Barr, W. M. (1976) Boundaries, Strategies, and Power Relations: Political Anthropology and Language. In W. M. O'Barr and J. F. O'Barr (eds) *Language and Politics*. The Hague: Mouton.

O'Hanlon, M. (n.d.) 'Handsome is as Handsome Does.' Unpublished manuscript.

Paine, R. (ed.) (1981) *Politically Speaking*. Philadelphia: Institute for the Study of Human Issues.

Pike, K. (1948) *Tone Languages*. Ann Arbor: University of Michigan.

Pomerantz, A. (1978a) Attribution of Responsibility: Blamings. *Sociology* **12**: 115–21.

—— (1978b) Compliment Responses. In J. Schenkein (ed.) *Studies in the Organization of Conversational Interaction*. New York: Academic Press.

Pos, H. (1938) La Notion d'opposition en linguistique. *Onzième Congrès International de Psychologie*. Paris: University of Paris.

Pugh-Kitigan, J. (1975) 'Communication, Language and Huli Music: A Preliminary Survey.' Unpublished B.A. thesis: Monash University.

—— (1977) Huli Language and Instrumental Performance. *Ethnomusicology* **21** (2): 205–32.

—— (1979) The Huli and their Music. *Hemisphere* **23** (2): 84–8.

Reay, M. (1959) *The Kuma: Freedom and Conformity in the New Guinea Highlands*. Melbourne: Melbourne University Press.

Roberts, S. (1979) *Order and Dispute*. Harmondsworth: Penguin.

—— (1981) Review of P. H. Gulliver (ed.) *Cross-Examinations: Essays in*

Memory of Max Gluckman, Int. Stud. Social Anthrop. 27. Leiden: Brill. *Man* (N.S.) **16** (3).

Rosaldo, M. (1973) I have nothing to hide: The Language of Ilongot Oratory. *Language in Society* 2: 193–223.

Rule, M. (1964) 'Huli Grammar.' Unpublished manuscript: APCM Tari.

Sacks, H., Schegloff, E., and Jefferson, G. (1974) A Simplest Systematics for the Organization of Turn-Taking for Conversation. *Language* **50**: 696–735.

Schegloff, E. and Sacks, H. (1973) Opening up Closings. *Semiotica* **8**: 289–327.

Scheffler, H. (1965) *Choiseul Island Social Structure*. Berkeley: University of California Press.

—— (1971) Dravidian-Iroquois: The Melanesian Evidence. In L. R. Hiatt and C. Jayawardena (eds) *Anthropology in Oceania*. Sydney: Angus & Robertson.

Schieffelin, B. B. (1979) Getting It Together: An Ethnographic Approach to the Study of the Development of Communicative Competence. In E. Ochs and B. B. Schieffelin (eds) *Developmental Pragmatics*. New York: Academic Press.

Seitel, P. (1974) Haya Metaphors for Speech. *Language in Society* **3**: 51–67.

Sinclair, J. P. (1955) N. W. Tari Patrol Report: Tari.

—— (1957a) Koroba Patrol Report No. 2. Supplementary confidential report: Koroba.

—— (1957b) Patrol Report No. 4: Koroba.

—— (1966) *Behind the Ranges*. Victoria: Melbourne University Press.

—— (1973) *Wigmen of Papua*. Milton Queensland: Jacaranda Press.

Starr, J. (1978) *Dispute and Settlement in Rural Turkey: An Ethnography of Law*. Leiden: Brill.

Strathern, A. J. (1972) *One Father One Blood*. London: Tavistock.

—— (1975) Veiled Speech in Mount Hagen. In M. Bloch (ed.) *Political Language and Oratory in Traditional Society*. London: Academic Press.

—— (1981) Compensation: Should There Be a New Law? In R. Scaglion (ed.) *Homicide Compensation in Papua New Guinea*. Law Reform Commission of Papua New Guinea Monograph No. 1.

Strathern, M. (1972) *Official and Unofficial Courts*. New Guinea Research Bulletin No. 47, ANU Press.

Stross, B. (1974) Speaking of Speaking: Tenejepa Tzeltal Metalinguistics. In R. Baumann and R. Sherzer (eds) *Explorations in the Ethnography of Speaking*. New York: Cambridge University Press.

Wagner, R. (1967) *The Curse of Souw: Principles of Daribi Clan Definition and Alliance in New Guinea*. Chicago: University of Chicago Press.

—— (1972) *Habu: The Innovation of Meaning in Daribi Religion*. Chicago: University of Chicago Press.

Wurm, S. A. (1961) The Languages of the Eastern, Western and Southern Highlands, TPNG. In A. Capell, *Linguistic Survey of the South-Western Pacific*. Noumea South-Pacific Commission.

Young, M. (1971) *Fighting with Food*. Cambridge: Cambridge University Press.

Name index

Subject index